A

CRITICAL AND GRAMMATICAL

COMMENTARY

ON ST. PAUL'S

EPISTLE TO THE EPHESIANS.

WITH A

REVISED TRANSLATION.

BY

CHARLES J. ELLICOTT, B.D.,

DEAN OF EXETER, AND PROFESSOR OF DIVINITY, KING'S COLLEGE,
LONDON.

Wipf & Stock
PUBLISHERS
Eugene, Oregon

Wipf and Stock Publishers
199 West 8th Avenue, Suite 3
Eugene, Oregon 97401

A Critical & Grammatical Commentary on St. Paul's Epistle to the Ephesians
By Ellicott, Charles J.
ISBN: 1-57910-081-3
Publication date 11/12/1997
Previously published by Warren F. Draper, 1997

PREFACE TO THE FIRST EDITION.

THE following pages form the second part of a commentary on St. Paul's Epistles, founded on the same principles and constructed on the same plan as that of the Epistle to the Galatians.

As I explained, somewhat at length, in the preface to that Epistle, the general principles, critical, grammatical, and exegetical, upon which this commentary has been attempted, I will now only make a few special observations on this present portion of the work, and record my obligations to those expositors who have more particularly devoted themselves to this Epistle.

With regard to the present commentary, I will only remind the reader, that as in style, matter, and logical connection, this sublime Epistle differs considerably from that to the Galatians, so the commentary must necessarily, in many respects, reflect these differences and distinctions. Several points of grammatical interest which particularly characterized the former Epistle are scarcely perceptible in the present; while difficulties which made themselves but slightly felt in the vivid, argumentative, expostulatory language of the Epistle to the Galatians, are here, amidst the earnest hortatory comments, the deeper doctrinal expositions, and the more profound enarrations of the primal counsels of God, ever maintaining a distinct and visible prominence. In the Epistle to the Galatians, for example, the explanation of the uses of the cases did not commonly involve many points of interest: in this Epistle, the cases, *especially the genitive,* present almost every phase and form of difficulty ; the uses are most various, the combinations most subtle and significant. In the Epistle to the Galatians, again, the particles, causal, illative, or adversative, which connected the clauses were constantly claiming the reader's attention, while the subordination or coördination of the clauses themselves and the inter-dependence of the different members and factors of the sentence were generally simple and perspicuous. In the present Epistle these difficulties are exactly reversed ; the use of the particles is more simple, while the intertexture of sentences and the connection of clauses, especially in the earlier portions of the Epistle, try the powers and principles of grammatical and logical analysis to the very uttermost.

In the first chapter more particularly, when we are permitted, as it were, to gaze upon the evolution of the archetypal dispensation of God, amidst those linked and blended clauses that, like the enwreathed smoke of some sweet-smelling sacrifice, mount and mount upwards to the very heaven of heavens, in that group of sentences of rarest harmony and more than mortal eloquence, these difficulties are so great and so deep, that the most exact language and the most discriminating analysis seem, as they truly are, too poor and too weak to convey the force or connection of expressions so august, and thoughts so unspeakably profound.

It is in this part that I have been deeply conscious that the system of exposition which I have adopted has passed through its sorest and severest trial, and though I have labored with anxious and unremitting industry, though I have spared neither toil nor time, but with fear and trembling, and not without many prayers have devoted every power to the endeavor to develop the outward meaning and connection of this stupendous revelation, I yet feel, from my very heart, how feeble that effort has been, how inexpressive my words, how powerless my grasp, how imperfect my delineation.

Still, in other portions of this Epistle, I trust I am not presumptuous in saying that I have been more cheered and hopeful, and that I have felt increased confidence in the system of exposition I was enabled to pursue in the commentary on the preceding Epistle. I have thus (especially after the kind notices my former work has received) studiously maintained in the present notes the same critical and grammatical characteristics which marked the former commentary. The only difference that I am aware of will be found in the still greater attention I have paid to the Greek Expositors, a slight decrease in the references to some modern commentators in whom I have felt a diminishing confidence, a slight increase in the references to our best English Divines which the nature of this profound Epistle has seemed to require. I deeply regret that the limits which I have prescribed to myself in this commentary have prevented my embodying the substance of these references in the notes, as I well know the disinclination to pause and consult other authors which every reader, save the most earnest and truth-seeking, is certain to feel. Yet this I will say, that I think the student will not often regret the trouble he may have to take in reading those few portions of our great English Divines to which I have directed his attention, and which, for his sake, I could wish had been more numerous. Such as they are, they are the results of my own private reading and observation.

In the grammatical portion of the commentary I must entreat the reader to bear with me, if for the sake of brevity, and, I might even say, perspicuity, I have been forced to avail myself of the current forms of expression adopted by modern grammatical writers. They will all be found elucidated in the treatises to which I have referred, and of these, every one, to the best of my belief, is well known and accessible, and will probably occupy a place in the library of most scholars.

I must now briefly notice the authors to whom, in addition to those mentioned in the preface to the *Galatians*, I am indebted in the present Epistle.

Of the patristic commentators I have derived great benefit from some *exceedingly* valuable annotations of Origen, which are to be found in Cramer's *Catenæ*, and which have hitherto scarcely received any notice from recent expositors, though they most eminently deserve it.

Of modern commentators on this Epistle, I am deeply indebted to the admirable exposition of Harless, which, for accurate scholarship, learning, candor, and ability, may be pronounced one of the best, if not the very best commentary that has ever yet appeared on any single portion of Holy Scripture. A second edition has long been promised, but, as far as I could learn from catalogues, and the foreign booksellers in this country, it had not made its appearance when I commenced this Epistle, nor, up to the present time, have I seen any notice of its publication.

The exposition of this Epistle by Dr. Stier, under the title of *Die Gemeinde in Christo Jesu*, is very complete and comprehensive, but so depressingly voluminous as to weary out the patience of the most devoted reader. When I mention that it extends to upwards of 1050 closely printed pages, and that some single verses (e. g. ch. i. 23, ii. 15) are commented on to the extent of nearly thirty pages, I may be excused if I express my regret that a writer so earnest, so reverential, and so favorably known to the world as Dr. Rudolph Stier, should not have endeavored to have confined his commentary to somewhat more moderate dimensions. The chief fault I venture to find with Dr. Stier's system of interpretation is his constant and (in this work) characteristic endeavor to blend together two or more explanations, and, in his earnest and most praiseworthy attempt to exhibit the many deeper meanings which a passage may involve, to unite what is often dissimilar and inharmonious. Still his commentary is the production of a learned and devout mind, and no reader will consult it in vain. A review of it may be found in the seventy-ninth volume of Reuter's *Repertorium*.

The third special commentary I desire to mention, is the full and laborious commentary of Professor Eadie. I have derived from it little *directly*, as it is, to a great degree, confessedly a compilation from existing materials, and these I have, in all cases, thought it my duty to examine and to use for myself; still I have never failed to give Professor Eadie's decisions my best consideration, and have in many cases felt myself edified by the devoutness, and, not unfrequently, the eloquence of his expositions. I trust, however, the learned author will excuse me when I say that I do not think the grammatical portion of the commentary is by any means so well executed as the exegetical, and that I cannot but regard this otherwise able work, as, to a certain extent, an example of the truth of an opinion which I ventured to express in the preface to the *Galatians*, viz., that theological as well as grammatical learning is now so much increased, that it is hard to find a commentator who is able satisfactorily to undertake, at one and the same time, a critical, grammatical, exegetical, and dogmatical exposition of any portion of the New Testament. In his cumulative representation of the opinions of other commentators, as my notes will occasionally testify, Professor Eadie is also not always exact: with these abatements, however, which candor compels me to make, I can heartily and conscientiously recommend this commentary as both judicious and comprehensive, and as a great and important addition to the exegetical labors of this country.

I need hardly add that the last edition of the accurate, perspicuous, and learned commentary of Dr. Meyer, has been most carefully consulted throughout, and I must again, as in the preface to the *Galatians*, avow my great obligations to the acumen and scholarship of the learned editor. In many doctrinal questions I differ widely from Dr. Meyer, but, as a critical and grammatical expositor, I entertain for him a very great respect.

I have now only to commit my work to the reader, with the humble prayer to Almighty God, through Jesus Christ, that it may receive a blessing from above, and, though feebly and imperfectly, may still be permitted to minister somewhat to the more accurate knowledge of His blessed Word, and to the clearer perception of the outward forms and expressions of His everlasting Truth.

C. J. ELLICOTT.

CAMBRIDGE, JUNE 1855.

PREFACE TO THE SECOND EDITION.

THE second edition of the present Epistle is in all respects similar to the second edition of the Epistle to the Galatians, which appeared a few months since, and is brought up, I sincerely hope, fully to the same standard.

It is perhaps right to say that little has been substantially altered, and that the reader of the first edition will scarcely find more than half a dozen passages[1] where the opinions formerly maintained are either retracted or modified; still the additions are great, and the number of notes that have been recast or re-written by no means inconsiderable. By this means space has been obtained for the introduction of new matter; weaker arguments in contested passages have been made to give place to what might seem to put in a clearer light the stronger argument; logical and grammatical observations have been more grouped, and the links of thought that connect clause with clause or sentence with sentence, more studiously exhibited. In this last respect the additions will be found great, and will, I trust, by the blessing of God, be of no little use to the reader in properly pursuing the train of sublime thought that runs through this transcendent Epistle. This, alas! is the point most commonly neglected in our general study of Scripture: we trust to general impressions, and carry away general ideas, but the exact sequence of thought in the mind of the inspired writer is what, I fear, is only too frequently neglected. It is useless to disguise that this close analysis of the sacred text is *very* difficult,—that it requires a calm judgment, and a disciplined mind no less than a loving and teachable heart,—that it is not a power we can acquire in a week or in a month,—yet if Scripture be, what I for one believe it to be, the writing of men inspired by the third Person of the adorable Trinity, then we may well conceive no labor in this direction can be too severe, no exercise of thought too close or persistent. Let it also be not forgotten that no intelligent reader can now fairly say that he is without proper assistance; that the well is deep and he has nothing to draw with.

Setting aside all mention of the general improvement in the Commentaries of the day, and supposing the tacit objector to be either unable or unwilling

---

[1] I may specify for the sake of those who have the first edition, ch. i. 10, 12, 22; ii. 15; iv. 6; iv. 23 (amplified view); v. 25 (critical note).

to face the labor of reading the great patristic expositors, let him still remember that the science of grammar is now so much advanced,[1] that syntax
and logic are now so well and so happily combined, that no one who is really
in earnest, and to whom God has given a fair measure of ability, can for a
moment justly plead that an accurate knowledge of the Greek of the New
Testament is beyond his grasp, and a power of analyzing the connection of
its weighty sentences not abundantly ministered to him. I studiously limit
myself to saying the Greek *of the New Testament:* individual industry, however steadily exercised, may sometimes fail in making a student a good general
Greek scholar ; he may have no natural power of appreciating those felicities
of expression, no ready ability for discriminating between those subtle uses
of particles which mark the best age of Attic Greek; but the language of the
New Testament, its plain, hearty, truly simple, but truly Greek diction, is, I
am confident, above the reach of no one who will soundly study the general
rules of thought and language, as they are now put before us by the gram-
marians of our own time.   And this I say, partly to encourage the humbler
reader who might have thought such acquirements decidedly out of his reach,
partly for the sake of augmenting that kind and considerate company of students that have given these commentaries a hearing, and have borne patiently
with the constant notice and repetition of grammatical details. I venture
thus to dwell upon this topic,— a topic in part alluded to in the preface to
the first edition, as four years of hard study since that was written, and,
what is more valuable for testing opinions, one year of responsible *teaching*
have convinced me that a really accurate knowledge of the language of the
Greek Testament may be acquired far more easily than might at first have
been imagined; and have further confirmed me in the belief that it is by
these accurate investigations of the language of the Inspired Volume that
we are enabled really to penetrate into its deeper mysteries, and thence to
learn to appreciate the more convincing certainty of our highest hopes, and
the more assured reality of our truest consolations.

But to return to the present volume.   The student will find a great, and,
I trust, a welcome addition in the constant citations from nine ancient versions, viz., the Old Latin, the two Syriac Versions, the Vulgate, the Coptic,
the Gothic, the two Ethiopic Versions, and the Armenian.[2] All these have

---

1 I may here remark that the Greek Grammar of Dr. Donaldson, noticed in the Preface
to the *Galatians*, has now reached a second and enlarged edition, and is so complete in all
its parts, and so felicitous in its combination of logic with grammar, as to form a most important contribution to the accurate study of the Greek language.

2 I may take this opportunity of noticing, for the benefit of those who may be disposed
to study this interesting and not very difficult language, that I have derived much useful
assistance from the *Brevis Linguæ Armeniacæ Grammatica* (Berl. 1841) of J. H. Petermann.
It is furnished with a good Chrestomathy and a useful glossary, and has the great advantage of being perspicuous and brief.

been carefully studied, their opinions maturely considered, and their views of debated passages exhibited in brief and unpretending, but (if labor may be allowed to make me hopeful) in correct and trustworthy enumerations.

Considerable additions have been made in the way of short critical notes, especially in those cases in which the Received Text differs from the reading which I have thought it right to follow. Here I have received some welcome assistance from the last, the so-called *seventh* edition of Dr. Tischendorf's *New Testament*,[1] though I regret to say I am still obliged to reiterate the opinion which I have formerly expressed, that at any rate in the citations from the Ancient Versions, Dr. Tischendorf is not always to be depended upon. His own preface, though marked by great assumption of tone, will indeed itself confirm this; as he has, by his own admissions, depended nearly entirely on Leusden and Schaaf for the Peshito-Syriac, — on the incorrect edition of Wilkins for the Coptic Version of the Epistles, to the complete neglect of the more recent edition of Bötticher, — on a collator for Platt's Ethiopic, — and for the Armenian, on the edition of a man whose general inaccuracies he has unsparingly denounced, Dr. Scholz. The subjective criticisms mixed up in the notes, cannot be pronounced as either very useful or very satisfactory, and will serve to show how hard it is to find in one and the same person the patient and laborious palæographer and the sound and sagacious critic. Still we owe much to Dr. Tischendorf, and it is probable shall have to owe much more;[2] his unwearied labors command our highest respect, and may only the more make us regret that they are not set off by a greater Christian courtesy in his general tone, and by more forbearance towards those who feel it their duty to differ from him.

The last addition to the present edition which it is here necessary to specify is, perhaps, the most important, — *systematic* reference to the sermons and treatises of our best English divines. This, it will be remembered, appeared to some extent in the first edition, and has always formed a feature of these commentaries; still I am now enabled to give to the reader the results of a wider reading, and to entertain the hope that he will find but few really valuable illustrations from our *best* divines overlooked in the present volume. All I have done, however, is only in the way of reference. Much I regret that neither space, nor the general character of the commentary, enable me to make long quotations: I will repeat, however, what I have said elsewhere, that, as the references have been made with great care and consideration, I venture to think that the reader who will take the trouble of consulting the writers in the places referred to, will find himself abundantly rewarded for his labor.

1 In deference to the opinion and present usage of this critic, I now designate the MS. of St. Paul's Epp. formerly marked J. in the critical editions, by the new mark L.

2 For a brief notice of the discovery by Dr. Tischendorf of a MS. of the *whole* New Test. of an antiquity *said to be* as great as that of B, see the *Literary Churchman* for July 16, 1859, p. 258; *Bib. Sacra*, vol. xvi. 669.   2

I have already received many kind recognitions of the use which this class of references has proved to students in Theology; and I now continue them with renewed interest, feeling day by day more assured that in these latter times it is to our own great divines of the sixteenth and seventeenth centuries we must go for our Theology; and that it is from them alone that we can provide ourselves with preservatives against the unsound, vaunting, and humanitarian theosophy that is such a melancholy and yet such a popular characteristic of our own times.

Nothing now remains for me, except to notice briefly the works of fellow-laborers that have appeared since the publication of the first edition.

A new edition has recently appeared by Harless, but, as the author himself apprizes us, too little changed to need any further notice than what has already appeared in the original Preface to this work. A very useful edition for the general reader has also appeared in America, from the pen of the estimable Dr. Turner, but is too different in its principles of interpretation to have been of much use to me in a critical and grammatical commentary such as the present. To two commentaries, however, which have appeared in this country, during the interval I have alluded to, I have paid very great attention. The first is the Third Volume of my friend Dean Alford's *Commentary;* the second is the Third Part of Canon Wordsworth's *Commentary,* — works which both deserve and have received the high approbation of all biblical students; the former for its able and attractive exegesis, the latter for its valuable citations from Patristic and English Divinity, and both for their accurate scholarship, and sound and intelligent criticism.

I now commend myself to the kind judgment of my readers; and with the hope, that some time in the course of the following year, if God be pleased to give me health and strength, I may be able to complete another portion of my laborious undertaking, I here bring to its close a work that has claimed my incessant attention for some months.

May the blessing of God rest on this reäppearance of a lowly tribute to His Honor and Glory; — may its errors and shortcomings be forgiven, and its broken and partial glimpses of Divine Truth be permitted to excite in others a deeper reverence for the Eternal Word, and a more earnest longing for the full and perfect Day.

CAMBRIDGE, AUGUST, 1859.

INTRODUCTION.

THE sublime epistle to the Ephesians was written by St. Paul during his first captivity at Rome (Acts xxviii. 16), and stands second or more probably third in the third of the four groups into which the Epistles of St. Paul may be conveniently divided. The Ep. to the Colossians (Meyer *Einleit.* p. 18, Wieseler, *Chronol.* p. 450 sq.), and also that to Philemon, appear to have immediately *preceded*, while that to the Philippians seems to have *succeeded* after an interval of perhaps a year, when the Apostle's confinement assumed a harsher character, and his prospects seemed in some measure more cheerless (Phil. i. 20).

It was thus written about the year A. D. 62, and was conveyed to the Church of Ephesus by Tychicus (Eph. vi. 21), either *while on his way* to deliver the Epistles addressed respectively to the Colossians and to Philemon, or, as has been thought more probable (Meyer *Einleit.* p. 17), *on his return* after having performed that duty.

That the Epistle was addressed to the Christians of the important city of Ephesus seems scarcely open to serious doubt. Both the critical arguments (see note on ch. i. 1) and the nearly unanimous consent of the early Church (Iren. *Hær.* v. 2, 3, Clem. Alex. *Strom.* iv. 8, Vol. I. p. 592, ed. Pott., Orig. *Cels.* Vol. I. p. 458, ed. Bened.) are so decidedly in favor of such a destination, that we scarcely seem warranted in calling in question a statement so strongly supported. Still the omission of greetings and personal notices in an Epistle sent from the founder of the Church of Ephesus (Acts xix. i. sq., comp. xviii. 19) to converts with whom he had abode nearly three years (Acts xx. 31) seems so very striking and noticeable, that we may perhaps so far adopt the opinion of Usher (*Annal.* ann. 4068) and of several recent expositors, that this Epistle, though addressed to the Christians at Ephesus, was still designed for circulation in all the churches conterminous to or dependent on that city, and was thus left studiously general in form, and free from distinctive notices. Individual greetings and other messages of affection might well have been entrusted to a bearer who was specially commissioned to inform the receivers of the Epistle upon all points connected with the personal state of the Apostle (ch. vi. 21).

The Epistle does not appear to have been called forth by any particular. circumstances, nor to have involved any warning against the peculiarities of Jewish or Eastern Philosophy, but was designed to set forth the origin and development of the Church of Christ, and to display to the Christian dweller under the shadow of the great temple of Diana the unity and beauty of that transcendently more glorious spiritual temple (ch. ii. 20) of which Christ Himself was the head corner-stone, and the saints portions of the superstructure. That it should also contain many thoughts nearly identical with those expressed in the Epistle to the Colossians is readily accounted for by the fact that both were written nearly at the same time, and both addressed to Churches which were sufficiently near to each other to have had many things in common, especially in the relations of social and domestic life.

The *genuineness* and *authenticity* admit of no reasonable doubt. The testimonies of the Early Church are unusually strong and persistent (see reff. above, and add Tertull. *de Præscr.* ch. xxxvi., Hippol. *Refut. Hær.* p. 193, ed. Oxf.), and have never been called in question till comparatively recent times. The objections are purely of a subjective character, being mainly founded on imaginary weaknesses in style or equally imaginary references to early Gnosticism, and have been so fairly and fully confuted that they can no longer be considered to deserve any serious attention; see esp. Meyer, *Einleit.* p. 19 sq., Davidson, *Introd.* Vol. II. p. 352 sq., Alford, *Prolegom.* p. 8.

The arguments in favor of the Epistle having been written at Cæsarea will be found in Meyer, *Einleit.* § 2, but are far from convincing.

THE EPISTLE TO THE EPHESIANS.

CHAPTER I. 1.

Apostolic address and salutation.

ΠΑΥΛΟΣ ἀπόστολος Χριστοῦ Ἰησοῦ διὰ
Θελήματος Θεοῦ τοῖς ἁγίοις τοῖς

1. ἐν Ἐφέσῳ] *Tisch.* and *Alf.* have enclosed these words in brackets, but scarcely with sufficient reason. Without entering into detailed arguments, it may be sufficient to remark, that the facts about which all now seem agreed are as follows : — (1) As far as our present collations can be depended upon, all the MSS., mss., and Vv., are unanimous in favor of the insertion, except B, where the words are supplied on the margin by a *second* hand (*Tisch.*), and 67, where they appear in the text, but with diacritical marks indicative of suspicion : — (2) Basil of Cappad. *certainly* did not find the words ἐν τοῖς παλαιοῖς τῶν ἀντιγράφων, *Eunom.* II. 19. Bp. Middleton supposes Basil only appeals to the ancient MSS. as containing τοῖς οὖσιν ἐν Ἐφ., not simply τοῖς ἐν Ἐφ.; comp. Wiggers, *Stud. u. Krit.* for 1841, p. 423 : this opinion, however, has no diplomatic support of any kind, and cannot fairly and logically be deduced from the words of Basil ; see Meyer, *Einleit.* p. 2, note : — (3) Tertullian (*Marc.* v. 11. 17) *possibly* was not aware of their existence ; it is uncritical to say more. His words, ' veritas Ecclesiæ,' do not necessarily imply an absence of diplomatic evidence, nor can ' interpolare' (comp. *Marc.* IV. 1, v. 21) be pressed : — (4) Origen (*Caten.* Vol. II. p. 102) appears to have accepted the omission, as he comments on the peculiarity of the expression τοῖς ἁγίοις τοῖς οὖσι ; see *Tisch.* (ed. 7). The *internal* evidence, such as absence of greetings and personal notices, is of more importance. Still, both combined cannot be considered sufficient to overthrow the vast preponderance of external authority, and the appy. unanimous tradition of the early Church, that this Ep. was addressed to

CHAP. I. 1. ἀπόστολος X. Ἰ.] ' an *apostle of Jesus Christ :* ' gen. not of *ablation* (the source from which his commission proceeded ; comp. Stier *in loc.*), but simply of *possession,* in ref. to the Master whose servant and minister he was ; see

Acts xxvii. 23, οὗ εἰμί, Rom. i. 1, δοῦλος Ἰ. X., and comp. notes *on Phil.* i. 1. The distinction between these forms of the gen. (which Eadie appears not to have fully felt) is often faintly marked (compare Scheuerl. *Synt.* § 16, 17) ; still

οὖσιν ἐν Ἐφέσῳ καὶ πιστοῖς ἐν Χριστῷ Ἰησοῦ.

the Ephesians (Iren. *Hær*, v. 2, 3, Clem. Al. *Strom*. IV. 8, Tertull. *l. c.*, Origen, *Cels*. III. p. 458, ed. Ben.). We therefore retain the words as genuine, and ascribe their omission in B to an early exercise of criticism founded on supposed internal evidence, traces of which are found in Theodoret, *Præf. in Eph.*: comp. Wieseler, *Chronol*. p. 442 sq. The different theories and attempts to reconcile conflicting evidence will be found in Meyer, *Einleit.* § 1, Wieseler, *Chronol*. p. 432 sq., and Davidson, *Introd.* Vol. II. p. 328 sq. Of the many *hypotheses*, that of Harless (*Einleit.* p. 57) — that the Ep. was designed not only for the Ephesians, but for the Churches dependent on Ephesus, or the Christians who had already been converted there — is perhaps the most plausible.

Harless seems quite correct in saying that the idea of *authorization* does not depend simply on the gen., but on the modal clauses κατ᾿ ἐπιταγήν, 1 Tim. i. 1, which are commonly attached : comp. Gal. i. 1, where the nature of the relations between the Apostle and his converts suggests language of unusual precision. διὰ θελήματος] '*by the will of God ;*' modal clause appended to the preceding words, not so much to enhance his apostolic authority (comp. Alf.), as in that thankful remembrance of God's power and grace, which any allusion to his ministerial office was sure to awaken in the Apostle's heart: comp. 1 Cor. xv. 10, Gal. i. 15. These and the preceding words occur in the same order and connection in 2 Cor. i. 1, Col. i. 1, 2 Tim. i. 1; compare 1 Cor. i. 1. Though it is not possible to doubt that the Apostle, in addressing different Churches or individuals, *designedly* adopted the same or different modes of salutation, still it is not in all cases easy to trace, from external considerations, the reasons for the choice ; comp. notes on *Col.* i. 1. Rückert, who has slightly touched on the subject (*on Gal.* i. 1), refers the Apostle's present specification of his authority, διὰ θελ. Θ., to the encyclical character of the Epistle. As this character, though probable (see crit. note), is merely hypothetical, it will be safer, and perhaps more natural, to adopt the more general explanation

above alluded to ; see Meyer *on* 1 *Cor.* i. 1. τοῖς ἁγίοις] '*to the Saints.*' Christians are appy. called ἅγιοι in the N. T. in three senses ; (*a*) *generally*, as members of a visible and local community devoted to God's service (Acts ix. 32, xxvi. 10, Rom. xv. 20), and, as such, united in a common outward profession of faith (1 Cor. i. 2 ; see Chrys. *on Rom.* i. 7) ; (*b*) more *specifically*, as members of a spiritual community (Col. iii. 12, 1 Pet. ii. 9) ; and (*c*) as also in many cases having personal and individual sanctity ; comp. ver. 4, see Fell, *in loc.* The context will generally show which of these ideas predominates. In salutations like the present, ἅγιος appears used in its most comprehensive sense, as involving the idea of a *visible* (hence the local predicate), and also (as the complementary clause καὶ πιστοῖς ἐν Χρ. Ἰ. suggests) that of a *spiritual* and holy community ; see Col. i. 1, and esp. 1 Cor. i. 2, where defining clauses involving these different ideas are grouped round κλητοῖς ἁγίοις : comp. Thorndike, *Review*, I. 33, Vol. I. p. 656 (A. C. Libr.), and Davenant *on Col.* i. 2. πιστοῖς ἐν Χ. Ἰ.] '*faithful, sc. believing, in Jesus Christ.*' Πιστός is not here in its general and classical sense, 'qui fidem præstat' (Grot., Alf.), but its particular and theological sense, 'qui fidem habet' comp. Syr.), a meaning which it indisputably bears in several passages in the N. T.; *e. g.* John xx. 27, 2 Cor. vi.

² χάρις ὑμῖν καὶ εἰρήνη ἀπὸ Θεοῦ πατρὸς ἡμῶν καὶ Κυρίου
Ἰησοῦ Χριστοῦ.

Blessed be *God* who has predestinated us to the adoption of sons, redeemed us by *Christ's* blood, revealed to us His eternal purpose of uniting all in Him, and has commenced its fulfilment by sealing with his *Spirit* both Jew and Gentile.

³ Εὐλογητὸς ὁ Θεὸς καὶ πατὴρ τοῦ Κυρίου

15, Gal. iii. 9, 1 Tim. iv. 3 (not 1 Tim. i. 12, Eadie), Titus i. 6, etc.; compare Wisdom i. 14, Psalm c. 6, and see Suicer, *Thesaur.* s. v. Vol. ii. p. 741. ἐν Χριστῷ implies union, fellowship, with Christ (see notes *on Gal.* ii. 17), and qualifies only the more restricted term, πιστός, not ἅγιος (Phil. i. 1.) *and* πιστός (Harl., Meier). The clause is not, however, on the one hand, a mere epexegesis of ἁγίοις (Beza), nor, on the other, a specification of another and separate class (Stier), but completes the description of the ἅγιοι, by the *addition* of a second and more distinctive predication; see Meyer *in loc.* Πιστὸς ἐν Χρ. thus approximates in meaning to πιστεύων εἰς Χρ. (Gal. ii. 16), except that the latter involves a closer connection of the verb and the prep. (πιστ. εἰς — Χρ.), and points rather to an *act* of the will, while the former involves a closer connection of the prep. and the noun (πιστ. — ἐν Χρ.), and marks a *state* and condition: see Fritz. *Marc.* p. 175, and Eadie *in loc.*, where the full force of the preposition is eloquently expanded.

2. χάρις ὑμῖν καὶ εἰρήνη] 'Grace *to you and peace;*' scil. εἴη not ἔστω (Meier, Holzh.), which, though not untenable (Bernhardy, *Synt.* xi. 5, p. 392 : comp. 2 Chron. ix. 8), is far less suitable and even less usual than the *optative;* see 1 Pet. i. 2, 2 Pet. i. 2, Jude 2, and comp. 2 John 3, where, however, ἔσται gives the wish the character of a definite expectation. The suggestion of Stier that χάρις and εἰρήνη refer respectively to the ἅγιοι and πιστοί does not seem tenable, as the formula is so common without any such antecedents (Rom. i. 7, 1 Cor. i. 3, 2 Cor. i. 2, al.); still they must not be diluted into mere equiva-

lents of the ordinary forms of salutation (Fritz. *Rom.* i. 7, Vol. i. p. 23). Χάρις expresses God's love toward man; εἰρήνη, the state of peace and blessedness which results from it; εἰρηνεύει γὰρ πρὸς τὸν Θεὸν ὁ τὴν εὐαγγελικὴν ἀσπασάμενος πολιτείαν, Theodoret, *Rom.* i. 8 : see notes *on Gal.* i. 3. It may be observed that as *this* form is regularly maintained in all St. Paul's Epp. to Churches (Philem. 3 is no exception, being addressed also τῇ κατ' οἶκον ἐκκλησίᾳ), while in 1 Tim. i. 2, 2 Tim. i. 2, Tit. i. 4 (*Rec.*, *Lachm.*), the more personal term ἔλεος is added; the latter might seem the form addressed to *individuals,* the former to *communities;* comp. too Rev. i. 4, 2 John 3, but consider Jude 2, Gal. vi. 16, and observe that in Tit. *l. c.* the longer reading is more than doubtful. St. James alone adopts the usual formula, χαίρειν : in 3 John i. 2 the salutation passes into a prayer.　　καὶ Κυρίου] Scil. καὶ ἀπὸ Κυρίου κ. τ. λ., so expressly Syr., Arm., both of which repeat the preposition. The Socinian interpretation, καὶ (πατρὸς) Κυρ., is grammatically admissible, but in a high degree forced and improbable: see esp. Tit. i. 4, and compare 1 Thess. iii. 11, 2 Thess. ii. 16.

3. εὐλογητός] '*Blessed,*'— scil. ἔστω (2 Chron. ix. 8), or εἴη (Job i. 21, Psalm cxii. 2): the verb is, however, commonly omitted in this and similar forms of doxology; comp. 2 Cor. i. 3. In this solemn ascription of praise εὐλογητός (ἐπαινεῖσθαι καὶ θαυμάζεσθαι ἄξιος, Theod.-Mops.), as its position shows, has the principal emphasis, the rule of Fritz. (*Rom.* ix. 5, Vol. ii. 274) being appy. reasonable — that εὐλογητός or εὐλογημένος will occupy the first or some succeeding place in the sentence, according

ἡμῶν Ἰησοῦ Χριστοῦ ὁ εὐλογήσας ἡμᾶς ἐν πάσῃ εὐλογίᾳ πνευ-

·as the emphasis rests on the predicate (as it commonly does), or on the substantive ; comp. 1 Kings x. 9, 2 Chron. *l. c.*, Job *l. c.*, and esp. Psalm *l. c.*, which are thus more satisfactorily explained than by a supposed limitation of position in consequence of the inserted copula (Alf. *on Rom.* ix. 5).   It has been remarked by Steiger *on* 1 *Pet.* i. 3 (comp. Harless), that in the N. T. εὐλογητός is only applied to God, εὐλογημένος to man: it may be added that in the LXX, the latter is occasionally applied to God, but never the former to man. For a good analysis of the present paragraph, in which the relations of the Church to the three persons of the blessed Trinity are distinctly unfolded, see Alford *in loc.* Θεὸς καὶ πατήρ κ. τ. λ.] '*God and the Father of our Lord Jesus Christ.*' It is doubtful whether in this formula (which Rück. needlessly terms 'paulinisch,' see 1 Pet. i. 3) the gen. depends (*a*) on both (Theoph.), or (*b*) only on the latter (Syr., Æth., Theod.-Mops. 1, Theodoret) of the two nominatives. Chrys. leaves it undecided. Grammatical considerations do not assist us ; for, on the one hand, the position of the article before Θεὸs rather than Πατήρ (Olsh.) does not invalidate the latter interpretation (compare Winer. *Gr.* § 19. 3, p. 115 note), nor the omission of τέ before καὶ (Harless) the former ; the usual 'preparative force of τὲ (Hartung, *Partik.* Vol. I. p. 98, Klotz, *Devar.* Vol. II. p. 730) here obviously out of place. To the former interpretation, Θεὸs μέν, ὡς σαρκωθέντος, πατὴρ δέ, ὡς Θεοῦ λόγου, there can be no doctrinal objections (see verse 17, John xx. 17, and compare Olsh. *on Matth.* xxi. 31, 32), but from the considerations suggested *on Gal.* i. 4, as well as from the fact that, except in ver. 17, St. Paul has not elsewhere so designated the Father, the latter construction seems

decidedly preferable.   On the most suitable translation, see notes *on Gal.* i. 4. (*Transl.*).   ὁ εὐλογήσας ἡμᾶς] '*who blessed us ;*' 'antanaclasis ; aliter nobis benedixit Deus, aliter nos benedicimus Illi,' Bengel. The aorist *participle* (where the aoristic force is always least obscure, Bernhardy, *Synt.* x. 9, p. 383) refers to the counsels of the Father as graciously completed in the Redemption, and is thus neither used (*a*) for a pres. (Holzh.) — an untenable position, except in a sense and under limitations (Scheuerl. *Syntax*, § 32. 2, p. 331) which would here be doctrinally unsuitable ; nor (*b*) as marking 'a customary or repeated act' (Eadie) — a meaning which the aorist never appears to bear in the N. T.; see Winer, *Gr.* § 40. 4. I. p. 248. The reference of ἡμᾶς can scarcely be doubtful : it cannot refer to St. Paul (Koppe), — for comp. κἀγώ, ver. 15, — but, as the inclusive nature of the context (ver. 14, 11, 12) distinctly implies, must be extended to Christians generally. No fixed rules can be laid down for the reference of the plural pronoun : this must always be determined by the context.   ἐν πάσῃ εὐλογίᾳ πνευματικῇ] '*with every blessing of the Spirit ;* agency by which the blessing was imparted, ἐν here being appy. instrumental (see notes *on* 1 *Thess.* iv. 18), and perhaps not without some parallelism to the Hebrew בְ : comp. the analogous construction, Tobit viii. 15, and James iii. 9, where, however, the instrumental sense is much more distinct. The meaning and force of πνευματικῇ is slightly doubtful. Chrys. and Theod.-Mops. find in it an antithesis to the blessings of the Old Covenant (τὴν Ἰουδαϊκὴν ἐνταῦθα αἰνίττεται· εὐλογία μὲν γὰρ ἦν ἀλλ' οὐ πνευματική ; Chrys.; comp. Schoettg. *Hor.* Vol. I. p. 756) ; so distinctly Syr., Æth., and with a detailed

μ̇ατικῇ ἐν τοῖς ἐπουρανίοις ἐν Χριστῷ, ⁴ καϑὼς ἐξελέξατο ἡμᾶς ἐν

enumeration of the blessings, Theodoret, *in loc.* It seems, however, much more in accordance both with the present context and with the prevailing usage of the N. T. (see Rom. i. 11, χάρισμα πνευματικόν, and 1 Cor. xii. 1 τῶν πνευματικῶν, compared with ver. 11), to refer the epithet directly to the Holy Spirit (Joel iii. 1 sq., Acts ii. 16). Bengel has not failed to notice the allusion to the Trinity, which, as Stier (Vol. I. p. 57) has clearly shown, pervades the whole of this sublime Epistle.   ἐ ν τ ο ῖ ς ἐ π ο υ ρ α ν ί ο ι ς] *in heavenly regions;* ܒ̣ܫ̣ܡ̣ܝ̣ܐ [in cœlo], Syr., 'in cœlis,' Æth. The exact meaning of these words is doubtful. Many of the ancient, and several modern expositors, explain τὰ ἐπουράνια, as 'heavenly blessings' (ἐπουράνια γὰρ τὰ δῶρα ταῦτα, Theodoret), 'heavenly institutions' (J. Johnson, *Unbl. Sacr.* Vol. I. p. 198, A. C. Libr.), and thus, as in *ethical* contrast to τὰ ἐπίγεια (Chrys.); see John iii. 12, but comp. 1 Cor. xv. 40, where the same words are in physical contrast. This is not grammatically untenable, and would not require the omission of τοῖς (Rück., Eadie, al.), as the article would thus only correctly designate the class; see Middleton, *Greek Art.* III. 2. 2, p. 40, and comp. Winer, *Gr.* § 18. 3, p. 99. As, however, such a specification of the sphere, and thence of the spiritual character of the action would seem superfluous after the definite words immediately preceding, — as in the four other passages in this Ep. (i. 20, ii. 6, iii. 10, and vi. 12, but contr. Chrys.) the expression seems obviously *local,* and lastly, — as throughout St. Paul's Epp. (even 2 Tim. iv. 18) ἐπουράνιος has that local or physical force which the preposition ἐπὶ (Harless) would also seem further to suggest, it will be best, both from contextual and

lexical reasons to retain that meaning in the present case. 'Εν τοῖς ἐπουρ. must then here be referred as a *local* predication to εὐλογ. πνευμ., defining, broadly and comprehensively the region and sphere where our true home is (Phil. iii. 20), where our hope is laid up (Col. i. 5), and whence the blessings of the Spirit, the δωρεὰ ἡ ἐπουράνιος (Heb. vi. 4), truly come : see notes to *Transl.* ἐ ν Χ ρ ι σ τ ῷ] Not for διὰ Χρ. (Chrys., Hamm.), but, as in ver. 1, '*in Christ;*' 'in quo uno spirituali et sanctificâ benedictione donamur,' Beza. Thus εὐλογήσας contains the predication of *time* (Donalds. *Gr.* § 574 sq.), ἐν εὐλογ. πνευμ. the predication of *manner,* more exactly defined by the *local* predication ἐν τοῖς ἐπούρ., while ἐν Χρ. is that mystical predication which, as Stier well observes, 'is the very soul of this Epistle,' and involves all other conceptions in itself. For a good example of this species of analysis of clauses and sentences, see Donalds. *Crat.* § 304.

4. κ α ϑ ώ s] '*even as,*' 'sicut' Clarom., Vulg., Copt., al.; explanation and expansion of the preceding εὐλογήσας κ. τ. λ., the particle καϑώς, which in most cases has a purely modal, appearing here to have also a slightly explanatory or even casual force ('inasmuch as'), and to mark not only the accordance, but the necessary connection of the εὐλογία with the ἐκλογή; see Rom. i. 28, 1 Cor. i. 6, and compare καϑότι (used only by St. Luke), which has both a modal (Acts ii. 45, iv. 35) and a causal (Acts ii. 24) meaning. The form καϑώς is not found in the older Attic writers, or in Lucian; see Lobeck, *Phryn.* p. 426, and notes *on Gal.* iii. 6.   ἐ ξ ε λ έ ξ α τ ο ἡ μ ᾶ s] '*chose us out for Himself;*' 'elegit,' Clarom., Vulg., al., — but with some sacrifice of the fullest meaning. Without entering into the profound dogmat-

αὐτῷ πρὸ καταβολῆς κόσμου, εἶναι ἡμᾶς ἁγίους καὶ ἀμώμους

ical questions connected with the meaning of this verb (only used by St. Paul, here and 1 Cor. i. 27), it may be simply observed that in ἐξελέξατο three ideas are suggested ; — (a) selection (not necessarily of *individuals*; see Ebrard, *Dogm.* § 560), from, out of, others not chosen (ἐκ τοῦ κόσμου, John xv. 19; contr. Hofmann, *Schriftb.* Vol. i. p. 198), suggested by the plain *meaning* of the word ; — (b) simple unrestricted preterition of the act (alike irrespective of duration or relation, Bernhardy, *Syntax*, x. 8, p. 380, and esp. Fritz. *de Aor.* p. 17 sq.), conveyed by the *tense*, and further heightened by the 'timelessness' (Olsh.) of the quasi-temporal predication πρὸ καταβολῆς; compare 2 Thess. ii. 13, εἵλατο ἀπ᾽ ἀρχῆς: God is ὁ καλῶν (1 Thess. ii. 2), as well as ὁ καλέσας (Gal. i. 6), but not ὁ ἐκλεγόμενος; — (c) reflexive action (for Himself; comp. Eph. v. 27, Rev. xxi. 2), implied by the *voice*. While the primary meaning of ἐκλέγ. and similar words is undoubtedly to be looked for in their general and national references in the O. T. (Usteri *Lehrbegr.* ii. 2. 2, p. 271, Knapp, *Script. Var. Arg.* p. 556), the modal clauses with which they are combined show the deeper and more distinctive sense in which they are used in the New Testament. On this profound subject, and on the estate of man (the estate of wrath, of reconciliation, and of election) see esp. Jackson, *Creed*, x. 37, 11 sq., Vol. ix. p. 312 sq., and comp. Hammond *on God's Grace*, Vol. i. p. 667 sq. (Lond. 1674), and Laurence, *Bampt. Lect.* for 1804. ἐν αὐτῷ] Not for δι᾽ αὐτοῦ, scil. διὰ τῆς εἰς αὐτὸν πίστεως (Chrys., Hamm.), nor for εἰς αὐτὸν (comp. Æth.). nor yet with an instrumental force (Arm.), but, as Olsh. correctly and profoundly explains it, 'in Him,'—in Christ, as the head and repre-

sentative of spiritual, as Adam was the representative of natural humanity ; comp. 1 Cor. xv. 22. πρό καταβολῆς κόσμου] This expression, used three times in the N. T. (John xvii, 24, 1 Pet. i. 20), here serves to define the archetypal character of the New Dispensation, and the wide gulf that separated the πρόθεσις πρὸ χρόνων αἰωνίων (2 Tim. i. 9) of God with respect to Christians, from His temporal ἐκλογὴ of the Jews ; see Neander, *Planting*, Vol. i. p. 522 (Bohn). εἶναι ἡμᾶς κ. τ. λ.] '*that we should be holy and blameless;*' object contemplated by God in His gracious ἐκλογή, the infin. being that of intention ; scil. ἐπὶ τούτῳ ἵνα ἅγιοι ὦμεν καὶ ἄμωμοι, Chrys.; comp 2 Cor. xi. 2, Col. i. 22, and see Winer, *Gr.* § 45. 1, p. 284. Donalds. *Gr.* § 607. a, p. 598. ἁγίους καὶ ἀμώμους '*holy and blameless;*' positive and negative aspects of true Christian life. The meaning of ἄμωμος (ἄμεμπτος· καθαρός· ἄψεκτος, Hesych.) is slightly doubtful; it may be (a) '*inculpatus,*' ὁ ἀνεπίληπτον βίον ἔχων, Chrys., in accordance with its derivation (μῶμος μέμφομαι), or (b) '*immaculatus*' (Vulg., Clarom., Arm. ; comp. Syr., Goth.), with possible reference to its application in the LXX to victims, Lev. i. 10, xxii. 19; comp. 1 Macc. iv. 42, ἱερεῖς ἀμώμους, and see Tittm. *Synon.* p. 29. The latter meaning is strongly supported by 1 Pet. i. 19, ἀμνοῦ ἀμώμου καὶ ἀσπίλου, and Heb. ix. 14 : still, as there is here no sacrificial allusion directly or indirectly (comp. ch. v. 27), it seems best to retain the simple etymological meaning; see Col. i. 22, ἀμώμους καὶ ἀνεγκλήτους, and compare Wisd. x. 15, λαὸν ὅσιον καὶ σπέρμα ἄμεμπτον. It is more doubtful whether these epithets point to a moral condition, *i. e.* to the righteousness of sanctification (Chrys., Hamm.), or to the imputed

κατενώπιον αὐτοῦ, ἐν ἀγάπῃ ⁵ προορίσας ἡμᾶς εἰς υἱοθεσίαν διὰ

righteousness of Christ, (Olsh., Mey.)
The former reference seems most consonant both with St. Paul's general teaching (1 Thess. iv. 7) and the obvious
inferences that may be drawn from other
passages in the N. T., 1 Pet. i. 16, Rev.
xxii. 11; see Stier *in loc.*, and on the
distinction between sanctifying and justifying righteousness, the excellent remarks of Hooker, *Serm.* II. 6. Vol. III.
p. 611.   κ α τ ε ν ώ π ι ο ν α ὐ τ ο ῦ]
'*before Him;*' 'id est vere, sincere,'
Beza; not what men, but what God
esteems as such. ἀγιωσύνην ζητεῖ ἦν ὁ
τοῦ Θεοῦ ὀφθαλμὸς ὁρᾷ Chrys. The form
αὐτοῦ is here to be preferred, as the reference to the subject is obviously remote
and unemphatic; comp. Bremi, *Jahrb.
der Philol.* ix. p. 171 (Winer). The distinction, however, between the proper
use of these two forms cannot be rigorously defined; see Buttm. *Mid.* (Excurs.
x) p. 140, and Tisch. *Prolegom.* p.
LVIII. ἐν ἀγάπῃ *may* be joined with
ἐξελέξατο; more probably with ἀγ. καὶ
ἀμώμ. (Vulg., Copt.); but appy. *most*
probably with προορίσας (Syr., Chrys.,
Theod.), as St Paul's object seems here
not so much to define the nature of the
required ἀγιωσύνη and ἀμεμφία on the
part of man, as to reveal the transcendent principle of Love which informed
the προορισμὸς of God; καὶ προεῖδεν ἡμᾶς
καὶ ἠγάπησε, Theod., compare Theod.-
Mops. The arguments derived from
the collocation of the words are not decisive, for ἐν ἀγάπῃ could as well be joined
with ἀγ. καὶ ἀμ. here, as ἐν ἁγιωσύνῃ with
ἀμέμπτους, 1 Thess. iii. 13; and again
could as easily precede (emphatically)
προορίσας here, as it does ἐῤῥιζωμένοι ch.
iii. 18. Lastly, it cannot be said that
the second modal clause, κατὰ τὴν εὐδ.
is thus superfluous (Meier): the two
clauses point to two different attributes;
ἐν ἀγάπῃ to the loving Mercy, κατὰ τὴν

εὐδ. to the sovereign Power of God.
For a good defence of the second form
of connection see Alford *in loc.*
    5. π ρ ο ο ρ ί σ α ς ἡ μ ᾶ ς] '*having fore-
ordained us*' i. e. not '*prædestinans*,'
Beng., but '*quum prædestinasset*,' Syr.-
Phil., the participle being most naturally
regarded as *temporal*, not modal, and its
action as *prior to*, not synchronous with
(as in ver. 9) that of ἐξελ.; comp. Rom.
viii. 29, 30, and see Bernhardy, *Synt.* III.
9, p. 383, Donalds. *Gr.* § 574 sq. With
regard to the prep. it would certainly
seem that πρὸ does not refer to others
(Baumg.), nor, appy., to existence before time (Eadie), but simply to the
realization of the event: the decree existed *before* the object of it came into
outward manifestation; comp. προηλπι
κότας, ver. 12, and see Olsh. *on Rom.* ix.
1. The distinction between ἐκλογὴ and
προορισμὸς is thus drawn by Scherzer
(cited by Wolf); 'differunt tantum ratione ordinativâ et objectivâ,'—the ἐκ of
the former referring to the mass from
whom the selection was made, the πρὸ
of the latter to the preëxistence and priority of the decree. On προορισμός, etc.,
see Petavius, *Theol. Dogm.* ix. 1, Vol. I.
p. 565 sq., and Laurence, *Bampt. Lect.*
VIII. p. 169 sq.   ε ἰ ς υ ἱ ο θ ε σ ί α]
'*for adoption*,' scil. ἵνα αὐτοῦ υἱοὶ λεγοί[ω]
μεθα καὶ χρηματίζωμεν, Theod.-Mops.;
υἱοθεσία, however, not being merely *sonship* (Ust. *Lehrb.* II. 1, 2, p. 186), but as
usual, '*adoptionem* filiorum, Vulg.; see
notes *on Gal.* iv. 5, and Neander, *Planting,* Vol. I. p. 477 (Bohn).   ε ἰ ς
α ὐ τ ό ν], '*unto Him;*' comp. Col. i. 20,
ἀποκαταλλάξαι τὰ πάντα εἰς αὐτόν. As
the exact meaning of these words is
slightly obscure, it will be best to premise the following statements. (a) Εἰς
υἱοθ. .... εἰς αὐτὸν must be regarded as a
single compound clause expressive of
the manner and nature of the προορισ·

'Ιησοῦ Χριστοῦ εἰς αὐτόν, κατὰ τὴν εὐδοκίαν τοῦ θελήματος αὐτοῦ, ⁶ εἰς ἔπαινον δόξης τῆς χάριτος αὐτοῦ, ἐν ᾗ ἐχαρίτωσεν

6. ἐν ᾗ] So *Tisch.* (ed. 2, 7) with DEF (om. ᾗ) GKL; great majority of mss.; Clarom., Vulg., Goth., Syr.-Phil., Arm., al.; Bas., Chrys., Theod., al. and rightly; for ᾗs, though found in AB; mss.; Syr., Æth.; Orig. (Cat.), Chrys. (1), al. (*Lachm., Mey., Alf.*), has weaker external support; and on internal grounds, as a grammatical correction, seems very suspicious. The statement of Alf., that 'a relative following a substantive is as often in a different case as the same, certainly cannot be substantiated; see Winer, *Gr.* § 24. 1, p. 197.

μός; δι' Ιησ. and εἰς αὐτ. being *separate* sub-clauses further defining the prominent idea εἰς υἱοθεσίαν. (*b*) Αὐτὸν (not αὐτὸν) is not to be referred to *Christ* (De W.), but, with the Greek expositors, to *God.* (*c*) Εἰς αὐτὸν is not merely equivalent to ἐν αὐτῷ (Beza), or לֹו, scil. לְבַהֲבָה (Holzh.); nor is the favorite transl. of Meyer, 'in reference to Him' (comp. Rück), though, grammatically tenable (Winer, *Gr.* § 49. a, p. 354), by any means sufficient. In these deeper theological passages the prep. seems to bear its primary (εἰς = ἐνs Donalds. *Crat.* § 170) and most comprehensive sense of '*to* and *into*' (see Rost u. Palm, *Lex.* s.v.); the idea of *approach* (τὴν εἰς αὐτὸν ἀνάγουσαν, Theoph.) being also blended with, and heightened by, that of *inward union;* comp. notes on *Gal.* iii. 27. We may thus paraphrase, 'God predestinated us to be adopted as His sons; and that adoption came to us through Christ, and was to lead us unto, and unite us to God.' Stier compares what he terms the bold expression, 2 Pet. i. 4. κατὰ τὴν εὐδοκίαν κ. τ. λ.] '*according to the good pleasure of His will,' 'in or rather 'secundum placitum (propositum, Vulg.) voluntatis suæ,' Clarom.; the prep. κατά, as usual, marking 'rule, measure, accordance to,' Winer, *Gr.* § 49 d, p. 357. The exact meaning of εὐδοκία is here doubtful. The Greek expositors (not Chrys.) refer it to the *benevolentia* (ἡ ἐπ' εὐεργεσίᾳ βούλησις Œcum.), the Vulg., Syr., Goth. ('leikainai'), al. to

the *voluntas liberrima* of God. The latter meaning rarely, if ever (not even Ecclus. i. 27, xxxii. 5), occurs in the *LXX;* in the *N. T.*, however, though there are decided instances of the former meaning, *e. g.* Luke ii. 14 (not 'lætitia,' Fritz.), Phil. i. 15 (δι' εὐδ. opp. to διὰ φθόνον), still there is no reason to doubt (Harl.) that the latter occurs in Matth. xi. 26 (θέλησις καὶ ἀρέσκεια, Theoph.) Luke x. 21, and, probably, Phil. ii. 13. Thus the context must decide. As here and ver. 9 εὐδοκία seems to refer exclusively to the actor (προορίσας, γνωρίσας), not to the objects of the action; it seems best with De Wette (mis-cited by Eadie) to adopt the latter meaning, though not in the extreme sense, τὸ σφοδρὸν θέλημα, as advocated by Chrys. In this the idea of *goodness* (ἡ ἀρίστη καὶ καλλίστη τοῦ Θεοῦ ἑκούσιος θέλησις, Etym. M.) is of course necessarily involved, but it does not form the prominent idea. For further details, see esp. Fritz. *on Rom.* x. 1, Vol. II. p. 369 sq., and Wordsw. *in loc.*

6. εἰς ἔπαινον κ. τ. λ.] '*for the praise of the glory of His grace,' 'in or rather 'ad [Clarom.; see Madvig, *Opusc. Acad.* p. 167 sq.; comp. Hand, *Tursell.* Vol. III. p. 317] laudem gloriæ gratiæ suæ,' Vulg.; ἵνα ἡ τῆς χάριτος αὐτοῦ δόξα δειχθῇ, Chrys.: divine purpose of the προορισμός; εἰς here denoting the 'finis primarius' (Phil. i. 11), not 'consequens aliquid' Grot., as in 1 Pet. i. 7. It is scarcely necessary to say that neither is

ἡμᾶς ἐν τῷ ἠγαπημένῳ, ⁷ ἐν ᾧ ἔχομεν τὴν ἀπολύτρωσιν διὰ τοῦ

ἔπαινος δόξης for ἔπαινος ἐνδοξος (Grot.), nor δόξα τῆς χάριτος for ἔνδοξος χάρις (Beza), — both of them weak, and, here especially, wholly inadmissible solutions. As Chrys. appears rightly to have felt, δόξης is a pure subst., and serves to specify that peculiar *quality* or *attribute* of the χάρις which forms the subject of praise ; comp. Winer, *Gr.* § 34. 3. obs. p. 211. Thus, then, of the three genitives, the first is that 'of the object,' or, more strictly speaking, 'of the point of view' (Scheuerl. *Synt.* § 18, p. 129), while the two last are united (Winer, *Gr.* § 30. 3. 1, p. 172), and form a common possessive genitive. Owing to the defining gen., the article is not indispensable ;. see Winer, *Gr.* § 19. 2. b, p. 113, and compare Madvig, *Synt.*, § 10. 2.　　ἐν ᾗ] '*in quâ*,' Vulg., Clarom., not 'e quâ,' Beza, or 'qua,' Arm. (instrum. case) ; the antecedent here much more naturally marking the state *in* which, than the means *by* which God showed us His favor.　　ἐχαρίτω-σεν] '*He imparted His grace to us*,' 'gratificavit,' Clarom., Vulg., 'largitus est,' Æth. The exact meaning of χαριτόω is doubtful. From the analogy of verbs in όω, whether in reference to what is material (*e. g.* χρυσόω, etc.) or what is immaterial (*e. g.* θανατόω, etc., see Harless), χαριτόω must mean '*χάριτι aliquem afficio.*' As, however, χάρις is indeterminate, and may mean either the subjective state of the individual or the objective grace of God, ἐχαρίτωσε may still have two meanings ;— (a) ἐπεράστους ἐποίησε, Chrys., 'gratis sibi acceptos effecit,' Beza ; comp. Ecclus. ix. 8 (*Alex.*), appy. xviii. 17, Symm. Psalm xvii. 28, and see Suicer, *Thesaur.* s. v. Vol. II. p. 1504 ;— or (b) *gratiâ amplexus est*, Beng., sim. Syr., 'gratiæ, quam effudit ;' comp. Luke i. 28. Both the context (comp. Alf.) and the prevailing meaning of

χάρις in St. Paul's Epp. seem distinctly in favor of the latter meaning. On the use of the aor., comp. note on ἐξελέξατο, ver. 4.　　ἐν τῷ ἠγαπημένῳ] '*in the Beloved ;*' see Matth. iii. 17, John iii. 16, and comp. Col. i. 13. Ἐν is not here interchangeable with διά (comp. Chrys.), or equivalent to *propter* (Grot., Locke), but retains its full primary meaning. Christ, as Olsh. well observes, is regarded not only as the mediator, but as the true representative of mankind.

7. ἐν ᾧ] '*in whom ;*' further illustration and expansion of the preceding ἐχαρίτωσεν. Here again ἐν is neither instrumental (Arm.), nor identical in meaning with διά (Vatabl.). Fritz, indeed (*Opusc.* p. 184), adduces this passage as an instance of this identity, and regards διὰ τοῦ αἵμ. as a sort of epexegesis of ἐν ᾧ, 'per quem,' *i. e.*, eo quod sanguinem effudit,' but such an explanation falls greatly short of the true meaning. As usual, ἐν has here its primary and fullest theological meaning : it implies more than *union with* (Rück., Eadie) ; it points to Christ as the living *sphere* of redemption, while διὰ κ. τ. λ. refers to the outward *means* of it ; comp. Rom. iii. 24. As Olsh. profoundly observes : 'we have not redemption in His work *without* His person, but *in* His person, with which His work forms a living unity ;' see Winer, *Gr.* § 48. a, p. 347 note.　　ἔχομεν] '*are having ;*' present, and not without emphasis ; 'we are ever needing and are ever having it,' Eadie.　　τὴν ἀπολύτρωσιν] '*the* (not *our*, Conyb.) *redemption ;*' scil. the long-promised, and now known and realized redemption. The use of this word is thus briefly but perspicuously elucidated by Usteri *in loc.*: 'Who is ransomed ? Men, from the punishment they deserved. What is the λύτρον (Matth. xx. 28, Mark x. 45, 1 Tim. ii.

αἵματος αὐτοῦ, τὴν ἄφεσιν τῶν παραπτωμάτων, κατὰ τὸ πλοῦτος
τῆς χάριτος αὐτοῦ, ⁸ ἧς ἐπερίσσευσεν εἰς ἡμᾶς ἐν πάσῃ σοφίᾳ καὶ

6)? The blood of Christ. To whom is it paid? To God. Who pays it? Christ in the first place; though strictly God who sent Him; so, God through Christ;' *Lehrb.* II. I. 1, p. 107 ; see collection of texts, Waterl. *Doctrine of Euch.* IV. 3, Vol. IV. p. 513. We must not, however, too much limit the application of this important word. As the art. renders it impossible to explain it merely metonymice, 'a redeemed state' (comp. Corn. a Lap.), so it presents to us the conception of 'redemption' in its most general and abstract sense, alike from Satan, sin, and death; comp. Middleton, *Greek Art.* V. I., p. 90 (ed. Bose). διὰ τοῦ αἵματος αὐτοῦ] '*through His blood;*' closer definition of the ἐν ᾧ, by a notice of the 'causa medians,' the blood of Christ, — that, without which there could have been no ἄφεσις : comp. Heb. x. 22, and see the sound remarks of Alf. and Wordsw. in *h. l.* τὴν ἄφεσιν κ. τ. λ.] '*the forgiveness of our transgressions;*' apposition to, and specification of the essential character of the preceding ἀπολύτρωσις. The distinction between ἄφεσις (condonatio) and πάρεσις (prætermissio, Rom. iii. 25) is noticed by Trench, *Synonym.* § 33; more briefly but most acutely by Fritz. *Rom.* Vol. I. p. 199. Too much stress need not here be laid on the distinction between παραπτώματα and ἁμαρτίαι, for compare Col. i. 14. Still the former so naturally point to sins on the side of commission, *sinful acts,* the latter to sins as the result of a state, *sinful conditions,* that it seems best (with Beza) to preserve the distinction in translation; comp. notes on ch. ii. 1. τὸ πλοῦτος τῆς χάριτος] '*the riches of His grace ;*' certainly not per Hebraismum, for 'abundans bonitas,' (Grot.), but, with the usual meaning of the *possessive* gen., the riches which ap-

pertain to, are the property of His χάρις. On the form πλοῦτος, here rightly retained by *Tisch.*, see Winer, *Gr.* § 9. 2. 2, p. 61. It occurs again, Col. i. 27 (strongly supported), Eph. iii. 8, 16 (well supported), Eph. ii. 7, Phil. iv. 19, Col. ii. 2 (fairly), 2 Cor. viii. 2 (doubtfully) ; comp. Tisch. *Prolegom.* p. LV.

8. ἧς ἐπερίσσευσε] '*which He made to abound;*' 'ufarassau ganohida' [abundanter concessit], Goth., 'abundare fecit,' Æth. Though περισσεύω is used intransitively by St. Paul, no less than twenty-two times, yet as it is certainly transitive in 2 Cor. iv. 15, ix. 8, 1 Thess. iii. 12 (comp. Athen. *Deipn.* II. 16 (42), περιττεύει τὰς ὥρας), and as there is no *satisfactory* instance in the N. T. of attraction in the case of a verb joined with a dat. (Fritzsche's explanation of Rom. iv. 17 is more than doubtful, and 1 Tim. iv. 6. ἧς (*Lachm.*) is only supported by A in opp. to CDFGKL), it seems better to adopt the latter meaning with Theod. (ἡμᾶς περικλύει) and the Vv. above cited, than the intrans., with Syr., Vulg., Arm., and appy. Chrys. *in loc.* On the apparent violations of the law of attraction in the N. T., see Winer, *Gr.* § 24. 1, p. 148. ἐν πάσῃ σοφίᾳ καὶ φρονήσει] '*in all wisdom and intelligence;*' sphere and element in which the περίσσευσεν is evinced and realized. As there is some difficulty in (1) the meaning, (2) reference, and (3) connection of these words, it will be best to consider these points separately. (1) Πᾶσα σοφία can only mean '*all wisdom,*' i. e., 'every kind of,' 'all possible wisdom,' not 'summa sapientia' (Rosenm., Eadie), πᾶς, as Harless correctly observes, always denoting *extension* rather than *intension,* and thus often giving a concrete application to abstract nouns; comp. Col. iv. 12, and see Winer, *Gr.* § 18. 4, p.

φρονήσει, ⁹ γνωρίσας ἡμῖν τὸ μυστήριον τοῦ θελήματος αὐτοῦ,

101. The examples adduced by Eadie (Matth. xxviii. 18, Acts v. 25 (23), 1 Tim. i. 15), do not in any way invalidate this principle. Σοφία and φρόνησις are not synonymous* (Homb.; compare Plato, Symp. 202 A) but may be thus distinguished : σ ο φ ί α (cognate with σά-φης, sapio) denotes 'wisdom' in its general sense, κοινῶς ἁπάντων μάθησιν, Suid. (see 4 Macc. i. 16); φ ρ ό ν η σ ι s is rather 'intelligentia,' 'a right application of the φρήν' (τὸ δύνασθαι καλῶς βου-λεύσασθαι περὶ τὰ αὑτῷ ἀγαθὰ καὶ συμφέ-ροντα, Aristot.), — in a word, an attribute or result of σοφία (ἡ δὲ σοφία ἀνδρὶ τίκτει φρόνησιν, Prov. x. 23), thus serving here (like ἀποκάλυψις ver. 17, σύνεσις Col. i. 9) to define and limit the reference of the more general and comprehensive word. That σοφία is theoretical, φρόνησις practical (Krebs; comp. Aristot. Ethic. vi. 5, 7, Cicero, Off. II. 2), is too bald a distinction ; for σοφία in its Christian application necessarily wears a practical aspect, and may, in this respect, be as much contrasted with γνῶσις (1 Cor. viii. 1), as φρόνησις with the more nearly synonymous σύνεσις, (Col. i. 9); see notes to Transl., and comp. Beck, Seelenl. II. 19, p. 61. (2) The reference is to man, not God (Alf.), for though φρόνη-σις might be applied to God (see Prov. iii. 19, Jer. x. 12, 1 Kings iii. 28), and ἐν σοφ. καὶ φρον. might, symmetrically with ἐν ἀγάπη ver. 4, denote the principle in which God was pleased to act, yet, (a) πάσῃ seems incompatible with such a reference ; (b) the introduction of these attributes in reference to God disturbs the pervading reference to the Divine χάρις ; (c) the analogy of Col. i. 9 (urged by Olsh.) forcibly suggests the reference to man. (3) The connection (left undecided by Lachm., Tisch.) must, then, be that of the text. If the arguments, a, b, c, be not considered valid, ἐν

πάσῃ κ. τ. λ. must be joined with γνωρί-σας, as Theod. (μετὰ πολλῆς σοφίας ἐγνώρισεν) Griesb., al. The reference to God, combined with the ordinary punctuation (De Wette), is in the highest degree unsatisfactory.

9. γ ν ω ρ ί σ α s] 'having made known ;' participle explanatory of the preceding ἐπερίσσευσεν — ἐν πάσῃ σοφίᾳ καὶ φρον., esp. of the latter words, and appy. denoting an act coincident, and terminating synchronously, with the finite verb ; see Bernhardy, Synt. x. 9, p. 383, Donalds. Gr. § 576, and esp. Herm. Viger, No 224, Stalbaum, Plato, Phædo, 62 D. The 'ut notum faceret' of Vulg. (comp. Clarom., Goth.) is due to the reading γνωρίσαι found in FG; 76; Hil., and some Latin Ff. τ ὸ μ υ σ τ ή ρ ι ο ν κ. τ. λ.] 'the mystery of His will ;' not 'Hebræo loquendi genere' for consilium arcanum, Grot., but 'the mystery pertaining to it,' τοῦ θελήμ. being neither a gen. of apposition (τὸ ἀποκεκρυμμένον αὑτοῦ θέλημα καὶ ἄδηλον τοῖς πᾶσι μυστήριον αὑτὸ καλῶν, Theod.-Mops.), nor a gen. subjecti ('as it has its origin in,' Eadie), but simply a gen. objecti ('concerning His will,' Meyer), marking that to which the mystery was referred, and on which it turned ; see Krüger, Sprachl. § 47. 7. 1, Scheuerl. Synt., § 17. 1, p. 127. The incarnation of Christ and the redemption He wrought for us, though an actual revelation considered as a matter of fact, was a μυστήριον considered with reference to the depths of the divine will : see above Theod.-Mops., and comp. Olsh. in loc. κ α τ ὰ τ ὴ ν ε ὐ δ ο κ ί α ν] 'according to His good pleasure ;' specification of the γνωρίσας as having taken place in strict dependence both in time and manner on the will of God ; comp. ver. 5. To refer this to what follows ('to wit, His intention according to his good pleasure to gather,' Eadie) seems

κατὰ τὴν εὐδοκίαν αὐτοῦ, ἣν προέθετο ἐν αὐτῷ ¹⁰ *εἰς οἰκονομίαν*

10. *ἐν τοῖς οὐρανοῖς*] Tisch. is undoubtedly right in maintaining this reading with AFGK; appy. majority of mss.; Copt.; Chrys., Theodoret (1) Theophyl. al. (*Rec. Griesb., Scholz., Harless, De W.*) against *ἐπὶ τοῖς οὐρανοῖς* with BDEL; about 40 mss.; Goth.; Theodoret (1), Dam., Œc., al. (*Lachm., Rück., Meyer, Alf.,*): for, conceding that it may be grammatically correct (comp. exx. Rost u. Palm, *Lex. ἐπί*, II. 1, Vol. I. p. 1035), it must be said that the internal objections, — that *ἐπὶ* is never joined in the N. T. with *οὐρανὸς* or *οὐρανοί*, and that *ἐν οὐρανῷ* and *ἐπὶ γῆς* (probably not without significance) are invariably found in antithesis, — are decisive: see Harless *in loc.*

obviously incorrect, involved, and out of harmony with ver. 5; as *κατὰ κ. τ. λ.* formed a modal clause to *προορίσας* there, so it naturally qualifies *γνωρίσας* here.

προέθετο] '*purposed;*' 'proposuit,' Vulg., not 'præstituerat,' Beza. The verb *προτίθεσθαι* only occurs in the N. T. in two other passages, viz., Rom. i. 13 (ethical, as here), and Rom. iii. 25 (quasi-local, 'set forth'); the force of the prep. in both cases being *local* rather than temporal.(Elsner, *Obs.* Vol. II. p. 20), and analogous to the use of the prep. in *προαιρεῖσθαι* (2 Cor. ix. 7) and *προχειρίζεσθαι* (Acts iii. 20). It may indeed be doubted whether any instance can be found of *προτίθεσθαι* in a *purely* temporal sense: Polyb. *Hist.* VIII. 13. 1. is not in point. *ἐν αὐτῷ*] '*in Himself*'; not *αὐτῷ* as Tisch. (ed. 2, 7). Though it is often difficult to decide between the reflexive and non-reflexive pronoun (see Buttm. *Mid.* Excurs. x. p. 140), yet as a general rule, where the attention is principally directed to the subject, the former is most natural; where it is diverted by the importance of the details, the latter. Thus, in ver. 5, *υἱοθεσία* is so distinctly the important word that *αὐτὸν* is sufficiently explicit; here, the connection with *προέθετο* is so immediate that the reflexive form alone seems admissible.

10. *εἰς οἰκονομίαν*] '*for with a view to, the dispensation;*' *εἰς* being not for *ἐν* (Vulg., Auth.), or temporal, 'us-

que ad,' Erasm. (a more justifiable translation), but simply indicative of the *purpose, intention*, of the *πρόθεσις*; compare Winer, *Gr.* § 49. a, p. 354. The meaning of *οἰκονομία* has been much debated. It occurs nine times in the N. T.; (*a*) in the simple sense of *stewardship* Luke xvi. 2 sq.), a meaning which Wieseler (*Chron.* p. 448) maintains even in this place; (*b*) in reference to the apostolic office, to the *οἶκος Θεοῦ*, 1 Cor. ix. 17, Col. i. 25, and (more remotely) 1 Tim. i. 4; (*c*) in reference to the Divine government of the world, *disposition, dispensation,* — here, and ch. iii. 2, 9; see exx. in Rost u. Palm, *Lex.* s. v. Vol. II. p. 417, and esp. Schweigh. *Lex. Polyb.* s. v. The special meanings 'dispensatio gratiæ,' 'redemptionis mysterium,' scil. Christi *ἀνανθρώπησις* (Suicer, *Thesaur.* s. v.; comp. Valesius, Euseb. *Hist.* I. 1, Petav. *de Incarn.* II. 1, Vol. IV. p. 110), which was probably deduced from the *whole* clause, cannot be admitted as explanations of the simple word. The article is not required, as the governing substantive is sufficiently defined by the gen. which follows; see Winer, *Gr.* § 19. 2. b, p. 113 sq. *τοῦ πληρώματος τῶν καιρῶν*] '*of the fulness of the seasons;*' scil. that moment which completes, and, as it were, fills up the ordained *καιροὶ* (time estimated in reference to the *epochs* in the Divine government), of the Gospel dispensation: compare the somewhat similar expression, *τοῦ πληρώματος τῶν καιρῶν, ἀνακεφαλαιώσασϑαι τὰ πάντα ἐν*

πλήρωσις ἡμερῶν (Dan. x. 3, Ezek. v. 2), where, however, the completion is estimated relatively to the *act*, rather than to the *exact moment* that made the remaining temporal void full; see notes *on Gal. l.* 4. The genitival relation of these words to οἰκονομία is very obscure. It would certainly seem that πληρώματος κ. τ. λ. cannot be (*a*) a gen. of the *object* (Theod.-Mops.), for, as Meyer justly observes, the πλήρωμα may be said ἐλϑεῖν (Gal. *l. c.*), but not οἰκονομεῖσϑαι: nor again (*b*) can it be an explanatory gen. or gen. of *identity* (Harless; comp. Scheuerl. *Synt.* § 12. 1, p. 82), for an essentially temporal conception can scarcely be used in explanation of an ethical notion. It may, however, be plausibly considered as (*c*) a gen. of the *characterizing quality* (Scheuerl. § 16. 3, p. 115), which, especially in local and temporal reference, admits considerable latitude of application; comp. Jude 6, κρίσις μεγάλης ἡμέρας, and see exx. in Winer, *Gr.* § 30. 2, p. 168 sq.; and in Hartung, *Casus*, p. 27. The difficult expression οἰκον. τοῦ πληρ. κ. τ. λ. will thus seem to imply not merely the 'full-timed dispensation,' (Eadie), but more exactly, ' the dispensation that was *characterized by*, that was to be set forth in, the fulness of time' ('propria plenitudini temp.' Calov.), and must be referred not only to the period of the coming of Christ (ed. 1, Ust. *Lehrb.* II. 1, p. 83; comp. Chrys. πλήρωμα τῶν καιρῶν· ἡ παρουσία αὐτοῦ ἦν), but, appy., as the more extended ref. of the context seems to suggest, the whole duration of the Gospel dispensation (Alf.); Stier *in loc.* (p. 96), and contrast Gal. iv. 4, where, as the context shows, the reference is more restricted. The use and meaning of the term is noticed by Hall, *Bampt. Lect.* for 1797. ἀνακεφαλαιώσασϑαι] '*to sum up again together*,' 'restaurare,' Clarom.,

'summatim recolligere,' Beza; not dependent on προέϑετο, but explanatory infinitive, defining the nature and purpose of the πρόϑεσις; comp. 1 Thess. iv. 4, and see notes *on Col.* i. 22. The article is not necessary, see Winer, *Gr.* § 44. 2. obs. p. 286, notes *on* 1 *Thess.* iii. 3, and comp. Madvig, *Syntax* § 144. The meaning of this word, connected as it here is with the counsels of Omnipotence, must be investigated with the most anxious care. Viewed simply, κεφαλαιῶσαι (συντόμως συναγαγεῖν, Hesych. means '*summatim colligere*,' Thucyd. III. 67, VI. 91, VIII. 53; ἀνακεφαλαιώσασϑαι '*summatim* (*sibi*) *recolligere ;*' comp. συγκεφαλαιοῦσϑαι ('in brevem summam contrahere'), Polyb. *Hist.* III· 3. 1, I. 66. 11, etc.; see Schweigh. *Lex. Polyb.*, and Raphel *in loc.* Viewed in connection with the context, two important questions arise. (1) Is there any allusion to Christ as the κεφαλή (Chrys.)? In a writer so profound as St. Paul this is far from impossible. The derivation of the word, however (κεφάλαιον not κεφαλή), — St. Paul's use of it in its common meaning, Rom. xiii. 9, — and most of all the context, which points to a union '*in* Christo,' not '*sub* Christo' (Beng.), to His atonement rather than His sovereignty (Col. ii. 10), render it improbable. (2) What is the force of ἀνά? From Rom. *l. c.* (see Fritz.) it has plausibly been considered latent; still, as even there this is very doubtful (see Meyer *in loc.*), it must not here be lightly passed over. What, then, is this force? Obviously not simple *repetition ;* nor again (from reasons above) summation *upwards*, in reference to Christ as the Head (σύνδεσμον ἄνωϑεν ἐπικειμένον, Chrys.), but *re-union*, *re-collection*, a ' partium divulsarum conjunctio' in reference to a state of previous and primal unity; so far, then, but *so far only*, a 'restora-

τῷ Χριστῷ, τὰ ἐν τοῖς οὐρανοῖς καὶ τὰ ἐπὶ τῆς γῆς, ἐν αὐτῷ, ¹¹ ἐν

tion' (Syr., Vulg.) to that state; comp. Beng. *in loc. University Sermons*, p. 162, and see an excellent discussion on the word in Andrewes, *Serm.* xvi. Vol. i. p. 265, 270 (A. C. Libr.). The force of the middle voice must also, appy., not be overlooked.　τὰ πάντα may imply 'all intelligent beings' (compare notes *on Gal.* iii. 22), but, on account of the clauses which follow, is best taken in its widest sense, 'all things and beings,' Meyer; comp. Andrewes, *Serm.* Vol. i. p. 269.　τὰ ἐν τοῖς οὐρανοῖς κ. τ. λ.] '*the things in heaven and the things upon earth;*' widest expression of universality designed to show the extent of the preceding τὰ πάντα (Andr.); comp. Col. i. 20, and see notes *in loc.* Without entering into the profound questions which have been connected with these words, it may be said, — that as on the one hand all limiting interpretations — *e. g.* Jews and Gentiles (Schoettg.), ἀγγέλους καὶ ἀνθρώπους, (Chrys.), the world of spirits and the race of men (Meier), — are opposed to the generalizing neuter (Winer, *Gr.* § 27. 5, p. 160), and the comprehensiveness of the expressions; so, on the other hand, any reference to the redemption or restoration of those spirits (Crellius), for whom our Lord Himself said τὸ πῦρ τὸ αἰώνιον (Matth. xxv. 4) was prepared, must be pronounced fundamentally impossible: comp. Bramhall, *Castigations*, etc., Disc. ii. Vol. iv. p. 354 (Angl. Cath. Lib.), Hofmann, *Schriftb.* Vol. i. p. 192 and *University Sermons* p. 91 sq. The reading ἐπὶ τοῖς οὐρ. (*Lachm. Alf.*), though fairly supported [BDEL], is scarcely probable; see crit. note. ἐν αὐτῷ] '*in Him;*' not added merely 'explicationis causâ (Herm. *Viger.* 123 b. 5), but as re-asseverating with great solemnity and emphasis (see Jelf, *Gr.* § 658), the only blessed sphere *in* which

this ἀνακεφαλαίωσις can be regarded as operative, and *apart* from which and *without* which, its energies cannot be conceived as acting; see *Univ. Serm.* p. 89, 90. It forms also an easy transition to the following relative.

11. ἐν ᾧ καὶ ἐκληρώθ.] '*in whom we were also chosen as His inheritance;*' καὶ obviously qualifying ἐκληρ., not the unexpressed pronoun (Auth.), and specifying the gracious carrying out and realization of the divine πρόθεσις, v. 9. This ascensive force may sometimes be expressed by 'really,' see Hartung, *Partik.* καὶ, 2. 7, p. 132 sq.; the exact shade of meaning, however, will be best defined by a consideration of the exact tenor and *tacit comparisons* of the context; see Klotz, *Devar.* Vol. ii. p. 636. The exact meaning of ἐκληρώθ. is very doubtful. Passing over the more obviously untenable interpretations of Bretsch., Wahl, Koppe, and others, we find four translations which deserve attention: (*a*) Pass. for middle; '*we have obtained an inheritance,*' Auth., Conyb.; comp. Elsner, *Obs.* Vol. ii. p. 204: this, however, is not fairly substantiated by the citations adduced, and is distinctly at variance with the significant *passives* which prevail throughout this profound paragraph in reference to man. Even προσεκληρώθησαν, Acts xvii. 4, is best taken passively; see Winer, *Gr.* § 39. 2, p. 234.　(*b*) Simple pass.; '*sorte vocati sumus,*' Vulg., Syr., Goth. (1 Sam. xiv. 41, see exx. in Elsner, *l. c.*), *i. e.* 'as though by lot,' in allusion to the sovereign *freedom* of God's choice; κλήρου γενομένου ἡμᾶς ἐξελέξατο, Chrys.: this, however, is seriously at variance with St. Paul's modes of thought and the regular forms of expression (καλεῖν, ἐκλέγεσθαι) which he uses on this subject: see Harless and Meyer *in loc.* (*c*) Passive, used like πιστεύομαι, μαρτυροῦμαι

ᾧ καὶ ἐκληρώθημεν προορισθέντες κατὰ πρόθεσιν τοῦ τὰ πάντα ἐνεργοῦντος κατὰ τὴν βουλὴν τοῦ θελήματος αὐτοῦ, [12] *εἰς τὸ εἶναι*

(comp. ἀποροῦμαι, Gal. iv. 20, and see Winer, *Gr.* § 39. 1, p. 233), with an implied accus., scil. '*in hæreditatem adsciti sumus,*' Grot. 2, Harl., Meyer ('were enfeoffed,' Eadie), — with allusion to Josh. xiv. 1 sq. and reference to the κλῆρος τῶν ἁγίων, Col. i. 12.   (d) Pass., in a special sense; '*eramus facti hæreditas (Domini),*' Beng., Hamm. [mis-cited by De W.], *i. e.* λαὸς ἔγκληρος, Deut. iv. 20; see ch. ix. 29, xxxii. 6. Between (c) and (d) it is somewhat hard to decide. While both present some difficulties, (c) in point of structure, (d) in the special character of its meaning, both harmonize well with the context, the former in its allusion to κληρονομία, ver. 14, the latter with reference to περιποίησις, ver. *ib.* As however (c) is doubtful in point of usage, and as the force of καὶ is well maintained by (d) in the gentle contrast it suggests between the general ἐκλογὴ and the more specially gracious κλήρωσις, this latter interpretation is certainly to be preferred; 'we were not only chosen out, but chosen out as a λαὸς ἔγκληρος;' εἶπεν, ἐξελέξατο ἡμᾶς, ἀνωτέρω ἐνταῦθα φησιν, ἐκληρώθημεν, Chrys. The reading ἐκλήθημεν though found in ADEFG; Clarom., Sang., Boern, al. (*Lachm.*) seems almost certainly a sort of gloss for the more difficult and appy. ill-understood ἐκληρώθημεν.   βουλὴν τοῦ θελήματος] '*the counsel of His will,* 'consilium voluntatis,' Vulg., Clarom.; assertion of the unconditioned and sovereign will of God appropriately introduced after ἐκληρώθημεν; ὥστε οὐκ ἐπειδὴ Ἰουδαῖοι οὐ προσεῖχον, διὰ τοῦτο τὰ ἔθνη ἐκάλεσεν, οὐδὲ ἀναγκασθείς, Chrys. The expression βουλὴ θελήματος is not either pleonastic, or expressive of 'consilium liberrimum' (Beng.), but solemnly represents the Almighty Will as displaying itself in action; θέλημα designating the *will* generally, βουλὴ the more special expression of it. The distinction of Buttmann (*Lexil.* s. v. § 35, compare Tittm. *Synon.* p. 124 sq.), that 'βούλομαι is confined to the *inclination*, ἐθέλω to that kind of wish in which there lies a *purpose* or *design*, does not seem generally applicable to the N. T. (see Matt. i. 19, and comp. 1 Cor. iv. 5 with Eph. ii. 3), and probably not *always* to classical Greek; see Pape, *Lex.* s. v. βούλομαι, Vol. I. p. 383, Donalds. *Crat.* § 463. For further illustrations see notes *on* 1 *Tim.* v. 14.

12. εἰς τὸ εἶναι κ. τ. λ.] '*that we should be to the praise of His glory;*' final cause of the κλήρωσις on the part of God mentioned in the preceding verse, εἰς τὸ κ. τ. λ. depending on ἐκληρ., and τοὺς προηλπικ. forming an opposition to ἡμᾶς. To refer this clause to προορισθέντες, and to connect εἶναι with προηλπικότας (Harl.) is highly involved and artificial; see Meyer *in loc.*   The reference of the pronoun is somewhat doubtful. Up to the present verse, ἡμεῖς has designated the community of believers, Jews and Gentiles. It would seem most natural to continue it in the same sense; the meaning, however, assigned to ἐκληρ., that of προηλπ., and most of all the opposition καὶ ὑμεῖς (which De Wette does not invalidate by ref. to ch. ii. 1, Col. i. 8), seem convincingly to prove that ἡμεῖς refers especially to *Jewish Christians,* ὑμεῖς to *Gentile Christians.* Chrys. has not *expressed* this, but the citation above (on ἐκληρ.) would seem to imply distinctly that he felt it.   It may be observed that the insertion of the art. τῆς before δόξης, with A; many mss.; Chrys., al. (*Rec.*), is opposed to the bulk of Mss. and rejected by all recent editors.   τοὺς προηλπικ.] '*we, I*

ἡμᾶς εἰς ἔπαινον δόξης αὐτοῦ, τοὺς προηλπικότας ἐν τῷ Χριστῷ·
¹³ ἐν ᾧ καὶ ὑμεῖς, ἀκούσαντες τὸν λόγον τῆς ἀληθείας, τὸ εὐαγγέλ-

say, who have before hoped;' Þai faura venjandans [hi ante sperantes], Goth. ; the article with the part. standing in distinct and emphatic apposition to ἡμᾶς, and defining more fully their spiritual attitude; comp. Winer, Gr. § 20. i. c, p. 121, but observe that the transl. 'quippe qui speravimus' (ed. 1, Winer, Meyer, al.) is inexact, as this would imply a part. without, not as here with the article; on these distinctions of predication, see esp. Donalds. Crat. § 304 sq., Gr. § 492 sq. The prep. πρὸ has received many different explanations, several of which, e. g. πρὶν ἢ ἐπιστῇ ὁ μέλλων αἰών, Theoph., 'qui priores speravimus,' Beza, 'already, prior to the time of writing,' Eadie — appear to have resulted rather from preconceived opinions of the reference of ἡμεῖς, than from a simple investigation of the word. As προορίζω, ver. 5, implies an ὁρισμὸς before the object of it appeared, so προελπίζω seems to imply an exercise of ἐλπὶς before the object of it, i. e. Christ, appeared. The perf. part., as usual, indicates that the action which is described as past still continues, see exx. Winer, Gr. § 40. 4. a, p. 244. ἐν Χριστῷ denotes the object in whom the hope was placed; compare 1 Cor. xv. 9, and see notes on 1 Tim. iv. 10, Reuss, Théol. Chrét. IV. 22, Vol. II. p. 222. The preceding reference of the fore-hope in the Messiah to the Jews (comp. Acts xxviii. 20) is in no way incompatible with the use of ἐν Χριστῷ rather than of εἰς Χριστόν (Holzh., Eadie): to have hoped in Christ was a higher characteristic than to have directed hope towards Christ, and designated them as more worthy exponents of the praise of God's glory; compare Stier in loc. p. 112, 114.

13. ἐν ᾧ καὶ ὑμεῖς κ. τ. λ.] The construction of this verse is somewhat doubtful. A finite verb is commonly supposed, either from ἐκληρώθημεν, ver. 11, or προηλπικότας. If from the former (Harless), it would now limit ἐκληρ. to the Gentile Christians, which formerly referred to both them and Jewish Christians: the regression, too, would seem unduly great. If from the latter, πρ οηλπίκατε (not ἠλπίκατε, Beza) must be supplied, which would imply what was contrary to the fact. Others (Meyer, Alf., al.) supply the verb subst., ' in whom ye are,' but thus introduce a statement singularly frigid and out of harmony with the linked and ever-rising character of the context. It can scarcely then be doubted that we have here a form of the 'oratio suspensa ' (Beng.), according to which the second ἐν ᾧ does not refer to a fresh subject (Mey.), but is simply resumptive of the first. The full force and meaning of this anacoluthon have scarcely been sufficiently expanded. Καὶ ὑμεῖς [ἡμεῖς, A K L; mss., but with no probability] directs the attention to the contrast between the pronouns; ἀκούσαντες κ. τ. λ. suggests a further reference to those who had hoped on less convincing evidence. This might have been followed at once by the finite verb ἐσφράγ. κ. τ. λ.: but was so important a clause to follow at once on ἀκούσαντες? Surely ἀκοὴ must be expanded into something more vital before it could be so blessed. Καὶ πιστ. is thus intercalated with all the ascensive force of καὶ (οὐ γὰρ μόνον ἠκούσατε ἀλλὰ καὶ ἐπιστεύσατε, Theod.), and thus, far from becoming superfluous (Meyer), is truly a necessary and vital member of the sentence. So appy. Syr., Copt., Goth., Æth., which though suppressing the καὶ, and converting the participles into finite verbs retain substantially the correct structure. 'Εν ᾧ may be joined with

ιον τῆς σωτηρίας ὑμῶν, ἐν ᾧ καὶ πιστεύσαντες ἐσφραγίσθητε τῷ

πιστεύσαντες (Mark i. 15) as well as ἐσφραγ. (Scholef.), but as πιστεύειν ἔν τινι is not used by St. Paul, and as ἐν ᾧ in ver. 11 is not joined with the participle but the finite verb, it seems best, in this somewhat parallel verse, to preserve the same construction; see Rück, and Harl. *in loc.*   τὸν λόγον τῆς ἀληϑείας] '*the word of the truth;*' not the gen. of *apposition* (Harless), but the gen. *substantiæ;* see Scheuerl. *Synt.* 12. 1, p. 82, Hartung, *Casus,* p. 21. The truth did not only form the subject (Meyer), but was its very substance and essence. The remark of Chrys. is thus perfectly in point, — τῆς ἀληϑείας, οὐκέτι τὸν τοῦ τύπου, οὐδὲ τὸν τῆς εἰκόνος; see notes *on Col.* i. 5.   τὸ εὐαγγέλιον τῆς σωτηρ.] '*the Gospel of your salvation;*' not a gen. of *apposition,* nor exactly, as above, a gen. of the *substance,* but rather a gen. of the (spiritual) *contents* or *subject-matter* (Bernhardy, *Synt.* III. 44, p. 161, Scheuerl, *Synt.* § 17, 1, p. 126), scil. 'the Gospel (τὸ κήρυγμα, Chrys.) which turns upon, which reveals salvation;' thus forming one of that large class of genitives of remoter reference (see exx. in Winer, *Gr.* § 30. 2. β, p. 169 sq.), and belonging appy. to the general category of the genitive of *relation;* see Donalds. *Gr.* § 453, p. 475 sq. For a list of the various substantives with which εὐαγγέλιον is associated (Θεοῦ, Rom. i. 1, xv. 16, al., Χριστοῦ, Rom. xv. 19, Gal. i. 7, al., τῆς χάριτος, Acts xx.· 24, τῆς εἰρήνης, Eph. vi. 19), see esp. Reuss, *Théol. Chrét.* IV. 8, Vol. II. p. 81.   πιστεύσαντες is not present (Eadie), and contemporaneous with ἐσφραγ. (Harl.), but *antecedent;* comp. Acts xix. 2, and see Usteri, *Lehrb.* II. 2. 2, p. 267; the ordinary sequence, as Meyer observes, is (*a*) Hearing; (*b*) Faith, which of course implies preventing grace; (*c*) Baptism; (*d*) Communi

cation of the Holy Spirit; compare together, esp. Acts ii. 37 (*a, c, d*); viii. 6, 12, 17 (*a, b, c, d*); xix. 5, 6 (*c, d*): Acts x. 44 (*d, c*) and *perhaps* ix. 17 are exceptional cases. On the divine order or method mercifully used by God in our salvation, see the brief but weighty remarks of Hammond, *Pract. Catech.* I. 4, p. 83 (A. C. Libr.).   ἐσφραγίσθητε] '*were sealed;*' τὴν βεβαίωσιν ἐδέξασθε, Theodor.-Mops.: see Suicer, *Thesaurus,* s. v. Vol. II. p. 1197. The seal of the Spirit is that blessed hope and assurance which the Holy Spirit imparts to our spirit, ὅτι ἐσμὲν τέκνα Θεοῦ, Rom. viii. 16: see esp. Bull, *Disc.* III. p. 397 (Engl. Works, Oxf. 1844). Any purely objective meaning in reference to heathen (Grot.), or even to Jewish customs (Schoettg. *Hor.* Vol. II. p. 508, compare Chrys.), seems *here* very doubtful: ἡ σφραγὶς is undoubtedly used by ecclesiastical writers simply for Baptism (Grabe, *Spicil.* Vol. I. p. 331 sq., comp. Rom. iv. 11), but any special reference of this nature would not appear in harmony with the present context.
τῷ Πνεύματι τῆς ἐπαγγελίας] '*the Spirit of promise,*' ܪܘܚܐ ܕܡܘܠܟܢܐ [qui promissus erat], Syr., 'quem promisit,' Æth. The genitival relation has here again received different explanations. The simple meaning derived from the most general use of the gen., as the case of *ablation* (Donalds. *Gr.* § 451), the 'whence-case' (Hartung, *Casus,* p. 12) requires but little modification. Τὸ Πν. τῆς ἐπ. is 'the Spirit which came from, *i. e.* was announced by, promise;' ὅτι κατὰ ἐπαγγ. αὐτὸ ἐλάβομεν, Chrys., or as Theoph. 1, still more literally, ὅτι ἐξ ἐπαγγ. ἐδόθη: so in effect Syr. The active sense, ὅτι βεβαιοῖ τὴν ἐπαγγελ. (Theoph. 2), is grammatically doubtful (as there is no such verbal basis in

Πνεύματι τῆς ἐπαγγελίας τῷ ἁγίῳ, ¹⁴ ὅς ἐστιν ἀρραβὼν τῆς κληρονομίας ἡμῶν, εἰς ἀπολύτρωσιν τῆς περιποιήσεως, εἰς ἔπαινον τῆς
δόξης αὐτοῦ.

Πνεῦμα; compare Scheuerl. *Synt.* § 17.
1, p. 126), and is exegetically unnecessary, as the idea of βεβαίωσις lies in ἐσφραγίσθητε. See Suicer, *Thesaur.* Vol.
II. p. 1767, and comp. *notes on Gal.* iii.
14.   τῷ ἁγίῳ marks, with solemn
emphasis, Him by whom they were
sealed — Him whose essence was holiness — the personal Holy Spirit of God.
For a weighty and practical sermon on
this verse, see Usher, *Serm.* XII. Vol.
XIII. p. 175 (ed. Elringt.), and for three
discourses of a more general character
Barrow, *Serm.* XIII. XIV. XV. Vol. I. p.
1—59 (Oxf. 1830).

14. ὅς] As the noun in the explanatory
clause (ὅς — ἐστί) gains a prominence
by being not only an elucidation or amplification (chap. i. 23), but a *definition*
and *specification* of that in the antecedent, the relative agrees with it in gender : see esp. Winer, *Gr.* § 24. 3, p. 192,
Madvig, *Synt.* § 98. b. Ὅς need not
therefore be referred to Christ (Poly-
carp. *Phil.* § 8), nor indeed to the personal nature of the Holy Spirit (John
xiv. 26), as τὸ Πν. in its most distinct
personal sense is invariably used with
the neuter relative ; compare the collection of exx. in Bruder, *Concord.* s. v. ὅς,
II. p. 619. The reading ὅ, adopted by
Lachm. with ABFGL ; 15 mss. ; Athan.
(2), al., seems clearly a grammatical
gloss, and is rejected by most recent editors.   ἀρραβών] 'earnest,' Auth.,
Arm.; a word used in the N. T. only
here and 2 Cor. i. 22, v. 5, comp. עֵרָבוֹן
Gen xxviii. 17 sq. 'arrhabo,' Plaut. *Most.*
III. 1. 3, *Rud.* Prol. 45. It is a term
probably of Phœnician origin (Gesen.
Lex. s. v.) and denotes (1) a portion of
the purchase money, an *earnest* of future
payment, πρόδομα, Hesych., ἡ ἐπὶ ταῖς
ὠναῖς παρὰ τῶν ὠνουμένων διδομένη προ-

καταβολή, *Etym. M.*; (2) *pignus*, Clarom., Vulg., 'vadi,' Goth.; see esp.
Kypke, *Obs.* Vol. II. p. 239. The word
has here its primary meaning : the gifts
and υἱοθεσία, of which the Spirit assures
us now, are the *earnest*, the ἀπαρχὴ (Basil) of the κληρονομία (ἐν τῇ βασιλείᾳ τοῦ
Χρ. καὶ Θεοῦ, ch. v. 5) hereafter : see
Rom. viii. 23, and comp. Reuss, *Théol.
Chrét.* IV. 22, Vol. II. p. 248. Christ,
somewhat similarly, is termed the ἀρρ.
τῆς ἀναστάσεως ἡμῶν, *Constit. Apost.* v.
6 : Suicer, *Thesaur.* s. v. Vol. I. p. 512.
εἰς ἀπολύτρωσιν κ. τ. λ.] '*for the
redemption of the purchased possession,*'

ܟܗܘܢ ܕܐܝܬܝܗܘܢ [eorum
qui vivunt, sc. servantur] Syr., 'in re-
demptionem adquisitionis' Vulg.; first
of the two final clauses, expressive of
the divine purpose involved in the ἐσφραγίσθητε κ. τ. λ.; see below (2).
The explanations of these difficult
clauses are very varied. Passing over
those founded on questionable constructions, whether by participial solution
(Koppe, Wahl), apposition (ἀπολύτρ.
scil. περιπ., comp. Chrys., Theophl. 1,),
conjunction (ἀπολ. καὶ περιπ., compare
Holzh.), or virtual interchange (περιπ.
τῆς ἀπολ. Beza, Steph. *Thesaur.* s. v.
περιπ.), we will notice (1) the probable
meaning of the words, (2) the probable
connection of the clause with the sentence.   (1) ἀπολύτρωσις, a
word always (*e. g.* ch. iv. 30, Rom. viii.
23), and here especially, modified by
the context, appears to denote the final
and complete redemption (ἡ καθαρὰ
ἀπολ. Chrys.) from sufferings and sins,
from Satan and from death ; see Usteri,
Lehrb. II. 1. 1, p. 106, Neand. *Planting,*
Vol. I. p. 456, and comp. Reuss, *Théol.
Chrét.* IV. 17, Vol. II. p. 183 sq. who,

I ever give thanks and pray that ye may be enlightened to know the hope of His calling, the riches of His inheritance, and the greatness of His power, which was especially displayed in the resurrection and supreme exaltation of Christ.

^{15} Διὰ τοῦτο κἀγώ, ἀκούσας τὴν καθ' ὑμᾶς

however, is appy. unduly restrictive. περιποίησις is much more obscure; while its etymological form and syntactic use (comp. 1 Thess. v. 9, 2 Thess. ii. 14, Heb. x. 39) suggest an active and abstract interpretation (Beng.), the genitival relation with ἀπολύτρ. renders this in the present case wholly untenable. The same may be said of the concrete passive explanation ' hæreditas acquisita ' (Calov.) even if that explanation be lexically demonstrable. The most ancient interpretation (Syr.), according to which ἡ περιπ. = οἱ περιποιηθέντες, scil. λαὸς εἰς περίπ. 1 Pet. ii. 9 (comp. Isaiah xliii. 21, and esp. Mal. iii. 7), and is a Christian application of the סְגֻלַּה יְהֹוָה, the λαὸς περιούσιος LXX, of the Old Testament, is on the whole most satisfactory. The objection that περιπ. is never *absolutely* so used is of weight, and is not to be diluted by a forced reference to αὐτοῦ (Mey.); still, while the exx. adduced show such a meaning to be possible, the context, and esp. the genitival relation, render it in a high degree probable. The discussions of the other interpretations by Harless and the comments of Stier (p. 129) on ἀπολύτρ. will repay perusal. (2) *Connection:* εἰς may be joined with ὅς ἐστιν κ. τ. λ. (*Tisch.*, Rück.) in a temporal sense, 'until,' Auth. Ver., but much more probably belongs to ἐσφραγίσθητε. Εἰς ἀπολ. is thus a clause coördinate with εἰς ἔπαινον κ. τ. λ., the former expressing the final clause in reference to *man*, the latter in more especial and ultimate reference to God.

15. διὰ τοῦτο κἀγώ] 'On this account *I also;*' ref. to the preceding verses as a reason for thanks to God for the spiritual state of the Ephesians, with a prayer (ver. 17) for their further enlightenment. The *exact* reference of these words is doubtful. Harless (after Chrys.) refers διὰ τοῦτο to the whole paragraph; as, however, the Ephesians are first specially addressed in ver. 13 (καὶ ὑμεῖς), it seems best, with Theophyl., to connect διὰ τοῦτο only with ver. 13, 14; 'on account of thus having heard, believed, and having been sealed in Christ.' Κἀγὼ ('*I also, I too,*' not ' I indeed,' Eadie) is thus faintly corresponsive with καὶ ὑμεῖς, and hints at the union in prayer and praise which subsisted between the Apostle and his converts. De Wette refers καὶ to διὰ τοῦτο, adducing Col. i. 9, but this example (comp. verse 4 with verse 9) certainly confirms the strict union of particle and pronoun; see notes *in loc.* Eadie and Bretschneider cite Rom. iii. 7, 1 Cor. vii. 8, xi. 1, Gal. iv. 12, 1 Thess. iii. 5, al., but in all these instances καὶ has its full and proper comparative force: see Klotz, *Devar.* Vol. II. p. 635.   ἀκούσας] '*having heard.*' All historical arguments (ὡς μηδέπω θεασάμενος αὐτούς, — noticed, but rejected by Theodoret) derived, on the one hand, from pressing the meaning of the *verb* (D. W.) or, on the other, the improbable (see Winer, *Gr.* § 40. 5. b. 1, comp. *on Gal.* v. 24) frequentative force of the *tense* (Eadie), must be pronounced extremely precarious. St. Paul certainly uses ἀκούσας, Col. i. 4, in reference to converts he had not seen; but this alone would not have proved it, and thus does not prevent our here referring ἀκούσας to the progress the Ephesians had made in the four or five years since he had last seen them; see Wieseler, *Chronol.*, p. 445, Wiggers, *Stud. u. Krit.* 1841, p. 431 sq.   τὴν καθ' ὑμᾶς πίστιν is commonly regarded as a mere periphrasis for τὴν ὑμετέραν π., or rather τὴν π. ὑμῶν, the possessive ὑμέτερος (comp. ἡμέτ.) being used sparingly

πίστιν ἐν τῷ Κυρίῳ Ἰησοῦ καὶ τὴν ἀγάπην τὴν εἰς πάντας τοὺς
ἁγίους, ¹⁶ οὐ παύομαι εὐχαριστῶν ὑπὲρ ὑμῶν, μνείαν ὑμῶν ποιού-

16. μνείαν ὑμῶν ποιούμενος] So *Tisch.* with D³EKL (FG ; Boern. transpose ὑμῶν
and ποιούμ.) great majority of mss.; Sangerm., Aug., Vulg., Syr. (both), Copt.,
al.; Chrys., Theod., Dam., al. (*Rec., Griesb., De W.* (e sil.), *Wordsw.*). The
omission of ὑμῶν is well supported by external evidence, viz. ABD¹ (*not* C, Eadie;
this is one of its lacunæ); about 10 mss.; Clarom., Goth.; Hil. (*Rück. Lachm.,
Mey.*, approved by *Mill*, Prolegom. p. 144?), but is perhaps slightly less probable;
esp. as an omission of ὑμῶν owing to the preceding ὑμῶν is more likely than an
explanatory insertion, where the meaning is so obvious, and as 1 Thess. i. 2 (where
AB similarly omit ὑμῶν) is appy. an instructive parallel.

(only 4 times) in St. Paul's Epp. It must be admitted that later writers appear to use κατὰ with acc. as equivalent to possess. pronoun or gen. (see Bernhardy, *Synt.* v. 20. b, p. 241, Winer, *Gr.* § 22. 7, obs. p. 178), still, as St. Paul uses ἡ πίστ. ὑμῶν at least 17 times, and ἡ καθ᾽ ὑμ. π. only once, there would *seem* to be a distinction; the latter (κατὰ distributive) probably denoting the faith of the community viewed objectively, '*the faith which is among you,*' the former the subjective faith of individuals : see Harless and Stier *in loc.*, and comp. John viii. 17, τῷ νόμῳ τῷ ὑμετέρῳ (addressed to *Pharisees*), with Acts xviii. 15, νομοῦ τοῦ καθ᾽ ὑμᾶς (in reference to Jews in Achaia), which seem to convey a parallel distinction, and at any rate to invert the supposition of Eadie, that ἡ καθ᾽ ὑμ. π. denotes more distinctive, characteristic possession than the former.
ἐν τῷ Κυρίῳ] '*in the Lord;*' definition of the holy sphere and object of the πίστις; the omission of the article giving a more complete unity to the conception, as it were, 'Christ-centred faith,' '*fidem erga Deum in Domino Jesu,*' Beng.; see notes *on Gal.* iii. 26. It is instructive to compare with this the subsequent clause, τὴν ἀγάπην τὴν κ. τ. λ., where the second article [*Lachm.* omits with AB; 17 al.] seems inserted to convey *two* momenta of thought, love generally, further defined by that amplitude (οὐ

τοὺς ἐπιχωρίους, φησί, μόνον, Chrys.) which is its true Christian characteristic; see Fritz. *Rom.* iii. 25, Vol. I. p. 195. As a general rule, it may be observed, that when the defining prepositional clause is so incorporated with (*e. g.* ch. ii. 11),—appended to (Col. iv. 8), — or, as here, structurally assimilated πίστις (πιστεύω) ἐν, compare ch. iii. 13, Rom. vi. 4) with the subst. it defines as to form only a single conception, the article is correctly omitted; see Harless *in loc.*, and Winer, *Gr.* § 20. 2, p. 123.
εἰς πάντας τοὺς ἁγίους] '*towards all the Saints;*' objects towards whom the love was directed; *omnes* character Christianismi; Bengel: compare ch. vi. 18, Philem. 5. On the meaning of ἁγίους, see notes on ch. i. 1.
16. οὐ παύομαι εὐχαριστῶν] '*I cease not giving thanks.*' In this simple and well-known formula the participle points to a state supposed to be already *in existence*; see Winer, *Gr.* § 45. 4, p. 308 sq., Scheuerl. *Synt.* § 45. 5, p. 481. In many verbs *e. g.* αἰσχύνομαι, Luke xvi. 3) this distinction between part. and inf. may be made palpable; in others, as in the present case, the verb is such as *rarely* to admit any other idiomatic structure; see Herm. *Viger*, No. 218, Donalds. *Gr.* § 591, and for a good paper on the general distinction between the uses of the participle and of the infin., Weller, *Bemerk. z. Gr. Synt.*

μενος ἐπὶ τῶν προσευχῶν μου,   ¹⁷ ἵνα ὁ Θεὸς τοῦ Κυρίου ἡμῶν

μνείαν ὑμῶν ποιούμ.] ‘making mention of you;’ limitation, or rather specification of the further direction of the εὐχαριστία: comp. 1 Thess. i. 2, Philem. 4, and see notes in locc.   ἐπὶ τῶν προσευχ. μου] ‘in my prayers,’ ‘in orationibus,’ Clarom., Vulg., Goth.; ἐπὶ here being not simply and crudely temporal, ‘at the time of my prayers’ (Eadie), but retaining also that shade of local reference of which even the more distinctly temporal examples are not wholly divested: see Bernhardy, Synt. v. 23. a, p. 246, and notes on 1 Thess. i. 2. The prep. thus serves to express the concurrent circumstances and relations in which, and under which an event took place ; see Winer, Gr. § 47, g, p. 336.

17. ἵνα ὁ Θεὸς κ. τ. λ.] ‘that God etc.;’ subject of the prayer blended with the purpose of making it. The exact meaning of this particle both here and in similar passages requires a brief notice. The uses of ἵνα in the N. T. appear to be three, — (1) Final, or indicative of the end, purpose, or object of the action, — the primary and principal meaning, and never to be given up except on the most distinct counter-arguments.   (2) Sub-final, — occasionally, especially after verbs of entreaty (not of command), the subject of the prayer being blended with, and even in some cases obscuring the purpose of making it; see esp. Winer, Gr. § 44. 8, p. 299, and notes on Phil. i. 9.   (3) Eventual, or indicative of result, — appy. in a few cases, and due, perhaps, more to what is called ‘Hebrew teleology’ (i. e. the reverential aspect under which the Jews regarded prophecy and its fulfilment) than grammatical depravation; comp. Winer, Gr. § 53. 6, p. 406 sq. After maturely weighing the evidence adduced by Winer and others, few, perhaps, will hesitate to characterize Fritzsche’s and Meyer’s strenuous

denial of (2) and (3) as perverse, and the criticism of Eadie, who admitting (3), denies (2) after verbs of entreaty, as somewhat illogical.   In the present case, independent of the parallelism afforded by numerous similar passages (ch. iii. 16, Phil. i. 9, Col. i. 9, iv. 3, 1 Thess. iv. 1, 2 Thess. i. 11), the presence of the opt. δῴη after the pres. (hoped for, dependent realization, Klotz, Devar. Vol. II. p. 622, Bernhardy, Synt. xi. 11, p. 407) inclines us distinctly to this sub-final or secondary telic use; compare Winer, § 41. 1. obs. p. 260. On the late and incorrect form δῴη for δοίη, see Lobeck, Phryn. p. 345, Sturz, de Dial. Maced. p. 52.   ὁ Θεὸς τοῦ Κυρίου] ‘the God of our Lord ;’ see John xx. 17, Matth. xxvii. 46. ‘Deus ejus est qua ex eo natus in Deum est,’ Hilar. de Trin. IV. 35, p. 96. The somewhat contorted explanations of this and the following clause, cited by Suicer (Thes. Vol. I. p. 944), may be dispensed with if this only be observed, that ‘the word God was never looked upon as a word of office or dominion, but of nature and substance,’ Waterland, Sec. Def. Qu. II. Vol. II. p. 399. The admirably perspicuous distinctions of the same author, in Ans. to Pref. Vol. II. p. 415, deserve perusal. ὁ πατὴρ τῆς δόξης] ‘the Father of glory;’ comp. Psalm xxviii. 3, Acts vii. 2, 1 Cor. ii. 8, Heb. ix. 5 ; gen. of the characteristic quality, see Scheuerl. Synt. § 16. 3, p. 115, Winer, Gr. § 34. 2. b, p. 211. It is singular that a mere adjectival resolution (Rückert), or a poetical and less usual meaning of πατὴρ (sc. ‘auctor,’ Job xxxviii. 28, probably Jas. i. 17, and perhaps Heb. xii. 9, but see context; not 2 Cor. i. 3 [Eadie], see De W., and Mey.), should so generally have been adopted instead of this simple and grammatical explanation. The use of πατὴρ was probably suggested by the

Ἰησοῦ Χριστοῦ, ὁ πατὴρ τῆς δόξης, δώῃ ὑμῖν Πνεῦμα σοφίας καὶ
ἀποκαλύψεως, ἐν ἐπιγνώσει αὐτοῦ, [18] πεφωτισμένους τοὺς ὀφ-

foregoing mention of our Lord, while the qualifying gen. δόξης serves appropriately to carry on the ref. to the eternal glory of God which pervades the whole of the first paragraph. The reference, then, of δόξα to the glorified humanity (Stier), or to the divine nature of Christ (Athan., Greg.-Naz., see Suicer, *Thesaur.* Vol. I. p. 944) is by no means necessary.

Πνεῦμα σοφίας κ. τ. λ.] '*the Spirit of wisdom and revelation ;*' the characterizing genitives denoting the special forms and peculiar *manifestations* in which the Apostle prayed for the gift of the Spirit to his converts; compare Rom. i. 4, 2 Cor. iv. 13, 2 Tim. i. 7, see notes *on Gal.* vi. 1, and on the omission of the article with Πνεῦμα, notes *on ib.*, ch. v. 5. The favorite subjective and objective distinctions of Harl., viz. that σοφ. is the subjective state, ἀποκάλ. the objective medium, are not necessary, nor even, as the order (state to means, not *vice versâ*) suggests, logically satisfactory; σοφία is simply the general gift of illumination; ἀποκάλ. the more special gift of insight into the divine mysteries; see further remarks in notes *on* 1 *Tim.* ii. 7.

ἐν ἐπιγνώσει αὐτοῦ] '*in the (full) knowledge of Him,*' 'in agnitione [or rather *cognitione*] ejus,' Clarom., Vulg.; ἐν not being for εἰς (Grot., Wolf) or διά (Beza), but, as usual, marking the *sphere* or element in which the action takes place ; the knowledge of God (not *Christ*, Calv., to whom the first ref. is in ver. 20) was to be the sphere, the circumambient element in which they were to receive wisdom and revelation; compare 2 Pet. i. 2, and see esp. Winer, *Gr.* § 48. a, p. 345. Ἐν ἐπιγν. thus belongs to the whole *preceding* clause, not specially to ἀποκάλ., still less to what *follows* (Chrys. *Lachm.*, al.), both of which connections would interfere with the paral-

lelism of ver. 15 and 16 ; πνεῦμα κ. τ. λ. being symmetrical with πεφωτ. κ. τ. λ., — ἐν ἐπιγν. with εἰς τὸ εἰδέναι. The ἐπὶ in ἐπίγνωσις may be either *additive* (Eadie), in ref. to the increments of knowledge continually received, or, more probably, simply *intensive*, scil. 'cognitio accurata et certa,' Bretschn., *erkenntniss* ; comp. 1 Cor. xiii. 12, see Rost u. Palm, *Lex.* s. v. ἐπὶ, iv. c. 5, and Delitzsch. *on Heb.* x. 26.

18. πεφωτισμένους τοὺς ὀφθαλμοὺς] '*having the eyes of your heart enlightened.*' Three constructions are here possible : (*a*) Accus. absolute, πεφωτισμένους agreeing with ὀφθαλμούς, Peile, Eadie. (*b*) Accusatival clause after, δώῃ. καὶ being omitted to give the clause an emphatically appositional aspect; see Harless and Stier. (*c*) Lax construction of part. ; πεφωτ. referring to ὑμῖν, and τοὺς ὀφθαλμοὺς being accus. of limiting reference ; Winer, *Gr.* § 32. 5. 6, p. 205, Madvig, *Synt.* § 31, comp. Hartung, *Casus*, p. 62. Of these (*a*) is grammatically doubtful, for though such accusatives undoubtedly *do* exist, esp. in later writers, — see Wannowski's elaborate treatise *de Construct. Abs.* IV. 5, p. 146 sq., — still they far more generally admit of an explanation from the context; see Winer, § 32. 7, p. 206, comp. Bernh. *Synt.* III. 30, p. 133. Again (*b*), is somewhat grammatically doubtful, on account of the article (see Beng.), and certainly exegetically unsatisfactory, 'enlightened eyes' rather defining the effect of the Spirit than forming any sort of apposition to It; see Meyer *in loc.* In (*c*) the connection of the accusatives is less simple, but the other syntactic difficulties are but slight, as a permutation of case, esp. in participial clauses, is not uncommon in the N. T. (*e. g.* Acts xv. 22, Winer, § 63. 1. 1, p. 500), nor with-

ϑαλμοὺς τῆς καρδίας ὑμῶν, εἰς τὸ εἰδέναι ὑμᾶς τίς ἐστιν ἡ ἐλπὶς

out distinct parallel in classical Greek; see exx. in Wannowski, IV. 6, p. 169 sq., Jelf, *Gr.* § 711. This then seems the most probable constr.: πεφωτ. κ. τ. λ. serves to define the result of the gift of the Spirit (comp. Phil. iii. 15, 1 Thess. iii. 13, Winer, *Gr.* § 66. 3, p. 549 sq), and owing to the subsequent inf. (εἰς τὸ εἰδέναι) which expresses the *purpose* of the illumination, not unnaturally lapses into the accusative.

τοὺς ὀφϑ. τῆς καρδίας] '*the eyes of your heart;*' a somewhat unusual and figurative expression denoting the inward intelligence of that portion of our immaterial nature (the ψυχή), of which the καρδία is the imaginary seat; comp. *Acta Thom.* § 28, τοὺς τῆς ψυχῆς ὀφϑαλμούς, and see esp. Beck, *Seelenl.* III. 24. 3, p. 94 sq., and notes *on* 1 *Tim.* i. 5. On the use and meaning of φωτίζειν, here, to illuminate with the brightness of *inner* light, see esp. Harl. *in loc.*, and contrast Eph. iii. 9, where, as the context shows, the illumination is of a nature less inward and vital; comp. Beck, *Seelenl.* II. 13. 2, p. 37.   The reading of *Rec.*, ὀφϑ. τῆς διανοίας, has only the support of some cursive mss.: Theod., Œcum. al.   τίς] '*what.*' There appears no reason to adopt in this verse either a qualitative ('cujusnam naturæ, Wahl, Harl.), or, what is appy. more questionable, a quantitative (ποταπή, πόση, Holzh., Stier) translation; the ordinary meaning 'what' ('quæ spes,' Vulg.), is fully sufficient, and includes all more special interpretations.   The articles with ἐλπὶς and πλοῦτος only serve to point them out as well-known and recognized, and as indirectly alluded to throughout the preceding paragraph; comp. Bernhardy, *Synt.* VI. 27, p. 324, Stalb. Plato, *Crit.* 43 c.

ἡ ἐλπὶς κ. τ. λ.] '*the hope of His calling,*' i. e. the hope which the calling works in the heart; κλήσεως being the gen. of the *causa efficiens*, Scheuerl. *Synt.* § 17, p. 125. Ἐλπὶς is thus not objective, τὸ ἐλπιζόμενον (Olsh., Eadie), a meaning scarcely *fully* substantiated even in Col. i. 5 (comp. notes *in loc.*), and here certainly unnecessary, but as usual *subjective*; ἐπὶ ποίαις ἐλπίσι κεκλήμεϑα παρ' αὐτοῦ, Theod. Like πίστις, it is probably occasionally used in an objective aspect ('objectivirt'), as 'the grounds, the state of hope,' but just as πίστις is not used in the N. T. for 'religio Christiana' (see *on Gal.* i. 23), so it is very doubtful whether ἐλπὶς ever *fully* amounts to 'res sperata,' as asserted by Suicer, *Thesaur.* s. v. Vol. I. p. 1095.   τίς ὁ πλοῦτος κ. τ. λ. '*what the riches of the glory of His inheritance;*' a noble accumulation of (possessive) genitives, setting forth the κληρονομία on the side of its glory, and that glory on the side of its riches. All adjectival solutions, it need scarcely be said, are wholly inadmissible; see notes on ver. 6, and Winer, *Gr.* § 30. 3. 1, p. 171 sq.   The prefixed καὶ is omitted by Lachm. with ABD¹FG; 59: Clarom., Sangerm., Amit., Goth., al, but appy. rightly retained by Tisch., Mey., al., with D⁸EKL; nearly all mss.; Copt., Syr. (both), al.; Orig. (Cat.), Chrys., Theod., — as the καὶ in the third member (ver. 19) might have so easily suggested an omission in the second.

ἐν τοῖς ἁγίοις] '*among the saints;*' a semi-local clause appended to τίς (ἐστιν) ὁ πλοῦτος κ. τ. λ., defining the sphere (the whole community of the faithful, comp. Acts xx. 32, xxvi. 18) in which the πλοῦτος τῆς δόξ. τῆς κληρ. is peculiarly found, felt, and realized: compare Col. i. 27, and see Meyer, *h. l.* Harless connects ἐν τοῖς ἁγίοις with κληρ. αὐτοῦ, an interpretation exegetically tenable (see Stier *in loc.* p. 161 sq.), but,

τῆς κλήσεως αὐτοῦ, καὶ τίς ὁ πλοῦτος τῆς δόξης τῆς κληρονομίας
αὐτοῦ ἐν τοῖς ἁγίοις, ¹⁹ καὶ τί τὸ ὑπερβάλλον μέγεθος τῆς δυνά-

on account of the omission of the article, by no means so grammatically admissible, even in Hellenistic Greek, as the somewhat sweeping language of Alf. *in loc.* would lead us to conclude. For as the former clause contains a defined and self-subsistent idea (not merely κληρον. ἐν κ. τ. λ. Job xlii. 15, etc., but κληρον. αὐτοῦ, sc. Θεοῦ, a very distinct expression), the latter cannot easily be regarded as supplemental, and thus, as legitimately anarthrous; see notes on ver. 15. If, however, ἐν τοῖς ἁγ. be immediately connected with the unexpressed ἐστί, the omission of the article will be less sensibly felt (comp. Winer, *Gr.* § 19. 2. b, p. 155), and the harmony in the three clauses fully preserved; the first, ἐλπὶς κ. τ. λ. being stated generally, the second, πλοῦτος κ. τ. λ., more nearly specialized by ἐν τοῖς ἁγ., the sphere in which it is found; the third, τὸ ὑπερβάλ-λον κ. τ. λ., by εἰς ἡμᾶς, the living objects towards whom it is, and will be, exercised.

19. καὶ τί τὸ ὑπερβ. κ. τ. λ.] '*and what (is) the exceeding greatness of His power;*' specification of .that by which hope becomes quickened and realized; ὅση τίς περίεσται κτῆσις ἀγαθῶν τοῖς τοῦ Θεοῦ ἁγίοις ἐπὶ τοῦ μέλλοντος αἰῶνος, Theodorus, Chrys., Theoph., and Œcum. refer this clause simply to the present life. This is doubtful, as the foregoing expressions, ἐλπὶς and κληρο-νομία (ch. v. 5, comp. 1 Cor. vi. 9, Gal. v. 21), and the reference in the following verse seem to point *primarily* to the power of God which shall *hereafter* quicken us even as it did Christ, and shall install us in our inheritance as it enthroned Him on the right hand of God. There is thus a kind of climax, — the *hope* which the calling awakens, — the exhaustless and inexpressible

glory (Chrys.) of that inheritance to which hope is directed, — the limitless *power* that shall bestow it. Still the individualizing εἰς ἡμᾶς seems to show that a *secondary* reference to the *present* quickening power in the hearts of believers (ch. ii. 1, 5) is by no means to be excluded. εἰς ἡμᾶς τοὺς πιστ.] '*to us-ward who are believing;*' objects towards whom the exceeding greatness of the power is displayed; the εἰς ἡμᾶς not being dependent on τῆς δυ-νάμ. αὐτοῦ (Harl., citing 2 Cor. xiii. 4, where however εἰς ὑμᾶς is most probably to be joined with ζήσομεν; see Meyer *in loc.*) but, as in the preceding member, on τί (ἐστί) and εἰς having its regular and primary sense of ethical direction, admirably expressed by '*to us-ward,*' Auth. Ver.; comp. Winer, *Gr.* § 49.·c. δ, p. 353. The second and third clauses τίς ὁ πλοῦτος κ. τ. λ., and τί τὸ ὑπερβ. κ. τ. λ., are thus perfectly symmetrical, the substantival sub-clauses forming a parallelism to each other, and the prepositional sub-clause εἰς ἡμᾶς being structurally parallel to the preceding ἐν τοῖς ἁγίοις, while at the same time it prepares us for the latent apposition suggested by the ἐν Χρ. which follows; see Stier *in loc.*, p. 155. κατὰ τὴν ἐνέρ-γειαν does not refer to all three clauses (Harl.), but, as the correspondence of ideas and language distinctly suggests, to that immediately preceding; not, however, especially to πιστεύοντας (Rück.), for such a connection, though doctrinally unexceptionable (see Col. ii. 12), is *exegetically* unsatisfactory from its interpolation of an unlooked-for idea, — viz., the origin and antecedents of faith. The reference, then, is simply to the whole clause, not, however, as an explanation (Chrys.) or amplification (Calv.) of this power, but, in accordance with

μεως αὐτοῦ εἰς ἡμᾶς τοὺς πιστεύοντας κατὰ τὴν ἐνέργειαν τοῦ κράτους τῆς ἰσχύος αὐτοῦ, ²⁰ἣν ἐνήργησεν ἐν τῷ Χριστῷ, ἐγείρας

the full ethical force of κατά ('measure,' 'proportion,' Bernhardy, *Synt.* v. 20. b, p. 239), as a definition of its mode of operation (Eadie), a mighty *measure*, a stupendous *exemplar* by which its infinite powers towards the believing, in its future, yea, and its present manifestations, might be felt, acknowledged, estimated, and realized; comp. Ignat. *Trall.* 9, where, however, the ὁμοίωμα of the ἔγερ-σις is more alluded to than in the present passage. As the meaning of κατὰ here falls short of 'propter' (compare Griesb. *Opuscula*, II. 5), so it certainly transcends that of mere similitude.

τοῦ κράτους τῆς ἰσχύος] 'the .strength of His might,' 'robur potentiæ,' Æth., scil. the strength which appertains to, is evinced by His ἰσχύς; neither a Hebraism (Holzh.), nor a mere cumulative form of expression (Küttn.), but a specification of the outcoming and exhibition of that power which is the divine attribute; see ch. vi. 10, Dan. iv. 27. Each word has thus its distinct and proper force; ἰσχυς, as its derivation (ἴσχω, ἔχω) implies, refers rather to *passive*, inherent power (Mark xii. 30); κρά-τος (ΚΡΑ, ΚΑΡ, cogn. with κάρα, comp. Benfey, *Wurzellex.* Vol. II. 178) to power evinced in *action;* see Luke i. 51. The striking force of the expressions here used to specify this 'eminent act of God's omnipotence' is well illustrated by Pearson, *Creed,* Art. v. Vol. II. p. 222 (ed. Burt.).

20. ἣν ἐνήργησεν] 'which He *wrought*,' scil. ἣν ἐνέργειαν,—which act of omnipotence God, as the principal cause (see Pearson, *Creed,* Art. v. Vol. I. p. 301, ed. Burt.), displayed in Christ, and in Him in us ('innuit efficaciam Dei in credentibus,' Cocc.) who share the humanity He vouchsafed to take, and are spiritually risen with our risen Lord;

see Stier *in loc.* p. 172.　The reading ἐνήργηκεν (AB; Cyr., Procop.) is adopted by Lachm., *Mey.*, but, as nearly the same authorities [AB; mss.; Aug., Vulg.; Eus., al.] also read καθίσας, must be regarded as very suspicious, and as a not unlikely emendation of style.

ἐν τῷ Χριστῷ] 'in Christ,' in Him as our spiritual Head; ἐν here being no mere 'nota dativi,' a construction now exploded in the N. T. (see Winer, *Gr.* § 31. 8, p. 195), but correctly indicating the *substratum* of the action; see notes on Gal. i. 24. It is scarcely necessary to recapitulate the caution of Theodoret and Theophyl., δῆλον δέ ὅτι ταῦτα πάντα ὡς περὶ ἀνθρώπου τέθεικε (Theod.), τὸ γὰρ ἀναστὰν ἄνθρωπος, εἰ καὶ Θεῷ ἥνωτο (Theophyl.). In this passage, Phil. ii. 6—11, and Col. i. 14—19, as Olsh. well observes, we find the entire Christology of St. Paul.　ἐγείρας] 'when He raised Him,' Auth., or perhaps better ' *in that* He raised Him, Arm.; contemporaneous act with ἐνήργησεν, see notes on γνωρίσας, ver. 9.　καὶ ἐκάθισεν] '*and He set Him;*' change from the participial structure to the finite verb, especially designed to enhance the importance of the truth conveyed by the participle; see exx. in Winer, *Gr.* § 63. 2. b, p. 505 sq. The distinctive and emphatic mention of the consequent and connected acts heightens the conception of the almighty ἐνέργεια of God (Father, Son, and Spirit, Pearson *on Creed,* Art. v. Vol. I. p. 302), displayed in the resurrection of Christ from the dead.　On the session of Christ at the right hand of God, see Knapp, *Scripta Var. Argum.* Art. II.; let these words of Bp. Pearson's, however, never be forgotten, '*He shall reign for ever and ever,* not only to the modified eternity of His mediatorship, but also to the complete eternity

αὐτὸν ἐκ νεκρῶν, καὶ ἐκάθισεν ἐν δεξιᾷ αὐτοῦ ἐν τοῖς ἐπουρανίοις
²¹ ὑπεράνω πάσης ἀρχῆς καὶ ἐξουσίας καὶ δυνάμεως καὶ κυριότη

of the duration of His humanity, which for the future is coëternal to His Divinity,' Art. vi. Vol. i. p. 335.

ἐν τοῖς ἐπουρανίοις] 'in the heavenly places' ܒܣܡܝܐ [in cœlo] Syr., Goth., Æth.; see notes on ver. 3. It is scarcely possible to doubt that these words have here a local reference. The distinctly local expressions, ἐκάθισεν, ἐν δεξιᾷ, — the Scripture doctrine of Christ's literal and local ascent (Mark xvi. 19, al.), — His regal session in heaven in his glorified and resplendent Body (Acts vii. 56, ἑστῶτα ἐκ δεξίων, al., see Phil. iii. 20), — His future literal and local judiciary descent (Acts i. 11, ὃν τρόπον ἐθεάσασθε αὐτὸν πορευόμενον), — all tend to invalidate the vague and idealistic 'status cælestis' urged by Harless in loc. The choice of the more general expression, ἐν τοῖς ἐπουρ., 'in the heavenly regions' (comp. ch. iv. 10), rather than the more specific ἐν τοῖς οὐρανοῖς was perhaps suggested by the nature of the details in ver. 21. The reading οὐρανοῖς (Lachm. with B; al.; Victorin., Hil.), has weak external support, and seems an almost self-evident gloss.

21. ὑπεράνω] 'over above,' 'supra,' Clarom., Vulg., 'ufaro,' Goth.; not 'longe supra,' Beza, Auth., Alf., al.: specification of the nature and extent of the exaltation. The intensive force which Chrys. and Theophyl. find in this word, ἵνα τὸ ἀκρότατον ὕψος δηλώσῃ, and which has recently been adopted by Stier and Eadie, is very doubtful; as is also the assertion (Eadie) that this prevails 'in the majority of passages' in the LXX.: cons. Ezek. i. 26, viii. 2, x. 19, xi. 22, xiii. 10, and even Deut. xxvi. 19, xxviii. 1. Such distinct instances as Ezek. xliii. 15, and in the N. T., Heb. ix. 5, — the similarly unemphatic use of the antitheton ὑποκάτω, John i. 51, Luke viii. 10, — and the tendencies of Alexandrian and later Greek to form duplicated compounds (see Peyron, ad Pap. Taurin. Vol. i. p. 89) make it highly probable that ὑπεράνω, both here and ch. iv. 10, implies little more than simple local elevation. So too Syr. and appy. all the ancient Vv.   πάσης ἀρχῆς κ. τ. λ.] 'all (every) rule and authority and power and lordship;' no parenthesis, but a fuller explanation of ἐν τοῖς ἐπουρανίοις; see Winer, Gr. § 64, 1. 2, p. 614 (ed. 5). The context and the illustrations afforded by ch. iii. 10, Col. i. 16, and 1 Pet. iii. 22, seem to preclude any mere generic reference to all forms of power and dominion (Olsh.), or any specific reference to the orders of the Jewish hierarchy (Schoettg.), or the grades of authority among men (see ap. Pol. Syn.). The abstract words (δυνάμεών τινων ὀνόματα ἡμῖν ἄσημα, Chrys.) seem to be designations of the orders of heavenly Intelligences, and are used by St. Paul in preference to any concrete terms (ἀγγέλων, ἀρχαγγέλων κ. τ. λ.) to express with the greatest aptitude and comprehensiveness the sovereign power and majesty of Christ; εἴ τι ἐστὶν ἐν τῷ οὐρανῷ, πάντων ἀνώτερος γέγονε, Chrys., see Calv. in loc. As this verse relates to Christ's exaltation in heaven rather than His victory over the powers of hell (1 Cor. xv. 24, comp. Rom. viii. 38), the reference is, probably, exclusively to good Angels and Intelligences, 1 Tim. v. 21. Any attempt to define more closely (see authors cited in Hagenbach, Hist. of Doctr. § 131, Petavius, de Angelis, ii. 1, Vol. iii. p. 101 sq.) is alike presumptuous and precarious: see the excellen remarks of Bp. Hall, Invisible World, Book i. § 7. On the nature of Angels, consult the able treatise by Twesten,

τος, καὶ παντὸς ὀνόματος ὀνομαζομένου οὐ μόνον ἐν τῷ αἰῶνι τούτῳ ἀλλὰ καὶ ἐν τῷ μέλλοντι, ²² καὶ πάντα ὑπέταξεν ὑπὸ τοὺς πόδας

Dogmatik, Vol. ii. esp. § 1. 4, the essay by Stuart, *Bibliotheca Sacra* for 1843, pp. 88—154, Ebrard, *Dogmatik*, § 228 sq. Vol. i. p. 276, and the remarks of Lange, *Leb. Jes.* Part. ii. p. 41 sq. καὶ παντὸς ὀνόματος] 'and, in a word, every name named;' concluding and comprehensive designation; καὶ having here that species of *adjunctive* force according to which a general term is appended to foregoing details; see Winer, *Gr.* § 53. 3, p. 388, notes *on Phil.* iv. 12, Fritz. *Matth.* p. 786. Πᾶν ὄνομα is not 'every title of honor,' (Grinf. *Scholl. Hell.*), a particular explanation to which ὀνομαζ. (which has always its simple meaning in the N. T., even in Rom. xv. 20, see Fritz.) is distinctly opposed, — nor again, in reference to Heavenly Powers which are ἀκατονόμαστοι (Theophyl.), — nor even as a generic representation of the foregoing abstract nouns (Wahl, Harless), — but simply with reference to everything in existence ('quicquid existit,' Beza), personal or impersonal, 'everything bearing a name and admitting designation;' comp. Col. i. 16, where a similar latitude is implied by the four times repeated εἴτε, and see notes *in loc.* οὐ μόνον κ. τ. λ.] clause appended not to ἐκάθισεν (Beza Koppe), but to παντὸς ὀνόμ. ὀνομαζ., to which it gives a still further expansion, both in respect of time and locality, — everything named, whether now or hereafter, in the present state of things or the world to come; παντὸς ῥητοῦ καὶ ὀνομαστοῦ, οὐ μόνον τοῦ ἐνταῦθα ὀνομαζομένου, ἀλλὰ καὶ τοῦ ἐκεῖθεν δυναμένου ῥηθῆναι καὶ ὀνομασθῆναι, Œcum. τῷ αἰῶνι τούτῳ] 'this world,' scil. 'this present state of things,' 'systema rerum,' Beng. With regard to the meaning of αἰῶν it may be observed that in all pas-

sages where it occurs, a *temporal* notion is more or less apparent. To this, in the majority, an *ethical* idea is united, so that αἰὼν οὗτος, as Olsh. has observed, is 'the temporary and terrestrial order of things, in which sin predominates (comp. Gesen. *Lex.* s. v. עוֹלָם, в), to which αἰὼν μέλλων (= βασιλεία Θεοῦ), the holy state of things founded by Christ, is the exact contrast; see *Comment on Matth.* xii. 31, 32, Neander, *Planting*, Vol. i. p. 500, 501 (Bohn). In a few passages, like the present, a *semi-local* meaning seems also superadded, causing αἰὼν to approach in meaning to κόσμος, though it still may be always distinguished from it by the temporal and commonly ethical notions which ever form its background; see notes, ch. ii. 2.

22. καὶ πάντα ὑπέταξεν] 'and put all things under His feet;' further specification of the majesty of Christ, — not only the highest conceivable exaltation (ver. 21), but the most unbounded sovereignty. The strong similarity of the language scarcely leaves a doubt that here and Heb. ii. 8, there is a distinct *allusion* to Psalm viii. 7, πάντα ὑπέταξας ὑποκάτω τῶν ποδῶν αὐτοῦ; comp. Gen. i. 28. Nor is this due to any 'rabbinischtypischer Interpretationsweise,' (Mey.) on the part of St. Paul, but to a direct reference under the guidance of the Spirit, to a passage in the O. T., which, in its primary application to man, involves a secondary and more profound application to Christ. In the grant of terrestrial sovereignty the Psalmist saw and felt the antitypical mystery of man's future exaltation in Christ, even more fully than Tholuck and even Hengstenberg *in loc.* appear to admit. The reference thus seems less to the subjugation of foes, as in 1 Cor. xv. 27 (Hamm., Stier), than to the limitless

αὐτοῦ, καὶ αὐτὸν ἔδωκεν κεφαλὴν ὑπὲρ πάντα τῇ ἐκκλησίᾳ, ²³ ἥτις

nature of Christ's sovereignty, which the words ὑπὸ τοὺς κ. τ. λ. (ἡ ἐσχάτη ὑποταγή, Chrys.) still more heighten and enhance. On this and the next verse see a sound sermon by Beveridge, in which the three points, Christ's headship over all things, His headship to the Church, and His relation to it as His body, are well discussed, *Serm.* XXXII. Vol. II. p. 124 sq. (A. C. Libr.) ἔδωκεν is not synonymous with נָתַן, ἔθηκεν, ἔστησεν (Wolf, Holzh., and even Harl.), either here or ch. iv. 11, but (as the dat. ἐκκλησίᾳ and the emphatic position of αὐτὸν seem to suggest) retains its primary and proper sense. The meaning then seems to be, though so exalted and so glorified, yet even HIM did God, out of his boundless mercy and beneficence, *give* to the Church to be its head. κεφαλὴν ὑπὲρ πάντα] '*head over all things.*' The exact construction and immediate reference of these words is not perfectly clear. Ὑπὲρ πάντα evidently qualifies κεφ., not, however, an immediate and adjectival epithet ('summum caput,' Beza, Conyb.), but as an accessory and quasi-participial definition, i. e. ὑπερέχουσαν πάντων; πάντα being used in exactly the same general sense as before, without any limiting reference to τῇ ἐκκλ. (Harl.), or any implied contrast to other subordinate heads, apostles, prophets, etc. (Olsh.). The accus. κεφ. may be regarded either as (a) a simple appositional accus. to the preceding αὐτόν, a second κεφ. being supplied (per brachylogiam) before τῇ ἐκκλ., — ' He gave Him, Head over all, (as Head) to his Church;' comp. Jelf, *Gr.* § 893. c.; or (b) as an accus. of further predication, serving to complete the notion of the verb, and forming a species of tertiary predicate (Donalds. *Gr.* § 489), — 'He gave Him as head over all,' *i. e.* 'in the capacity of head over all; compare

Madvig, *Synt.* § 24. a, and see the various exx. in Donalds. *Gr.* § 490. Of these (a) was adopted in ed. 1 (so also Stier, Mey.), and coincides in *meaning* with the ungrammatical order (ἔδωκεν αὐτὸν [ὄντα] ὑπὲρ πάντα κεφ. τῇ ἐκκλ.) of Syr., Æth.-Platt, Chrys., al., but is, grammatically considered, less simple than (b), and, considered exegetically, but little different in meaning : if God gives Christ to the Church, and Christ at the same time is Head over all things (tertiary predication) He becomes necessarily head to the Church. It seems best, then, with (appy.) Syr.-Phil., Vulg., Clarom., Arm., to adopt the latter view; comp. Alf. *in loc.*

23. ἥτις] '*which indeed;*' not exactly 'ut quæ,' Meyer, but '*quæ quidem,*' the force of the indef. relative being here rather *explanatory* than causal, and serving to elucidate the use and meaning of κεφαλὴ by the introduction of the corresponding term σῶμα. On the uses of ὅστις, see notes *on* Gal. iv. 24. τὸ σῶμα αὐτοῦ] '*His body;*' not in any merely figurative sense, but really and truly; the Church is the veritable body of Christ mystical (ch. iv. 12, 16, esp. v. 30), no mere institution subject to Him as to a κεφαλὴ used in any ethical sense, but united to Him as to a κεφαλὴ used in its simple and literal sense; ἵνα γὰρ μὴ, ἀκούσας κεφαλὴν, ἀρχήν τινα καὶ ἐξουσίαν νομίσῃς, σωματικῶς φησίν, ἡμῶν ἐστί κεφαλή, Œcum. This great and vital truth, and the nature of our union with Christ which it involves and implies, is well illustrated in the beautiful treatise of Bp. Hall, *Christ Mystical,* esp. ch. VII. τὸ πλήρωμα κ. τ. λ.] '*the fulness of Him that filleth all things with all things;*' apposition to the preceding τὸ σῶμα αὐτοῦ designed still more to expand the full meaning of the preceding identification of the Church with

ἐστὶν τὸ σῶμα αὐτοῦ, τὸ πλήρωμα τοῦ τὰ πάντα ἐν πᾶσιν πληρουμένου.

the Lord's body, the general truth conveyed being τὸ πλήρωμα τοῦ Χριστοῦ ἡ ἐκκλησία, Chrys. The special meaning and reference of these mysterious words has been greatly contested. This, however, seems clear (esp. after the long and careful note of Fritz. on Rom. xi. 12, Vol ii. p. 469), that πλήρωμα is here used passively, and that of its two passive meanings, (a) id quod impletum est, and (b) id quo res impletur (see notes on Gal. iv. 4), the former, sc. τὸ πεπληρωμένων, though less common (compare Lucian, Ver. Hist. ii. 37, δύο πληρωμάτων, 'manned ships'), is here alone applicable. The Church, then, is τὸ πεπληρωμένον, — not, however, in the sense 'plenum Christi agmen,' 'hominum a Christo impletorum caterva,' as Fritz. paraphrases, but in a simple and almost local sense, 'that which is filled up by Christ,' 'the receptacle' (Eadie), as it were, of all the gifts, graces, and blessings of Christ; comp. Philo, de Præm. et Pœn. p. 920, where the soul is called a πλήρωμα ἀρετῶν, and contrast the opposed κένωμα, as used by the Gnostics to express the void world of sense; Baur Gnosis, p. 157, 462 (cited by Mey.).   ἐν πᾶσιν πληρουμ.] 'Of Him who filleth all things with all things,' 'qui rerum universitatem omnibus rebus [sibi] implet,' Fritz.; ἐν being here used in its instrumental sense (see notes on 1 Thess. iv. 18), as serving to specify that with which the filling takes place (see ch. v. 18), and πᾶσιν being used with an equal latitude to τὰ πάντα (ver. 22) as implying, not only 'all blessings' (Eadie), but 'all things' unrestrictedly; for by Christ was the whole Universe made, and all things therein; see Col. i. 16, and comp. in ref. generally to the terms of the expression, Philo, Sacrif. Cain, § 18, Vol. i. p. 175 (ed. Mang.), πεπληρωκὼς πάντα διὰ πάν-

των. It has been doubted whether πληροῦσθαι is (a) passive as Vulg., Clarom., Chrys., al., or (b) middle, as Syr., Copt., Goth., Arm., whether in a purely active sense (Xen. Hell. vi. 2. 14, 35, see exx. in Rost u. Palm, Lex. s. v. Vol. ii. p. 956), or, perhaps, as this unique use of the middle in the N. T. suggests, in a specially reciprocal sense 'sibi implere.' Of these the latter alone seems admissible, as the idea of Christ receiving completion in His members (Est., compare Harl.) implies restrictions little accordant with the inclusive τὰ πάντα. The meaning of the whole then would seem to be, — that the Church is the veritable mystical Body of Christ, yea the recipient of the plenitudes of Him who filleth all things, whether in heaven or in earth, with all the things, elements, and entities of which they are composed. And this, as both the parallelism of τὸ σῶμα αὐτοῦ and τὸ πληρ. κ. τ. λ. and the absence of any hint of a change of person seem distinctly to suggest, must be referred, not to God (Theod. Alf.) but to Christ; see esp. ch. iv. 10.   On the doctrine of the omnipresence of Christ, an eternal truth of vital importance (Bull, Def. Fid. Nic. §4. 3. 1 sq., Waterland, Sermon vii. 3, Vol. ii. p. 164), to which this verse seems to allude, see notes on ch. iv. 10, Jackson, Creed, Book xi. 3, 10 sq, and the calm and conciliatory observations of Martensen, Dogmatik, § 177 sq. Well and clearly has it been said by Andrews, 'Christ is both in Heaven and earth: as He is called the Head of His Church, He is in Heaven, but in respect of His body which is called Christ He is on earth,' Serm. xii. Vol v. p. 407. The omission of τὰ (Rec.) is opposed to all the MSS. and to the majority of mss., and adopted by none of the best recent editors.

II. Καὶ ὑμᾶς ὄντας νεκροὺς τοῖς παραπτώ-

1. ὑμῶν] This word was omitted in ed. 1 with *Rec.* and *Tisch.* (ed. 2) on the authority of KL; great majority of mss.; Chrys. Dam., al., — but, though somewhat doubtful on account of the variation of A (ἑαυτῶν), is appy. to be restored on the greatly preponderating authority of BDEFG; 15 mss.: nearly all Vv.; ·Theod., al. So *Lachm.* and *Tisch.* (ed. 1 and 3.)

CHAPTER II. 1. καὶ ὑμᾶς] 'And *you also,*' ' *you too ;* ' special address and application of the foregoing to the case of the readers; καὶ neither (a) simply connecting the verse with what precedes, sc. καὶ ὑπέταξεν, καὶ ἔδωκεν, καὶ ὑμᾶς κ. τ. λ. (*Lachm.*), — as ver. 23 is plainly a conclusion of the foregoing clause, nor (b) serving to introduce a special exemplification of the general act of grace in ver. 23 (Peile), — as the force of the correlation between νεκροὺς and συνεζωπ. is thus seriously impaired, but rather (c) applying what has been said to the ὑμᾶς, to which word it gives emphasis and prominence. The Ephesians are reminded how they *also* had experienced in their moral death the energy of the same quickening power which raised Christ from physical death (ch. i. 20), the ascensive force of καὶ being just perceptible in the implied parallelism between the νέκρωσις ψυχικὴ in the case of the Ephesians (see next note), and the νέκρωσις σωματικὴ on the part of Christ (ch. i. 20); comp. Klotz, *Devar.* Vol. II. p. 636. The *connection* has also its difficulties. According to the most simple view, ver. 1, after having its structure interrupted by the two relatival sentences, ver. 2, 3, is renewed in ver. 4 (not ver. 5, Schott.), by means of δὲ resumptive (Herm. *Viger*, No. 544), and there further elucidated by the interpolated nominat. Θεός, expanded in application by the more comprehensive ἡμᾶς, and concluded in ver. 5; see Theophyl. *in loc.* ὄντας νεκρούς] '*being dead,*' sc. spiritually; νέκρωσις οὐκ

ἡ σωματική, ἡ ἐκ τοῦ Ἀδὰμ ἀρξαμένη, ἀλλὰ ἡ ψυχική, ἡ ἐξ ἡμῶν συνισταμένη, Theophyl.; compare Bramhall, *Castig.* III. 2, Vol. IV. 233 (Angl. Cath. Lib.). The proleptic reference to physical death, scil. 'certo morituri' (Mey.), seems irreconcilable with the context. The πλούσιος ὢν ἐν ἐλέει, which seems to specify God's mercy in extending the exercise of His resurrectional power, would thus lose much of its appropriateness, and the particle καὶ (ver. 5) its proper ascensive force. On this and the two following verses, see a good practical sermon by Usher, *Serm.* IV. Vol. XIII. p. 45 (ed. Elringt.) τοῖς παραπτώμασιν κ. τ. λ.] '*by the trespasses and sins* which ye had committed,' 'delictis et peccatis,' Vulg., Goth.; not 'in delictis,' etc., Arm.; the dat. being appy. that of the *causa instrumentalis;* see Hartung, *Casus,* p. 79, Winer, *Gr.* § 31. 7, p. 194. In the closely parallel passage Col. ii. 13, νεκροὺς ὄντας ἐν τοῖς παραπτώμασιν, the same general sentiment is expressed under slightly different relations; here sin is conceived as that which kills (Olsh.); there it is described as the element or state in which the νέκρωσις shows and reveals itself; comp. notes *in loc.* It is doubtful whether the distinction drawn by Tittmann (*Synon.* p. 45) between παραπτ., sins *rashly* ('a nolente facere injuriam'), and ἁμαρτίαι sins *designedly* committed, can be fully substantiated; both equally referring to 'peccata actualia,' whether in thought, word, or deed, and differing more in the images ('missing,' 'stum-

μασιν καὶ ταῖς ἁμαρτίαις ὑμῶν, ² ἐν αἷς ποτὲ περιεπατήσατε

bling') under which they are presented to our conception, than in the degree of intention ascribed to the perpetrator; see Fritz. *Rom.* v. 15, Vol. i. p. 324, comp. Müller, *Doctr. of Sin,* i. 1. 2, Vol. i. p. 92 (Clark). Perhaps we may say *generally,* that παραπτώματα, as its derivation suggests, is the more *limited* term, viz. particular, special acts of sin; ἁμαρτίαι [ἁ μέρυς, μείρω, Buttm. *Lexil.* No. 15, note], the more *inclusive* and abstract, viz. all forms, phases and movements of sin, whether entertained in thought or consummated in act; compare notes *on Col.* ii. 16.

2. ἐν αἷς] '*in which;*' not so much with ref. to the prevailing *direction* (De Wette), as the *sphere* in which they habitually moved. It does not, however, seem necessary to press the meaning of περιπατεῖν ('sphere in which they *trod,*' Eadie) this being one of those words in the N. T. which are used with so strong a Hebraistic coloring (see the list, Winer, *Gr.* § 3, p. 31), that in several passages it denotes little more than 'vivere;' see Fritz. *Rom.* xiii. 12, Vol. iii. p. 141, Suicer, *Thesaur.* s. v. Vol. ii. p. 679. τὸν αἰῶνα κ. τ. λ.] '*according to the course of this world,*' Auth. ܠܥܠ ܕܥܠܡܐ ܗܢܐ [mundanitatem mundi hujus] Syr.; the ethical meaning of αἰὼν here appy. predominating; see on ch. i. 22. In such cases as the present the meaning seems to approach that of 'tendency, spirit, of the age' (Olsh.), yet still not without distinct trace of the regular *temporal* notion, which, even in those passages where αἰὼν seems to imply little more than our 'world' (comp. 2 Tim. iv. 10), may still be felt in the idea of the (evil) *course,* development, and progress ('ubi ætas mala malam excipit') that is tacitly associated with the term; see Beng.

in loc., and comp. Reuss, *Théol. Chrét.* iv. 20, Vol. ii. p. 228. Any Gnostic reference (Baur, *Paulus,* p. 433), as St. Paul's frequent use of the word satisfactorily proves, is completely out of the question. κατὰ τὸν ἄρχοντα κ. τ. λ.] '*according to the prince of the power* or *empire of the air,*' scil. the devil; climax to the foregoing member, the contrast being κατὰ Θεόν, ch. iv. 24. Without entering into the various interpretations these difficult words have received, we will here only notice briefly, (1) the simple *meaning* of the words; (2) their grammatical *connection;* (3) their probable *explanation.* (1) the two cardinal words are ἐξουσία and ἀήρ. The former, like many words in –ία (Bernhardy, *Synt.* i. 2, p. 47), appears used, not exactly for ἐξουσίαι, scil. as an abstract implying the concrete possessors of the ἐξουσία (comp. Dionys. Hal. viii. 44), but as a *collective* designation of their empire and sovereignty, see esp. Lobeck *Phryn.* p. 469. Ἀὴρ is used thrice by St. Paul besides this place, thrice in the rest of the N. T., — (a) 'the air' simply and generally, Acts xxii. 23, 1 Cor. ix. 26, xiv. 9, and appy. Rev. ix. 2, — (β) as 'the air,' with, probably, strict physical reference, Rev. xvi. 17, — (γ) as 'the air or sky,' appy. tacitly correlative to γῆ (the seat of the περιλειπόμενοι), 1 Thess. iv. 17. We seem, then, bound to reject all partial interpretations, *e. g.* σκότος (Heinsius, Küttn. ap. Peile), πνεῦμα (Hofmann *Schriftb.* Vol. i. p. 403), and to leave the context to define the specific meaning and application of the word. (2) The gen. ἀέρος is not a gen. *objecti,* 'cui potestas est aeris,' Beza; nor *qualitatis,* scil. ἀέριος, ἀσώματος (so Phrys., appy., but not the Greek Fathers generally), but a gen. *of place,* denoting their ἐναέριον διατριβήν (Œcum.), the seat of their

κατὰ τὸν αἰῶνα τοῦ κόσμου τούτου, κατὰ τὸν ἄρχοντα τῆς ἐξουσίας τοῦ ἀέρος, τοῦ πνεύματος τοῦ νῦν ἐνεργοῦντος ἐν τοῖς υἱοῖς τῆς

spiritual empire; οὐχ ὡς τοῦ ἀέρος δεσ-πόζοντα, ἀλλ' ὡς αὐτῷ ἐμφιλοχωροῦντα, Theophyl.; compare Bernhardy, *Synt.* III. 33. a, p. 137. (3) The *explanation* really turns on the latitude of meaning assigned to ἀήρ. Without venturing to deny that the word may mysteriously intimate a near propinquity of the spirits of evil, it may still be said that the limitation to the physical atmosphere (Mey.) is as precarious in doctrine as the reference to some ideal 'atmosphere belting a death-world' (Eadie), or to the common parlance of mankind (Alf.), is too vague and undefined. The natural explanation seems to be this, — that as οὐρανὸς is used in a limited and partial (Matt. vi. 26), as well as an uncircumscribed meaning, so conversely ἀήρ, which is commonly confined to the region of the air or atmosphere, may be extended to all that supra-terrestrial but sub-celestial region (ὁ ὑπουράνιος τόπος, Chrys.) which seems to be, if not the abode, yet the haunt of evil spirits; see esp. LXX., Job i. 7, ἐμπεριπατήσας τὴν ὑπ' οὐρανόν; compare Olsh. *in loc.*, and Stuart, *Bibl. Sacra* for 1843, p. 139; see also Hagenbach, *Stud. u. Krit.* Vol. I. 479. Quotations out of Rabbinical writings and Greek philsophers will be found in Wetst., and Harl. *in loc.*, but that St. Paul drew his conceptions from the former (Mey.) or the latter (Wetst.), we are slow indeed to believe; see the remarks *on Gal.* ch. iv. 24. τοῦ πνεύματος] 'the spirit;' scil. the evil principle of action, more specially defined by the succeeding words. The explanation of this gen. is not easy, as exegesis appears to suggest one construction, grammar another. The most convenient assumption, an anomaly of case (gen. for accus. in apposition to τὸν ἄρχ. κ. τ. λ., Heinichen, Euseb. *Hist. Eccl.* v.

20, Vol. ii. p. 99), is so doubtful, that it seems best, with Winer (*Gr.* 67. 3, p. 558), to regard the gen. as dependent on τὸν ἄρχοντα, and in apposition with ἐξουσίας; πμεῦμα not referring, like ἐξουσία, to the aggregate of individual πνεύματα (πάντος ἐναερίου πνεύματος, Theophyl., compare Eadie, Alf.), a *very* doubtful meaning, owing to the difference of termination, but to the evil principle which animated the empire, and emanated from Satan, the ruler of it. There is confessedly an exegetical difficulty in the expression τὸν ἄρχ. τοῦ πνεύμ.; this, however, may be removed either by supplying a similar but more appropriate substantive out of τὸν ἄρχ., or (what is in effect the same) by observing that τοῦ πνεύματος has a species of objective meaning reflected on it from the words with which it is in apposition. There is probably, as Harless and Meyer suggest, a tacit antithesis in τοῦ πν. to the Πνεῦμα τὸ ἐκ Θεοῦ; comp. 1 Cor. ii. 12. νῦν is commonly referred to the period since the redemption, the time of increased satanic energy and of hottest strife (De Wette); comp. Rev. xii. 12. This, however, is more than the words seem intended to convey. As ποτέ, ver. 1, is again repeated ver. 3, the natural antithesis appears νῦν—ποτέ; the Apostle specifies the *still* active existence in one class, the children of disobedience, of the same spirit which *formerly* wrought not only in his readers, but in all; sim. Hammond and Harless *in loc.* τοῖς υἱοῖς τῆς ἀπειθ.] '*the sons of disobedience;*' a Hebraistic circumlocution nearly equivalent to οἱ ἐξ ἀπειθείας (compare Fritz. *Rom.* ii. 16, Vol. i. p. 105), and serving to mark more vividly than the adjectival construction the essential and innate disobedience of the subjects, — a disobedience to which they

ἀπειθείας, ³ *ἐν οἷς καὶ ἡμεῖς πάντες ἀνεστράφημέν ποτε ἐν ταῖς*
ἐπιθυμίαις τῆς σαρκὸς ἡμῶν, ποιοῦντες τὰ θελήματα τῆς σαρκὸς

belong as chidren to a parent; comp. ch.
v. 6, Col. iii. 6 (notes), 1 Thess. v. 5
(notes), 2 Thess. ii. 3, and see Winer,
Gr. § 34. 3. b, 2, p. 153, and Gurlitt,
Stud. u. Krit. 1829, p. 728. 'Απειθεία,
as in Col. iii. 6 (see critical note *in loc.*),
is obviously neither 'diffidentia' (Vulg.,
Clarom., 'ungalaubeinais,' Goth.; compare Æth.), nor ἀπάτη (Chrysost.), but
'disobedience,' ܠܡܰܣܰܪܠܳܐ ܡܰ
[inobedientiæ] (Syr., Arm.), whether to
the message of the Gospel or the man-
dates of the conscience, — sin, in fact, in
its most enhanced form, the violation of
the dependence of the creature on the
Creator; see Müller, *Doctr. of Sin,* I. 1.
2, Vol. I. p. 91 (Clark).

3. *ἐν οἷς*] '*among whom,*' Auth.,
scil. ὧν καὶ αὐτοὶ ὄντες, Rück.; not ἐν οἷς
sc. παραπτώμασιν (Syr., Hier.), in which
case ver. 2 would illustrate the ἁμαρτ.,
ver 3 the παραπτ. The parallelism (ἐν
αἷς—ἐν οἷς) is a specious argument for
such a reference (see Stier *in loc.*, p.
252); still, grammatical perspicuity, the
studied change to ἀνεστράφ., and still
more the *very general* nature of the distinction between παραπτώματα and ἁμαρτίαι are seriously opposed to it; comp.
2 Cor. i. 12, where ἀνεστρ. is similarly
used with a double ἐν, the first (semi-
local) referring to the surrounding objects, 1 Tim. iii. 15, the second (ethical)
to the element in which they moved, 2
Pet. ii. 18. *καὶ ἡμεῖς πάντες*]
'*even we all;*' Jews and Gentiles, not
Jews alone (Mey.). As ὑμεῖς (ver. 1, 2)
denotes the Gentile world, so it might be
argued ἡμεῖς would seem naturally to
refer to the Jews. To this, however,
the addition of πάντες presents an insuperable objection, as almost obviously
designed to preclude any such limitation, and to expand the reference to both

classes (συντάττει καὶ ἑαυτόν, Theod.);
we all, called and reclaimed Jews and
converted Gentiles, were once members
of that fearful company, the υἱοὶ τῆς
ἀπειθείας; comp. Alf. *in loc.*   *τὰ*
θελήματα τῆς σαρκός] '*the (va-*
rious) desires of the flesh.' The plural
is not elsewhere found in the N. T. (Acts
xiii. 22 is a quotation), though not unusual in the LXX; Psalm. cx. 2, 2
Chron. ix. 12, Isaiah xliv. 28, lviii. 13,
al. It here probably denotes the various
exhibitions and manifestations of the
will, and is thus symmetrical with, but a
fuller expansion of ἐπιθυμίαις. On the
true meaning of σάρξ, 'the life and
movement of man in the things of the
world of sense,' see Müller, *Doctr. of
Sin,* II. 2, Vol. I. p. 352 sq., and esp.
notes *on Gal.* v. 16.   *τῶν διανοιῶν*]
'*of the thoughts,*' scil. ' of the *evil* thoughts '
(compare διαλογισμοὶ, πονηροί Matth. xv.
19); the ethical meaning, however, not
being due to the plural ('die schwan-
kenden wechselnden Meinungen,' Harl.),
but, as Mey. justly observes, to the context; comp. τὰ διανοήματα, Luke xi. 17.
It is added, not to strengthen the meaning of σάρξ (Holzh.), but to include
both sources whence our evil desires
emanate, the worldly (sensual) tendency
of our life on the one hand, and the spiritual sins of our thoughts and intentions
on the other; so Theod. *in loc.*, except
that he too much limits the meaning of
σάρξ. On the meaning of διανοίαι, as
usually marking the motions of the
thoughts and will on the side of their
outward manifestations, see Beck, *Seelenl.*
II. 19, p. 58.   *καὶ ἦμεν*] '*and we
were;*' with great definiteness as to the
relation of time, the change of construction from the (*present*) part. to the *oratio
directa* being intended to give emphasis
to the weighty clause which follows (see

καὶ τῶν διανοιῶν, καὶ ἦμεν τέκνα φύσει ὀργῆς, ὡς καὶ οἱ λοιποί·
⁴ ὁ δὲ Θεὸς, πλούσιος ὢν ἐν ἐλέει, διὰ τὴν πολλὴν ἀγάπην αὐτοῦ

notes, ch. i. 20), and also to disconnect it from any possible relation to the present; 'we *were* children of wrath by nature, — it was once our state and condition, it is now so no longer.'

τέκνα φύσει ὀργῆς] '*children by nature — of wrath.*' This important clause can only be properly investigated by noticing separately (1) the simple *meaning* of the words; (2) their *grammatical connection;* (3) their probable *dogmatical application.* (1) We begin with (*a*) τέκνα, which is not simply identical with the Hebraistic υἱοὶ, ver. 2, but, as Bengel obviously felt, is more significant and suggestive; see Steiger *on* 1 *Pet.* i. 14. The word arouses the attention; 'we were τέκνα,' — that bespeaks a near and close relation, — but of what? Of God? No, — '*of wrath;*' its actual and definite objects; see Stier *in loc.* p. 256, and comp. Hofm. *Schriftb.* Vol. i. p. 497. (*b*) Ὀργὴ has its proper meaning, and denotes, not τιμωρία or κόλασις itself (Suicer, *Thesaur.* s. v. Vol. II. p. 505), but the moving principle of it, God's holy hatred of sin, which reveals itself in His punitive justice; compare Rom. i. 18. (*c*) The meaning of φύσει has been much contested. The *general* distinction of Waterland (*Second Defence* Qu. xxiv. Vol. II. p. 723) seems perfectly satisfactory that φύσει in Scripture relates to something inherent, innate, fixed, and implanted from the first, and is in opposition to something accessional, superinduced, accidental; ·or, as Harl. more briefly expresses it, 'das Gewordene in Gegensatz zum Gemachten;' compare Thorndike, *Covenant of Grace,* II. 10, Vol. III. p. 170 (A. C. Libr.). The more exact meaning must be determined by the context: compare Gal. ii. 15, Rom. ii. 14, Gal. iv. 8, where φύσει respectively means, (*a*) transmit-

ted, inborn nature; (β) inherent nature; (γ) essential nature. The connection must here guide us. (2) *Connection.* Φύσει is to be joined with τέκνα, not ὀργῆς (Holzh., Hofm. *Schriftb.* Vol. i. p. 497), and defines the aspect under which the predicate shows itself (see Madvig, *Synt.* § 40); the unusual order [ADEFGL reverse it but appy. by way of emendation] appearing to have arisen from a limitation of a judgment which St. Paul was about to express unlimitedly; the Jews were the covenant people of God; Jews and Gentiles (ἡμεῖς) could not then equally and unrestrictedly be called τέκνα ὀργῆς; see Müller, *Doctr. of Sin,* iv. 2, Vol. II. p. 306. (3) The *doctrinal reference* turns on the meaning of φύσει. · This the limiting connection seems to show *must* imply what is *innate;* for if it implied 'habitual or developed character' (*e. g.* Ælian, *Var. Hist.* ix. 1, φύσει φιλάργυρος; see exx. in Wetst., and compare Fritz. *Rom.* Vol. i. p. 116), there would be little need of the limitation, and little meaning in the assumed contrast, 'filii adoptione,' Estius ap. Poli *Syn.* This is further confirmed by the tense (see above) and the argument 'ex simili' in ὡς καὶ οἱ λοιποί (ἦσαν), for·it must have been some universal state to have applied to all the rest of mankind. Still it must fairly be said the unemphatic position of φύσει renders it doubtful whether there is any special contrast to χάριτι, or any *direct* assertion of the doctrine of Original Sin; but that the clause contains an *indirect,* and therefore even more convincing assertion of that profound truth, it seems impossible to deny. The very long but instructive note of Harless *in loc.* may be consulted ·with profit.

4. ὁ δὲ Θεός] '*but God.*' Resumption of ver. 1 after the two relatival

ἢν ἠγάπησεν ἡμᾶς, ⁵ *καὶ ὄντας ἡμᾶς νεκροὺς τοῖς παραπτώμασιν*

sentences, ἐν αἷς ver. 2, and ἐν οἷς ver. 3; δέ being correctly used rather than οὖν, as the resumption also involves a *contrast* to the preceding verse. The declaration of the ἔλεος of God forms an assuring and consoling antithesis to the foregoing statement that by nature all were the subjects of His ὀργή. On the use of δὲ after a parenthesis, see Klotz, *Devar.* Vol ii. p. 377, Hartung, *Partik.* δὲ, 3. 2, Vol. p. 173; the use of 'autem' in Latin is exactly similar, see esp. Hand, *Tursell.* s. v. § 9, Vol. i. p. 569; Beza's correction of the Vulg., 'sed' instead of 'autem' is therefore not necessary.　πλούσιος ὢν κ. τ. λ.] '*being rich in mercy,*' scarcely 'ut qui dives sit,' Beza (comp. Madvig, *Lat. Gramm.* § 366. 2), as the participial clause does not here so much assign the reason, as characterize, in the form of a secondary predicate of time, 'being as He is' (compare Donalds. *Gr.* § 442. *a*) the *general* principle under which the divine compassion was exhibited. The more *particular* motive (De W.) is stated in the succeeding clause. The expression πλούσιος ἐν (οὐχ ἁπλῶς ἐλεήμων, Chrys.) occurs James ii. 5, and points to the object or sphere in which the richness is apparent; compare 1 Cor. i. 5. On the distinction between ἔλεος ('ipsum miseris succurrere studium') and οἰκτιρμὸς ('ipsa tantum misericordia'), see Tittm. *Synon.* p. 69 sq.　ἢν ἠγάπησεν ἡμᾶς] '*wherewith He loved us;*' cognate accus., serving to add force and emphasis to the meaning of the verb; see exx. in Winer, *Gr.* § 32. 2, p. 200, and in Donalds. *Gr.* § 466. The pronoun ἡμᾶς obviously includes both Jewish and Gentile Christians, and is coëxtensive with ἡμεῖς πάντες, ver. 3.

5. καὶ ὄντας ἡμᾶς νεκρ.] '*even while we were dead;*' καὶ not being otiose (comp Syr., Æth.), nor simple copula

(Mey.), nor as a mere repetition of καί, ver. 1, but qualifying ὄντας (Syr.-Phil.), and suggesting more forcibly than in ver. 1 (where it qualifies ὑμᾶς) the might of the quickening power of God which extended even to a state of moral death. Καὶ νεκροὺς κ. τ. λ. would certainly seem a more natural order (Fritz. *Conject. in N. T.* p. 45; comp. Chrys. τοὺς νεκροὺς . . . τούτους ἐζωοπ.), but as St. Paul seems to wish to make their *state* of death its permanence and its endurance, more felt than the mere *fact* of it, the ascensive particle is joined with the participle rather than with the predicate; see Klotz, *Devar.* Vol. ii. p. 638.

συνεζωοποίησεν τῷ Χρ.] '*He together quickened with Christ,*' not 'in Christ,' Copt., Arm. (perhaps following the reading συνεζ. ἐν, B; 17, al.), but 'with Christ,' ܘ ܠܡ ܫܝܚ Syr. al.; ἐζωοποίησε κἀκεῖνον καὶ ἡμᾶς, Chrysost. The previous statement of the spiritual nature of their death, and the similar (but, owing to the mention of baptism, not wholly parallel) passage, Col. ii. 13, seem to show that συνεζ. has reference to *spiritual* life, the life of grace. It is thus not necessary to consider the realization as future (Theod.), nor even with Theophyl. (ἡμᾶς δυνάμει νῦν μετ' ὀλίγον δὲ καὶ ἐνεργείᾳ), to limit the present degree of it: the aorist has its proper and characteristic force; what God wrought in Christ he wrought 'ipso facto' in all who are united with Him. Meyer aptly cites Fritz. *Rom.* Vol. ii. p. 206, 'ponitur aoristus de re, quæ quamvis futura sit, tamen pro peractâ recte censeatur . . . . cum aliâ re jam factâ contineatur.' It is then just possible that συνεζ. *may* include *also* a future and physical reference (Rom. viii. 10, 11, see notes ver. 6). but that its primary reference is to an actually existent and spiritual state, it seems

συνεζωοποίησεν τῷ Χριστῷ (χάριτί ἐστε σεσωσμένοι), ⁶ καὶ
συνήγειρεν, καὶ συνεκάθισεν ἐν τοῖς ἐπουρανίοις ἐν Χριστῷ Ἰησοῦ,
⁷ ἵνα ἐνδείξηται ἐν τοῖς αἰῶσιν τοῖς ἐπερχομένοις τὸ ὑπερβάλλον

very difficult to deny.   Χ ά ρ ι τ ί
ἐ σ τ ε σ ε σ ω σ μ έ ν ο ι] 'by grace have ye
been (and are ye) saved;' see notes on
ver. 8.   This emphatic mention of grace
(grace, not works) is to make the readers
feel what their own hearts might otherwise have caused them to doubt, — the
real and vital truth, that they have present and actual fellowship with Christ in
the quickening, — yea, and even in the
resurrectionary and glorifying power of
God; see esp. Origen (Cram. Caten.),
and comp. Bp. Hall, Christ Mystical, ch.
v. 1 (ad. init.).

6. σ υ ν ή γ ε ι ρ ε ν . . . . σ υ ν ε κ ά θ ι -
σ ε ν] 'He raised us with (Him), He enthroned us with (Him).' The simple
meaning of these verbs, and esp. of the
latter, seems to confine the reference to
what is future and objective. Still, as
συνεζωοποίησεν, though primarily spiritual and present, may have a physical
and future reference, — so here conversely, a present spiritual resurrection
and enthronement may also be alluded
to; as Andrewes truly says, 'even now
we sit there in Him, and shall sit with
Him in the end,' Serm. VII. in Vol. I. p.
115 (A. C. Libr.). This may be referred
(a) to the close nature of our union with
Christ, so that His resurrection and exaltation may be said, in Him, to be actually ours (κεφαλὴ γὰρ ἡμῶν ὁ συνεδρεύων,
ἀπαρχὴ ἡμῶν ὁ συμβασιλεύων, Theod.),
or, more simply, (b) to that divine effi-
cacy of the quickening power of God
which extends itself to issues spiritually
indeed present (Phil. iii. 20, Rev. i. 6),
but, strictly speaking, future and contin-
gent; comp. esp. Rom. viii. 30, where the
aorists are used with equal significance
and effect.   ἐ ν τ ο ῖ ς ἐ π ο υ ρ α ν ί -
ο ι ς] 'in the heavenly places;' see notes,
ch. i. 3, 20.   Bengel has noticed how

appropriately St. Paul omits the specific
ἐν δεξιᾷ, of ch. i. 20; 'non dicit in dex-
trâ; Christo sua manet excellentia;'
comp. Est. in loc.   ἐ ν Χ ρ . Ἰ η σ ο ῦ
must not be connected simply with ἐν
τοῖς ἐπουρ. (Peile, Eadie), but with συνήγειρεν and συνεκάθισεν ἐν τοῖς ἐπουρ.;
comp. ch. i. 3.   At first sight the clause
might seem superfluous, but more atten-
tively considered, it will be found to
define the deep, mystical nature of the
union; God ἤγειρεν, ἐκάθισεν, ἡμᾶς, not
only σὺν Χρ., but ἐν Χρ.; not only with
Christ by virtue of our fellowship, but
in Christ by virtue of our mystical, cen-
tral, and organic union with Him.   On
the nature of this union, see Hooker,
Serm. III. Vol. iii. p. 762 (ed Keble),
Ebrard, Dogmatik, § 445, Vol. II. p. 323,
Martensen, Dogmatik, § 176. obs.

7. ἵ ν α ἐ ν δ ε ί ξ η τ α ι] 'in order that
He might show forth;' divine purpose of
the gracious acts specified in ver. 5, 6.
The middle voice ἐνδείξασθαι is not used
(either here or Rom. ii. 15, ix. 17, 22, 2
Cor. viii. 24) with any reference to 'a
sample or specimen of what belonged to
Him' (Rück., Eadie), but either simply
implies 'for Himself,' i. e., 'for His
glory' (comp. Jelf, Gr. § 363. 1), 'let be
seen, (Peile), or, still more probably, is
used with only that general subjective
reference, 'show forth his, etc.' (the
'dynamic' middle of Krüger, Sprachl.
§ 52. 8. 5; see Kuster de Verb. Med. §
58, and exx. in Rost. u. Palm. Lex. s.
v.), which, owing to the following αὐτοῦ,
can hardly be retained in translation.
The word occurs eleven times in the N.
T. (only in St. Paul's Epp. and Heb.),
always in the middle voice.   In fact, as
δείκνυμι is but rarely used in the middle
voice, though in a few formulæ (see Ast,
Lex. Plat. s. v.) it involves a middle

πλοῦτος τῆς χάριτος αὐτοῦ ἐν χρηστότητι ἐφ' ἡμᾶς ἐν Χριστῷ
Ἰησοῦ. ⁸ τῇ γὰρ χάριτί ἐστε σεσωσμένοι διὰ τῆς πίστεως· καὶ

sense; so ἐνδείκνυμαι, which is not common in the act., except in legal forms, may in the middle involve little more than an active meaning; comp. Donalds. Gr. § 434, p. 447.　τοῖς αἰῶσιν τοῖς ἐπερχ.] 'to the ages which are coming.' These words have been unduly limited. Any special reference to the then present and immediately coming age ('per omne vestrum tempus,' Mor.), or to the still future kingdom of Christ, the αἰὼν ὁ μέλλων, ch. i. 21 (Harl., Olsh.), seems precluded respectively by the use of the plural and the appended pres. part. ἐπερχομ. The most simple meaning appears to be 'the successively arriving ages and generations from that time to the second coming of Christ,' 'tempora inde ab apostolicis illis ad finem mundi secutura,' Wolf. Such expressions as the present deserve especial notice, as they incidentally prove how very ill-founded is the popular opinion adopted by Meyer and others, that St. Paul believed the Advent of the Lord to be close at hand; see *on* 1 *Thess.* iv. 15.　τὸ ὑπερβάλλον πλοῦτος] 'the exceeding riches;' an especially and studiedly strong expression designed to mark the 'satis superque' of God's grace in our redemption by Christ; comp. ch. iii. 20, 1 Tim. i. 14, and see Andrewes, *Serm.* I. Vol. II. p. 197 (A. C. Libr.). The neuter πλοῦτος is adopted with ABD¹FG; 17 67**: Orig. (1), and by *Lachm., Tisch.*, and most recent editors.　ἐν χρηστότητι ἐφ' ἡμᾶς ἐν Χρ. Ἰησ.] 'in goodness towards us in Christ Jesus;' a single compound modal clause appended to ἐνδειξ.; ἐν χρ. ἐφ' ἡμ. being closely connected (comp. Luke vi. 35; the art. is not necessary, see notes, ch. i. 6), and defining accurately the manner in which God displays 'the riches of His grace,' while ἐν Χ. 'Ι.

('in,' not 'through Christ Jesus,' Auth.; see Winer, *Gr.* § 48. a, p. 347 note) specifies, as it were, the ever-blessed sphere to which its manifestations are confined, and in which alone its operations are felt. Well do Calvin and Stier call attention to this 'notanda repetitio nominis Christi' (contrast the melancholy want of appreciation of this in De W.), and the reiteration of that eternal truth which pervades this divine epistle, — 'nur in *Christo Jesu* das alles, und anders nicht,' Stier, p. 273 ; see notes on ch. i. 3.　　On the meaning of χρηστότης see notes *on Gal.* v. 22.

8.　τῇ γὰρ χάριτί] 'For by grace;' confirmatory explanation of the truth and justice of the expression τὸ ὑπερβ. κ. τ. λ., by a recurrence to statement made parenthetically in ver. 5. The article is thus not added merely because χάρις 'expresses an idea which is familiar, distinctive, and monadic in its nature' (Eadie), but because there a retrospective reference to χάριτι, ver. 5, where the noun, being used adverbially, is properly anarthrous ; see Middleton, *Greek Art.* v. 2, p. 96 (ed. Rose). It may be observed that the emphasis rests on τῇ χάριτι, the further member διὰ τῆς πίστεως being added to define the weighty ἐστε σεσωσμένοι: χάρις is the objective, operating and *instrumental* cause of salvation, πίστις the subjective *medium* by which it is received, the *causa apprehendens*, or to use the language of Hooker, 'the hand which putteth on Christ, to justification,' *Serm.* II. 31 ; comp. Waterland, *Justif.* Vol. VI. p. 22, and a good sermon by Sherlock, Vol. I. p. 323 sq. (ed. Oxf.).　ἐστε σεσωσμένοι] 'ye have been (and are) saved.' It is highly improper to attempt to dilute either the normal meaning of the verb ('salvum facio,' 'ad eternam vitam per-

τοῦτο οὐκ ἐξ ὑμῶν, Θεοῦ τὸ δῶρον· ⁹ οὐκ ἐξ ἔργων, ἵνα μή τις

duco,' see Suicer, *Thesaur.* s. v.) or the proper force of the tense. The perfect indicates 'actionem plane præteritam, quæ aut nunc ipsum seu modo finita est, *aut per effectus suos durat*' (Poppo, *Progr. de emend. Matth. Gramm.* p. 6), and, in a word, serves to connect the past and the present, while the aorist leaves such a connection wholly unnoticed; see esp. Schmalfeld, *Synt.* § 56, and compare Scheuerl. *Synt.* § 32. 5, p. 342. Thus, then, ἐστὲ σεσωσμ. denotes a present state as well as a terminated action; for, as Eadie justly observes, 'Salvation is a present blessing, though it may not be fully realized.' On the other hand, ἐσώ-θημεν (Rom. viii. 24) is not · ἐν τοῖς σωζομένοις ἐσμέν (Peile), but simply 'we were saved,' the context (ἐλπίδι) supplying the necessary explanation.   διὰ τῆς πίστεως] 'through your faith;' subjective medium and condition; see above, and compare Hammond, *Pract. Catech.* p. 42 (A. C. Libr.). The modification suggested by Bull ('per fidem hic intelligit obedientiam evangelio præstitam cujus fides specialiter sic dicta non tantum initium est sed et radix et fundamentum,' *Harm. Apost.* I. 12. 8) is here not necessary. The contrast with ἐξ ἔργων and connection with χάριτι, seem to show that πίστις is 'reliance on the divine grace' (Waterland, *Justif.* Vol. VI p. 37), 'the living capacity,' as it is termed by Olsh., 'for receiving the powers of a higher world;' χάρις being thus identical with *imparting*, πίστις with *receiving* love; see Olshaus. *on Rom.* iii. 21, and comp. Usteri, *Lehrb.* II. 1. 1, p. 151.   *Lachm.* omits the article with BD¹FG; 4 mss.; Chrys., al.; the external authority, however [AD³EKL; nearly all mss.; Theod., Dam., al.], seems slightly in favor of the text.   καὶ τοῦτο] '*and this*,' sc. τὸ σεσωσμ. εἶναι (Theoph. 2), not 'nempe hoc quod

credidistis,' Bull, *loc. cit.*, with Chrys., Theod., Theoph. 1, al.; see Suicer, *Thesaur.* Vol. II. p. 728. Grammatically considered, καὶ τοῦτο (= καὶ ταῦτα, Rost u. Palm, *Lex.* s. v. οὗτος, Vol. II. p. 599) *might* be referred to a verbal notion (τὸ πιστεύειν) derived from πίστις, but the logical difficulty of such a connection with ἐξ ἔργων (parallel and explanatory to ἐξ ὑμῶν) seems insuperable. Still it may be said that the clause καὶ τοῦτο κ. τ. λ. was *suggested* by the mention of the subjective medium πίστις, which might be thought to imply *some* independent action on the part of the subject (compare Theod.); to prevent even this supposition, the Apostle has recourse to language still more rigorously exclusive.   Θεοῦ τὸ δῶρον] '*of God is the gift*,' scil. Θεοῦ δῶρον τὸ δῶρον ἐστί; the gen. Θεοῦ (emphatic, on account of antithesis to ὑμῶν) being thus the *predicate*, τὸ δῶρον ('the peculiar gift in question,' τὸ σεσωσμ. εἶναι διὰ τῆς πίστ.), the *subject* of the clause; see Rückert *in loc.* Harl., *Lachm.*, and De W. inclose these words in a parenthesis, but certainly without reason; the slight want of connection seems designed to add force and emphasis.

9. οὐκ ἐξ ἔργων] '*not of works*;' more exact explanation of the preceding οὐκ ἐξ ὑμῶν, and thus standing more naturally in connection with καὶ τοῦτο than with τὸ δῶρον ἐστί (Meyer). The sense, however, in either case is the same. The grammatical meaning of ἐξ ἔργων is investigated in notes *on Gal.* ii. 16; its doctrinal applications are noticed by Neander, *Planting*, Vol. I. p. 419 (Bohn).   ἵνα μή τις καυχ.] '*that no man should boast*;' purpose of God, involved in and included in the 'lex suprema' alluded to in the foregoing οὐκ ἐξ ἔργων; comp. Rom. iii. 27. The repression of boasting was not the

καυχήσηται· ¹⁰ αὐτοῦ γάρ ἐσμεν ποίημα, κτισθέντες ἐν Χριστῷ

primary and special object of God's appointment of salvation by grace through faith (compare Mackn.), still less was it merely the *result* (Peile), but was a purpose (*ἵνα εὐγνώμονας περὶ τὴν χάριν ποιήσῃ,* Chrys.), that was necessarily inseparable from His gracious plan of man's salvation. On the force and use of *ἵνα*, see notes on ch. i. 17.

10. *αὐτοῦ γάρ κ. τ. λ.*] '*for we are His handiwork,*' 'ipsius enim sumus factura,' Vulg.; proof of the foregoing sentences *καὶ τοῦτο—δῶρον* and *οὐκ ἐξ ἔργων*; the emphatic *αὐτοῦ* pointing to the positive statement that the gift of salvation comes from God, and the assertion of our being His (spiritual) *ποίημα*, to the negative statement that salvation is not *ἐξ ὑμῶν*, or as further explained, *οὐκ ἐξ ἔργων*. If we are *God's ποίημα*, our salvation, our all must be due to. Him (comp. Bramhall, *Castig.* Vol. iv. 232, A. C. Libr.); if we are a spiritual *ποίημα* (*τὴν ἀναγέννησιν ἐνταῦθα αἰνίττεται,* Chrys.), spiritually formed and designed for good works, our salvation can never be *ἐξ ἔργων* (whether of the natural, moral, or ritual law which preceded that *ἀνάκτισις*); see Neander, *Planting*, Vol. i. p. 476 note (ed. Bohn). *κτισθέντες ἐν Χρ. Ἰησ.*] '*created in Christ Jesus;*' defining clause, explaining the true application and meaning of the preceding *ποίημα*; compare ver. 15, the expression *καινὴ κτίσις*, 2 Cor. v. 17, Gal. vi. 15, and notes *in loc.* That the reference of *ποίημα* is not to the physical, and that of *κτισθ.* to the spiritual creation ('quantum ad substantiam fecit, quantum ad gratiam condidit,' Tertull. *Marc.* v. 17), but that *both* refer to the *spiritual ἀνάκτισις*, seems contextually necessary, and is asserted by the best ancient (*οὐ κατὰ τὴν πρώτην λέγει δημιουργίαν, ἀλλὰ κατὰ τὴν δευτέραν,* Theod., compare Œcum.), and accepted by the best mod-

ern commentators; still it does not seem improbable that the more general and inclusive word *ποίημα* was designed to *suggest* the analogy (Harl.) between the physical creation and the spiritual re-creation of man. For a sound sermon on this text see Beveridge, *Serm.* iv. Vol. ii. p. 417 sq. (A. C. Libr.). *ἐπὶ ἔργοις ἀγαθοῖς*] '*for good works,*' *i. e.*, 'to do good works;' *ἐπὶ* denoting the object or purpose for which they were created; see Winer, *Gr.* § 48. c, p. 351, notes *on Gal.* v. 13, 1 *Thess.* iv. 7, and exx. in Raphel, *Annot.* Vol. ii. p. 546. On the doctrinal and practical aspects of the clause, see Beveridge, *Serm.* l. Vol. ii. p. 418. *οἷς προητοίμασεν*] '*which God afore prepared,*'

ܩܰܕܶܡ ܛܰܝܶܒ [ab initio paravit] Syr., 'prius paravit,' Copt. Æth., 'præparavit,' Vulg., Clarom. The construction, meaning, and doctrinal significance of these words has been much discussed. We may remark briefly, (1) that owing to the absence of the usual accus. after *προητοίμ.* (Isaiah xxviii. 24, Wisdom ix. 8, Rom. ix. 23), *οἷς* cannot be 'the dative of the object,' 'for which God hath from the first provided,' Peile, but is simply (by the usual attraction) for *ἅ*; Winer, *Gr.* § 24. 1, p. 188, and § 22. 4. obs. p. 173. So Vulg., Syr., Copt., al., and the majority of commentators. (2) *Προητοίμ.* is not neuter (Beng., Stier); the simple verb is so used Luke ix. 52, 2 Chron. i. 4 (?), but there is no evidence of a similar use of the compound. Nor is it equivalent (in regard to things) with *προορίζω* (in regard to persons), Harl., a paraphrastic translation rightly condemned by Fritz. *Rom.* ix. 23, 'aliud est enim *parare*, ἑτοιμάζειν [to make ἕτοιμα, ἔτα, see Rost u. Palm, *Lex.* s. v. *ἕτοιμος*], aliud *definire*, '*ὁρίζειν,*' Vol. ii. p. 339. Lastly, neither

Ἰησοῦ ἐπὶ ἔργοις ἀγαθοῖς, οἷς προητοίμασεν ὁ Θεὸς ἵνα ἐν αὐτοῖς
περιπατήσωμεν.

Remember that ye were once aliens, but have now been brought nigh. [11] Διὸ μνημονεύετε ὅτι ποτὲ ὑμεῖς τὰ ἔθνη ἐν σαρκί, οἱ λεγόμενοι ἀκροβυστία ὑπὸ τῆς λεγομέ-

here nor Rom. *l. c.* must the force of πρὸ be neglected; comp. Philo, *de Opif.* § 25, Vol. I. p. 18 (ed. Mang.), ὡς οἰκειοτάτῳ . . . ζώῳ τὰ ἐν κόσμῳ πάντα προητοιμάσατο, rightly translated by Fritz., 'ante paravit quam conderet.' (3) Thus, then, we adhere to the simplest meaning of the words, using the latter part of the clause to explain any ambiguity of expression in the former: ' God, *before* we were created in Christ, *made ready* for us, pre-arranged, prepared a sphere of moral action; or (to use the simile of Chrys.) a road, with the intent *that we should walk in it*, and not leave it; this sphere, this road was ἔργα ἀγαθά; comp. Beveridge, *Serm. l. c.* p. 428. On the important doctrinal statement fairly deducible from this text, — ' bona opera sequuntur hominem justificatum, non præcedunt in homine justificando,' see Jackson, *Creed*, XI. 30. 6.

11. διό] ' *Wherefore*,' ' since God has vouchsafed such blessings to you and to all of us;' not in exclusive reference to ver. 10, ὅτι ἐκτίσθημεν ἐπ' ἔργοις ἀγαθοῖς, Chrys., nor alone to ver. 4—10 (Meyer), but, as the use of ὑμεῖς (compare ver. 1) suggests, to the whole, or rather to the declaratory portion of the foregoing paragraph, ver. 1—7; ver. 7—10 being an argumentative and explanatory addition. On St. Paul's use of διό, comp. notes *on Gal.* iv. 31.   The construction, which is not perfectly clear, is commonly explained by the introduction of ὄντες before τὰ ἔθνη (Fuld.), or ἦτε before (Syr.), or after (Goth.) ἐν σαρκί. This is not necessary; the position of ποτὲ (as rightly maintained by *Lachm.* *Tisch.*, with ABD¹E; Clarom., Sang., Aug., Vulg., al.) seem to suggest that τὰ ἔθνη κ. τ. λ. is simply in *apposition* to

ὑμεῖς. Ὅτι and ποτὲ are then respectively resumed by ὅτι and τῷ καιρῷ ἐκείνῳ in ver. 12; see Meyer *in loc.* τὰ ἔθνη ἐν σαρκί] ' *Gentiles in the flesh.*' On the correct insertion of the article before ἔθνη (to denote class, category), see Middl. *Gr. Art.* III. 2. 2, p. 40 (Rose); and on its equally correct omission before ἐν (τὰ ἔθν. ἐν σ. forming only one idea), see Winer, *Gr.* § 20. 2, p. 123, notes ch. i. 15, and Fritz. *Rom.* iii. 25, Vol. I. p. 195. Ἐν σαρκὶ is not in reference ' to their natural descent' (Hamm.), nor to their corrupted state (οὐκ ἐν πνεύματι, Theoph., ' unregenerate Gentiles,'. Peile; compare Syr.), but, as the use of the word below distinctly suggests, to the *corporeal* mark : ' præputium profani hominis indicium erat,' Calv. They bore the proof of their Gentilism in their flesh and on their bodies.

οἱ λεγόμενοι ἀκροβυστία κ.τ.λ.] ' *who are called (contemptuously) the Uncircumcision by the so-called Circumcision.*' Both ἀκροβ. and περιτ. are used as the distinctive names or titles of the two classes, Gentiles and Jews. On the omission of the art. before ἀκροβυστ. (a verb ' vocandi' having preceded), see Middl. *Gr. Art.* III. 3. 2, p. 43 (Rose), and on the derivation of the word (an Alexandrian corruption of ἀκροποσθία), Fritz. *Rom.* ii. 26, Vol. I. p. 136.

ἐν σαρκὶ χειροποιήτου] ' *wrought by hand in the flesh*,' ' et est opus manuum in carne,' Syr.; a tertiary predication (see Donalds. *Gr.* § 479 sq., and observe the idiomatically exact transl. of Syr.), added by the Apostle reflectively rather than descriptively ; ' the circumcision, — yes, hand-wrought in the flesh, only a visible manual operation on the flesh, when it ought to be a secret spiritual

νης περιτομῆς ἐν σαρκὶ χειροποιήτου, ^{12} ὅτι ἦτε τῷ καιρῷ ἐκείνῳ

process in the heart, only κατατομή, not περιτομή;' comp. Rom. ii. 28, 29, Phil. iii. 3, Col. ii. 11. Thus, then, as Calvin rightly felt, the Apostle expresses no contempt for the outward rite, which he himself calls a σφραγῖδα τῆς δικαιοσύνης, Rom. iv. 11, but only (as the present words suggest) at the assumption of such a title (observe τῆς λεγομ., not τῶν λεγομ.) by a people who had no conception of its true and deep significance. The Gentiles were called, *and were* the ἀκροβυστία; the Jews were called, but were not truly the περιτομή.

12. ὅτι ἦτε] 'that ye were;' resumption of the ὅτι in ver. 11, and continuation of the suspended sentence; see notes on ver. 11. τῷ καιρῷ ἐκείνῳ] 'at that time;' 'in your heathen state.' The prep. ἐν (here rightly omitted by *Lachm., Tisch.*, with ABD[1] FG; mss.; Clarom., Sang., Aug.; al.; Chrys.), though occasionally omitted (2 Cor. vi. 2 quotation, Gal. vi. 9), is more commonly, and indeed more correctly inserted in this and similar forms; compare Rom. iii. 26, xi. 5, 2 Cor. viii. 13, 2 Thess. ii. 6, and see Wannowski, *Constr. Abs.* iii. 1, p. 88, Madvig, *Synt.* § 39, and comp. ib. *Lat. Gr.* § 276.

ἦτε.... χωρὶς Χριστοῦ] 'ye were .... without Christ;' χωρὶς Χρ. forming a predicate (Syr.; 'et nesciebatis Christum,' Æth.), not a limiting clause to ἦτε ἀπηλλοτρ. (De W., Eadie), — a singularly harsh construction. The Ephesians, whom St Paul here views as the representatives of Gentilism (Olshaus.), were, in their heathen ante-Christian state, truly χωρὶς Χρ., without *the Messiah*, without the promised Seed (contrast Rom. ix. 4 sq.); now, however, 'eum possidetis non minus quam ii quibus promissus fuerat,' Grot. *in loc.* The two following clauses, each of two parts, then more exactly elucidate the signifi-

cance of the expression. On the distinction between ἄνευ ('absence of object from subject') and χωρὶς ('separation of subject from object'), see Tittm., *Synon.* p. 94. This distinction, however, does not appear perfectly certain (comp. Phil. ii. 14, with 1 Pet. iv. 9), and must, at all events, be applied with caution, when it is remembered that χωρὶς is used forty times in the N. T., and ἄνευ only three times, viz., Matt. x. 29, 1 Pet. iii. 1, iv. 9. Where, in any given writer or writers, there is such a marked preference for one rather than another of two perfectly simple words, it is well not to be hypercritical. ἀπηλλοτριωμένοι κ. τ. λ.] '*being aliens*, or *in a state of alienation, from the commonwealth of Israel;*' in opp. to συμπολῖται τῶν ἁγίων, ver. 19. There is a slight difficulty in the exact meaning and application of the words. Reversing the order, for the sake of making the simpler word define the more doubtful, we may observe that Ἰσραὴλ is clearly the theocratic name of the Jewish people, the title which marks their *religious* and *spiritual*, rather than their national or political distinctions; see Rom. ix. 6. 1 Cor. x. 18, Gal. vi. 16. From this it would seem to follow that πολιτεία, which may be either (*a*) '*reipublicæ forma, status,*' τῶν τὴν πόλιν οἰκούντων τάξις τις, Aristot. *Pol.* iii. 1. 1 (compare 2 Macc. iv. 11, νομίμους πολιτείας opp. to παρανόμους ἐθισμούς, viii. 17, προγονικὴ πολιτεία), — or (*b*) '*jus civitatis*' (compare Acts xxii. 28, 3 Macc. iii. 21), — or (*c*) '*vivendi ratio*' (comp. Vulg., Clarom., 'conversatione' — ; see Theoph. on ver. 13, and Suiçer, *Thesaur.* s. v. Vol. ii. p. 795), is here used only in the first sense, and with a distinctly spiritual application; so Æth.-Platt, Arm., and most modern commentators. The gen. is thus, not that of the 'identical motion,' *e. g.* ἄστυ

χωρὶς Χριστοῦ, ἀπηλλοτριωμένοι τῆς πολιτείας τοῦ Ἰσραὴλ καὶ

Ἀθηνῶν (Harl.), but a simple *possessive* gen., — the 'reipublicæ status' which belonged to Israel. ἀπηλλοτρι- ωμένοι, a noticeable and emphatic word (οὐκ εἶπε κεχωρισμένοι .... πολλὴ τῶν ῥημάτων ἡ ἔμφασις πολὺν δεικνῦσα τὸν χωρισμόν, Chrys.), seems to hint at a state of former unity and fellowship, and a lapse or separation (ἀπὸ) from it; comp. ch. iv. 18, Col. i. 21, Ecclus. xi. 34, 3 Macc. i. 3, Joseph. *Antiq.* xi. 5. 4, and exx. in Kypke, *Obs.* Vol. ii. p. 295, and Schweigh. *Polyb. Lex.* s. v. This union, though not historically demonstrable, is no less spiritually true. Jew and Gentile were once under one *spiritual* πολιτεία, of which the Jewish was a subsequent visible manifestation. The Gentile lapsed from it, the Jew made it invalid (Matt. xv. 6, compare Chrys.); and they parted, only to unite again, ἔθνη καὶ λαοὶ Ἰσραήλ (Acts iv. 27), in one act of uttermost rebellion, and yet, through the mystery of redeeming Love, to remain thereby (ver. 15, 16) united in Christ forever. ξένοι τῶν δια- θηκῶν] '*strangers from the covenants;*' second and more specializing part of the first explanatory clause. The gen. after ξένος is not due to any quasi-participial power (Eadie), but belongs to the category of the (inverted) *possessive* gen. (Bernhardy, *Synt.* iii. 49, p. 171), or perhaps rather to the gen. of 'the point of view' ('extraneos quod ad pactorum promissiones attinet,' Beza); see Scheuerl. *Synt.* § 18. 3, a, p. 135. The use of the plural διαθῆκαι must not be limited, either here or Rom. ix. 4, to the two tables of the law (Elsn., Wolf), nor again unnecessarily extended to God's various covenant promises to David and the people (comp. De W.), but appears simply to refer to the several renewals of the covenant with the *patriarchs;* see esp. Wisdom xviii. 22, ὅρκους πατέρων καὶ

διαθήκας, 2 Macc. viii. 15, τὰς πρὸς τοὺς πατέρας αὐτῶν διαθήκας; compare Rom. xv. 8. The great Messianic promise (Gen. xiii. 15, xv. 18, xvii. 8; Chrys. Theophyl.) was the subject and substratum of all. ἐλπίδα μὴ ἔχον- τες] '*not having hope,*' Auth., 'spem non habentes,' Vulg., Clarom., comp. Syr.; general consequence of the alienation mentioned in the preceding member; not however with any special dependence on that clause, scil. ὥστε μὴ ἔχειν ἐλπίδα, 'so that you had no (covenanted) hope,' 'spem promissioni respondentem,' (Bengel, comp. Harl.), — for (a) the absence of the article shows that ἐλπίδα cannot here be in any way limited, but is simply 'hope' in its most general meaning, and (b) μὴ can be no further pressed than as simply referring to the thought and feeling of the subject introduced by μνημο- νεύετε, ver. 11, 'having (as you must have felt) no hope;' comp. Winer, *Gr.* § 55. 5, p. 428, Herm. *Viger,* No. 267, and the good collection of exx. in Gayler, *Partic. Neg.* ch. ix. p. 275 sq. On the general use in the N. T. of μὴ with participles, see notes *on* 1 *Thess.* ii. 15. ἄθεοι ἐν τῷ κόσμῳ] '*without God in the world;*' objective negation (ἀ being here equivalent to οὐ with an adjective, Harl.; see, however, Gayler, *Partic. Neg.* p. 35), forming the climax and accumulation of the misery involved in χωρὶς Χριστοῦ; they were without church and without promise, without hope, and, in the profane wicked world (ἐν τῷ κόσμῳ being in contrast to πολιτ. τοῦ Ἰσρ., and like it ethical in its reference), — without God. Ἄθεος may be taken either with active, neuter, or passive reference, *i. e.,* either denying (see exx. Suicer, *Thes.* s. v.), ignorant of (Gal. iv. 8; 'nesciebatis Deum,' Æth., ἔρημοι τῆς θεογνω- σίας, Theod., comp. Clem. Alex. *Protrept.* 14), or *forsaken* by God (Soph.

ξένοι τῶν διαθηκῶν τῆς ἐπαγγελίας, ἐλπίδα μὴ ἔχοντες καὶ ἄθεοι ἐν τῷ κόσμῳ· ¹³ νυνὶ δὲ ἐν Χριστῷ Ἰησοῦ, ὑμεῖς οἵ ποτε ὄντες μακρὰν ἐγγὺς ἐγενήθητε ἐν τῷ αἵματι τοῦ Χριστοῦ. ¹⁴ αὐτὸς γάρ

Œd. Rex, 661, ἄθεος, ἄφιλος); the last meaning seems best to suit the passive tenor of the passage, and to enhance the dreariness and gloom of the picture. On the religious aspects of heathenism, see the good note of Harless *in loc.*

13. νυνὶ δέ] '*But now;*' in antithesis to τῷ καιρῷ ἐκείνῳ, ver. 12.　ἐν Χρ. Ἰησοῦ] '*in Christ* JESUS;' prominent and emphatic; standing in *immediate* connection with νυνί (not ἐγενήθητε, Mey.), which it both qualifies and characterizes, and forming a contrast to χωρὶς Χρ., ver. 12. The addition of Ἰησοῦ, far from being an argument against such a contrast (Mey.), is, in fact, almost confirmatory of it. Such an addition was necessary to make the circumstances of the contrast fully felt. Then, they were χωρὶς Χρ., separate from and without part in the Messiah, — now they were not only ἐν Χριστῷ but ἐν Χριστῷ Ἰησοῦ, in a *personal Saviour,* — in One who was no longer their future hope, but their present salvation. The personal reference is appropriately continued by ἐν τῷ αἵματι, — not merely αὐτοῦ, but τοῦ Χρ.; He who poured out His blood, Jesus of Nazareth, was truly Christ.　ἐγγὺς ἐγενήθητε] '*became nigh,*' were brought nigh to God's holy and spiritual πολιτεία; οἱ μακρὰν ὄντες τῆς πολιτ. τοῦ Ἰσρ., τῆς κατὰ Θεὸν ἐγγὺς ἐγενήθητε, Œcum. On the passive *form* ἐγενήθ. see notes on ch. iii. 7, and on the use of the words μακράν and ἐγγὺς in designating Gentiles and Jews (comp. the term προσήλυτοι), see the very good illustrations of Schoettgen, *Hor. Heb.* Vol. I. p. 761 sq. and of Wetst. *in loc.;* comp. also Isaiah lvii. 19, Dan. ix. 7, and Valck. *on Acts.* ii. 39 (cited by Grinfield, *Schol. Hell.*). The order ἐγεν. ἐγγὺς is adopted by *Lachm.* with

AB; mss.; Aug., Vulg., Goth., al. but seems due to a mistaken correction of the emphatic juxtaposition μακρὰν ἐγγύς. ἐν τῷ αἵματι] '*by the blood;*' ἐν having here appy. its instrumental force; see Winer, *Gr.* § 48. a, p. 346. No very precise distinction can be drawn between this use and διὰ τοῦ αἵμ. ch. i. 7. We may perhaps say the latter implies mediate and more simple, the former, *immanent* instrumentality; comp. Jelf, *Gr.* § 622. 3, Winer, *l. c.* p. 347 note, and notes *on* 1 *Thess.* iv. 418.

14. αὐτὸς γάρ] '*For He* — and none other than He;' confirmatory explanation of ver. 13, the emphasis resting, not on εἰρήνη ἡμῶν (De W.), but, as the prominent position of ἐν Χρ. Ἰησ. and repetition of Χριστοῦ, ver. 13, seem *decisively* to show, — on αὐτός, which is thus no mere otiose pronoun. (compare Thiersch, *de Pentat.* p. 98), but is used with its regular and classical significance; see Winer, *Gr.* § 22. 4, obs. p. 135, and comp. Herm. *de Pronom.* αὐτός, ch. x.　εἰρήνη ἡμῶν] '*our Peace.*' Though the context, and participle defining ὁ ποιήσας seem very distinctly to prove that εἰρήνη is here used in some degree ' per metonymiam ' (compare 1 Cor. i. 30, Col. i. 27), and so in a sense but little differing from εἰρηνοποιός (Usteri, *Lehrb.* II. 2, p. 253), the abstract subst. still has and admits of a fuller and more general application. Not only was Christ our ' Pacificator,' but our ' Pax,' the true שַׂר שָׁלוֹם (Isaiah ix. 5), the very essence as well as the cause of it; comp. Olsh. *in loc.* Thus considered, εἰρήνη seems to have here its widest meaning, — not only peace between Jew and Gentile, but *also* between both and God. In ver. 15 the context limits it to the former reference; in ver. 17 it reverts

ἐστιν ἡ εἰρήνη ἡμῶν, ὁ ποιήσας τὰ ἀμφότερα ἓν καὶ τὸ μεσότοιχον
τοῦ φραγμοῦ λύσας, ¹⁵ τὴν ἔχθραν, ἐν τῇ σαρκὶ αὐτοῦ, τὸν νόμον

to its present and more inclusive reference.   τ ὰ ἀ μ φ ό τ ε ρ α] 'both,' Jews and Gentiles; explained by τοὺς δύο and τοὺς ἀμφοτέρους, ver. 15, 16. We have here no ellipsis of γένη, ἔθνη κ. τ. λ., but only the abstract and generalizing neuter; see exx. in Winer, *Gr.* § 27. 5, p. 160.   κ α ί] 'and,' sc. 'namely;' the particle having here its *explanatory* force; see Fritz. *Rom.* ix. 23, Vol. ii. p. 339, Winer, *Gr.* § 53. 3. obs. p. 388, and notes on *Phil.* iv. 11. τ ὸ μ ε σ ό τ ο ι χ ο ν τ ο ῦ φ ρ α γ μ ο ῦ] '*the middle wall of the fence* or *partition*,' scil. between Jew and Gentile. The genitival relation has been differently explained. There is of course no real (Pisc.) or virtual (Beza) interchange of words for τὸν φρ. τοῦ μεσοτ.; nor does τοῦ φραγμοῦ appear to be here either (*a*) a gen. of the characterizing *quality*, scil. τὸ διαφράσσον, τὸ διατειχίζον (Chrys. i., Harl.; comp. Clem. Alex. *Strom.* vi. 13, p. 793, τὸ μεσότοιχον τὸ διορίζον) or (*b*) a gen. of *identity*, 'the middle wall which was or formed the φραγμός' (Mey.), but either (*c*) a gen. of *origin*, τὸ ἀπὸ φραγμοῦ (Chrys. 2), or still more simply (*d*) a common *possessive* gen., 'the wall which pertained to, belonged to the fence,' — a use of the case which is far from uncommon in the N. T., and admits of some latitude of application; comp. Donalds. *Gr.* § 454. *aa*, p. 481 sq. The exact reference of the φραγμὸς (גָּדֵר, Buxtorf *Lex.* s. v. Vol. i. p. 1447) is also somewhat difficult to fix, as both εἰρήνη and ἔχθρα (ver. 15) and indeed the whole tenor of the passage seem to imply something more than the relations of Jews and Gentiles to *each other*, and must include the relations of both to God; comp. Alf. *in loc.* If this be so, the φραγμὸς would seem to mean the Law generally (Zonaras, *Lex.* p. 1822),

not merely the ceremonial law (Neander, *Planting*, Vol. i. p. 49, ed. Bohn), nor the 'discrimen præputii' (Beng.) but the *whole* Mosaic Law, esp. in its aspects as a *system of separation;* comp. Chrys. *in loc.*, who appositely cites Isaiah v. 2. Whether there is any direct reference to the ἑρκίον δρυφράκτου λιθίνου (Joseph. *Antiq.* xv. 11. 6) between the courts of the Jews and Gentiles (Hamm.) is perhaps doubtful; see Meyer. We may well admit, however, as indeed the specific and so to say localizing φραγμὸς seems to suggest, an allusion both to this and to the veil which was rent (Matth. xxvii. 51) at our Lord's crucifixion; the former illustrating the separation between Jew and Gentile, the latter between both and God. As it has been well remarked, the temple was, as it were, a material embodiment of the law, and in its very outward structure was a symbol of spiritual distinctions; see Stier *in loc.* p. 322, 323.

15.   τ ὴ ν ἔ χ θ ρ α ν] '*the enmity;*' 'ponenda hic ὑποστιγμή,' Grot.; in apposition to, and a further explanation of τὸ μεσ. τοῦ φρ., 'to wit, the root of the enmity ('parietem, qui est odium,' Æth.) between Jew and Gentile, and between both and God. The exact reference of ἔχθραν has been greatly debated. That it cannot imply exclusively (*a*) 'the enmity of Jews and Gentiles against God' (Chrys.), seems clear from the foregoing context (compare ὁ ποιήσας τὰ ἀμφότερα ἕν, ver. 14), in which the enmity between Jew and Gentile is distinctly alluded to. That it also cannot denote simply (*b*) 'the reciprocal enmity of Jew and Gentile' (Meyer, compare Usteri, *Lehrb.* ii. 2. 1, p. 253), seems also clear from its appositional relation to μεσ. τοῦ φρ., from the preceding term εἰρήνη, and from the subsequent explana-

τῶν ἐντολῶν ἐν δόγμασιν καταργήσας, ἵνα τοὺς δύο κτίσῃ ἐν ἑαυτῷ

tion afforded by τὸν νόμον τῶν ἐντ. κ. τ. λ. The reference then must be to *both*, sc. to the ἔχθρα which was the result and working of the law regarded as a system of separation, — the enmity due not only to Judaical limitations and antagonisms, but also and, as the widening context shows, *more especially* to the. alienation of both Jew and Gentile from God; ἑκατέραν ἔχθραν καὶ ἑκάτερον μεσότοιχον ἔλυσε Χριστὸς ὁ Θεὸς ἡμῶν, Phot. ap. Œcum. This, though not distinctly put forward in ed. 1, and peremptorily rejected by De W. and Meyer, seems, on reconsideration, the only explanation that satisfies the strong term ἔχθρα, and the very inclusive context. ἐν τῇ σαρκὶ αὐτοῦ] '*in His* crucified *flesh;*' comp. Col. i. 22, ἐν τῷ σώματι τῆς σαρκὸς αὐτοῦ, διὰ τοῦ θανάτου. These words cannot be connected with τὴν ἔχθραν (Arm., Chrys., Cocc.), as in such a case the article could not be dispensed with even in the dialect of the N. T., but must be joined as a specification of the manner, or perhaps rather of the *instrument* — either (*a*) with καταργήσας, to which this clause is emphatically prefixed (ed. 1, De W., Mey.), or perhaps more naturally (*b*) with λύσας (Syr. Æth., Theod., Theoph., Œcum.), to which it subjoins an equally emphatic specification. Stier (compare Chrys.) extends the ref. of σάρξ to Christ's incarnate state and the whole tenor of His earthly life ('Fleisches-lebens'); comp. Schulz, *Abendm.* p. 95 sq. This is doubtful; the context appears to refer alone to His death; compare ver. 13, ἐν τῷ αἵματι, ver. 16, διὰ τοῦ σταυροῦ. On the distinction between the σάρξ and the σῶμα (the σὰρξ δοθεῖσα) of Christ, compare Lücke *on John* vi. 51, Vol. II. p. 149 sq. τὸν νόμον τῶν ἐντ. ἐν δόγμ.] '*the law of ordinances* expressed *in decrees*,' scil. '*the law of*

decretory ordinances;' compare Col. ii. 14. The Greek commentators join ἐν δόγμ. with καταργ., referring δόγματα (scil. τὴν πίστιν, Chrys. τὴν εὐαγγελικὴν διδασκαλίαν, Theod.) to Christian doctrines; this meaning of δόγμα in the N. T. is, however, untenable. Harless (comp. Syr.) retains the same construction, but regards ἐν δόγμ. as defining the sphere in which the action of Christ's death was manifested, 'on the side of, in the matter of decrees.' This is plausible, and much to be preferred to Fritzsche's expl. 'nova præcepta stabiliendo' (*Dissert. ad* 2 *Cor.* p. 168); still the article (τοῖς δόγμ.) seems indispensable, for, as Winer observes (*Gr.* p. 250, ed. 5) both the law and the side or aspect under which it is viewed are fairly definite. We retain, therefore, the ordinary explanation, according to which ἐν δόγμ. is closely united with τῶν ἐντολῶν, and therefore correctly anarthrous; see Winer, *Gr.* § 20. 2, and notes ch. i. 15. The gen. ἐντολ. thus serves to express the *contents* (Bernhardy. *Synt.* III. 45, p. 163), ἐν δόγμ. the definite mandatory *form* ('legem imperiosam,' Erasm.) in which the ἐντολαί were expressed; see Tholuck, *Beiträge*, p. 93 sq., and esp. Winer, *Gr.* § 31. 10. obs. I. p. 196 (ed. 6), but more fully in ed. 5, p. 250. ἵνα τοὺς δύο κ. τ. λ.] '*that He might make the two in Himself into one new man;*' purpose of the abrogation; peace between Jew and Gentile by *making* them (οὐκ εἶπε, 'μεταβάλῃ' ἵνα δείξῃ τὸ ἐνεργὲς τοῦ γενομένου, Chrys.) in Himself, in His person (not δι' ἑαυτοῦ, Chrys.), into — not merely one man, but one *new* man; ἕνα ἀνήνεγκε θαυμαστόν, αὐτὸς τοῦτο πρῶτον γενόμενος, Chrys. Meier's assertion that καινὸς has here no moral significance is obviously untenable; comp. ch. iv. 24, and notes *in loc.* The reading is slightly doubtful. *Lachm.*

εἰς ἕνα καινὸν ἄνθρωπον, ποιῶν εἰρήνην, ¹⁶ καὶ ἀποκαταλλάξῃ

adopts αὐτῷ with ABF; ten mss.; Procop.,—a more difficult reading, but appy. less strongly attested than ἑαυτῷ [DEGKL; bulk of mss.], and not improbably due to the frequent confusion between the oblique cases of αὐτὸς and those of the reflexive pronoun.

ποιῶν εἰρήνην] 'so making peace,' scil. between Jews and Gentiles, and between both and God, πρὸς τὸν Θεόν, καὶ πρὸς ἀλλήλους, Chrys.; contrast τὴν ἔχθραν, ver. 15. It may be observed that the aorist is not used (as in ver. 16), but the present; the 'pacificatio' is not mentioned as in modal or causal dependence on the 'creatio,' but simply as extending over, and contemporaneous with, the whole process of it; compare Scheuerl. Synt. § 31, 2. a, p. 310.

16. καὶ ἀποκαταλλάξῃ] 'and might reconcile us;' parallel purpose to the foregoing, and stated second in order, though really from the nature of the case the first; the divine procedure being, as De W. observes, stated regressively, ἵνα κτίσῃ . . . . . ἵνα ἀποκατ. . . . . ἀποκτείνας. The double compound ἀποκατ. is used only here and Col. i. 20, 21. In both cases ἀπὸ does not simply strengthen (e. g. ἀποθαυμάζω, ἀπεργάζομαι. Meyer, Eadie), but hints at a restoration to a primal unity, 'reduxerit in unum gregem,' Calv.; compare ver. 13, and Winer, de Verb. Comp. iv. p. 7, 8. Chrys. gives rather a different and perhaps doubtful turn, δεικνὺς ὅτι πρὸ τούτου ἡ ἀνθρωπίνη φύσις εὐκατάλλακτος ἦν, οἷον ἐπὶ τῶν ἁγίων καὶ πρὸ τοῦ νόμου. The profound dogmatical considerations connected with καταλλαγὴ (alike active and objective, and passive and subjective, comp. 2 Cor. v. 18 with ib. 20) are treated perspicuously by Usteri, Lehrb. ii. 1. 1, p. 102 sq.; see also Jackson, Creed, Book x. 49. 3, Pearson, ibid. Vol. i. p. 430 sq. (Burton). ἐν

ἐνὶ σώματι] 'in one (corporate) body,' scil. in the Church. The reference to the human σῶμα τοῦ Χρ. (Chrys.) is plausible, but on nearer examination not tenable. Had this been intended, the order (comp. the position of ἐν τῇ σαρκὶ αὐτοῦ) would surely have been different, if only to prevent this very connection of τοὺς ἀμφοτ. and ἐνὶ σώμ. which their present juxtaposition so obviously suggests. Moreover, the query of B. Crus., why Christ's human body should be here designated ἓν σῶμα, has not been satisfactorily answered, even by Stier; the application of it to the mystical body is intelligible and appropriate, comp. ch. iv. 4. Ἐν does not thus become equivalent to εἰς, but preserves its proper meaning; they were κτισθέντας εἰς ἕνα ἄνθρ.; thus κτισθέντας, Christ reconciles them both ἐν ἑνὶ σώμ. (scil. ὄντας, Olsh.) to God; see Winer, Gr. § 50 5, p. 370.

ἀποκτείνας] 'having slain,' i. e., 'after He had slain;' temporal participle, standing in contrast with ποιῶν, ver. 15. The use of the particular word has evidently been suggested by διὰ σταυροῦ; not λύσας, not ἀνελών, but ἀποκτείνας, 'quia crux mortem adfert,' Grot.; and thus in the words, though not the application of Chrys., ὥστε μηκέτι αὐτὴν ἀναστῆναι. The ἔχθρα here specified is not merely and exclusively the enmity between Jew and Gentile (comp. ed. 1), but also, as in ver. 15, and here even still more distinctly and primarily, the enmity between both and God; μᾶλλον πρὸς τὸν Θεόν· τὸ γὰρ ἑξῆς τοῦτο δηλοῖ, Chrys., comp. Alf. in loc. ἐν αὐτῷ] 'in it,' scil. 'upon it,' Hamm.—not 'in corpore suo,' Bengel; see Col. ii. 15 and notes in loc. In FG; Vulg. ('in semet ipso') Syr.-Philox., and several Latin Ff., we find ἐν ἑαυτῷ; the reading probably owes its origin and support to the reference ἓν σῶμα to Christ.

τοὺς ἀμφοτέρους ἐν ἑνὶ σώματι τῷ Θεῷ διὰ τοῦ σταυροῦ, ἀποκτείνας τὴν ἔχθραν ἐν αὐτῷ. ¹⁷ καὶ ἐλθὼν εὐηγγελίσατο εἰρήνην ὑμῖν
τοῖς μακρὰν καὶ εἰρήνην τοῖς ἐγγύς, ¹⁸ ὅτι δι' αὐτοῦ ἔχομεν τὴν

17. καὶ ἐλθών] 'And having come, etc.;' not 'and came' (Auth.), as this obscures the commencement of the new sentence (see Scholef. Hints, p. 100), nor 'and coming' (Eadie), as the action described by ἐλθὼν is not here contemporaneous with, but prior to that of εὐηγγελίσατο; comp. Bernhardy, Synt. x. 9, p. 382. This verse seems clearly to refer back to ver. 14, αὐτὸς γάρ κ. τ. λ., there being, as B. Crus. suggests, a faint apposition between Χρ. ἐστιν εἰρήνη, ver. 14, and εὐηγγελ. εἰρήνην, ver. 17 ; still, as ver. 15 and 16 cannot be considered parenthetical, the connection is carried on by καί, and the verse is linked with what immediately precedes. 'Ελθὼν thus following ἀποκτείνας will more naturally refer to a spiritual advent (see esp. Acts xxvi. 23), or a mediate advent in the person of His Apostles, than to our Lord's preaching when on earth.; compare Acts xxvi. 23. The participle ἐλθὼν (no mere redundancy, Raphel, Annot. Vol. ii. p. 471) in fact serves to give a realistic touch to the whole group of clauses ; 'Christ is our peace; yes, and He came and by His Spirit and the mouths of His Apostles He preached it;' see Hofm. Schriftb. Vol. ii. 1, p. 338.

εἰρήνην] 'peace,' not only τὴν πρὸς τὸν Θεόν (Chrys.), but also τὴν πρὸς ἀλλή-λους; see notes ver. 14. The repetition of εἰρήνην is rightly maintained by Tisch. with ABDEFG; mss.; Vulg., Clarom., Goth., Copt., Æth., Arm., and many Ff. It gives an emphasis and solemnity to the passage, which is here (though denied by Stier, p. 370, comp. Bengel) especially appropriate. Meyer compares Rom. iii. 31, viii. 15.

18. ὅτι δι' αὐτοῦ] 'seeing that through Him,' not merely explanatory, 'to wit, that we have,' (Baumg.), nor yet strongly causal, 'because we have, (Bengel), but with somewhat more of a demonstrative or confirmatory force, 'as it is a fact that, etc.;' compare 2 Cor i. 5, and see notes on 2 Thess. iii. 7. The 'probatio,' as Calvin observes, is 'ab effectu;' the principal moment of thought, however, does not rest on ἔχο-μεν, on the reality of the possession (Harl.), or on any appeal to inward experience, 'for — is it not so ?' (Stier), but, as the order suggests, on δι' αὐτοῦ, on the matter of fact that it was 'through Him, and none but Him' that we have this προσαγωγή. For a sound sermon on this text, see Sherlock, Serm. xvi. Vol. i. p. 288 sq. (ed. Hughes).

ἔχομεν] 'we are having,' present; the action is still going on ; contrast ἐσχήκα-μεν, Rom. v. 2, where the reference is to the period when they became Christians, and where, consequently, the προσαγωγὴ is spoken of as a thing past. τὴν προσαγωγήν] 'our introduction, admis-sion, 'quia ipse adduxit,' Æth.; not intran-sitively, either here or Rom. v. 2, scil. 'access,' Auth., 'accessum,' Vulg., ad-ventum (dshini), Copt., 'atgagg,' Goth., — but transitively, 'adeundi copiam,' 'admissionem,' the latter being the pri-mary and proper meaning of the word ; see Meyer on Rom. v. 2, and compare (appy.) Xen. Cyrop. vii. 5. 45, τοὺς ἐμοὺς φίλους δεομένους προσαγωγῆς, ib. i. 3. 8, and the various applications of the word in Polybius, e. g. Hist. i. 48. 2, τῶν μηχανημάτων πρ., xiv. 10. 9, τῶν ὀργά-νων. Christ is thus our προσαγωγεὺς to the Father; οὐκ εἶπεν 'πρόσοδον' ἀλλὰ 'προσαγωγήν,' οὐ γὰρ ἀφ' ἑαυτῶν προσῆλ-θομεν, ἀλλ' ὑπ' αὐτοῦ προσήχθημεν, Chrys. on ver. 21; see 1 Pet. iii. 18, ἵνα ἡμᾶς προσαγάγῃ τῷ Θεῷ. There may possibly be here (less probably, however,

προσαγωγὴν οἱ ἀμφότεροι ἐν ἑνὶ Πνεύματι πρὸς τὸν πατέρα.
¹⁹ ἄρα οὖν οὐκέτι ἐστὲ ξένοι καὶ πάροικοι, ἀλλ' ἐστὲ συνπολῖται

Rom. v. 2) an allusion to the προσαγωγεὺς ('admissionalis,' Lampridius, Sever. 4) at oriental courts, Tholuck, Rom. l. c., and Usteri, Lehrb. ii. 1. 1, p. 101; at any rate, the supposition does not merit the contempt with which it has been treated by Rückert. The uses of προσαγωγὴ are well illustrated by Wakefield, in Steph. Thes. s. v. Vol. ii. p. 86 (ed. Valpy), and by Bos, Obs. Misc. 35, p. 149 sq.   ἐν ἕνι Πνεύματι] 'in one Spirit, common to Jew and Gentile;' not for διά, (Chrys.; compare Œcum., Calv., al.), but, as usual, 'united in' (Olsh.); compare 1 Cor. xii. 13. The Holy Spirit is, as it were, the vital sphere or element in which both parties have their common προσαγωγὴ to the Father. The mention of the three Persons in the blessed Trinity, with the three prepp. διά, ἐν, πρός, is especially noticeable and distinct.

19. ἄρα οὖν] 'Accordingly then,' 'so then;' 'rebus ita comparatis igitur;' conclusion and consequence from the declarations of ver. 14—13, with a further expansion of the ideas ·of ver. 13. On the use of ἄρα οὖν, see notes on Gal. vi. 10, and compare Rom. v. 18, vii. 3, 25, viii. 12, ix. 16, 18; in all these cases the weaker ratiocinative force of ἄρα is supported by the collective οὖν. This union of the two particles is not found in classical Greek, except in the case of the interrogative form ἆρα; see Herm. Viger, No. 292.   ξένοι καὶ πάροικοι] 'strangers and sojourners;' 'peregrini atque incolæ,' Cic. Offic. i. 34. The two expressions seem to constitute a full antithesis to συνπολῖται, and to include all who, whether by national and territorial demarcation, or by the absence of civic privileges, were not citizens. Πάροικος then is here (compare Acts vii. 6, 29, 1 Pet. ii. 11) simply the same as the

classical μέτοικος (a form which does not occur in the N. T., and only once, Jer. xx. 3, in the LXX), and was probably its Alexandrian equivalent. It is used frequently in the LXX, in eleven passages as a translation of גֵּר, and in nine of תּוֹשָׁב: 'accolas fuisse dicit gentiles quatenus multi ex illis morabantur inter Judæos, ... non tamen iisdem legibus aut moribus aut religione utentes,' Estius. Harless (after Beng.) regards πάρ. as in antithesis to οἰκεῖοι, ξένοι to συνπολῖται, the former relating to domestic, the latter to civic privileges; this is plausible, — see Lev. xxii. 10 sq., Ecclus. xxix. 26 sq., — but owing to the frequent use of πάροικος simply for μέτοικος, not completely demonstrable.   An allusion to proselytes (Whitby) is certainly contrary to the context; see ver. 11 sq.   συνπολῖται, though partially vindicated by Raphelius, Annot. Vol. ii. p. 472, belongs principally to later Greek, e. g. Ælian, Var. Hist. iii. 44, Joseph. Antiq. xix. 2. 2; but also Eur. Heracl. 826; see Lobeck, Phryn. p. 172. The tendency to compound forms without an adequate increase of meaning is appy. a very distinct characteristic of 'fatiscens Græcitas;' comp. Thiersch, de Pentat. ii. 1, p. 83.   With regard to the orthography we may observe that the form συνπολ. is adopted by Tisch. (ed. 7) with AB¹CDEFG, and must appy. be adopted, as supported by such very distinctly preponderating uncial authority; see Tisch. Prolegom. p. xlvii. τῶν ἁγίων] 'the saints:' not inclusively the holy 'of all times and lands' (Eadie), for the mention of the πολιτεία τοῦ Ἰσρ., ver. 12, is distinct and specific; nor exclusively the Jews as a nation (Hamm.), or the saints of the Old Testament (Chrys.), for this the nature of the argument seems to preclude, — but,

τῶν ἁγίων καὶ οἰκεῖοι τοῦ Θεοῦ, ²⁰ ἐποικοδομηθέντες ἐπὶ τῷ θεμε-

20. Ἰησοῦ Χριστοῦ] So CDEFGKL; many Vv.; Orig. (1) and many Ff.; Chrys. (text) omits Ἰησ. (*Rec., Griesb., Scholz, De W., Meyer*). *Tisch.* inverts the order with AB; Vulg., Goth., Copt.; Orig. (2), Theophyl.; Ambrosiast., August. (frequently), and many others (*Rück., Lachm., Alf.*). The evidence of the seven uncial MSS. seems to preponderate.

the members of that spiritual community in which Jew and Gentile Christians were now united and incorporated, and to which the external theocracy formed a typical and preparatory institution. The expression is further heightened and defined by οἰκεῖοι τοῦ Θεοῦ. On this use of οἰκεῖος, see notes *on Gal.* vi. 10, and for a good sermon on this text, Beveridge, *Serm.* XLVIII. Vol. II. p. 381 sq.

20. ἐποικοδομηθέντες] '*built up,*' '*superædificati,*' Vulg.; the preposition being not otiose, but correctly marking the *super-position,* superstructure; comp. 1 Cor. iii. 10, 12, 14, Col. ii. 7. The accus. is not used here (as in 1 Cor. iii. 12) because the idea of *rest* predominates over that of *motion* or *direction.* That the dat. rather than the gen. of rest is here used, can hardly be said to be 'purely accidental' (Meyer), as the former denotes absolute and less separable, the latter partial and more separable super-position; see esp. Donalds. *Gr.* § 483. *a*, Krüger, *Sprachl.* II. § 68. 41. 1. Though this distinction must not be over-pressed in the N. T. (see Luke iv. 29), or even in classical writers (see exx. in Rost u. Palm, *Lex.* s. v. ἐπί, II. Vol. I. p. 1035), it still *appears* to have been correctly observed by St. Paul. The reading ἐπὶ τοῖς οὐρανοῖς, ch. i. 10 (*Lachm.*), which would apparently form an exception in this very Ep., is of doubtful authority. τῶν ἀποστόλων καὶ προφητῶν] '*of the Apostles and Prophets.*' Two questions of some interest present themselves, (1) the nature of the gen.; (2) the meaning of προφητῶν. With regard to (1) it may

be said, that though the gen. of *apposition* (θεμέλιος οἱ ἀπόστ. καὶ οἱ προφ., Chrys., comp. Theoph., Œcum.) is perfectly tenable on grammatical grounds, (compare Winer, *Gr.* § 59. 8, p. 470), and supported by the best ancient commentators, all exegetical considerations seem opposed to it. The Apostles were not the foundations (Rev. xxi. 14 is not, like the present, a dogmatical passage, see Harl.), but laid them; see 1 Cor. iii. 10. The gen. will therefore more probably be a gen. *subjecti,* not however in a *possessive* sense (Calv. 2, Cocc., Alf.), as this seems tacitly to mix up the θεμέλιος and the ἀκρογων. (comp. Jackson, *Creed,* XI. 5. 2), but simply as a gen. of the *agent* or *originating cause* (Scheul. *Synt.* § 17. 1, p. 125; see *on Thess.* i. 6); what the Apostles and prophets preached formed the θεμέλιος; compare Rom. xv. 20, Heb. vi. 1. Thus all seems consistent, and in accordance with the analogy of other passages; the doctrine of the Apostles, *i. e.,* Christ *preached,* is the θεμέλιος; Christ *personal* (αὐτ. Ἰησ. Χρ.) the ἀκρογωνιαῖος; Christ *mystical* the πλήρωμα; comp. ch. i. 23. (2) That the prophets of the New (Grot. al.) and not of the Old Testament (Chrys., Theod.) are now alluded to, seems here rendered highly probable by the order of the two classes (arbitrarily inverted by Calv., and insufficiently accounted for by Theod.), — by the analogous passages, ch. iii. 5, iv. 11, — by the known prophetic gifts in the early Church, 1 Cor. xii. 16, al., — and still more by the apparent nature of the *gen. subjecti*; see above. No great stress can be laid on

λίῳ τῶν ἀποστόλων καὶ προφητῶν, ὄντος ἀκρογωνιαίου αὐτοῦ
Ἰησοῦ Χριστοῦ, ²¹ ἐν ᾧ πᾶσα οἰκοδομὴ συναρμολογουμένη αὔξει

the absence of the article; this only shows that the Apostles and Prophets were regarded as one class (Winer, *Gr.* § 19. 4. d, p. 116), not that they were identical (Harl.); Sharp's rule cannot be regularly applied to plurals; see Middleton, *Art.* III. 4. 2, p. 65 (ed. Rose). This prominence of 'prophets' has been urged by Baur (*Paulus.* p. 438) as a proof of the later and Montanist origin of this Ep.; surely δεύτερον προφήτας, 1 Cor. xii. 20, is an indisputable proof that such a distinct order existed in the time of St. Paul. On the nature of their office, see notes on ch. iv. 11. ἀκρογωνιαίου] 'head-corner stone;' ἀκρογων. scil. λίθου; 'summus angularis lapis is dicitur qui, in extremo angulo fundamenti positus, duos parietes ex diverso venientes conjungit et continet,' Estius; comp. Psalm cxviii. 22, Jer. li. 26 (Heb.), Isaiah xxviii. 16, Matth. xxi. 42, 1 Pet. ii. 6. In 1 Cor. iii. 11, Christ is represented as the θεμέλιος; the image is slightly changed, but the idea is the same, — Christ is in one sense the substratum and in another the binding-stone of the building; ὁ λίθος ὁ ἀκρ. καὶ τοὺς τοίχους συνέχει καὶ τοὺς θεμελίους, Chrys.; see Suicer, *Thes.* s. v. and Vol. II. p. 242. On the doctrinal meaning and application of this attribute of Christ, see the excellent discussion of Jackson, *Creed*, XI. 51 sq. αὐτοῦ Ἰησ. Χρ.] '*Jesus Christ Himself*,' no human teachers; the pronoun being obviously referred not to θεμελίῳ ('angulari ejus,' Beng.) or to ἀκρογων., as possibly Vulg. ('ipso summo angulari lapide Chr. Jesu'), but to Christ; so rightly Auth., Syr., Clarom., and appy. Goth.; Copt., Æth., Arm. omit. The art. before Ἰησ. Χρ. (the absence of which is pressed by Beng.) may not only be dispensed with (see Luke xx. 42),

but would even, as Harl. suggests, be here incorrect; it would strictly then be 'He Himself, viz. Christ' (see Fritz. *Matth.* iii. 4, p. 117), and would imply a previous mention of Christ; whereas Christ is mentioned for the first time in the clause, and as in emphatic contrast with those who laid the foundations; see Stier *in loc.*, p. 394.

21. ἐν ᾧ] '*in whom*;' further and more specific explanation of the preceding clause; the pronoun referring, not to ἀκρογωνιαίῳ (Œcum.), but to Ἰησ. Χρ.; ὁ τὸ πᾶν συνέχων ἐστὶν ὁ Χριστός, Chrysost. πᾶσα οἰκοδομή] '*all the building*;' [totum ædificium] Syr., 'omne illud æd.,' Copt., Arm. (with the distinctive *n*), Syr.-Phil. There is here some difficulty owing to the omission of the article; the *strictly* grammatical translation of πᾶσα οἰκοδ. (scil. 'every building') being wholly irreconcilable with the context, which clearly implies a reference to one single building. Nor can it be readily explained away; for πᾶσα οἰκ. can never mean 'every part of the building' (Chrys.), nor can οἰκοδ. (per se) be regarded as implying 'a church' (Mey.). We seem, therefore, compelled either to adopt the reading of *Rec.*, and insert ἡ [with AC; many mss.; Chrys. (text), Theoph., but opp. to BDEFGKL; majority of mss.; Clem., al.], or, with more probability, to class οἰκοδομὴ in the present case with those numerous nouns (see the list in Winer, *Gr.* § 19), which, from referring to what is well known and defined (e. g. πᾶσα γῆ, Thucyd. II. 43, see Poppo *in loc.* p. 233) can, like proper names, dispense with the art. comp. πᾶσα ἐπιστολή, Ignat. *Eph.* § 12, Pearson, *Vind. Ignat.* II. 10. 1, and Winer, *Gr.* § 18. 4, p. 101. It must be

εἰς ναὸν ἅγιον ἐν Κυρίῳ, ²² ἐν ᾧ καὶ ὑμεῖς συνοικοδομεῖσθε εἰς κατοικητήριον τοῦ Θεοῦ ἐν Πνεύματι.

admitted that there appears no other equally *distinct* instance in the N. T. (Matth. ii. 3, Luke iv. 13, Acts ii. 36, vii. 22, cited by Eadie, are not in point, as being either exx. of proper names or abstract substt.), nor appy. even in the Greek Pentateuch (most of the exx. of Thiersch. *Pentat.* iii. 2, p. 121, admit of other explanations); still in the present case this partial laxity of usage can scarcely be denied. The late and non-Attic form οἰκοδομή (Lobeck, *Phryn.* p. 421, 487), used both for οἰκοδόμημα and οἰκοδόμησις (Rost u. Palm, *Lex.* s. v.), is here perhaps adopted in preference to οἶκος as less distinctly implying the notion of a completed building; see Harl. *in loc.* συναρμολογουμένη] *'fitly framed together,'* Auth., *'compaginata,'* Jerome; present part.; the process was still going on. The rare verb συναρμολογ. (= συναρμόζειν) is only found here and iv. 16. Wetst. cites *Anthol.* iii. 32. 4, ἡρμολόγησε τάφον. αὔξει] *'groweth;'* the present marking not only the actual progress, but the normal, perpetual, unconditioned nature of the organic increase; see Scheuerl. *Synt.* § 32. p. 339, 340. This increase must undoubtedly be understood as *extensive* (opp. to Harl.) as well as intensive, and as referring to the enlargement and development of the Church, as well as to its purity or holiness; compare Thiersch, *Apostol. Church,* p. 52 sq. (Transl.). The pres. αὔξω (more common in poetry) is not found in the LXX, and in the N. T. only here and Col. ii. 19. ἐν Κυρίῳ] *'in the Lord (Jesus Christ),'* the usual meaning of Κύρ. in St. Paul's Epp.; see Winer, *Gr.* § 19. 1, p. 113. It is difficult to decide how these words are to be connected; whether (a) with αὔξει, Meyer; (b) with ἅγιον, Harl., Usteri, *Lehrb.* ii. 1, p. 249,

or (c) with ναὸν ἅγιον (comp. Stier), to which it is to be regarded as a kind of tertiary predicate; comp. Donalds. *Gr.* § 489 sq. Of these, (a) seems tautologous; (b) gives perhaps a greater prominence to the special nature of the holiness than the context requires; (c) on the contrary, as the order shows (ναὸν ἅγ., not ἅγ. ναόν; comp. Gersdorf, *Beiträge,* v. p. 334 sq.), gives no special prominence to the idea of holiness, but defines almost, as a further predication of manner, how the whole subsists and is realized, — 'and it is a holy temple in the Lord, and in Him alone;' comp. notes on ver. 11. On this account, and from the harmony with ἐν Πνεύματι, ver. 22, (c) is to be preferred.

22. ἐν ᾧ καὶ ὑμεῖς] *'in whom ye also;'* further specification in ref. to those whom the Apostle is addressing; ἐν ᾧ not being temporal ('dum,' Syr., but not Philox.), nor referring to the more remote ναὸν ἐν Κύρ. (Eadie), but, as in ver. 21, to the preceding ἐν Κυρίῳ, and καὶ with its ascensive and *slightly* contrasting force (comp. notes *on Phil.* iv. 12) marking the exalted nature of the association in which the Ephesians shared; they also were living stones of the great building; comp. Alf. *in loc.* συνοικοδομεῖσθε] *'are builded together;'* clearly not imperative (Calv.), as St. Paul is evidently impressing on his readers what they are, the mystical body they actually belong to, not what they ought to be. The force of σὺν appears similar to that in συνέκλεισεν, Gal. iii. 22 (see notes), and to refer to the *close* and compact union of the component parts of the building. Meyer aptly cites Philo, *de Præm.* § 20, Vol. ii. p. 427 (ed. Mang.), οἰκίαν εὖ συνῳκοδομημένην καὶ συνηρμοσμένην. The comma after συνοικοδ. (*Griesb.*) which would refer εἰς

So I pray for you, believing
ye know how God revealed

III. Τούτου χάριν ἐγὼ Παῦλος ὁ δέσμιος

to me the mystery of the call of the Gentiles, and gave me grace to preach it, that men and angels might learn
God's manifold wisdom. Faint not then at my troubles.

κατοικ. to αὔξει, does not seem necessary. ἐν Πνεύματι] 'in the Spirit;' tertiary predication ('and it is in the Spirit') exactly similar and parallel to ἐν Κυρίῳ, ver. 21. Two other translations have been proposed : (a) 'through the spirit,' Auth., Theophyl., Meyer; (b) 'in a spiritual manner,' opp. to ἐν σαρκί; i. e., the κατοικ. is πνευματικόν, not a ναὸς χειροποίητος, Acts vii. 48 (Olsh.). Of these (a) violates the apparent parallelism with ἐν Κυρ., and presupposes, in order to account for the position of ἐν Πν., an emphasis in it which does not seem to exist, while again (b) introduces an idea not hinted at in the context, and obscures the reference to the Holy Trinity, which here can scarcely be pronounced doubtful. It has been urged by Meyer, that in the interpr. here adopted, the 'continens' and 'contentum' are confounded together; but see Rom. viii. 9, and observe that the second ἐν refers rather to the act of κατοικεῖν involved in the verbal subst.; 'we are built in Christ, form a habitation of God, and are so inhabited in and by the influence of the Spirit;' see Alf. in loc., and compare Hofm. Schriftb. Vol. ii. 2, p. 105 sq. Lastly, no argument in favor of (b) can be founded on the absence of the article, as Πνεῦμα is used with the same latitude as proper names; see notes on Gal. v. 5, p. 83. The opinion also there expressed against the distinction of Harless (h. l.), between the 'subjective' and 'objective' Holy Spirit, seems perfectly valid. For a practical sermon on this verse ('the essence of religion a disposition to God'), see Whichcote, Serm. XLVIII. Vol. ii. p. 383.

CHAPTER III. 1. τούτου χάριν] 'For this reason,' 'hujus rei gratiâ,' Vulg., Clarom.; sc. 'because ye are so

called and so built together in Christ.' The exact meaning of these words will of course be modified by the view taken of the construction. Out of the many explanations of this passage, two deserve attention. (a) That of Syr. and Chrys., according to which εἰμί is supplied after ὁ δέσμ. ʼΙ. Χ., ὁ δέσμιος being the predicate, — 'I am the prisoner of the Lord,' the prisoner κατʼ ἐξοχήν ('multa enim erat istius captivitatis celebritas,' Beza); τούτου χάριν then being 'for the sake of this edification of yours,' ch. ii. 22: (b) that of Theodoret, al., according to which ὁ δέσμιος is in apposition, and the construction resumed, ver. 14; τούτου χάριν then implying on this account, 'because ye are so built together' (De W.), or, more probably, as above, with a wider ref. to the whole foregoing subject; ἀκριβῶς ἐπιστάμενος, καί τινες ἦτε, καὶ πῶς ἐκλήθητε, καὶ ἐπὶ τίσιν ἐκλήθητε, δέομαι καὶ ἱκετεύω τὸν τῶν ὅλων Θεὸν βεβαιῶσαι ὑμᾶς τῇ πίστει, Theodoret. The interpretation 'per brachylogiam,' according to which, δέσμ. εἰμι is to be supplied (Wiggers, Stud. u. Krit. p. 841. p. 431 note, Meyer, ed. 1), is so clearly untenable, that Meyer (ed. 2) has now given it up in favor of (a). This former interpr. deserves consideration, but on account of the virtual tautology in τούτ. χάρ. and ὑπὲρ ὑμῶν, — the analogy of ch. iv. 1, — and still more the improbability that St. Paul would style himself ὁ δέσμιος, when he so well knew others were suffering like himself (1 Cor. iv. 9 sq.), the latter is to be preferred; see Winer, Gr. § 62. 4, p. 499. The recent explanation of Wieseler, which makes ὁ δέσμιος in be in apposition, but dispenses with all assumption of a parenthesis, or of an abbreviated structure is not very satisfactory or intelligible; see Chron. Synops. p. 446.   τοῦ Χρ. ʼΙησοῦ]

τοῦ Χριστοῦ Ἰησοῦ ὑπὲρ ὑμῶν τῶν ἐϑνῶν — ² εἴγε ἠκούσατε τὴν
οἰκονομίαν τῆς χάριτος τοῦ Θεοῦ τῆς δοϑείσης μοι εἰς ὑμᾶς,   ³ ὅτι

'Of Jesus Christ,' scil. 'whom Christ
and His cause have made a prisoner,'
Olsh.; gen. of the *author* or *originating
cause* of the captivity; compare Philem.
13, δεσμοὶ τοῦ εὐαγγελίου, and see Winer,
Gr. § 30. 20, obs. p. 170, Hartung,
Casus, p. 17, and notes *on* 1 *Thess.* i. 6.
ὑπὲρ ὑμ. τῶν ἐϑνῶν] '*in behalf of
you Gentiles;*' introductory of the subject
of the Apostle's calling as an Apostle of
the Gentiles, and resumed ver. 12.

2. εἴγε] '*if indeed,*' 'as I may suppose,' 'on the assumption that;' gentle
appeal, expressed in a hypothetical form,
and conveying the hope that his words
had not been quite forgotten. Εἴγε is
properly '*si quidem*,' and if resolved,
'*tum certe si*,' (see Klotz, *Devar.* Vol. II.
p. 308); it does not *in itself* imply the
rectitude of the assumption made ('εἴγε
usurpatur de re quæ jure sumpta creditur,' Herm. *Viger*, No. 310), but derives·
that shade of meaning from the context;
see notes *on Gal.* iii. 4. In the present
case there could be no real doubt; 'neque
enim ignorare, quod hic dicitur, poterant
Ephesii, quibus Paulus ipse evangelium
plusquam biennio prædicaverat,' Estius ;
comp. ch. iv. 21, 2 Cor. v. 3, Col. i. 23.
No argument, then, can be fairly deduced from these words against the
inscription of this Ep. to the Ephesians
(Mill, *Prolegom.* p. 9, De Wette), nor
can the hypothetical form be urged as
implying that the Apostle was personally
unknown to his readers.   τὴν
οἰκονομίαν κ. τ. λ.] '*the dispensation
of the grace of God which was given to me,
etc.*' In this passage two errors must be
avoided : first, τῆς δοϑείσης must not be
taken, virtually or expressly ('per hypal-
lagen '), for τὴν δοϑεῖσαν, comp. Col. i.
25 ; secondly, no special meanings must
be assigned either to οἰκονομία or χάρις.
Οἰκονομία is not 'the apostolic office'

(Wieseler, *Synops.* p. 448), but, as in ch.
i. 10 (see notes), 'disposition,' 'dispensation ;' τῆς χαρίτος being the gen., — not
subjecti, Œcum. (who reads ἐγνώρισε, as
in *Rec.*), but, as the pass. ἐγνωρίσϑε
seems rather to suggest, — *objecti*, or
rather the gen. of 'the point of view,'
which serves to complete the conception,
sc. 'the dispensation in respect of the
grace of God, etc.,' see Scheuerl. *Synt.*
§ 18, p. 129, comp. Winer, *Gr.* § 30. 2,
p. 175. This is further explained by
ὅτι κατὰ ἀποκ. ver. 3; οἰκονομίαν χάριτός
φησι τὴν ἀποκάλυψιν, Chrys. There is
thus no need to depart from the strict
meaning of χάρις; it is not 'munus
Apostolicum' (Estius), but the assisting
and qualifying grace of God for the performance of it.   εἰς ὑμᾶς is well
translated '*to youward,*' Auth.; it is not
'in vobis,' Vulg., or even 'for you' (dat.
commodi), but with the proper force of
εἰς (ethical direction), 'toward you,' 'to
work in you;' compare ch. i. 19, and
Winer, *Gr.* § 49. a. p. 354.

3. ὅτι κ. τ. λ.] '*that by way of revelation ;*' objective sentence (Donalds. *Gr.*
§ 584) dependent on the preceding ἠκούσατε κ. τ. λ. and explanatory of the
nature and peculiarity of the οἰκονομ.;
the emphasis obviously falling on the
predication of manner κατὰ ἀποκάλυψιν.
These latter words are used in a very
similar, though not perfectly identical
manner, Gal. ii. 2 (comp. 2 Cor. viii. 8,
Gal. iv. 29, see note, Phil. ii. 2); there,
however, the allusion is rather to the
norma or *rule*, here to the *manner*, 'by
way of revelation,' 'revelation-wise;'
comp. Bernhardy, *Synt.* v. 20. b, p. 239.
τὸ μυστήριον] '*the mystery,*' not of
redemption generally, nor of St. Paul's
special call, but, in accordance with the
context, of that which is the evident subject of the passage, — the admission of

9

κατὰ ἀποκάλυψιν ἐγνωρίσθη μοι τὸ μυστήριον, καθὼς προέγραψα
ἐν ὀλίγῳ, ⁴ πρὸς ὃ δύνασθε ἀναγινώσκοντες νοῆσαι τὴν σύνεσίν

the Gentiles to fellowship and heirship with Christ in common with the Jews; μυστήριον γάρ ἐστι τὸ τὰ ἔθνη ἐξαίφνης εἰς μείζονα τῶν Ἰουδαίων εὐγένειαν ἀναγαγεῖν, Chrys.; see Usteri, *Lehrb.* p. 252. On the use and meaning of the word μυστήριον see notes on ch. v. 32. The reading ἐγνωρίσθη [*Rec.* with DᵌE KL; many mss.; Æth. (both); Dam., Theoph., al.] is distinctly inferior to the text [ABCD¹FG; many mss.; Syr. (both), Vulg., Clarom., Goth., Copt., al.] in external authority, and seems to have been an intended emendation of structure. προέγραψα] 'have *afore written*,' Hamm.; a translation here preferable to the aoristic 'afore wrote' (Auth.), as serving better to define the reference, as not being to any earlier (Chrys., but not Theod., Theoph.), but simply to the present Epistle; comp. ch. i. 9 sq., ii. 13 sq. The clause seems introduced to confirm the readers, the ref. being, as ver. 4 clearly shows, neither to κατὰ ἀποκαλ. nor to μυστήρ. but to ἐγνωρίσθη μοι τὸ μυστ.; it was the *fact* of this knowledge having been imparted, not the manner in which he attained it, or the precise nature of it that the Apostle desires to specify and reiterate. To enclose this clause and ver. 4 in a parenthesis (*Wetst.*, *Griesb.*), is thus obviously unsatisfactory. ἐν ὀλίγῳ] [Syriac] [in paucis] Syr., 'in brevi,' Vulg., διὰ βραχέων, Chrys.; see Kypke, *Obs.* Vol. II. p. 293. The meaning, 'a short time before,' 'just now,' (comp. Theod.) is distinctly untenable: this would be πρὸ ὀλίγου: ἐν ὀλίγῳ in a temporal sense can only mean, as Mey. and Harl. correctly observe, 'in a short space of time:' see Acts xxvi. 28, where, however, as in the present case, the meaning, 'briefly,'

'with a compendious form of argument' (not 'lightly,' Alf.; see Meyer *in loc.*), is appy. more tenable. Stier alludes to the common epistolary expression, 'a few lines.' 4. πρὸς ὃ] '*in accordance to which*,' '*agreeably to which*,' scil. the προγεγραμμένον, not ἐν ὀλίγῳ (Kypke): from what the Apostle had written in this Epistle his insight into the mystery of Christ was to be inferred by his readers; 'ex ungue leonem,' Beng. The remark of Harl. that πρὸς (with acc.) in its *ethical* use denotes the relation of *conformity to*, seems correct and comprehensive. Whether this be in reference to *cause and effect* ('owing to,' Herod. IV. 161, comp. Matth. xix. 8; see exx. in Palm u. Rost, *Lex.* s. v. b. aa, Vol. II. p. 1157), *design and execution* ('in order to,' 1 Cor. xii. 7, al.), *simple comparison* (Rom. viii. 18; Herod. III. 34, cited by Bernhardy, *Synt.* v. 31, p. 265, or, as here *rule* and *measure* (see notes *on Gal.* ii. 14) must be determined by the context. If we add to these the indication of simple *mental direction* ('in regard to,' 'in reference to,' Heb. i. 7, see Winer, *Gr.* § 48. h. p. 360, comp. notes on ch. iv. 12), the ethical uses of πρὸς with acc. will be sufficiently delineated. For a good and comprehensive list of exx. see Rost and Palm, *Lex.* s. v. Vol. II. p. 1156 sq. δύνασθε ἀναγιν. νοῆσαι] '*you can while reading, or as you read. perceive;*' the temporal participle expressing the contemporary act, comp. Donalds. *Gr.* § 576. The aor. νοῆσαι is appy. here used as marking, not exactly the sudden and transitory nature of the act (Alf.; contrast Bernhardy, *Synt.* x. 9, p. 383), but the distinct manifestations of it, the single act being regarded, as it were, the commencement of a continuity; see

μου ἐν τῷ μυστηρίῳ τοῦ Χριστοῦ, ⁵ ὃ ἑτέραις γενεαῖς οὐκ ἐγνωρίσθη τοῖς υἱοῖς τῶν ἀνθρώπων, ὡς νῦν ἀπεκαλύφθη τοῖς ἁγίοις

esp. Schmalfeld, *Synt.* § 173. 4, Donalds. *Gr.* § 427. *d.* The student must be careful in pressing the aor. in this mood, as so much depends on the context and the mode in which the action is contemplated by the writer; see Bernhardy, *Synt. l. c.*, Krüger, *Sprachl.* 53. 6. 9, and observe that δύναμαι and similar verbs, ἔχω, δυνατός εἰμι, θέλω, are often idiomatically followed by the *aor.* rather than the present; see Winer, § 44. 7, p. 298, and the note of Mätzner in his ed. of Antiph. p. 153 sq.   τὴν σύνεσίν μου κ. τ. λ.] '*my insight, my understanding in the mystery of Christ.*' The article is not needed before the prep., as σύνεσις ἐν τῷ μυστ. forms a single composite idea; comp. 3 Esdr. i. 3, τῆς συνέσεως αὐτοῦ ἐν τῷ νόμῳ Κυρίου (Harl.), and see notes on ch. i. 15. The formula, συνιέναι ἐν (and εἰς) occurs several times in the LXX, 2 Chron. xxxiv. 12, Nehem. xiii. 7, al., and thus justifies the omission of the article with the derivative subst.: see Winer, § 20. 2, p. 123.   The distinction between συνιέναι ('to understand,' 'verstehn'), and νοεῖν ('to perceive,' 'merken'), is noticed by Tittmann, *Synon.* p. 191. τοῦ Χριστοῦ is commonly taken as a gen. *objecti*, 'the mystery relating to Christ,' sc. of which His reconciliation, and union of the Jews and Gentiles in Himself formed the subject; compare Theophyl. *in loc.* By comparing, however, the somewhat difficult passage, Col i. 27, τοῦ μυστηρ. ..... ὅς ἐστιν Χριστὸς ἐν ὑμῖν, it would certainly seem that it is rather a species of gen. *materiæ*, or *of identity*: 'Christus selbst ist das *Concretum* des göttlichen Geheimnisses,' Meyer; comp. Stier *in loc.*, and see exx. in Scheuerlein, *Synt.* § 12. 1, p. 82, 83.

5. ὅ] '*which*,' scil. which μυστήριον τοῦ Χρ. ver. 4; there being no parenthe-sis (see above), but that simple linked connection by means of relatives which is so characteristic of this Epistle.

ἑτέραις γενεαῖς] '*in other generations, ages,*' 'anþaraim aldim,' Goth.; dative of time; see Winer, *Gr.* § 31. 9, p. 195; comp. notes, ch. ii. 11. Meyer, maintaining the usual meaning of γενεά, explains the dat. as a simple dat. *commodi*, and τοῖς υἱοῖς as a further explanation. This is unnecessary precision, as in Col. i. 26, ἀπὸ τῶν αἰώνων καὶ ἀπὸ τῶν γενεῶν, the less usual meaning, 'age,' can scarcely be denied: see Acts xiv. 16, and, probably, Luke i. 50. In the LXX, γενεά is the usual translation of דּוֹר, which certainly (see Gesen. *Lex.* s. v.), admits both meanings. In one instance, Isaiah xxiv. 22, even רֹמִי is so translated.   The insertion of ἐν before ἑτέραις (*Rec.*) rests only on the authority of a few mss.; Copt., and Syr.-Phil.   τοῖς υἱοῖς τῶν ἀνθρ.] '*to the sons of men*;' 'latissima appellatio, causam exprimens ignorantiæ, ortum naturalem;' so Beng., who, however, proceeds less felicitously to refer the expression to the ancient prophets. This is neither fairly demonstrable from the use of בְּנֵי־אָדָם, (Ezek. vii. 1, al.), nor by any means consonant with the present passage, where no comparison is instituted between the prophets of the Old and of the New Test, but between the times,—the *then* and the *now.* The expression, υἱοὶ τῶν ἀνθρ. seems chosen to make the contrast with the ἅγιοι ἀπόστ. αὐτοῦ καὶ προφ., the Θεοῦ ἄνθρωποι (2 Pet. i. 21, Deut. xxxiii. 1) more fully felt.   ὡς] Observe the *comparison* which the particle introduces and suggests: ἐγνωρίσθη μὲν τοῖς πάλαι προφήταις, ἀλλ' οὐχ ὡς νῦν· οὐ γὰρ τὰ πράγματα εἶδον [comp. 1 John i. 1] ἀλλὰ τοὺς περὶ τῶν πραγμάτων προέ-

ἀποστόλοις αὐτοῦ καὶ προφήταις ἐν Πνεύματι, ⁶ εἶναι τὰ ἔθνη

γραψαν λόγους, Theodoret.　　　τ ο ῖ ς
ἁ γ ί ο ι ς ἀ π ο σ τ.] 'to His holy Apostles.'
The epithet ἁγίοις has been very unrea-
sonably urged by De Wette as a mark
of the post-apostolic age of the epistle.
It is obviously used to support and
strengthen the antithesis to the υἱοὶ τῶν
ἀνθρ. The Apostles were ἅγιοι in their
office as God's chosen messengers, ἅγιοι
in their personal character as the inspired preachers of Christ; compare
Luke i. 70, Acts iii. 21, 2 Pet. i. 21
(Lachm.), where the prophets are so
designated. The meaning of προφῆται
is here the same as in ch. ii. 20, the
'N. T. prophets;' see notes on ch. iv.
11.　　　ἐ ν Π ν ε ύ μ α τ ι] 'by the
Spirit;' Auth., Arm. (instrumental
case); Holy Agent by whom the ἀποκάλυψις was given, ἐν having here more of
its instrumental force; εἰ μὴ γὰρ τὸ
Πνεῦμα ἐδίδαξε τὸν Πέτρον, οὐκ ἂν τὸν
ἐθνικὸν Κορνήλιον μετὰ τῶν σὺν αὐτῷ
παρεδέξατο, Theophyl.; comp. Chrys.,
who certainly appears erroneously cited
(De W., Eadie) as joining ἐν Πν. with
προφ., 'prophets in the Spirit,' sc. θεο-
πνεύστους. This latter construction,
though fairly admissible (comp. Winer,
Gr. § 20. 4, p. 126), is open to the decisive exegetical objection that it is an
'idem per idem;' if prophets were not
divinely inspired, 'prophets in the Spirit,'
the name would be misapplied. On the
omission of the art. see ch. ii. 22. The
traces of Montanism which Baur
(Paulus, p. 440) finds in these words,
are so purely imaginary as not to deserve serious notice or confutation.

6. ε ἶ ν α ι τ ὰ ἔ θ ν η] 'to wit, that the
Gentiles are,' 'esse gentes,' Clarom.,
Vulg., Goth., not 'should be,' Auth.,
Eadie, the objective infin. here expressing not the design but the subject and
purport of the mystery: τοῦτ' ἔστι τὸ
μυστήριον τὸ εἶναι τὰ ἔθνη συγκληρονόμα

τῷ Ἰσραὴλ τῆς ἐπαγγελίας, καὶ συμμέ-
τοχα, Theoph.; compare Donalds. Gr.
§ 584.　　σ υ ν κ λ η ρ ο ν ό μ α κ. τ. λ.]
'fellow-heirs and fellow-members, and fel-
low-partakers of the promise.' It does not
seem correct to regard these three epithets, on the one hand, as merely cumulative and oratorical, or on the other as
studiedly mystical and significant (compare Stier, who here finds a special allusion to the Trinity). The general fact
of the συνκληρονομία is reasserted, in
accordance with the Apostle's previous
expressions, both in its outward and inward relations. The Gentiles were fellow-heirs with the believing Jews in the
most unrestricted sense; they belonged
to the same corporate body, the faithful;
they shared to the full in the same spiritual blessings, the ἐπαγγελία; see Theod.
in loc. The compounds σύνσωμος ('con-
corporalis,' see Suicer, Thes. s. v. Vol.
II. 1191) and συνμέτοχος ('comparti-
ceps,' ch. v. 7) appear to have been both
formed by St. Paul, being only found in
this Ep. and the Ecclesiast. writers.
The verb συμμετέχω occurs in classical
Greek, e. g. Eurip. Suppl. 648, Plato,
Theaet. 181 c, Xenoph. Anab. VII. 8. 17.
Tisch. (ed. 7) now adopts the forms συν-
κληρ. and συνσωμ. with ABᴵDEFG, and
συνμετ. with ABᴵCDᴵFG, — appy. on
right principles; see Prolegom. p. XLVII.
τ ῆ ς ἐ π α γ γ ε λ ί α ς] 'the promise of salvation,' not merely of the Holy Spirit
(Eadie); for though the promise of the
Spirit was one of the prominent gifts of
the New Covenant (Gal. iii. 14), it
would here be not only too restricted,
but even scarcely consonant with the
foregoing συνκληρονόμα. The addition of αὐτοῦ after τῆς ἐπαγγ. (Rec.) is
fairly supported [DᶻDᶟEFGKL; many
mss.; Vulg. (some edd.), Goth., Syr.-
Philox.; Theod., al.], but not found in
ABCDᴵ; mss.; Clarom., Sang., Amit.,

συνκληρονόμα καὶ σύνσωμα καὶ συνμέτοχα τῆς ἐπαγγελίας ἐν
Χριστῷ Ἰησοῦ διὰ τοῦ εὐαγγελίου, ⁷ οὗ ἐγενήθην διάκονος κατὰ
τὴν δωρεὰν τῆς χάριτος τοῦ Θεοῦ τὴν δοθεῖσάν μοι κατὰ τὴν ἐνέργειαν τῆς δυνάμεως αὐτοῦ. ⁸ ἐμοὶ τῷ ἐλαχιστοτέρῳ πάντων ἁγίων

Copt., Syr., and thus rightly rejected by the best recent editors. ἐν Χρ. 'and διὰ τοῦ εὐαγγ. both refer to the three foregoing epithets. The former points to the objective ground of the salvation, Him *in* whom it centred, the latter the *medium* by which it was to be subjectively applied (Mey.): τῷ πεμφθῆ-ναι καὶ πρὸς αὐτούς, καὶ τῷ πιστεῦσαι· οὐ γὰρ ἁπλῶς, ἀλλὰ διὰ τοῦ εὐαγγελίου, Chrysost. On the distinction between ἐν and διὰ in the same sentence, see Winer, *Gr.* § 48. a, p. 347 note, and comp. ch. i. 7.　　　The reading of *Rec.* ἐν τῷ Χρ. [DEFGKL; most mss.; Clarom., Sang., Boern.; Orig. (3), al.] is rejected by most recent editors in favor of the text which is found in ABC; some mss., and supported by Aug., Vulg., Goth., Copt., al.

7. ἐγενήθην] ʼ*I became;*ʼ this less usual form is rightly adopted by *Tisch.*, *Lachm.*, al., on the authority of ABD¹ FG against CD³EKL, which read ἐγενό-μην. The passive *form*, however, implies no corresponding difference of meaning (Rück., Eadie); γίγνομαι in the Doric dialect was a deponent pass.; ἐγενήθην was thus used in it for ἐγενόμην, and from thence occasionally crept into the language of later writers; see Buttmann, *Irreg. Verbs*, s. v. ΓΕΝ—, Lobeck, *Phryn.* p. 108, 109, and comp. notes *on Col.* iv. 11.　　　διάκονος] ʼ*a minister*,ʼ Col. i. 23, 2 Cor. iii. 6.　Meyer rightly impugns the distinction of Harless, that διάκ. points more to activity in relation to *the service*, ὑπηρέτης to activity in relation to *the master*. This certainly cannot be substantiated by the exx. in the N. T.; see 2 Cor. vi. 4, xi. 23, 1 Tim. iv. 6, where διάκ. is simply used in reference to

the master, and Luke i. 2, where ὑπηρέτης refers to the *service*. On the derivation of διάκ. (διήκω), see Buttm. *Lexil.* s. v. διάκτορος, § 40. 3; for its more remote affinities [ΑΚ-ΑΓΚ- ʼbendʼ], Benfey, *Wurzellex.* Vol. II. p. 22.　　τὴν δωρ. τῆς χάριτος] ʼthe gift of the grace;ʼ gen. *of identity;* that of which the gift (the apostolic office, the office of preaching to the Gentiles) consisted; compare Plato, *Leg.* VIII. 844, διττὰς δωρεὰς χάριτος, and see Scheuerl. *Synt.* § 12. 1, p. 82, Winer, *Gr.* § 59. 8, p. 470.　　τὴν δοθεῖσάν μοι] ʼwhich was given to me;ʼ not a mere reiteration of the preceding δωρεάν, but associated closely with the following words which define the *manner* of the δόσις. The reading τῆς δοθείσης (*Lachm.*) is supported by strong external authority [ABCD¹FG; 10 mss.; Vulg. Clarom., Copt.] but appears very likely to have arisen from a conformation to ver. 2. The accus. is found in D³EKL; majority of mss.; Syr. (both), Goth., al.; Chrys., Theod.. al., and is adopted by *Tisch.*, and most recent critics.　　κατὰ τὴν ἐνέργ.] ʼaccording to the working or operation of his power;ʼ defining preposit. clause, dependent, not on ἐγενόμην (Mey.) but on τὴν δοθεῖσάν μοι, which would otherwise seem an unnecessary addition: ʼthe mention of the *power* of God is founded on the circumstance that St. Paul sees in his change of heart, from a foe to a friend of Christ, an act of omnipotence,ʼ Olsh. On the proper force of κατά, see notes, ch. i. 19.

8. ἐμοὶ τῷ ἐλαχιστοτέρῳ] ʼ*To me who am less than the least*,ʼ Auth.; a most felicitous translation. No addition was required to the former period; the

ἐδόθη ἡ χάρις αὕτη, ἐν τοῖς ἔθνεσιν εὐαγγελίσασθαι τὸ ἀνεξιχνίαστον πλοῦτος τοῦ Χριστοῦ, ⁹ καὶ φωτίσαι πάντας τίς ἡ οἰκονομία

great Apostle, however, so truly, so ear-
nestly felt his own weakness and nothingness (εἰ καὶ οὐδέν εἰμι, 2 Cor. xv. 15),
that the mention of God's grace towards
him awakens within, by the forcible contrast it suggests, not only the remembrance of his former persecutions of the
church (1 Cor. xv. 10), but of his own
sinful nature (1 Tim. i. 15, εἰμί, not ἦν),
and unworthiness for so high an office.
Calvin and Harl. here expound with far
more vitality than Est., who refers this
ταπεινοφροσύνης ὑπερβολὴν (Chrysost.)
solely to the memory of his former persecutions. It is perfectly incredible how,
in such passages as these, which reveal
the truest depths of Christian experience,
Baur (Paulus, p. 447) can only see con-
tradictions and arguments against the
apostolic origin of the Epistle. On the
form ἐλαχιστ. see Winer, Gr. § 11. 2, p.
65, and the exx. collected by Wetst. in
loc., out of which, however, remove
Thucyd. IV. 118, as the true reading is
κάλλιον. ἐν τοῖς ἔθν. εὐαγ-
γελ.] 'to preach among the Gentiles;'
explanatory and partly appositional
clause, the emphatic ἐν τοῖς ἔθνεσιν
marking the Apostle's distinctive sphere
of action, and the inf. defining the preceding ἡ χάρις αὕτη; see Krüger, Sprachl.
§ 57. 10. 6, Schmalfeld, Synt. § 192,
Winer, Gr. § 44. 1, p. 284. To make
this clause dependent on δωρεάν, ver. 7,
and to regard ἐμοὶ — αὕτη as parenthetical (Harl.) seems a very improbable
connection, and is required neither by
grammar nor by the tenor of the passage. Lachm. omits ἐν with ABC;
3 mss.; Copt. (Alf.), but the authority
for retaining it [DEFGKL; nearly all
mss.; Syr. (both), Clarom., Vulgate,
Goth., al.; Chrys., Theod., al.] seems
fairly to preponderate. πλοῦτος
τοῦ Χρ.] 'riches of Christ,' i. e. the

exhaustless blessings of salvation; compare Rom. xi. 33. It is ἀνεξιχνίαστον
(חֵקֶר אֵין, Job v. 9, ix. 10) both in its
nature, extent, and application.

9. καὶ φωτίσαι πάντας] 'and
to illuminate all, make all see;' ܘܠܡܢܗܪܘ

ܠܟܠܢܫ [et in lucem proferam omni

homini] Syr.; expansion of the foregoing clause as to the process (the Apostle
had grace given not only outwardly to
preach the Gospel, but inwardly to en-
lighten), though appy. not as to the persons (ed. 1); as owing to its unemphatic
position the πάντας can scarcely be regarded more inclusive than the foregoing
τὰ ἔθνη; see Meyer. The significant
verb φωτίσαι must not be explained away
as synonymous with διδάξαι (De W.);
this derivative meaning is found in the
LXX, see Judges xiii. 8 (Alex.), 2 Kings
iv. 2, xvii. 27, 28, but not in the N. T.,
— where the reference is always to light,
either physical (Luke x., xi., 36), metaphorical (1 Cor. iv. 5), or spiritual (Heb.
vi. 4, al.); comp. Reuss., Théol. Chrét.
IV. 15, Vol. II. p. 156, note. Christ is
properly ὁ φωτίζων (John i. 9); His apostles illuminate 'participatione ac minis-
terio,' Estius. On the use of the word
in ref. to baptism, see Suicer, Thesaur.
Vol. II. p. 1491. Lachm. brackets
πάντας as being omitted by A; some
mss.; Cyr., Hill., al., but without sufficient authority. οἰκονομία τοῦ
μυστ.] 'the dispensation of the mystery,'
'dispositio sacramenti absconditi,' Clarom., — scil. the dispensation (arrange-
ment, regulation) of the mystery (the
union of Jews and Gentiles in Christ,
ver. 6), which was to be humbly traced
and acknowledged in the fact of its having secretly existed in the primal counsels of God, and now having been re-

τοῦ μυστηρίου τοῦ ἀποκεκρυμμένου ἀπὸ τῶν αἰώνων ἐν τῷ Θεῷ
τῷ τὰ πάντα κτίσαντι, ¹⁰ ἵνα γνωρισϑῇ νῦν ταῖς ἀρχαῖς καὶ ταῖς

vealed to the heavenly powers by means of the Church. On the meaning of οἰκονομία, see notes on ch. i. 10. The reading κοινωνία (*Rec.*) has only the support of cursive mss., and is a mere explanatory gloss. ἀπὸ τῶν αἰώνων] '*from the ages,*' scil. '*since the ages of the world began ;*' comp. בְּרֵאשִׁית, Gen. vi. 4 : *terminus a quo* of the concealment. The counsel itself was formed πρὸ τῶν αἰώνων, 1 Cor. ii. 7 ; the concealment of it dated ἀπὸ τῶν αἰώνων, — from the commencement of the ages when intelligent beings, from whom it could be concealed, were called into existence; compare Rom. xvi. 25, μυστηρίου χρόνοις αἰωνίοις σεσιγημένου. τῷ τὰ πάντα κτίσαντι] '*who created all things,*' '*qui omnia creavit,*' Clarom., Vulg., certainly not, 'quippe qui omnia creavit,' Meyer, — a translation which would require the absence of the article; compare notes on ch. i. 12, and see esp. Donalds. *Crat.* § 306. The exact reason for this particular designation being here appended to τῷ Θεῷ has been somewhat differently estimated. The most simple explanation would seem to be that it is added to enhance the idea of God's omnipotence; the emphatic position of τὰ πάντα ('nullâ re prorsus exceptâ,' Est.) being designed to give to the idea its widest extent and application, — 'who created *all* things,' and so, with His undoubted prerogative of sovereign and creative power, ordained the very μυστήριον itself. A reference to God's *omniscience* would more suitably have justified the concealment, the reference to His *omnipotence* more convincingly vindicates the εὐδοκία according to which it was included in, and formed part of his primal counsels. It is not necessary to limit τὰ πάντα, but the tense seems to show that it is rather

to the *physical* (οὐδὲν γὰρ χωρὶς αὐτοῦ πεποίηκε, Chrys.), than to the spiritual creation (Calv.) This latter view was perhaps suggested by the longer reading κτίσ. διὰ Ἰησοῦ Χρ. [*Rec.* with DᵃEJK; most mss.; Syr.-Phil. with asterisk; Chrys., Theod., al.], which, however, is rightly rejected by most recent editors with ABCD¹FG; a few mss.; Syr., Vulg., Goth., al.; Basil, Cyr., and many Ff.

10. ἵνα γνωρισϑῇ νῦν] '*in order that there might be made known now;*' divine object and purpose, — not of either the acts specified in the participial clauses immediately preceding, for neither the concealment of the mystery (Meyer), nor the past act of material creation (Harl.) could be properly said to have had as its purpose and design the *present* (νῦν opp. to ἀπὸ τῶν αἰώνων) exhibition of God's wisdom to angels, — but of the general dispensation described in the two foregoing verses. The Apostle (as Olsh. well remarks), in contrasting the greatness of his call with the nothingness of his personal self, pursues the theme of his labor through all its stages : the ἐλαχιστότερος has grace given him εὐαγγ. κ. τ. λ., nay more, φωτίσαι πάντας κ. τ. λ., and that, too, that heaven might see and acknowledge the πολυποίκιλος σοφία of God; see Neander, *Planting,* Vol. i. p. 518 (Bohn). ταῖς ἀρχαῖς κ. τ. λ.] '*to the principalities and to the powers in the heavenly regions,*' sc. to the *good* angels and intelligences ; a ref. to both classes (Hofm. *Schriftb.* Vol. i. p. 315) being excluded, not so much by ἐν τοῖς ἐπουρ. (Alf., for compare ch. vi. 12), as by the general tenor of the passage ; evil angels more naturally recognize the *power,* good angels the *wisdom* of God. On the term ἀρχαῖς καὶ ἐξουσ. (here to add weight to

ἐξουσίαις ἐν τοῖς ἐπουρανίοις διὰ τῆς ἐκκλησίας ἡ πολυποίκιλος
σοφία τοῦ Θεοῦ, ¹¹κατὰ πρόθεσιν τῶν αἰώνων, ἣν ἐποίησεν ἐν

the enumeration each with the art.), see notes ch. i. 21, and on τοῖς ἐπουρ. notes on ch. i. 3, 20.   διὰ τῆς ἐκκλησίας] 'through the Church,' scil. 'by means of,' the Church; διὰ τῆς περὶ τὴν ἐκκλησίαν οἰκονομίας, Theod. The Church, the community of believers in Christ (Col. i. 24), was the means by which these ministering spirits were to behold and contemplate God's wisdom: comp. Calvin, in loc., — 'ecclesia .... quasi speculum sit in quo contemplantur Angeli mirificam Dei sapientiam;' ὅτε ἡμεῖς ἐμάθομεν, τότε κἀκεῖνοι δι' ἡμῶν, Chrys. That the holy angels are capable of a specific increase of knowledge, and of a deepening insight into God's wisdom, seems from this passage clear and incontrovertible; comp. 1 Pet. i. 12, εἰς ἃ ἐπιθυμοῦσιν ἄγγελοι παρακύψαι, and see Petavius, Theol. Dogm. Vol. III. p. 44 sq., Suicer, Thesaur. Vol. i. p. 46. πολυποίκιλος] 'manifold,' 'multiformis,' Clarom., Vulg.; see Orph. Hymn. VI. 11, LXI. 4. This characteristic of God's wisdom is to be traced, not in the παράδοξον, by which issues were brought about by unlooked-for means (διὰ τῶν ἐναντίων τὰ ἐναντία κατωρθώθη, διὰ θανάτου ζωή, δι' ἀσθενείας δύναμις, δι' ἀτιμίας δόξα, Greg. Nyss. ap. Theoph.), but in the πολύτεχνον (Theoph.), the variety of the divine counsels, which nevertheless all mysteriously coöperated toward a single end, — the call of the Gentiles, and salvation of mankind by faith in Jesus Christ. The use of πολυποίκ. in reference to Gnosticism (Irenæus, Hær. I. 4. 1) does not give the slightest reason for supposing (Baur, Paulus, p. 429) that the use of the word here arose from any such allusions.

11. κατὰ πρόθ. τῶν αἰώνων] 'according to the purpose of the ages;' modal clause dependent on ἵνα γνωρισθῇ,

specifying the accordance of the revelation of the divine wisdom with God's eternal purpose; νῦν μὲν, φησί, γέγονεν, οὐ νῦν δὲ ὥριστο, ἀλλ' ἄνωθεν προτετύπωτο, Chrys. The gen. αἰώνων is somewhat obscure; it can scarcely be (a) a gen. objecti ('the foreordering of the ages,' Whitby, comp. Peile), or even (b) a gen. of the point of view (Scheuerl. Synt. § 18. 1, p. 129), — for the Apostle is not speaking of God's purpose in regard to different times or dispensations, but of His single purpose of uniting and saving mankind in Christ, — but will be most naturally regarded as (c) belonging to the general category of the gen. of possession ('the purpose which pertained to, existed in, was determined on in the ages'), and as serving to define the general relation of time; compare Jude 6, κρίσιν μεγάλης ἡμέρας, and see Winer, Gr. § 30. 2, p. 169. The meaning is thus nearly equivalent to that of the similar expression 2 Tim. i. 9, πρόθεσιν ...... πρὸ χρόνων αἰωνίων; God's purpose existed in His eternal being and was formed in the primal ages ('a sæculis,' Syr.) before the foundation of the world; comp. ch. i. 4.   ἣν ἐποίησεν] 'which he wrought,' 'quam fecit,' Clarom., Vulg., Copt., 'gatavida,' Goth. The exact meaning of ἐποίησεν is doubtful. The mention of the eternal purpose would seem to imply rather 'constituit' (Harl., Alf.), than 'exsecutus est' (De W., Mey.), as the general reference seems more to the appointment of the decree than to its historical realization (see Calv., Hofm. Schriftb. Vol. I. p. 204); still the words ἐν Χρ. Ἰησ. τῷ Κυρίῳ ἡμῶν seem so clearly to point to the realization, the carrying out of the purpose in Jesus Christ, — the Word made flesh (compare Olsh.), — that the latter (Matth. xxi. 31, John vi. 38, 1

$$Χριστῷ \ Ἰησοῦ \ τῷ \ Κυρίῳ \ ἡμῶν, \quad ^{12} ἐν \ ᾧ \ ἔχομεν \ τὴν \ παῤῥησίαν$$

Kings v. 8, Isaiah xliv. 28) must be considered preferable. As, however, St. Paul has used a middle term, neither προέθετο nor ἐπετέλεσε, a middle term (e. g. 'wrought,' 'made,' — not 'fulfilled,' Conyb.) should be retained in translation. The reading is slightly doubtful. *Tisch.* (ed. 1 and 7) inserts τῷ before Χρ. with ABC¹; 37. 116. al.; as, however, the title ὁ Χρ. ʼΙησ. ὁ Κυρ. ἡμῶν does not *appy.* occur elsewhere (Col. ii. 6 is the nearest approach to it; see Middl. *Gr. Art.* Append. II. p. 495, *ed. Rose*) and the omission is well supported [C³DEKL; most mss.; Ath., Chrys., Theod.] we still retain the reading of *Rec., Lachm., Tisch.* (ed. 2), and the majority of editors.

12. ἐν ᾧ ἔχομεν] 'in whom (grounded in whom) *we have;*' appeal to, and proof drawn from their Christian experience, the relative ᾧ having here a slightly demonstrative and explanatory force (ὅτι δὲ διὰ τοῦ Χρ. γέγονεν ἅπαν, 'ἐν ᾧ ἔχομεν' φησί κ. τ. λ. Chrys., compare Theod.), and being nearly equivalent to ἐν αὐτῷ γάρ; see Jelf, *Gr.* § 834. 2, Bernhardy, *Synt.* VI. 12, p. 293, and notes *on Col.* i. 27. τὴν παῤῥησίαν] 'our boldness,' 'fiduciam,' Clarom., Vulg.; not here 'libertatem oris,' whether in ref. to prayer (Beng.) or to preaching the Gospel (Vatabl.), as in many instances (Lev. xxvi. 13, μετὰ παῤῥ. דָּקוֹמְמִיּוּת, 1 Macc. iv. 18, Heb. iii. 6, 1 John ii. 28, al.) the primitive meaning has merged into that of 'cheerful boldness.' (θάῤῥος, Zonar. *Lex.* p. 1508, 'Freudigkeit,' Luth.); that 'freedom of spirit' ('freihals,' Goth.), which becomes those who are conscious of the redeeming love of Christ; ἁγιάσας γὰρ ἡμᾶς διὰ τοῦ ἰδίου αἵματος προσήγαγε θαῤῥοῦντας, Œcum.; see notes *on* 1 *Tim.* iii. 13. τὴν προσαγωγὴν] 'our admission;' οὐχ ὡς αἰχμάλωτοι, φησί, προσήχθη-

μεν, ἀλλʼ ὡς συγγνώμης ἀξιούμενοι, Chrys. and sim. the other Greek commentators; comp. Æth. 'ductorem nostrum,' and see notes on ch. ii. 18. The transitive meaning there advocated is appy. a little less certain in the present case, on account of the union with the intrans. παῤῥ.; still both lexical authority and the preceding ref. to our Lord seem to require and justify it; comp. Suicer, *Thesaur.* s. v. Vol. II. p. 850. How 'the use of the article before both nouns signalizes them as the *twin* elements of an unique privilege' (Eadie), is not clear; see, on the contrary, Winer, *Gr.* § 19. 5, p. 117. *Lachm.* omits the second art., with AB; 2 mss.; but in opp. to CDE (D¹E τὴν προσ. κ. τ. παῤῥ.) FG (FG τὴν προσ. εἰς τ. παῤῥ.) KL; nearly all mss.; Ath., Chrys., Theod., al., — authority distinctly preponderant. ἐν πεποιθήσει] 'in confidence,' μετὰ τοῦ θαῤῥεῖν, Chrys., — a noble example of which is afforded by St. Paul himself in the sublime words of Rom. viii. 38, 39 (Mey.). The present clause does not qualify προσαγωγή ('no 'timorous approach,' Eadie), but the predication of *manner,* and defines the tone and frame of mind ('alacriter libenterque, Calv.) in which the προσαγωγὴ is enjoyed and realized. Thus, then, ἐν Χρ. marks the objective ground of the possession, διὰ τῆς πίστ. the subjective medium *by which,* and ἐν πεποιθ. the subjective state *in which* it is apprehended; 'tres itaque gradus sunt faciendi, nam primum Dei promissionibus credimus, deinde his acquiescentes concipimus fiduciam ut bono simus tranquilloque animo : hinc sequitur audacia, quæ facit, ut, profligato metu, intrepide et constanter nos Deo commendemus,' Calv. Πεποίθησις (2 Kings xviii. 19) is only used in the N. T. by St. Paul (2 Cor. i. 15, iii. 4, viii. 22, x. 2, Phil. iii. 4), and is a word of

καὶ τὴν προσαγωγὴν ἐν πεποιϑήσει διὰ τῆς πίστεως αὐτοῦ. ¹³ διὸ
αἰτοῦμαι μὴ ἐγκακεῖν ἐν ταῖς ϑλίψεσίν μου ὑπὲρ ὑμῶν, ἥτις ἐστὶν
δόξα ὑμῶν.

later Greek; see Eustath. *on Odyss.* III.
p. 114. 41, Lobeck, *Phryn.* p. 294 sq.
πίστεως αὐτοῦ] '*faith on Him;*'
gen. *objecti*, virtually equivalent to πίστ.
εἰς αὐτόν; see Rom. iii. 22, Gal. ii. 16,
and compare notes *in loc.* It is doubtful
whether the deeper meaning which Stier
(compare Matth.) finds in the words, sc.
'faith of which Christ is not only the
object, but the ground,' can here be fully
substantiated. On the whole verse, see
three posthumous sermons of South,
Serm. XXIX. sq. Vol. IV. p. 413 sq.
(Tegg).

13. διό] '*On which account,*' '*wherefore,*' sc., since my charge is so important and our spiritual privileges so
great; διότι μέγα τὸ μυστήριον τῆς κλήσεως ἡμῶν, καὶ μεγάλα ἃ ἐνεπιστεύϑην
ἔγω, Theoph. The reference of this
particle has been very differently explained. Estius and Meyer, with some
plausibility, connect it simply with the
preceding verse, — 'cum igitur, ad tan-
tam dignitatem vocati sitis, ejusque con-
sequendæ fiduciam habeatis per Christum; rogo vos, etc.,' Est. As, however,
ver. 8—11 contain the principal thought
to which ver. 12 is only subordinate and
supplementary, the former alluding to
the *nature* and *dignity* of the Apostle's
commission, the latter to its *effects*
and *results*, in which both he and his
converts (ἔχομεν) share, the particle
will much more naturally refer to the
whole paragraph. The union of the
Apostle's own interests and those of his
converts in the following words then
becomes natural and appropriate. The
use of διό by St. Paul is too varied to
enable us safely to adduce any grammatical considerations; see notes *on Gal.* iv.
31. αἰτοῦμαι μὴ ἐγκακεῖν]
'*I entreat you not to lose heart;*' ὑμᾶς

(Æth.) not τὸν Θεόν (Theod.) being supplied after the verb; comp. 2 Cor. v. 20,
Heb. xiii. 19 (2 Cor. vi. 1, x. 2, cited by
De W., are less appropriate), where a
similar supplement is required. Such
constructions as 'I pray (God) that ye
lose not heart,' or 'that I lose not heart'
(Syr.), are both open to the objection
that the object of the verb and subject of
the inf. (both unexpressed) are thus
made different without sufficient reason.
Moreover, such a prayer as that in the
latter interpretation would here fall
strangely indeed from the lips of the
great Apostle who had learnt in his sufferings to rejoice (Col. i. 24), and in his
very weakness to find ground for boasting; compare 2 Cor. xi. 30, xii. 5. On
the form ἐγκακεῖν, not ἐκκακεῖν, see notes
on Gal. vi. 9. ἐν ταῖς ϑλίψε-
σιν κ. τ. λ.] '*in my tribulations for you,*'
'in (not 'ob,' Beza) tribulationibus meis,'
Clarom., Vulg.; ἐν as usual denoting
the *sphere*, as it were, in which the faint-
heartedness of the Ephesians might possibly be shown; see Winer, *Gr.* § 48. a,
p. 345. So close was their bond of
union in Christ, that the Apostle felt his
afflictions were theirs; they might be
faint-hearted in his, as if they were their
own. The article is not necessary before
ὑπέρ, as ϑλίψεσι can be considered in
structural union with ὑπὲρ ὑμῶν; comp.
ϑλίβεσϑαι ὑπέρ τινος, 2 Cor. i. 6; see
notes, ch. i. 15. ἥτις ἐστὶ δόξα
ὑμῶν] '*inasmuch as it is your glory;*'
reason (ὑμετέρα γὰρ δόξα κ. τ. λ. Theod.),
or rather explanation why they were not
to be faint-hearted; the indef. relative
being here explanatory (compare i. 23,
notes *on Gal.* iv. 24, and Hartung, *Casus*,
p. 286), and referring to ϑλίψεσιν on the
common principle of attraction by which
the relative assumes the gender of the

On this account (I say) I pray to God the Father to give you strength within, and teach you the incomprehensible love of Christ, and fill you with God's fulness.

^{14} Τούτου χάριν κάμπτω τὰ γόνατά μου πρὸς τὸν Πατέρα, ^{15} ἐξ οὗ πᾶσα πατριὰ ἐν οὐρανοῖς

predicate; see Winer, *Gr.* § 24. 3, p. 150, Madvig, *Synt.* § 98. The way in which St. Paul's tribulations could be said to tend to the glory of the Ephesians is simply but satisfactorily explained by Chrys.; ὅτι οὕτως αὐτοὺς ἠγάπησεν ὁ Θεός, ὥστε καὶ τὸν υἱὸν ὑπὲρ αὐτῶν δοῦναι καὶ τοὺς δούλους κακοῦν. ἵνα γὰρ οὗτοι τύχωσι τοσούτων ἀγαθῶν [see ver. 8] Παῦλος ἐδεσμεῖτο. The personal reason, 'quod doctorem habetis qui nullis calamitatibus frangitur' Calixt. (compare Theod.), in which case ἥτις must refer to μὴ ἐκκακεῖν, seems wholly out of the question. Glory accrued to the Ephesians from the official dignity, not the personal fortitude (καρτερία, Theod.) of the sufferer.

14. τούτου χάριν] 'On this account,' sc., 'because ye are so called and so built together in Christ,' resumption of ver. 1 (ταῦτα πάντα ἐν μέσῳ τεθεικώς, ἀναλαμβάνει τὸν περὶ προσευχῆς λόγον, Theod.); τούτου χάριν referring to the train of thought at the end of ch. ii., and to the ideas parallel to it in the digression; in brief, ἐπειδὴ οὕτως ἠγαπήθητε παρὰ Θεοῦ, Œcum. κάμπτω τὰ γόνατα κ. τ. λ.] '*I bend my knees (in prayer) to*;' expression indicative of the earnestness and fervency of his prayer; τὴν μετὰ κατανύξεως δέησιν ἐσήμανε, Theoph., comp. Chrys. Κάμπτειν γόνυ (usually κ. ἐπὶ γόνυ in the LXX) is joined with the dat. in its simple sense (Rom. xi. 4, xiv. 11, both quotations), but here, in the metaphorical sense of προσεύχεσθαι, is appropriately joined with πρὸς to denote the object towards whom (as it were) the knees were bowed, — the mental *direction* of the prayer; see Winer, *Gr.* § 49. h, p. 360. On the posture of kneeling in prayer, see Bingham, *Antiq.* XIII. 8. 4, and esp. Suicer,

Thesaur. Vol. i. p. 777. The interpolation, after πατέρα, of the words τοῦ Κυρίου ἡμῶν Ἰ. Χ., though undoubtedly ancient, and well supported [DEFGKL; nearly all mss.; Syr., Vulg., Goth., al.; Chrys., Theod., al.], is rightly rejected in favor of the text [ABC; 2 mss.; Demid., Copt., Æth. (both), al.; Orig., Cyr., al.] by nearly all modern editors except De Wette and Eadie.

15. ἐξ οὗ] '*from whom*,' '*after whom*;' ἐκ pointing to the *origin* or *source* whence the name was derived; see notes *on Gal.* ii. 16, and compare Xen. *Mem.* IV. 5. 8, ἔφη δὲ καὶ τὸ διαλέγεσθαι ὀνομασθῆναι ἐκ τοῦ συνιόντας κοινῇ βουλεύεσθαι, Hom. *Il.* x. 68, πατρόθεν ἐκ γενεῆς ὀνομάζων. Less direct origination is expressed by ἀπό; comp. ὀνομαζ. ἀπό, Herod. VI. 129. πᾶσα πατριά] '*every race, family*,' not 'the whole family,' Auth.; see Middleton *in loc.*, p. 361 (ed. Rose). The use of the particular term πατριά is evidently suggested by the preceding πατέρα (πατ. ἐξ οὗ πᾶσα πατριά), its exact *meaning*, however, and still more its present *reference*, are both very debatable. With regard to the first it may be said that πατριὰ does not imply (*a*) 'paternitas,' Syr., Vulg., al. (κυρίως πατήρ, καὶ ἀληθῶς πατὴρ ὁ Θεός, Theod., compare Tholuck, *Bergpr.* p. 394), a translation neither defensible in point of etymology or exegesis, but is either used in (*b*) the more limited sense of 'familia' (*metiôt*, Copt., compare Arm.), or more probably (*c*) that of the more inclusive '*gens*' (Heb. מִשְׁפָּחָה, less commonly בֵּית אָבוֹת, compare Gesen. *Lex.* s. v. בַּ֫יִת, 10); see Herod. I. 200, εἰσί τῶν Βαβυλωνίων πατριαὶ τρεῖς, and compare Acts iii. 25 with Gen. xii. 3, where πατριὰ and φυλὴ are interchanged. If, then, as seems most correct, we adopt this more inclusive

καὶ ἐπὶ γῆς ὀνομάζεται, ¹⁶ ἵνα δῴη ὑμῖν κατὰ τὸ πλοῦτος τῆς

meaning, the *reference* must be to those larger classes and communities into which, as we may also infer from other passages (comp. ch. i. 21, notes, Col. i. 16, notes), the celestial hosts appear to be divided, and to the races and tribes of men ('quæque regionum,' Æth.), every one of which owes the very title of πατριὰ, by which it is defined, to the great Πατὴρ of all the πατριαὶ both of angels and men; this title οὐκ ἀφ' ἡμῶν ἀνῆλθεν ἄνω, ἀλλ' ἄνωθεν ἦλθεν εἰς ἡμᾶς, Severian ap. Cramer, *Caten. (in loc.);* see Schoettg. *Hor.* Vol. ɪ. p. 1238, and Suicer, *Thesaur.* s. v. Vol. ɪɪ. p. 637. ὀνομάζεται is thus taken in its simple etymological sense, '*is named, bears the name,*' scil. of πατριά; 'dicitur,' Copt., al., 'namnajada,' Goth.; see Mey. *in loc.* All special interpolations, e. g. 'nominantur *filii Dei,*' (Beng., compare Beza), or arbitrary interpretations, of ὀνομαζ, e. g., 'existit, originem accipit' (Estius, al.; comp. Rück.), — meanings which even καλεῖσθαι (Eadie) never *directly* bears, — are wholly inadmissible.

16. ἵνα δῴη] '*that He would give to you;*' subject of the prayer being blended with the *purpose* of making it; see notes on ch. i. 17, where the unusual form δῴη is also briefly discussed. The reading is here somewhat doubtful. *Lachm.* adopts δῷ with ABCFG; 3 mss.; Orig. (*Cat.*), Bas., Method., al. (*Tisch.* ed. 1, *Rück., Mey.*), but perhaps not rightly, as it seems much more probable that δῷ was a grammatical correction of δῴη, than that δῴη was a correction of δῷ arising from a remembrance of ch. i. 17. We retain then the rarer form, δῴη, with DEJK; great majority of mss.; Ath., Mac., Chrysost., Theod., al. So *Rec., Tisch.,* (ed. 2, 7), Harl., De W., and most recent editors. κατὰ τὸ πλοῦτος κ. τ. λ.] '*according to the riches of His glory,*' according

to the abundance and plenitude of His own perfections; see notes on ch. i. 7. δυνάμει] '*with power,*' 'with (infused) strength;' 'ut virtute seu fortitudine ab eo acceptâ corroboremini,' Estius. This dative has been differently explained; it cannot be (*a*) the dat of 'reference to' or, more correctly speaking, of 'ethical locality' (see notes *on Gal.* i. 22, and exx. in Krüger, *Sprachl.* § 48. 15, *e. g.* χρήμασι δυνατοὶ εἶναι, etc.), for it was not one particular faculty, *power* as opp. to *knowledge,* etc., but the whole 'inner man,' which was to be strengthened. Harl. cites Acts iv. 33, but the example is inapplicable. Nor again (*b*) does it appear used adverbially (dat. of *manner,* Jelf, *Gr.* § 603. 2), for this, though a more plausible interpr. (see Rück.), is open to the objection of directing the thought to the strengthener rather than to the subject in whom strength is to be infused; see Meyer *in loc.* It is thus more correctly regarded as (*c*) the simple *instrumental* dat. (Arm.) defining the element or influence of which the Spirit is the 'causa medians;' comp. ἐν δυνάμει, Col. i. 11. εἰς τὸν ἔσω ἄνθρωπον] '*into the inner man;*' direction and destination of the prayed-for gift of infused strength; the clause being obviously connected with κραταιωθ. (Vulg., Goth., — appy.) not with κατοικῆσαι (Syr., Copt., Æth., and Gr. Ff.), and εἰς not being for ἐν (Beza), nor even in its more lax sense, 'in regard of' (Mey.; comp. Winer, *Gr.* § 49. a, p. 354), but in its more literal and expressive sense of '*to and into;*' 'the inner man' is the recipient of it (ὁ χωρῶν, Schol. ap. Cram. *Caten.*), the subject 'into whom' the δύναμις is infused; compare notes *on Gal.* iii. 27. The expression ὁ ἔσω ἄνθρ. (Rom. vii. 22) is nearly identical with, but somewhat more inclusive than ὁ κρυπτὸς τῆς καρδίας ἄνθρωπος (1 Pet.

δόξης αὐτοῦ δυνάμει κραταιωϑῆναι διὰ τοῦ Πνεύματος αὐτοῦ εἰς τὸν ἔσω ἄνϑρωπον, ¹⁷ κατοικῆσαι τὸν Χριστὸν διὰ τῆς πίστεως

iii. 4), and stands in antithesis to ὁ ἔξω ἄνϑρωπος (2 Cor. iv. 16); the former being practically equivalent to the νοῦς, or higher nature of man (Rom. vii. 23), the latter to the σάρξ or the μέλη; see Beck, *Seelenl.* III. 21. 3, p. 68. It is within this ἔσω ἄνϑρωπος that the powers of regeneration are exercised (Harless, *Christl. Ethik*, § 22. a), and it is from their operation in this province that the whole man ('secundum interna spectatus,' Beng.) becomes a νέος ἄνϑρωπος (as opp. to a former state), or a καινὸς ἄνϑρωπος (as opp. to a former corrupt state, ch. iv. 24), and is either ὁ κατὰ Θεὸν κτισϑείς (ch. iv. 24), or ὁ ἀνακαινούμενος εἰς ἐπίγνωσιν κατ᾽ εἰκόνα τοῦ κτίσαντος αὐτόν (Col. iii. 10), according to the point of view under which regeneration is regarded; see Harless, *Ethik*, § 24. c. The distinction between this and the partially synonymous terms πνεῦμα, and νοῦς, may perhaps be thus roughly stated: πνεῦμα is simply the highest of the three parts of which man is composed (see notes *on* 1 *Thess.* v. 23); νοῦς the πνεῦμα regarded more in its *moral* and *intellectual* aspects, 'quatenus intelligit, cogitat, et vult' (see notes *on Phil.* iv. 7); ὁ ἔσω ἄνϑρ., the πνεῦμα, or rather the whole immaterial portion, considered in its *theological* aspects, and as the seat of the inworking powers of grace; compare Olsh. *on Rom.* vii. 22, *Opusc. Theol.* p. 143 sq., Beck, *Seelenl.* II. 13, p. 35, and on the threefold nature of man generally, *University Serm.* v. p. 99—120. The attempt to connect St. Paul's inspired definitions with the terminology of earlier (ὁ ἐντὸς ἄνϑρ. Plato, *Republ.* IX. 589), or of later Platonism (ὁ ἔνδον ἄνϑρ. Plot. *Ennead.* I. 1. 10), as in Fritz. *Rom.* Vol. II. 63, will be found on examination to be untena-

ble. The dissimilarities are marked, the supposed parallelisms illusory.

17. κατοικῆσαι τὸν Χρ.] 'that Christ may dwell in your hearts;' issue and result (ὥστε κατοικῆσαι, Orig.), not purpose (Eadie), of the inward strengthening; the present clause not being parallel to δυνάμει κραταιωϑ. (Mey.), and dependent on δῷη, but as the emphatic position of κατοικῆσαι seems clearly to show, appended to κραταιωϑῆναι with a partially climactic force, but a somewhat lax grammatical connection; see Winer, *Gr.* § 44. 1, p. 284, compare Madvig, *Synt.* § 153. The meaning is thus perfectly clear and simple; the indwelling of Christ, the taking up of His *abode* [κατοικῆσαι, Matth. xii. 45, Luke xi. 26, Col. i. 19 (see notes), 2 Pet. iii. 13; the simple form is, however, used, Rom. viii. 9, 1 Cor. iii. 16] is the result of the working of the Holy Spirit on the one side, and the subjective reception of man (διὰ τῆς πίστ.) on the other; 'non procul intuendum esse Christum fide, sed recipiendum esse animæ nostræ complexu,' Calv. τὸν Χριστόν] The attempt of Fritz. (*Rom.* viii. 10, Vol. II. p. 118) to show that Χριστὸς is here merely 'mens quam Christus postulat,' by comparing such passages as Arist. *Acharn.* 484, καταπιὼν Εὐριπίδην, is as painful as it is unconvincing. What a contrast is the vital exegesis of Chrys., πῶς δὲ ὁ Χρ. κατοικεῖ ἐν ταῖς καρδίαις, ἄκουε αὐτοῦ λέγοντος τοῦ Χριστοῦ, Ἐλευσόμεϑα ἐγὼ καὶ ὁ πατήρ, καὶ μονὴν παρ᾽ αὐτῷ ποιήσομεν. ἐν ταῖς καρδίαις] 'in your hearts;' 'partem etiam designat ubi legitima est Christi sedes, nempe cor: ut sciamus non satis esse si in linguà versetur, aut in cerebro volitet,' Calv. On the meaning of καρδία (properly the imaginary seat of the

ἐν ταῖς καρδίαις ὑμῶν, ¹⁸ ἐν ἀγάπῃ ἐρριζωμένοι καὶ τεθεμελιωμέ-

ψυχή, and thence the seat and centre of the moral life viewed on the side of the *affections*), see Delitzsch, *Bibl. Psychol.* IV. 11, p. 203 sq., and notes *on Phil.* iv. 7.

18. ἐν ἀγάπῃ ἐρρ. καὶ τεθ.] '*ye having been rooted and grounded in love*;' state consequent on the indwelling of Christ, viz., one of fixedness and foundation in love, the participle reverting irregularly to the nominative for the sake of making the transition to the following clause more easy and natural: δοκεῖ μοι σαφῶς τὰ ἑξῆς ἐν σολοικίῳ εἰρῆσθαι, ὡς πρὸς τὴν φράσιν. πρὸς γὰρ τὸ δόφη ὑμῖν,' ἀκόλουθον ἦν εἰπεῖν ἐρριζωμένοις καὶ τεθεμελιωμένοις .... ὁ δὲ θέλων ἀποκαταστῆσαι τὰ κατὰ τὸν τόπον χωρὶς σολοικίας, σκέψαι εἰ μὴ βιάσεται οὕτω τὴν φράσιν ἀποκοτασστάς, Origen ap. Cramer, *Caten.* The assumed transposition of ἵνα (ἵνα ἐρρ. καὶ τεθ. ἐξισχ., Auth., Mey., — but adopted by none of the ancient Vv. except Goth.), which Origen thus properly rejects, cannot be justified by any necessity for emphasis, or by the passages adduced by Fritz (*Rom.* xi. 31, Vol. II. p. 541), viz. Acts xix. 4, John xiii. 29, 1 Cor. ix. 15, 2 Cor. ii. 4, Gal. ii. 10, 2 Thess. ii. 7, as in all of them (except Thess. *l. c.*, which is not analogous) the premised words are not, as here, connected with the subject, but form the objective factor of the sentence. The only argument of any real weight against the proposed interpr. is not so much *syntactic* (for see the numerous exx. of similar irregularities in Winer, *Gr.* § 63. 2, p. 620, Krüger, *Sprachl.* § 56. 9. 4) as *exegetical*, it being urged that the *perf.* part. which points to a completed state is inconsistent with a prayer which seems to refer to a state of progress, and to require the *present* part. (see Meyer). The answer, however, seems satisfactory, — that the clause *does*

express the *state* which must ensue upon the indwelling of Christ, before what is expressed in the next clause (ἵνα ἐξισχ.) can in any way be realized, and that therefore the perf. part. is perfectly correct. The Apostle prays that they may be strengthened, that the *result* of it may be the indwelling of Christ, the state naturally consequent on which would be fixedness in the principle of Christian love. We now notice the separate words. ἐν ἀγάπῃ] '*in love*,' — not either of Christ (compare Chrysost. ἀγάπη αὐτοῦ) or of God (Wolf), either of which references would certainly have required some defining gen., but the Christian principle of love, — love, ἥτις ἐστὶ σύνδεσμος τῆς τελειότητος, Col. iii. 4. This was to be their basis and foundation, in which alone they were to be fully enabled to realize all the majestic proportions of Christ's surpassing love to man; comp. 1 John iv. 7 sq. The absence of the article is unduly pressed both by Meyer (= 'in amando') and Harl. ('*subjective*' love,' ' man's love to Christ'), such omissions in the case of abstract nouns, esp. when preceded by prepp., being not uncommon in the N. T.; see exx. Winer, *Gr.* § 19. 1, p. 109, and comp. Middleton, *Greek Art.* VI. 1, p. 98 (ed. Rose). ἐρριζ. καὶ τεθεμ.] It has been said that there is here a mixture of metaphors; compare Olsh., Meyer, al. This is not strictly true; ῥιζόω is abundantly used both with an ethical (Herod. I. 64, Plutarch, *Mor.* 6 E) and a physical (Hom. *Od.* XIII. 163) reference, without any other allusion to its primitive meaning, than that of *fixedness, firmness*, at the *base* or *foundation*; see exx. in Rost. u. Palm, *Lex.* s. v. Vol. II. p. 1337, and Wetst. *in loc.* ἵνα ἐξισχύσητε] '*in order that ye may be fully able*;' object contemplated in the prayer for Christ's

νοι, ἵνα ἐξισχύσητε καταλαβέσθαι σὺν πᾶσιν τοῖς ἁγίοις, τί τὸ
πλάτος καὶ μῆκος καὶ βάθος καὶ ὕψος, 19 *γνῶναί τε τὴν ὑπερβάλ-*

indwelling in their hearts, and their consequent fixedness in love; ' ἐξισχύσ.' φησίν· ὥστε ἰσχύος πολλῆς δεῖ, Chrys.; comp. Ecclus. vii. 6, μὴ οὐκ ἐξισχύσεις ἐξᾶραι ἀδικίας.　καταλαβέσθαι] 'to comprehend;' the tense perhaps implying the singleness of the act (see exx. Winer, *Gr.* § 44. 7, p. 296, but see notes on ver. 4), and the voice the exercise of the mental power; see esp. Donalds. *Gr.* § 432. bb, where this is termed the *appropriative* middle, and Krüger, *Sprachl.* § 52. 8. 1 sq., where it is termed the *dynamic* middle, as indicating the earnestness or spiritual energy with which the action is performed. The meaning of the verb (κατανοεῖσθαι Hesych.) can scarcely be doubtful; the meaning 'occupare' (compare Goth. 'gafahan,' Coptic *taho*) adopted by Kypke (*Obs.* Vol. ii. p. 294), and supported only by one proper example, is here plainly untenable, as the middle voice only occurs in the N. T. in reference to the mental powers; comp. Acts iv. 13, x. 34, xxv. 25.　τί τὸ πλάτος κ. τ. λ.] '*what is the breadth, and length, and depth, and height;*' certainly not 'latitudinem quandam, etc.' Kypke (*Obs.* Vol. ii. p. 294), such a use of τί implying a transposition, and assigning a meaning here singularly improbable. The exact force and application of these words is somewhat doubtful. Without noticing the various spiritual applications (see Corn. a Lap., and Pol. *Syn. in loc.*) all of which seem more or less arbitrary, it may be said (1) that St. Paul is here expressing the idea of greatness, metaphysically considered, by the ordinary dimensions of space; διὰ γὰρ τοῦ μήκ. καὶ πλ. καὶ βάθ. καὶ ὕψ. τὸ μέγεθος παρεδήλωσεν· ἐπειδὴ ταῦτα μεγέθους δηλωτικά, Theod. It is, however, more difficult (2) to specify *what it is* of

which this greatness and dimensions are predicated. Setting again aside all arbitrary references (ἡ τοῦ σταυροῦ φύσις, Orig., Sever., 'contemplatio Ecclesiæ,' Beng., Eadie), we seem left to a choice between a reference to (a) ἡ ἀγάπη τοῦ Θεοῦ πῶς πανταχοῦ ἐκτέταται, Chrysost., τῆς χάριτος τὸ μέγεθος, Theod.-Mops.; or (b) ἡ ἀγάπη τοῦ Χρ., Calv., Mey. If the preceding ἀγάπη had referred to the love of God, (a) would have seemed most probable; as it does not, and as its general meaning *there* would be inapplicable *here*, (b) seems the most natural explanation. Thus then the consequent clause, without being dependent or explanatory, still practically supplies the defining gen.: St. Paul pauses on the word ὕψος, and then, perhaps feeling it the most appropriate characteristic of Christ's love, he appends, without finishing the construction, a parallel thought which hints at the same conception (ὑπερβάλλουσαν), and suggests the required genitive. The order βάθος κ. ὕψος, has only the support of AKL; most mss.; Syr.-Phil.; Orig., Chrys., Theod., al. (*Tisch., Meyer, Alf.*); but is appy. rightly maintained, even in opp. to BCDEFG; mss.; Vulg., Clarom., Syr., Goth., Copt.; Ath., Maced. (*Rec., Lachm.*) which adopt the more natural, and for this very reason, the more suspicious order.

19. γνῶναί τε] '*and to know;*' supplemental clause to καταλαβέσθαι κ. τ. λ., the former referring to the comprehensive knowledge of essentials (Olsh.), the latter further specifying the practical knowledge arising from religious experience. It may be remarked, that though the union of sentences by τε is characteristic of later Greek, (Bernhardy, *Synt.* xx. 17, p. 483), it is comparatively rare in the Gospels. In the Epistles, but most

λουσαν τῆς γνώσεως ἀγάπην τοῦ Χριστοῦ, ἵνα πληρωθῆτε εἰς πᾶν
τὸ πλήρωμα τοῦ Θεοῦ.

especially in the Acts, it is of more
common occurrence. Τε is to be distinguished from καὶ as being *adjunctive*
rather than *conjunctive ;* like 'que,' it
appends to the foregoing clause (which
is to be conceived as having a separate
and independent existence, Jelf, *Gr.* §
754. 6), an additional, and, very frequently, a ‧ new thought ; — a thought
which, though not necessary to (Herm.
Viger, No. 315), is yet often supplemental to, and partially involved in the
first clause; comp. Acts ii. 23, Heb. i. 3,
and see Winer, *Gr.* § 57. 3, p. 517
(ed. 5).   τ ὴ ν ὑ π ε ρ β ά λ λ. τ ῆ s
γ ν ώ σ ε ω s ἀ γ.] '*the knowledge-surpass-
ing love ;*' the gen. γνώσεως being due to
the notion of comparison involved in
ὑπερβάλλειν ; comp. Æsch. *Prom.* 944,
βροντῆς ὑπερβάλλοντα κτύπον, Arist. *Pol.*
III. 9, and see Jelf, *Gr.* § 504, Bernhardy, *Synt.* III. 48. b, p. 169. The
words can scarcely be twisted into meaning 'the exceeding love of God in be-
stowing on us the knowledge of Christ'
(Dobree, *Advers.* Vol. I. p. 573), nor
can the participle ὑπερβ. be explained in
an *infinitival* sense, ' to know that the
love of Christ is ἀνεξιχνίαστον' (comp.
Harl.), — a translation untenable in point
of grammar (Winer, *Gr.* § 45. 4, note,
p. 309), and unsatisfactory in exegesis,
— but, as its position shows, must be
regarded as simply *adjectival.* The sentence then contains an oxymoron or
apparent paradox (comp. 1 Cor. i. 21,
25, 2 Cor. viii. 2, Gal. ii. 19, 1 Tim. v.
6), thus simply and satisfactorily explained by Chrysost. (ed. Savile) and
Œcum., εἰ καὶ ὑπερκεῖται πάσης γνώσεως
ἀνθρωπίνης [this is too restricted] ἡ ἀγάπη
τοῦ Χρ. ὅμως ὑμεῖς γνώσεσθε εἰ τὸν Χρ.
σχοίητε ἐνοικοῦντα : comp. Theophylact.
Γνῶναι is thus contrasted with γνῶσις ;
the *former* being that knowledge which

arises from the depths of religious experience (τὸ γνῶναι ἀντὶ τοῦ ἀπολαῦσαι
λέγει, Theod.-Mops.), the knowledge
that is ever allied with love (Phil. i. 9) ;
the *latter* abstract knowledge, not merely
ἀνθρωπίνη (Chrys.), and most certainly
not ψευδώνυμος (Holzh.), but knowledge
without reference to religious consciousness or Christian love; comp. 1 Cor.
viii. 1 sq., xiii. 8.   ἀ γ ά π η ν τ ο ῦ
Χ ρ.] '*love of Christ* towards us ;' gen.
subjecti ; not 'love for Christ,' 1 John ii.
5, 15.   ἵ ν α π λ η ρ ώ θ η τ ε κ. τ. λ.]
'*that ye may be filled to all the fulness of
God ;*' object and purpose of ἐξισχύειν
καταλαβέσθαι : ὥστε πληροῦσθαι πάσης
ἀρετῆς ἧς πλήρης ἐστίν ὁ Θεός, Chrysost.
(ed. Sav.). There is some little difficulty in these words, arising from the
ambiguity of the meaning of πλήρωμα.
If we adhere (a) to the more strict meaning, 'id quo res impletur' (see Fritz.
Rom. Vol. II. p. 469 sq., notes *on Gal.*
iv. 4), the words must imply 'that ye
may be so filled as God is filled' (Olsh.),
τοῦ Θεοῦ being the *possessive* gen., and τὸ
πλήρ. referring, not to the essence, still
less to the δόξα (Harl.), but to the *spiritual perfections* of God. Owing to the
somewhat obvious objection, that such a
fulness could never be completely realized in this present state of human im-
perfection (1 Cor. xiii. 10 sq.), De W.
and Mey. adopt (b) the secondary meaning of πλήρωμα, scil. πλοῦτος, πλῆθος
(see Fritz. *Rom.* Vol. II. p. 471), the
translation being either, ' ut pleni fiatis
usque eo ut omnes Dei opes animis vestris recipiatis' (Fritz. *ib.*), or ' ut omnibus Dei donis abundetis' (Est.), according as Θεοῦ is regarded more as a
possessive gen. ; or as a gen. of the *originating* cause (notes on 1 *Thess.* i. 6).
Both these latter interpretations are,
however so frigid and so little in har-

Doxology.   ²⁰ Τῷ δὲ δυναμένῳ ὑπὲρ πάντα ποιῆσαι ὑπερεκπερισσοῦ ὧν αἰτούμεθα ἢ νοοῦμεν, κατὰ τὴν δύναμιν τὴν ἐνερ-
γουμένην ἐν ἡμῖν, ²¹ αὐτῷ ἡ δόξα ἐν τῇ ἐκκλησίᾳ ἐν Χριστῷ

mony with the climactic character of the passage (δυν. κρατ. διὰ τοῦ Πν . . . . . κατοικ. Χρ . . . . . . ἵνα πληρωθ. εἰς πᾶν τὸ πλήρ. τοῦ Θεοῦ), and the apparently well considered use of εἰς (not ἐν instrumental or an ablatival dat.), that we do not hesitate to adopt (a), and urge, with Olsh., that where Christ the living Son of God dwells, there surely πᾶν τὸ πλήρ. τοῦ Θεοῦ is already; comp. Col. ii. 19.

εἰς πᾶν τὸ πλήρ.] 'to all the fulness;' 'in omnem plenitudinem,' Clarom., Vulgate; εἰς not implying 'accordance to' (Eadie), but with its usual and proper force, denoting the end (here quantitatively considered), or limit of the πλήρωσις; see Rost u. Palm, Lex. s. v. εἰς, III., Vol. I. p. 803, compare Bernhardy, Synt. v. 11. b, p. 218.

20. τῷ δὲ δυναμένῳ] 'Now to Him that is able;' concluding doxology, not without some antithesis (δὲ) between Him who is the subject of the present verse, and the finite beings who are the subjects of the preceding verses.

ὑπὲρ πάντα ποιῆσαι] 'to do (effect, complete) beyond all things;' 'periphrasis Dei Patris emphatica,' Vorst. That ὑπὲρ cannot here be taken adverbially seems almost self-evident; the order would thus be needlessly artificial and the sentence tautologous; comp. Winer, Gr. § 50. 7. 2, p. 376. ὑπερεκπερισσοῦ ὧν κ. τ. λ.] 'superabundantly beyond what we ask or think;' second member explanatory of the preceding, ὧν not referring to πάντα, but forming with αἰτούμ. and νοοῦμ. a fresh and more specific subject: ὅρα δὲ δύο ὑπερβολάς. τὸ ὑπὲρ πάντα ποιῆσαι τὰ εἰρημένα, καὶ ὑπερεκπερισσοῦ ποιῆσαι ἃ ποιεῖ. ἔνι γὰρ καὶ πλείονα ποιοῦντα τῶν αἰτηθέντων κεφάλαια, μὴ πλουσίως μήτε δαψιλῶς ἕκαστον ποιῆσαι, Œcum. The cumula-

tive compound ὑπερεκ. occurs 1 Thess. iii. 10 (comp. notes) v. 13, and belongs to a class of compounds (those with ὑπέρ), for which the Apostle seems to have had a somewhat marked predilection; compare ὑπερνικάω, Rom. viii. 37; ὑπερπερισσεύω, Rom. v. 20, 2 Cor. vii. 4; ὑπερλίαν, ib. xi. 5; ὑπερυψόω, Phil. ii. 9; ὑπεραυξάνω, 2 Thess. i. 3; ὑπερπλεονάζω, 1 Tim. i. 14; and see Fritz. Rom. v. 20, Vol. I. p. 351. It is noticeable that ὑπὲρ occurs nearly thrice as many times in St. Paul's Epp. and the Ep. to the Heb. as in the rest of the N. T., and that, with a few exceptions (Mark vii. 37, Luke vi. 38, etc.), the compounds of ὑπὲρ are all found in St. Paul's Epp. The gen. ὧν is governed by ὑπερεκπ. as γνώσεως by ὑπερβάλλουσαν, ver. 19; comp. Bernh. Synt. III. 34, p. 139 sq. αἰτούμεθα ἢ νοοῦμεν] 'we ask or think;' not only the requests we actually prefer, but all that it might enter into the mind to conceive; 'cogitatio latius patet quam preces' Bengel; comp. Phil. iv. 7. τὴν ἐνεργ. ἐν ἡμῖν] 'which worketh in us, sc. in our souls', 'quæ operatur in nobis,' Clarom., Vulg.; ἐνεργ. not being here passive (Hamm., Bull, Exam. II. 3), but middle (Syr., Goth., Æth., Arm.), as in Gal. v. 6, where see notes. On the constructions of ἐνεργέω, see notes on Gal. ii. 8, and on the distinction between the uses of act. (mainly in personal ref.) and middle (mainly in non-personal ref.), Winer, Gr. § 38. 6, p. 231. The δύναμις, which so energizes, is the power of the Holy Ghost; comp. ver. 16, Rom. viii. 26.

21. αὐτῷ] 'to Him;' rhetorical repetition of the pronoun, — not, however, in accordance with 'Hebrew usage' (Eadie), but in agreement with the sim-

'Ιησοῦ, εἰς πάσας τὰς γενεὰς τοῦ αἰῶνος τῶν αἰώνων· ἀμήν.

21. ἐν τῇ ἐκκλησίᾳ ἐν Χριστῷ 'Ιησοῦ] So *Tisch.* (ed. 2, 7), *Harl, De Wette, Mey.*, al., with D² [E, Χρ. 'I. ἐν τῇ ἐκκ.] KL; great majority of mss.; Goth., Syr. (both), al.; Chrys., Theod., Dam. (text), Theoph., Œcum.; Vig. The variations can be so satisfactorily accounted for that there seems little doubt that this is the true reading. Assuming it to be so, the preëminence due to Christ would first have suggested a change of order (compare E): the insertion of καὶ would have easily followed, as in D₁FG; Clarom., Sang., Aug., Boern.; Ambrst.; it would thus have acquired such a footing in the text, as to be maintained even when the right order was observed. We have hence the fairly attested, though appy. spurious, reading, ἐν τῇ ἐκκ. καὶ ἐν Χρ. 'I. in ABC; 73, 80, 213; Vulg., Copt., Arm.; Dam. (comm.); Hier., Pel. (*Lachm., Rückert.*).

ple principles of emphasis; see Bernh., *Synt.* vi. 11. c, p. 290.   ἡ δόξα] '*the glory* that is due to Him, and redounds to Him from such gracious dealings towards us;' see notes *on Gal.* i. 5. ἐν τῇ ἐκκλ. ἐν Χρ. 'Ιησ.] '*in the Church, in Christ Jesus;*' the first member denoting the outward province, the second the inward and spiritual sphere in which God was to be praised. The second member ἐν Χρ. 'Ιησ. is thus not for διὰ Χρ. (Theoph.), nor for σὺν Χρ. (Œcum.), but retains its proper meaning, specifying, not exactly the manner (De W.), but the true *element* in which alone praise was duly to be ascribed to God; 'if any glory come from us to God it is by [in] Christ,' Sanders (cited by Wordsw. *in loc.*). The ordinary explanation, 'the Church (which is) in Christ Jesus,' is objectionable, not so much on account of the absence of the article (for comp. 1 Thess. i. 1, 2 Thess. i. 1), as on account of the then appy. superfluous character of the words (the ἐκκλ. here mentioned could only be the Christian Church), which in our present interpr. echo the preceding τοῦ Χριστοῦ (ver. 19) with special and appropriate force; contrast Alf. *in loc.*, who still partially connects the two members; but comp. Syr., which by its omission of the relative here, and its insertion in Thess. *ll. cc.*, seems not obscurely to favor our

present view.   *Laehm.* and *Rück.* insert καὶ (καὶ ἐν Χρ. 'Ιησ.) with a fair amount of authority (see crit. note), — but contrary to critical probability; as the insertion of the copula seems more naturally due to emendation (observe the variations *in loc.*), than its omission to an error in transcription.   εἰς πάσας γενεάς κ. τ. λ.] '*to all the generations of the age of the ages;*' compare Dan. vii. 18, ἕως αἰῶνος τῶν αἰώνων, 3 Esdr. iv. 38, εἰς τὸν αἰῶνα τοῦ αἰῶνος, and see notes *on Gal.* i. 5. The cumulative expression is somewhat peculiar. It is not improbable, as Grotius suggests, that the two formulæ expressive of endless continuity, γενεαὶ γενεῶν, Luke i. 50, and αἰῶνες τῶν αἰώνων, are here blended together. The use of γενεαὶ suggests the use of the singular αἰών, as the conception of the successive generations composing the entirety of the αἰών is thus more clearly presented, while again the subjoined plural marks that αἰὼν as also composed of a series of αἰῶνες (gen. of the *content*) of which it is the sum and aggregation. Harless finds a difference between the two expressions αἰῶνες τῶν αἰώνων and αἰὼν τῶν αἰώνων, the former being rather *extensive*, and conveying the idea of πάντες αἰῶνες, the latter being rather *intensive*, 'sæculum sæculorum, quod omnia sæcula in se continet' (Drus.), and more strictly in accordance

Walk worthy of your voca-
tion in lowliness, in love,
and especially in unity;
there is but one body, one
Spirit, one Lord, and one God.

*IV. Παρακαλῶ οὖν ὑμᾶς ἐγὼ ὁ δέσμιος ἐν
Κυρίῳ, ἀξίως περιπατῆσαι τῆς κλήσεως ἧς*

with the Hebrew superlative. This is in-
genious, but appy. of doubtful application,
as in actual practice the difference between
the two expressions is hardly apprecia-
ble. Baur (*Paulus*, p. 433) finds in this
expression distinct traces of Gnosticism:
it is unnecessary to refute such utterly
foregone conclusions.

CHAPTER IV. 1. *παρακαλῶ οὖν*]
'*I exhort you then;*' commencement of
the practical portion of the Epistle
(comp. Rom. xii. 1), following naturally
and with an appropriate *retrospective*
reference (*οὖν*) to what has preceded;
οὕτως αὐτοῖς ἐπιδείξας τῆς θείας εὐεργεσίας τὸν πλοῦτον, ἐπὶ τὰ εἴδη προτρέπει
τῆς ἀρετῆς, Theod. The meaning of
παρακαλῶ will thus be both here and in
Rom. *l. c.* more naturally 'hortor'
(παρακ. τὸ προτρέπω, ὡς ἐπὶ τὸ πολύ,
Thom. M. p. 684, ed. Bern.) than 'obse-
cro,' (Clarom., Vulg., Arm., and most
Vv.), — a meaning which it sometimes
bears, but which would seem inapplicable
in the present context; see Fritz. *Rom.*
Vol. III. p. 4, and, for a general notice
of the word, Knapp, *Script. Var. Arg.*
p. 127 sq.; comp. also notes *on* 1 *Thess.*
v. 11.　　The *exact* reference of *οὖν*
is more doubtful; Meyer refers it to the
verse immediately preceding, Winzer
and Alford (*Rom. l. c.*) to the whole
doctrinal portion of the Ep.; the former
view, however, seems too narrow, the
latter too vague. The more natural ref.
is appy. to those passages in the preceding chap. which relate to the spiritual
privileges and calling of the Ephesians,
e. g. ver. 6, 12, but especially to 14 sq.,
in which the tenor of the prayer incidentally discloses how high and how
great that calling really was. On the
true force of this particle, see Klotz,

Devar. Vol. II. p. 117, Donalds. *Gr.*, §
548. 31, and comp. notes on *Phil.* ii. 1.
ὁ δέσμιος ἐν Κυρίῳ] '*the prisoner
in the Lord,*' *i. e.*, as paraphrased by
Fritz., 'ego vinctus in Christi castris;'
not παρακ. ἐν Κυρ., a construction at
variance both with the grammatical
order of the words, and the apparent
force of the exhortation; see Winer, *Gr.*
§ 20. 2, p. 123. St. Paul exhorts not
merely as the prisoner, but as the prisoner *in the Lord;* 'a vinculis majorem
sibi auctoritatem vindicat,' Calv.; comp.
Gal. vi. 17. Thus ἐν Κυρ. is not for διὰ
Κυρ. (Chrysost., Theod.), or σὺν Κυρ.
(Œcum.), but denotes the sphere in
which captivity existed, and out of which
it did not exist; 'in Domini enim vinculis constrictus est, qui ἐν Κυρίῳ ὤν vinctus est,' Fritz. *Rom.* viii. 1, Vol. II. p.
82 sq.; comp. notes *on Gal.* i. 24. The
distinction between this and ὁ δέσμ. τοῦ
Χρ., ch. iii. 1, seems to be that in the latter the captivity is referred immediately
to Christ as its author and originator, in
the former to the union with Him and
devotion to His service. It must be
conceded, that occasionally ἐν Κυρίῳ
appears little more than a kind of qualitative definition (comp. Rom. xvi. 8, 13,
1 Cor. iv. 17, Phil. i. 14, al.); still the
student cannot be too much put on his
guard against the frigid and even unspir-
itual interpretations into which Fritz.
has been betrayed in his elaborate note
(Rom. *l. c.* Vol. II. p. 82 sq.) on this
and the similar formula ἐν Χριστῷ.
On the nature of this union with
Christ compare Hooker, *Serm.* III. Vol.
III. p. 762.　　ἧς ἐκλήθητε]
'*wherewith ye were called,*' 'quâ vocati
estis,' Clarom., Vulg., Goth.; ἧς here
appy. standing for ᾗ (comp. 2 Tim. i. 9,
but not 1 Cor. vii. 20 [De W.], as there

ἐκλήθητε, ² μετὰ πάσης ταπεινοφροσύνης καὶ πραΰτητος, μετὰ

ἐν precedes), and so slightly violating the usual law of attraction, unless, following the analogy of such phrases as κλῆσιν καλεῖν, παρακλήσιν παρακ., we suppose the relative standing as usual for the *accus.* ἥν; compare Winer, *Gr.* § 24. 1, p. 189. De W. indeed denies the existence of such a phrase as κλῆσιν καλεῖν, but see Arrian, *Epict.* p. 122 (Raphel), καταισχύνειν τὴν κλῆσιν ἥν κέκληκεν.

2. μετὰ πάσης ταπ.] 'with all *lowliness;*' dispositions with which their moral walk was to be associated (comp. Col. iii. 12), μετὰ (' *with*,' Vulg., Goth., not 'in,' Copt.) being used with ref. to the mental powers and dispositions with which an action is, as it were, *accompanied;* comp. Luke i. 39, 2 Cor. vii. 15, and see Winer, *Gr.* § 47. h. p. 337. Σὺν denotes rather *coherence* (Krüger, *Sprachl.* § 68. 13, 1), not uncommonly with some collateral idea of assistance; compare 1 Cor. v. 4.   On the use of πάσης, comp. notes, ch. i. 8; and on the meaning of the late word ταπεινοφροσύνη, ' the esteeming of ourselves small, *because we are so,*' ' the thinking truly, and, because truly, therefore lowlily of ourselves,' see Trench, *Synon.* § XLII., and Suicer, *Thesaur.* s. v., where several definitions of Chrysostom are cited. Most of these openly or tacitly ascribe to the ταπεινόφρων a consciousness of greatness (ταπ. ἐστίν, ὅταν μεγάλα τὶς ἑαυτῷ συνειδὼς μηδὲν μέγα περὶ αὑτοῦ φαντάζηται); this, however, as Trench observes, is alien to the true sense and spirit of the word.   πραΰτητος] '*meekness,*' in respect of God, and in the face of men; see Trench, *Synon.* § XLII., Tholuck, *Bergpr.* (Matth. v. 5), p. 82 sq., and notes *on Gal.* v. 23. The less definite meaning of ' gentleness' is appy. maintained by some of the Vv. (Vulg. 'mansuetudine' Goth. 'qairrein'

[comp. Lat. *cicur*], Arm., al.), and also by the Greek commentators (ἔσω ταπεινὸς ὁμοίως δὲ καὶ πρᾳος, ἔστι γὰρ ταπεινὸν μὲν εἶναι, ὀξὺν δὲ καὶ ὀργίλον, Chrysost.; compare Theophyl. *on Gal.* v. 3); the deeper and more biblical sense is, however, distinctly to be preferred.   A good general definition will be found in Stobæus, *Floril.* I. 1 (18).   The reading πρᾳΰτητος, though only supported by BC; mss., is appy. to be preferred to πραότητος (*Rec.*, Lachm. with ADEFGL; majority of mss.), as the best attested form in the dialect of the New Test. see Tischend. *Prolegom.* p. L. μετὰ μακροθυμίας] '*with long suffering;*' separate clause more fully elucidated by the following words, ἀνεχόμενοι κ. τ. λ. Two other constructions have been proposed; (*a*) the connection of μετὰ μακρ. with ἀνεχ. (Est. Harl.) so as to form a single clause; (*b*) the union of all the clauses in one single sentence. The objections to (*a*) are, (1) that ἀνεχ. is the natural expansion of μετὰ μακρ., — (2) that undue emphasis must thus (owing to the position) be ascribed to μετὰ μακρ., — (3) that the parallelism of the participial clauses would be needlessly violated; to the latter that the passage of the general ἀξίως περιπ.) into the special ἀνεχόμ. ἀλλ.) becomes sudden and abrupt, instead of being made easy and gradational by means of the interposed prepositional clauses; comp. Mey. *in loc.*   The fine word μακροθυμία (' long-suffering,' ' forbearance,' Goth. ' usbeisnai '), implies the reverse of ὀξυθυμία (James i. 19), and is well defined by. Fritz. (*Rom.* II. 4, Vol. I. p. 98) as '*clementiâ,* quâ iræ temperans, delictum non statim vindices, sed ei qui peccaverit pœnitendi locum relinquas.' The gloss of Chrys. (on *Cor.* xiii. 4), μακρόθυμος διὰ τοῦτο λέγεται, ἐπειδὴ μακράν τινα καὶ μεγάλην ἔχει ψυχήν (compare Clarom.

μακροθυμίας, ἀνεχόμενοι ἀλλήλων ἐν ἀγάπῃ, ³σπουδάζοντες

'magnanimitate'), is too inclusive and general; that of Beza, 'iræ cohibitione,' too limited and special. ἀνεχό-μενοι κ. τ. λ.] 'forbearing one another in love;' manifestation and exhibition of the μακροθυμία; compare Col. iii. 13. The relapse of the participle from its proper case into the nom. is here so perfectly intelligible, and natural, that any supplement of ἐστὲ or γίνεσθε (Heins., al.) must be regarded as wholly unnecessary; see notes on ch. iii. 18, and Elsner, Obs. Vol. ii. p. 211 sq. ἐν ἀγάπῃ is referred by Lachm. and Olsh. to σπου-δάζοντες. Such a punctuation, though supported by Origen (Caten.), seems wholly inadmissible, as disturbing the symmetry of the two participial clauses, and throwing a false emphasis on ἐν ἀγάπῃ.

3. σπουδάζ. τηρεῖν] 'using diligence to keep;' participial member parallel to the foregoing, specifying the inward feelings (Mey.) by which the ἀνέχεσθαι is to be characterized, and the inward efforts by which it is to be promoted; οὐκ ἀπόνως ἰσχύσομεν εἰρηνεύειν, Theoph. For two good discussions of this verse, though from somewhat different points of view, see Laud, Serm. vi. Vol. i. p. 155 sq. (A. C. Libr.), and Baxter, Works, Vol. xvi. p. 379 (ed. Orme). τὴν ἑνότητα τοῦ Πν.] 'the unity of the Spirit,' scil. 'wrought by the Spirit' (τὴν ἑνότ., ἣν τὸ Πνεῦμα ἔδωκεν ἡμῖν, Theoph., comp. Chrysost., Œcum.), τοῦ Πν. being the gen. of the originating cause (Scheuerl. Synt., § 17. 1, p. 125), not the possessive gen. (as appy. Origen, Caten.), or both united (as Stier, see Vol. ii. p. 18), neither of which seem here so pertinent; see notes on 1 Thess. i. 6, and on Col. i. 23. That the ref. is to the personal Holy Spirit, seems so clear that we may wonder how such able commentators as Calvin and Estius could regard τὸ Πν. as the human spirit, and acquiesce in an interpr. so frigid as 'animorum concordia,' 'animorum inter vos conjunctio.' De Wette, — whose own interpr. 'die Einheit des kirchlichen Gemeingeistes' (comp. Theod.-Mops., Πνεῦμ., τὸ ἀναγεννῆσαν σῶμα), is very far from satisfactory, urges ἑνότης πίστεως, ver. 13 (compare Origen), but the two passages are by no means so closely analogous as to suggest any modification here assigned to Πνεῦμα; see Land, Serm. vi. Vol. i. p. 162 (A. C. Libr.). ἐν τῷ συνδέσμῳ τῆς εἰρήνης] 'in the bond of peace;' element or principle in which the unity is maintained, viz. 'peace;' τῆς εἰρήν. being not the gen. objecti ('that which binds together, maintains, peace,' Rückert, 'vinculum quo pax retinetur,' Beng., scil. ἀγάπη, Col. iii. 14), but the gen. of identity or apposition; see Scheuerl. Synt. § 12. 1, p. 82, Winer, Gr. § 59. 8, p. 470. The former interpretation is plausible, and appy. as ancient as the time of Origen (τῆς ἀγάπης συνδεούσης κατὰ τὸ Πνεῦμα ἐνουμένους, ap. Cram. Caten. p. 165), but derives very doubtful support from Col. l. c., where ἀγάπη is specified, and was perhaps only due to the assumption that ἐν was here instrumental (διά Œcum.), and that συνδ. τῆς εἰρ. was a periphrasis for the agent (ἀγάπη) supposed to be referred to. Ἐν, however, correctly denotes the sphere, the element in which the ἑνότης is to be kept and manifested (see Winer, Gr. § 48. a, p. 345), thus preserving its parallelism with ἐν in ver. 2, and conveying a very simple and perspicuous meaning: the Ephesians were to evince their forbearance in love, and to preserve the Spirit-given unity in the true bond of union, the 'irrupta copula' of peace. The etymological identity of σύνδεσμος and εἰρήνη must not be

τηρεῖν τὴν ἑνότητα τοῦ Πνεύματος ἐν τῷ συνδέσμῳ τῆς εἰρήνης.
⁴ ἓν σῶμα καὶ ἓν Πνεῦμα, καθὼς καὶ ἐκλήθητε ἐν μιᾷ ἐλπίδι
τῆς κλήσεως ὑμῶν· ⁵ εἷς Κύριος, μία πίστις, ἓν βάπτισμα·

pressed (Reiners, ap. Wolf) as the derivation of εἰρήνη from ΕΙΡΩ 'necto' is less probable than from ΕΙΡΩ 'dico;' see Benfey, *Wurzellex.* Vol. ii. p. 7, Rost u. Palm, *Lex.* s. v. Vol. i. p. 799.

4. ἓν σῶμα] '*There is one body;*' assertory declaration of the unity pervading the Christian dispensation, designed to illustrate and enhance the foregoing exhortation; the simple verb ἐστί, not γίνεσθε or ἐστέ (οἵπερ ἐστέ, Camer.), being appy. the correct supplement; see Winer, *Gr.*, § 64. 2, p. 546. The connection of thought between ver. 3 and 4 is somewhat doubtful. That the verse is not *directly* hortatory, and connected with (*Lachm.*), dependent on ('ut sitis,' Syr. Est. 2), or in apposition to ('existentes,' Est. 1) what precedes, seems clear from the parallelism with ver. 5 and 6; still less does it introduce a *reason* for the previous statement by an ellipse of γάρ (Eadie), all such ellipses being wholly indemonstrable; 'nullâ in re magis pejusque errari quam in ellipsi particularum solet,' Herm. *Viger* Append ii. p. 701 (ed. Valpy). It seems then only to contain a simple assertion, the very unconnectedness of which adds weight and impressiveness, and seems designed to convey an echo of the former warning; 'remember, — there is one body, etc.;' comp. Hofm. *Schrift.* Vol. ii. p. 108.   In the explanation of the sentiment, the Greek commentators somewhat vacillate; we can, however, scarcely doubt that the σῶμα implies the whole community of Christians, the mystical body of Christ (ch. ii. 16, Rom. xii. 5, Col. i. 24, al.), and that the Πνεῦμα is the Holy Spirit which dwells in the Church (Eadie), and by which the σῶμα is moved and vivified (1 Cor. xii. 13); comp. Jackson, *Creed*, xii. 3.

4, Usteri, *Lehrb.* ii. 2. 1, p. 249, and Wordsw. *in loc.* On this text, see a good treatise by Barrow, *Works*, Vol. vii. p. 626 sq.   καθώς] '*even as;*' illustration and proof of the unity, as more especially afforded by the unity of the *hope* in which they were called. On the later form καθώς, see notes on *Gal.* iii. 6.   καὶ ἐκλήθητε ἐν μιᾷ ἐλπ.] '*ye were also called in one hope,*' 'vocati estis in unâ spe,' Clarom., Vulg., Arm.; καί marking the accordance of the calling with the previously-stated unity ('unitas spiritus ex unitate spei noscitur,' Cocc.), and ἐν being neither equiv. to ἐπί (Chrys.) or εἰς (Rück.), nor even instrumental, but simply specifying the *moral element* in which as it were the κλῆσις took place; compare Winer, *Gr.*, § 50. 5, p. 370. Meyer adopts the instrumental sense; as, however, there are not here, as in Gal. i. 6 (see notes), any prevailing dogmatical reasons for such an interpretation, and as the two remaining passages in which καλεῖν is joined with ἐν (1 Cor. vii. 15, 1 Thess. iv. 7) admit a similar explanation, it seems most correct to adhere to the strict, and so to say, theological meaning of this important preposition; we were called ἐπ' ἐλευθερίᾳ (Gal. v. 13), and εἰς ζωὴν αἰώνιον (1 Tim. vi. 12), but ἐν εἰρήνῃ (1 Cor. vii. 15), ἐν ἁγιασμῷ (1 Thess. iv. 7) and ἐν ἐλπίδι; compare Reuss, *Théol. Chrét.* iv. 15, p. 146.   τῆς κλήσεως ὑμῶν] '*of your calling,*' sc. arising from your calling; κλήσεως being not the gen. of possession (Eadie, Alf.), but of the *origin* or *originating cause*; κοινὴ ἐστὶν ἡμῶν ἐλπὶς ἐκ τῆς κλήσεως γενομένη, Œcum.; see notes on 1 *Thess.* i. 6.

5. εἷς Κύριος] '*one Lord,*' sc. Christ; placed prominently forward, as the Head

⁶ εἷς Θεὸς καὶ πατὴρ πάντων, ὁ ἐπὶ πάντων καὶ διὰ πάντων καὶ ἐν

of His one body, the Church, and the one divine object toward whom *faith* is directed, and into whom all Christians are baptized; comp. Rom. vi. 3, Gal. iii. 27, and for a good sermon on this text Barrow, *Serm.* xxii. Vol. v. p. 261 sq. μία πίστις] 'one *faith*;' not the 'fides *quæ* creditur,' and still less the 'regula fidei,' Grot., — this meaning in the N. T. being extremely doubtful, see notes *on Gal.* i. 23, — but the 'fides *quâ* creditur,' the 'fides salvifica,' which was the same in its essence and qualities for all Christians (Mey.). That this, however, must not be unduly limited to the feeling of the individual, sc. to faith in its` utterly *subjective* aspect, seems clear from the use of μία, and the general context. As there is one Lord, so the μία πίστις is not only a subjective recognition of this eternal truth (Usteri, *Lehrb.* ii. ·1. 4, p. 238), but also necessarily. involves a common objective profession of it; comp. Rom. x. 10; and see Stier, Vol. i. p. 33, Pearson, *Creed*, Art. iv. Vol. i. p. 399 (ed. Burt.).   ἐν βάπτισμα] 'one baptism;' a still further 'consequentia' to εἷς Κύριος; as there was one Lord and one faith in Him, so was there one and one only baptism into Him (Gal. iii. 27), one and one only *inward* element, one and one only *outward* seal. Commentators have dwelt, perhaps somewhat unprofitably, upon the reasons why no mention is made of the other sacrament, the εἷς ἄρτος (1 Cor. x. 17) of the Holy Communion. If it be thought necessary to assign any reason, it must certainly not be sought for in the mere historical fact (Mey.), that the Holy Communion was not at that time so separate and distinct in its administration (compare Bingham *Antiq.* xv. 7. 6, 7, Waterland, *Eucharist*, Ch. i. Vol. iv. p. 475) as Holy Baptism, for the words of inspiration are for all

times, but must be referred to the fundamental difference between the two sacraments. The one is rather the symbol of *union* (Usteri, *Lehrb.* ii. 2, p. 284); the other, from its single celebration and marked individual reference, presents more clearly the idea of *unity.* — the idea most in harmony with the context; see Kahnis, *Abendm.* p. 276, 249.

6. εἷς Θεὸς καὶ πατήρ] 'one God and *Father*;' climactic reference to the eternal *Father* (observe the distinct mention of the three Persons of the blessed Trinity, ver. 4, 5, 6) in whom unity finds its highest exemplification; 'etiamsi baptizamur in nomen Patris, Filii, et Spiritus Sancti, et filium unum Dominum nominamus, tamen non credimus nisi in unum Deum,' Cocc. On this solemn designation, see notes *on Gal.* i. 4, and for a discussion of the title 'Father,' Pearson, *Creed,* Art. i. Vol. i. p. 35 sq. (ed. Burt.), Barrow, *Creed,* Serm. x. Vol. iv. p. 493 sq.   ὁ ἐπὶ πάντων] 'who is over all;' ὁ κύριος καὶ ἐπάνω πάντων, Chrysost.; the relation expressed seems that of simple *sovereignty*, not only spiritual (Calv.), but general and universal (δεσποτείαν σημαίνει, Theod.); comp. Rom. ix. 5, and see Winer, *Gr.* § 50. 6, p. 370, where the associated reference to 'protection' (ed. 5), is now rightly excluded; this would have been more naturally expressed by ὑπέρ; see Krüger, *Sprachl.* § 68. 28. It is unnecessary to remark that the three clauses are no synonymous formulæ (Koppe), but that the prepositions mark with scrupulous accuracy the threefold relation in which God stands to his creatures; see notes *on Gal.* i. 1, and Winer, *Gr. l. c.,* and Stier, Vol. i. p. 44.   The gender of πάντων is doubtful. It seems arbitrary (Clarom., Vulg.) to regard the first πάντων and πᾶσιν as masc., the second πάντων as neuter, as there is nothing

Further, Christ gives His
grace in measure to each,
as the Scripture testifies. πᾶσιν. ⁷ Ἑνὶ δὲ ἑκάστῳ ἡμῶν ἐδόθη ἡ χάρις

in the context or in the meaning of the prepp. to require such a limitation; the gender of one may with propriety fix that of the rest. As πᾶσιν then certainly seems masculine, πάντων may be assumed of the same gender; so Copt., which by the omission of *hôb* seems here to express a definite opinion. In Rom. ix. 5, πάντων is commonly (and properly) interpreted as neuter (opp. to Fritz. *in loc.* Vol. ii. 272), there being no limitation or restriction implied in the context. The reading is very doubtful; ἡμῖν (*Rec.* ὑμῖν with mss.; Chrys. comment., al.) is added to πᾶσιν with DEF GKL; mss.; Clarom., Vulgate, Syr. (both), Goth.; Did., Dam., al., — but seems more rightly omitted with ABC; 10 mss.; Copt., Æth. (both); Ath., Greg.-Naz., Chrys. (text), al., as a not improbable gloss; so *Lachm., Tisch.,* and appy. the majority of recent editors. δ ι ὰ π ά ν τ ω ν κ α ὶ ἐ ν π ᾶ σ ι ν] '*through all and in all.*' These two last clauses are less easy to interpret, on account of the approximation in meaning of the two prepositions. Of these διὰ is referred (*a*) by the Greek expositors to God (*the Father*), in respect of his providence (ὁ προνοῶν καὶ διοικῶν, Chrysost.); (*b*) by Aquinas (ap. Est.), al., to God *the Son*, 'per quem omnia facta sunt,' comp. Olsh., — a very inverted interpretation; (*c*) by Calvin, Meyer, al. 'to the pervading charismatic influence and presence of God by means of the *Holy Spirit.*' This last interpretation seems at first sight most in unison with the strict meaning of both prepp., διὰ pointing to the influence of the Spirit which *passes through* ('transcurrit,' Jerome) and *pervades* all hearts [operative motion], ἐν His indwelling (ὁ οἰκῶν, Chrysost.) and informing influence [operative rest]; see ed. 1; still as the three Persons of the blessed Trinity have been so lately spec-

ified, as references to this holy Truth seem very noticeably to pervade this Ep. (see Stier, *Eph.* Vol. i. p. 35), and as the ancient interpr. of Irenæus ('super omn*ia* (?) quidem Pater, ... per omn*ia* (?) autem Verbum, ... in omnibus autem nobis Spiritus,' *Hær.* v. 18; compare Athan. *ad. Serap.* § 28, Vol. ii. p. 677, ed. Bened.), seems to have a just claim on our attention, it seems best and safest to maintain that allusion in the present case (opp. to Hofm. *Schriftb.* Vol. i. p. 184), and to refer δ ι ὰ π ά ν τ ω ν to the redeeming and reconciling influences of the Eternal *Son* which pervade all hearts, while ἐν πᾶσιν, as above, marks the indwelling *Spirit;* see Stier *in loc.,* and comp. Waterl. *Def. of Queries,* Vol. i. p. 280.

7. ἐ ν ὶ δ ὲ ἑ κ ά σ τ ῳ ἡ μ ῶ ν] '*But to each of us,*' ' to each one individually;' further inculcation of this unity in what might at first sight have seemed to militate against it: δὲ neither being transitional (comp. Eadie), nor encountering any objection (Grot., comp. Theoph.), but merely suggesting the *contrast* between the individual and the πάντες previously mentioned (ver. 6). In the general distribution of gifts (implied in the ὁ Θεὸς ἐν πᾶσιν), no single individual is overlooked (1 Cor. xii. 11, διαιροῦν ἰδίᾳ ἑκάστῳ); each has his peculiar gift, each can and ought to contribute his share to preserving 'the unity of the Spirit;' so in effect Chrys., who in the main has rightly felt and explained the connection, τὰ πάντων κεφαλαιωδέστερα, φησί, κοινὰ πάντων ἐστί, τὸ βάπτισμα κ. τ. λ. εἰ δέ τι ὁ δεῖνα πλέον ἔχει ἐν τῷ χαρίσματι, μὴ ἄλγει; see also Theod.-Mops. *in loc.*

ἐ δ ό θ η ἡ χ ά ρ ι ς] '*the grace was given,*' sc. by our Lord after His ascension; χάρις, however, not being simply equivalent to χάρισμα (= 'gift of grace, Peile),

κατὰ τὸ μέτρον τῆς δωρεᾶς τοῦ Χριστοῦ. ⁸ διὸ λέγει Ἀναβὰς

but, as De W. rightly observes, retaining some shade of a transitive force, and denoting the energizing grace which manifests itself in the peculiar gift; comp. Rom. xii. 6. The omission. of the art. (*Lachm.* with BD¹FGL; 5 mss.; Dam.) is due appy. to an error in transcription, caused by the preceding η, by which it became absorbed, and is retained by *Tisch.* (with ACD³EK; great majority of mss.; Chrys., Theod., al.), and most recent editors.

κ α τ ὰ   τ ὸ   μ έ τ ρ ο ν κ. τ. λ.] '*according to the measure of the gift of Christ,*' scil. 'in proportion to the amount of the gift which Christ gives,' καθὼς τὴν ἑαυτοῦ δωρεὰν ἑκάστῳ ἡμῶν ὁ δεσπότης ἐπεμέτρησε Χριστός, Theod.-Mops.; δωρεᾶς being thus a simple *possessive* gen. (the measure which the gift has, which belongs to and defines the gift), and Χριστοῦ the gen. of *ablation* (Donalds. *Gr.* § 451), or, more specifically, of the *agent,* the giver (comp. δωρεὰς χάριτος, Plato, *Leg.* viii. 844 d, and see notes *on 1 Thess.* i. 6) not of the *receiver* (Oeder ap. Wolf), — an idea which is in no sort of harmony with the context, ἔδωκεν δόματα, ver. 8; see 2 Cor. ix. 15. Stier very infelicitously (in point of grammar) endeavors to unite both.

8. δ ι ὸ λ έ γ ε ι] '*On which account He saith;*' on account of this bestowal of the gift of Christ, and that in differing measures, — ὅτι, φησίν, ἡ χάρις δωρεά ἐστι τοῦ Χρ. καὶ αὐτὸς μετρήσας ἔδωκεν, ἄκουε, φησί, τοῦ Δαυΐδ, Œcum. The difficulties of this verse, both in regard to the connection, the source, and the form of the citation, are very great, and must be separately, though briefly noticed. (1) *Connection.* There is clearly no parenthesis; verse 8 is to be closely connected with verse 7, and regarded as a scriptural confirmation of its assertions. These assertions involve two

separate moments of thought, (*a*) the primary, that each individual has his peculiar and appropriate gifts, further elucidated and exemplified, ver. 11; (*b*) the secondary, *that these gifts are conferred by Christ.* The intrinsic, though not so much contextual importance of (*b*) induces the Apostle to pause and add a special confirmation from Scripture. The cardinal words are thus so obviously ἐδόθη, δωρεά, ἔδωκε δόματα, that it is singular how so good a commentator as Olsh. could have supposed the stress of the citation to be on τοῖς ἄνθρ.　　　(2) The *source* of the citation is not any Christian hymn (Storr, *Opusc.* iii. p. 309), but Psalm lxviii., — a psalm of which the style, age, purport, and allusions have been most differently estimated and explained (for details see Reuss, *lxviii. Psalm*), but which may, with high probability, be deemed a hymn of victory in honor of Jehova, the God of Battles (Hengst. opp. to J. Olsh.), of high originality (Hitzig opp. to Ewald), and composed by David on the taking of Rabbah (Hengst. opp. to Reuss, J. Olsh.). We have therefore no reason whatever to entertain any doubt of its inspired and prophetic character; compare Phillips, *Psalms,* Vol. ii. p. 79.　　　(3) The *form* of citation is the real difficulty; the words of the Psalm are לָקַחְתָּ מַתָּנוֹת בָּאָדָם, in LXX, ἔλαβες δόματα ἐν ἀνθρώπῳ [-ποις, Alex., Compl., Ald.]. The difference in St. Paul's citation is palpable, and, we are bound in candor to say, does not appear diminished by any of the proposed reconciliations; for even assuming that לָקַח = 'danda sumsit,' 'he took only to give' (comp. Gen. xvi. 9, xviii. 5, xxvii. 13, xlii. 16, and see Surenhus. Βιβλ. Καταλλ., p. 585), still the nature of the gifts, which in one case were *reluctant* (see Hengst.), in the

εἰς ὕψος ᾐχμαλώτευσεν αἰχμαλωσίαν, ἔδωκεν δόματα τοῖς ἀνθρώ-

other *spontaneous*, appears essentially different. We admit, then, frankly and freely, the verbal difference, but remembering that the Apostle wrote under the inspiration of the Holy Ghost, we recognize here neither imperfect memory, precipitation (Rück.), arbitrary change (Calv., compare Theod.-Mops.), accommodation (Morus), nor Rabbinical interpretation (Meyer), but simply the *fact*, that the Psalm, and esp. ver. 18, *had* a Messianic reference, and bore within it a further, fuller, and deeper meaning. This meaning the inspired Apostle, by a slight change of language, and substitution of ἔδωκε for the more dubious חָקַל succinctly, suggestively, and *authoritatively* unfolds; comp. notes *on Gal.* iii. 16. We now proceed to the grammatical details. λ έ γ ε ι] '*He saith,*' sc. ὁ Θεός, not ἡ γραφή. This latter nominative is several times inserted by St. Paul (Rom. iv. 3, ix. 17, x. 11, Gal. iv. 30, 1 Tim. v. 18), but is not therefore to be regularly supplied whenever there is an ellipsis (Bos, *Ellips.* p. 54), without reference to the nature of the passage. The surest, and in fact only guide, is the context; where that affords no certain hint, we fall back upon the natural subject, ὁ Θεός, whose words the Scriptures are; see notes *on Gal.* iii. 16. ἀναβὰς εἰς ὕψος] '*Having ascended on high;*' not ' ascendens,' Clarom., Vulgate, but ' quum ascendisset,' Beza, — the reference being obviously to Christ's ascent into heaven (Barrow, *Creed*, Vol. vi. p. 358, Pearson, *Creed*, Art. vi. Vol. i. p. 323, ed. Burt.), and the aor. part. here being temporal, and, according to its more common use, denoting an action *preceding* [never, in the N. T. *subsequent to*, see Winer, *Gr.* § 45. 6. b, p. 316] that of the finite verb ; see Bernhardy, *Synt.* x. 9, p. 383, Krüger, *Sprachl.* § 56. 10. L Our Lord, it may

be urged, gave the Holy Spirit before his ascension (John xx. 22); but this was only an ' arrha Pentecostes,' Beng., a limited (Alford), and preparatory gift of the Holy Spirit; see Lücke *in loc.* On this text, as cited from Psalm lxviii., see a good sermon by Andrewes, *Serm.* vii. Vol. iii. p. 221 (A. C. Libr.). ᾐ χ μ α λ ώ τ. α ἰ χ μ α λ ω σ ί α ν] '*He led captivity captive,*' ' captivam duxit captivitatem,' Clarom., Vulg.; the abstract, αἰχμαλωσ. being used for the concrete αἰχμαλώτους (comp. Numbers xxxi. 12, 2 Chron. xxviii. 11, 13, and see exx. Jelf, *Gr.* § 353), and serving by its connection with the cognate verb to enhance and *slightly* intensify; compare Winer, *Gr.* § 32. 2. p. 201, and see the copious list of exx. in Lobeck, *Paralip.* p. 498 sq. *Who* constituted this αἰχμαλωσία has been much discussed. That the captives were not (*a*) Satan's prisoners (ἀνθρώπους ὑπὸ τὴν τοῦ διαβόλου τυραννίδα κατεχομένους, Theod.-Mops., comp. Just. Mart. *Trypho*, § 39, p. 128, ed. Otto, and Theod. *in loc.*) seems clear from the subsequent mention of ἀνθρώποις, which (though not so in the original) seems *here* to refer to a different class to the captives. Nor (*b*) can they be the souls of the righteous in Hades (Estius, compare *Evang. Nicod.* § 24, in Thilo, *Codex Apocryph.* p. 747), as, setting aside other reasons (' captivos non duci in libertatem, sed hostes, in captivitatem,' Calov.), the above interpr. of the part. ἀναβὰς seems seriously opposed to such a view. If, however, (*c*) we regard ' the captivity' as captive and subjugated enemies (Meyer, De W.), the enemies of Christ, — Satan, Sin, and Death, — we preserve the analogy of the comparison (compare Alf.), and gain a full and forcible meaning: so rightly Chrysost., αἰχμάλωτον γὰρ τὸν τύραννον ἔλαβε [not κατήργησε, which with regard to Death

ποις.   ⁹ τὸ δὲ ἀνέβη τί ἐστιν εἰ μὴ ὅτι καὶ κατέβη εἰς τὰ κατώτερα

is yet future, 1 Cor. xv. 26] τὸν διάβολον λέγω καὶ τὸν θάνατον, καὶ τὴν ἀράν, καὶ τὴν ἁμαρτίαν; comp. Œcum. 2, Theoph. ἔδωκεν δόματα] 'He gave gifts,' sc. spiritual gifts; comp. ἐδόθη ἡ χάρις, ver. 7, and as a special and particular illustration, Acts ii. 33.   The reading is very doubtful.   Tisch. (ed. 7) prefixes καὶ with BC¹(C³)D³KL; nearly all mss.; Goth., Syr. (both), al.; Orig., Chrys., Theod., al.   Rec., Alf.; Lachm. on the contrary omits with AC²D¹EFG; mss.; Vulg., Clarom., Copt.; Iren. (interpr.), Tertull., al. (Tisch. ed. 2); and appy. rightly, as an insertion for the sake of keeping up the connection seems more probable than a conformation to the LXX. where the καὶ is omitted.

9. τὸ δὲ ἀνέβη] 'Now (δὲ here marking a slight explanatory transition, Hartung, Partik., δέ, 2. 3, Vol. i. p. 165) that He ascended,' scil. ' now the predication of His ascent;' not 'the word ἀνέβη,' — as ἀναβάς, not ἀνέβη, precedes. To evince still more clearly the truth and correctness of the Messianic application of the words just cited, St. Paul urges the antithesis implied by ἀνέβη, viz. κατέβη, a predication only applicable to Christ; compare Hofm. Schriftb. Vol. ii. 1, p. 344, where this and the preceding verses are fully investigated.   τί ἐστιν εἰ μὴ κ.τ.λ.] 'what is it ('what does it imply,' Matth. ix. 13, John xvi. 17, comp. notes on Gal. iii. 19), except that He also (as well as ἀνέβη) descended;' the tacit assumption, as Meyer observes, being clearly this, — that He who is the subject of the citation is One whose seat was heaven, — no man, but a giver of gifts to men; especially comp. John iii. 13.   The insertion of πρῶτον after κατέβη (Rec. with BC³KL; most mss.; Aug., Vulg., Goth.; Theod., al.) seems clearly to have arisen from an explanatory gloss,

and that of μέρη after κατώτερα, though better supported (Rec., Lachm., with ABCD³KL; nearly all mss.; Vulg., al.) to be still fairly attributable to the same origin.   εἰς τὰ κατώτερα τῆς γῆς] 'to the lower (parts) of the earth,' 'in loca quæ subter terram,' Copt., 'subter terram,' Æth. This celebrated passage has received several different interpretations, two only of which, however, deserve serious consideration, and between which it is extremely difficult to decide; (a) the ancient explanation, according to which τὰ κατώτερα τῆς γῆς = τὰ καταχθόνια, and imply 'Hades' (ποῦ δὲ κατέβη; εἰς τὸν ἄδην· τοῦτον γὰρ κατώτερα μέρη τῆς γῆς λέγει, κατὰ τὴν κοινὴν ὑπόνοιαν, Theoph.), the gen. not being dependent on the comparative (Rück., — still less compatible with his insertion of μέρη), but being the regular possessive gen.; (b) the more modern interpretation, adopted by the majority of recent commentators, according to which τῆς γῆς is regarded as the gen. of apposition (see esp. Winer, Gr. § 59. 8, p. 410), and the expression as equivalent to εἰς τὴν κατωτέραν γῆν. Both sides claim the comparative κατώτερα, — (the תַּחְתִּיּ֥ות הָאָ֫רֶץ pressed by Olshaus. is appy. equally indeterminate with the Greek), — the one as suggesting a comparison with the earth, 'a lower depth than the earth;' the other as suggested by the comparison with the heaven (Acts ii. 19, John viii. 23, — but in this latter passage κάτω reaches lower than the earth, Stier, Reden Jesu, Vol. iv. p. 447 sq.); comp. Hofm. Schriftb. Vol. ii. 1, p. 345. These arguments must be nearly set off against one another, as the positive would have been most natural in the latter case, the superlative perhaps in the former. As, however, the superl. would have tended to fix the locality (comp. Nehem. iv. 13) more definitely

τῆς γῆς ;　¹⁰ ὁ καταβάς, αὐτός ἐστιν καὶ ὁ ἀναβὰς ὑπεράνω πάν-

than was suitable to the present context, and as the use of the term ᾅδης would have marred the antithesis (γῆ opp. to οὐρανός), it does not seem improbable that the more vague comparative was expressly chosen, and that thus its use is more in favor of (a) than (b). When to this we add the full antithesis that seems to lie in ὑπεράνω τῶν οὐρανῶν, ver. 10 ('sublimiora cælorum' opp. to 'inferiora terrarum,' Tertull.), surely more than a mere expansion of εἰς ὕψος (Winer, Mey.), and also observe the sort of exegetical necessity which ἵνα·πληρώσῃ τὰ πάντα (ver. 10) seems to impose on us of giving the fullest amplitude to every expression, we still more incline to (a), and with Irenæus (Hær. v. 31, comp. iv. 22), Tertullian (de Animâ, c. 55), and the principal ancient writers (see Pearson, Creed, Art. v. Vol. i. p. 269, and ref. on Vol. ii. p. 195, ed. Burt.), recognize in these words an allusion, not to Christ's death and burial (Chrys., Theod.), but definitely to His descent into hell; so also Olsh., Stier, Alf., Wordsw., and Baur (Paulus, p. 431), but it is to be feared that the judgment of the last writer is not unbiassed, as he urges the ref. as a proof of the gnostic origin of the Epistle.　　　On this clause and on ver. 10 see a good sermon by South, Serm. (Posth.) i. Vol. iii. p. 169 sq. (Lond. 1843), and for a general investigation of the doctrine of Christ's descent into hell, and its connection with the last things, Guder, Lehre von der Erscheinung J. C. unter den Todten, Bern, 1853.

10. ὁ καταβάς] 'He that descended;' emphatic, as its position shows; the absence of any connecting or illative particle gives a greater force and vigor to the conclusion. It may be observed that αὐτὸς is not 'the same,' Auth., — as no instance of an omission of the article,

though occasionally found in the earlier (Herm. Opusc. Vol. i. p. 332), and frequently in Byzantine authors, occurs in the N. T., but is simply the emphatic 'He,' — οὐ γὰρ ἄλλος κατελήλυθε καὶ ἄλλος ἀνελήλυθεν, Theod.; see Winer, Gr. § 22. 4. obs. p. 135.　　　πάντων τῶν οὐρανῶν] 'all the heavens,' 'cælos omnes penetravit ascendendo, usque ad summum cælum,' Est.; ὑψηλότερος τῶν οὐρανῶν, Heb. vii. 26, compare ib. iv. 4. There is no necessity whatever to connect this expression with the 'seven heavens' of the Jews (comp. Wetst. on 2 Cor. xii. 2, Hofm. Schriftb. Vol. ii. 1, p. 387); the words, both here and in Heb. ll. cc., have only a simple and general meaning, and are well paraphrased by Bp. Pearson, — 'whatsoever heaven is higher than all the rest which are called heavens, into that place did He ascend,' Creed, Art. vi. Vol. i. p. 320 (ed. Burton).　　　ἵνα πληρώσῃ τὰ πάντα] 'in order that He might fill all things;' more general purpose involved in the more special ἔδωκεν δόματα τοῖς ἀνθρώποις (ver. 8), though structurally dependent on the preceding participle. The subjunctive with ἵνα, after a past tense, is correctly used in the present case, to denote an act that still continues; see Herm. Viger, No. 350, and esp. Klotz, Devar. Vol. ii. p. 618, who has treated this and similar uses of the subj. with ἵνα after preterites, with considerable acumen ; for exx. see Gaylèr, Partic. Ney. p. 176, who has also correctly seized the general principle, 'subjunctivum usurpari si prævalet consilium, aut respectus ad eventum habendus,' p. 165. Great caution, however, must be used in applying these principles to the N. T., as the general and prevailing use of the subj. both in the N. T. and in later writers makes it very doubtful whether the finer distinction of mood was in all such cases

τῶν τῶν οὐρανῶν, ἵνα πληρώσῃ τὰ πάντα.   ¹¹ Καὶ αὐτὸς
He appointed divers min-   ἔδωκεν τοὺς μὲν ἀποστόλους, τοὺς δὲ προφήτας,
istering orders, till we all
come to the unity of faith, and in truth and love grow up into Christ, the head of the living body, the
Church.

as the present distinctly felt and intended.   It is not necessary either
to limit πάντα πληροῦν, the solemn predicate of the Deity (Jerem. xxiii. 22, see
Schoettg. *Hor. Heb.* Vol. I. p. 775), to
the gift of redemption (Rück.), or to
confine the comprehensive τὰ πάντα to
the faithful (Grot.), or to the church of
Jews and Gentiles (Meier); the expression is perfectly unrestricted, and refers
not only to the sustaining and ruling
power (τῆς δεσποτείας αὐτοῦ καὶ ἐνεργείας,
Chrys.), but also to the divine presence
('præsentiâ et operatione suâ *se ipso*,'
Beng.) of Christ.   The doctrine of the
ubiquity of Christ's *Body* derives no
support from this passage (*Form. Concord.* p. 767), as there is here no reference
to a diffused and ubiquitous corporeity,
but to a pervading and energizing omnipresence; compare Ebrard, *Dogmatik*, §
390, Vol. II. p. 139, and notes on ch. i.
20.   The true doctrine may perhaps be
thus briefly stated:—Christ is perfect
God, and perfect and glorified man; as
the former he is present *everywhere*, as
the latter he can be present *anywhere*;
see Jackson, *Creed*, Book XI. 3, and
comp. Stier, *Reden Jesu*, Vol. VI. p. 164.

11.   καὶ αὐτός] 'and He,' 'jah
silba,' Gothic; ἐμφατικῶς δὲ εἶπε τὸ,
αὐτός, Theophyl.   There is here no *direct* resumption of the subject of ver. 7,
as if ver. 8—10 were merely parenthetical, but a *regression* to it, while at the
same time the αὐτὸς is naturally and
emphatically linked on to the αὐτὸς in
the preceding verse.   This return to a
subject, without disturbing the harmony
of the immediate connection or the natural sequence of thought, constitutes one
of the high excellences, but at the same
time one of the difficulties in the style of
the great Apostle.   ἔδωκεν] 'gave,'

'dedit,' Clarom., Vulg., al.; not merely
Hebraistic (נָתַן, Olsh.), and equivalent
to ἔθετο (Acts xx. 28, 1 Cor. xii. 28),
'*dedit* Ecclesiæ id est posuit in Eccl.'
(Est.), but in the ordinary and regular
meaning of the word, and in harmony
with ἐδόθη, ver. 7, δόματα, ver. 8; comp.
notes on ch. ii. 22.   ἀποστόλους]
'*Apostles*,'—in the highest and most
special sense; comp. notes *on Gal.* i. 1.
The chief characteristics of an Apostle
were an immediate call from Christ
(compare Gal. i. 1), a destination for all
lands (Matth. xxviii. 19, 2 Cor. xi. 28),
and a *special* power of working miracles
(2 Cor. xii. 12); see Eadie *in loc.*, who
has grouped together, with proof texts,
the essential elements of the Apostolate.
προφήτας] '*Prophets*,'—not only in
the more special sense (as Agabus, Acts
xi. 27), but in the more general one of
preachers and expounders, who spoke
under the *immediate* impulse and influence of the Holy Spirit, and were thus
to be distinguished from the διδάσκαλοι;
ὁ μὲν προφητεύων πάντα ἀπὸ τοῦ Πνεύματος φθέγγεται· ὁ δὲ διδάσκων ἐστὶν ὅπου
καὶ ἐξ οἰκείας διανοίας διαλέγεται, Chrys.
on 1 Cor. v. 28; see Thorndike, *Relig.
Assemblies*, ch. v. 1 sq. Vol. I. p. 182 sq.
(A. C. Libr.), and comp. notes on ch. ii.
20.   εὐαγγελιστάς] '*Evangelists*,'—not τοὺς τὸ εὐαγγέλιον γραψάντας
(Œcum., Chrys. 2), but τοὺς εὐαγγελι-
ζομένους (Chrys. 1), preachers of the Gospel who περιϊόντες ἐκήρυττον (Theod.),
and yet, as μὴ περιϊόντες πανταχοῦ
(Chrys.), were distinguished from the
Apostles, to whom they acted as subor-
dinates and missionaries; compare Acts
viii. 14, and see Thorndike, *Relig. Assembl.* IV. 37, Vol. I. p. 176, ib. *Right of
Church*, II. 30, Vol. I. p. 451, Hofm.
Schriftb. Vol. II. 2, p. 249.

τοὺς δὲ εὐαγγελιστάς, τοὺς δὲ ποιμένας καὶ διδασκάλους, ¹² πρὸς
τὸν καταρτισμὸν τῶν ἁγίων εἰς ἔργον διακονίας, εἰς οἰκοδομὴν τοῦ

ποιμένας καὶ διδασκάλους] 'Pastors and Teachers.' It has been doubted
whether these words denote different
classes, or are different names of· the
same class. The absence of the disjunctive τοὺς δὲ (arbitrarily inserted in Syr.
but altered in Syr.-Phil.) seems clearly
to show that both ποιμ. and διδάσκ. had
some common distinctions, — probably
that of being *stationary* rather than *mis-
sionary*, οἱ καθήμενοι καὶ περὶ ἕνα τόπον
ἠσχολημένοι, Chrysost. — which plainly
separated them from each of the preceding classes. Thus far they might be said
to form one class ; but that the individuals who composed it bore either or both
names indifferently, is very doubtful.
The ποιμένες (a term probably including
ἐπίσκοποι and πρεσβύτεροι, Fritz. *Fritzsch.
Opusc.* p. 43 sq.) might be, and perhaps
always were διδάσκαλοι (comp. 1 Tim.
iii. 2, Tit. i. 9, *Martyr. Polyc.* § 16, see
Thorndike, *Relig. Assembl.* IV. 40, Vol.
I. p. 170); but it does not follow that the
converse was true. The χάρισμα of
κυβέρνησις is so distinct from that of
διδασκαλία, that it seems necessary to
recognize in the διδάσκ. a body of men
(scarcely a distinct *class*) who had the
gift of διδαχή, but who were not invested
with any administrative powers and authority ; see esp. Hooker, *Eccl. Pol.* v.
78. 8, and compare Neander, *Planting*,
Vol. I. p. 149 (Bohn).

12. πρὸς τὸν καταρτισμὸν κ.
τ. λ.] '*with a view to the perfecting of the
saints, for the work of ministration, for the
building up of the body of Christ ;*' more
ultimate and more immediate end of the
gifts specified in the preceding verse. It
is extremely difficult to fix the exact
shade of meaning which these prepp.
are intended to convey. It seems clear,
however, (a) that there is no 'trajection,'
Grot. ; — nor again (b) that the three

members are to be regarded as merely
parallel, and *coördinately* dependent on
ἔδωκε (ἕκαστος οἰκοδομεῖ, ἕκαστ. καταρ-
τίζει, ἕκαστ. διακονεῖ, Chrys.), for πρὸς
and εἰς must thus be regarded as synonymous (Syr., Goth., Arm.) ; and though
St. Paul studied prepositional variations
(see Winer, *Gr.* § 50. 6, p. 372), it still
does not appear from the exx. usually
cited that he did so except for the sake
of definition, limitation, or presentation
of the subject in a fresh point of view ;
see notes *on Gal.* i. 1. Moreover, as
Mey. justly observes, the second member, εἰς ἔργον κ. τ. λ., would thus much
more naturally and logically stand first.
It also seems (c) nearly equally unsatisfactory, with Æth. (expressly ; Vulg.,
Clarom., Copt. are equally ambiguous
with the Greek), De W., al., to connect
εἰς — εἰς closely with πρός, as we are
thus compelled to give διακονία the less
usual, and here (after the previous accurate definitions) extremely doubtful
meaning of 'christliche Dienstleitung,'
De W., 'genus omnium functionum in
Ecclesiâ,' Aret.; see below. It seems,
then (d) best and most consonant with
the fundamental (ethical) meaning of
the prepositions to connect εἰς—εἰς with
ἔδωκε, and, — as εἰς, with the idea of
destination, frequently involves that of
attainment (see Jelf, *Gr.* § 625. 3, Krüger,
Sprachl. § 68. 21. 5, and comp. Hand,
Tursell. ' in,' III. 23, Vol. III. 23), — to
regard εἰς—εἰς as two parallel members
referring to the more *immediate*, πρὸς to
the more *ultimate* and final purpose of
the action ; comp. Rom. xv. 2, ἀρεσκέτω
εἰς τὸ ἀγαθὸν πρὸς οἰκοδομήν, which seems
to admit a similar explanation, and see
notes *on Philem* 5. For distinctions
between εἰς, πρός, and ἐπί see notes *on* 2
Thess. ii. 4, and between εἰς, πρός, and
κατά, notes *on Tit.* i. 1. We may thus

σώματος τοῦ Χριστοῦ, ¹³ μέχρι καταντήσωμεν οἱ πάντες εἰς
τὴν ἑνότητα τῆς πίστεως καὶ τῆς ἐπιγνώσεως τοῦ υἱοῦ τοῦ Θεοῦ,

paraphrase: 'He gave apostles, etc., to fulfil the work of the ministry and to build up the body of Christ, His object being to perfect his saints;' compare Hofm. *Schriftb.* Vol. ii. 2, p. 109, where the same view is *practically* maintained. τ ὸ ν κ α τ α ρ τ ι σ μ ό ν] '*the perfecting,*' τὴν τελείωσιν, Theophyl.; comp. κατάρτισις, 2 Cor. xiii. 9; the nature of this (definite) perfecting is explained ver. 13. The *primary* (ethical) meaning of καταρτίζειν, 'reconcinnare' (Rost u. Palm, *Lex.* s. v.), appears only in Gal. vi. 1 (comp. notes); in all other passages in the N. T. of ethical reference (e. g. Luke vi. 40, 1 Cor. i. 10, 2 Cor. xiii. 11, Heb. xiii. 21, 1 Pet. v. 10), the *secondary* meaning, 'to make ἄρτιος,' 'to make perfect, complete' (τελειοῦν, Hesych.), appears to be the prevailing meaning; compare καταρτίζειν τριήρεις, Diod. Sic. xiii. 70, see exx. in Schweigh, *Lex. Polyb.* s. v. Any allusion to 'the accomplishment of the number of the elect,' Pelag. (compare Burial Service), would here be wholly out of place. ἔ ρ γ ο ν δ ι α κ ο ν ί α ς] '*the work of (the) ministry;*' scil. 'for the duties and functions of διάκονοι in the Church.' As the meaning of both these words has been unduly strained, we may remark briefly that ἔργον is not pleonastic (see Winer, *Gr.* § 65. 7, p. 541), or in the special sense of 'building' (compare 1 Cor. iii. 13), but has the simple meaning of 'business,' 'function' (1 Tim. iii. 1),—not 'res perfecta,' but 'res gerenda,' in exact parallelism with the use of οἰκοδομή. Again, διακονία is not 'service' generally, but, as its prevailing usage in the N. T. (Rom. xi. 13, 2 Cor. iv. 1, al.) and especially the present context suggest, 'spiritual service of an *official* nature;' see Meyer *in loc.*, Hofm. *Schriftb.* Vol. ii. 2, p. 109. The absence of both

articles has been pressed (Eadie, Peile), but appy. unduly; διακονία may possibly have been left studiedly anarthrous in reference to the different modes of exercising it alluded to in ver. 11, and the various spiritual wants of the Church (Hamm.); ἔργον, however, seems clearly definite in meaning, though by the principle of *correlation* (Middleton, *Art.* iii. 3, 6) it is necessarily anarthrous in form. ο ἰ κ ο δ. τ ο ῦ σ ώ μ α τ ο ς] '*building up of the body,*' parallel to, but at the same time more nearly defining the nature of the ἔργον. The article is not required (as with καταρτ.), as it was not any absolute, definite process of edifying, but edifying generally that was the object. The observation which some commentators make on 'the confusion of metaphors' is nugatory; as τὸ σῶμα τοῦ Χρ. has a distinct metaphorical sense, so has οἰκοδομή. On the nature of Christian οἰκοδομή, see Nitzsch, *Theologie*, § 39, Vol. i. p. 205.

13. μ έ χ ρ ι κ α τ α ν τ ή σ ω μ ε ν] '*until we come to, arrive at;*' specification of the time up to which this spiritual constitution was designed to last. Several recent commentators (Harl., Meyer, al.) notice the omission of ἄν as giving an air of less uncertainty to the subj.; see notes *on Gal.* iii. 19. As a general principle this is of course right (see Herm. *Partic.* ἄν, ii. 9, p. 109 sq., Hartung, *Partik.* ἄν, 3, Vol. ii. p. 291 sq.); we must be *cautious*, however, in applying the rule in the N. T., as the tendency of latter Greek to the nearly exclusive use of the subj., and esp. to the use of these temporal particles with that tense, without ἄν, is very discernible; see Winer, *Gr.* § 41. 3, p. 265. The use of the subj. (the mood of conditioned but objective possibility), not fut (as Chrys.), shows that the καταντᾶν is represented

εἰς ἄνδρα τέλειον, εἰς μέτρον ἡλικίας τοῦ πληρώματος τοῦ Χρισ-

not only as the eventual, but as the *expected* and *contemplated* result of the ἔδωκε; see Scheuerl. *Synt.* § 36. 1, p. 393, Jelf, *Gr.* § 842. 2, and compare Schmalfeld, *Synt.* § 128, p. 280. This use of the subj. deserves observation. The meaning of καταντᾶν with ἐπὶ or εἰς (only the latter in the N. T.) has been unduly pressed; it has no necessary reference to former wanderings or diverse *starting*-points (Zanch., Vatabl. ap. Poli *Syn.*), but simply implies 'pervenire ad' ('occurrere,' Vulg., Clarom.), with ref. only to the place, person, or point arrived at; see notes *on Phil.* iii. 11, and compare exx. in Schweigh. *Lex. Polyb.* s. v. οἱ πάντες] 'we all,' 'the *whole of us;*' scil. all Christians, implied in the τῶν ἁγίων, ver. 12. It is difficult to agree with Ellendt (*Lex. Soph.* s. v. πᾶς, III. 1, Vol. II. p. 519) in the assertion that in the *plural* the addition or omission of the article, 'cum sensus fert,' makes no difference. The distinction is not *always* obvious (see Middleton, *Art.* VII. 1), but may generally be deduced from the fundamental laws of the article. εἰς τὴν ἑνότητα τῆς πίστ.] 'to the unity of the faith;' '*that* oneness of faith' (Peile, see Wordsw.), which was the aim and object towards which the spiritual efforts of the various forms of ministry were all directed; ἕως ἂν δειχθῶμεν πάντες μίαν [rather, τὴν μίαν] πίστιν ἔχοντες· τοῦτο γάρ ἐστιν ἑνότης πίστεως ὅταν πάντες ἓν ὦμεν, ὅταν πάντες ὁμοίως τὸν σύνδεσμον ἐπιγινώσκωμεν, Chrys. καὶ τῆς ἐπιγνώσεως κ. τ. λ.] 'and of the (true) *knowledge* of the Son of God;' further development, — not only faith in the Son, but saving knowledge of Him; the gen. τοῦ υἱοῦ τοῦ Θεοῦ being the gen. *objecti* (Winer, *Gr.* § 30. obs. p. 168), and belonging to both substantives. The καὶ is thus not 'exegetice positum'

(Calv.), but simply copulative; the former interpr. though grammatically admissible (see *on Gal.* vi. 16), would here be contextually untenable, as πίστις and ἐπίγνωσις (see notes on ch. i. 17) obviously convey different ideas (Mey.), and are terms by no means mutually explanatory; 'cognitio perfectius quiddam *fide* sonat,' Beng. Such sentences as the present may serve to make us careful in obtruding too hastily on every passage the meaning of πίστις Ἰησοῦ Χρ. alluded to on ch. iii. 12, and noticed in notes *on Gal.* ii. 16. εἰς ἄνδρα τέλειον] 'to a perfect, full-grown, man;' metaphorical apposition to the foregoing member, the concrete term being probably selected rather than any abstract term (ἡ τελειοτέρα τῶν δογμάτων [better τοῦ Χριστοῦ] γνῶσις, Theoph.), as forming a good contrast to the following νήπιοι (ver. 14, compare 1 Cor. xiii. 9), and as suggesting by its singular the idea of the complete unity of the holy personality further explained in the next clause, into which they were united and consummated. Instances of a similar use of τέλειος are cited by Raphel, *Annot.* Vol. II. p. 447; see esp. Polyb. *Hist.* v. 29. 2, where παιδίον νήπιον and τέλειον ἄνδρα stand in studied contrast to each other. εἰς μέτρον κ. τ. λ.] 'to the measure of the stature of Christ's fulness,' i. e., 'of the fulness which Christ has,' τοῦ Χρ. being the gen. .*subjecti*; see esp. notes ch. iii. 19, and on the accumulation of genitives, Winer, *Gr.* § 30. 3, obs. 1, p. 172; comp. 2 Cor. iv. 4. It is doubtful whether ἡλικία is to be referred (a) to *age* (John ix. 21, so clearly Matth. vi. 27), or (b) to *stature* (Luke xix. 3), both being explanations here equally admissible; see Bos, *Exercit.* p. 183. In the former case, τοῦ πληρ. τ. Χρ. will be the qualifying, or rather *characterizing* gen. (Scheuerl. *Synt.* § 16, 3,

τοῦ, ¹⁴ ἵνα μηκέτι ὦμεν νήπιοι, κλυδωνιζόμενοι καὶ περιφερόμενοι

p. 115, and notes on ch. i. 10), and will more nearly define τῆς ἡλικ., — 'the age when the fulness of Christ is received;' in the latter the gen. is purely *possessive*. The antithesis (τέλειοι—νήπιοι) seems in favor of (a); still, — as both words are metaphorical, — as μέτρον is appropriately used in reference to 'stature' (see esp. Lucian, *Imag*. 6, cited by Wetst.; even in Hom. *Od*. xviii. 217, ἥβης μέτρ. is associated with the idea of *size*), and still more, as the separate words πλήρωμα, αὐξήσωμεν, etc., no less than the context ver. 16, all suggest ideas of *matured growth* in respect of *magnitude*, — the latter interpr. (b) seems most probable and satisfactory; so Syr., Goth. ('vahstaus'), Copt. (*maïē*), appy. Æth., and our own Auth. Version.   It has been considered a question whether the Apostle is here referring solely to *present* (Chrysost.), or to *future* life (Theod.). The mention of πίστις, and the tenor of ver. 14, 15, incline us to the former view; still it is probable (see Olsh.) that no special distinction was intended. St. Paul regards the Church as one; he declares its issue and destination as ἑνότης and τελειότης; on the realization of this, whensoever and wheresoever, the functions of the Christian ministry will cease.

14. ἵνα μηκέτι κ. τ. λ.] '*in order that we may be no longer children;*' purpose contemplated in the limitation as to duration of the gifts specified in ver. 11 sq. The connection is not perfectly clear. Is this verse (a) coördinate with ver. 13, and *immediately* dependent on 11, 12 (Harl.), or (b) is it *subordinate* to it, and *remotely* dependent on ver. 11, 12? The latter seems most probable; ver. 13 thus defines the 'terminus ad quem' which characterizes the functions of the Christian ministry; ver. 14 explains the object, viz., our ceasing to be

νήπιοι, contemplated in the appointment of such a 'terminus,' and thence more remotely in the bestowal of a ministry *so characterized;* see Meyer *in loc*., who has ably elucidated the connection. For a sound sermon on this text in reference to the case of 'Deceivers and Deceived,' see Waterl. *Serm*. xxix. Vol. v. p. 717 sq.   μηκέτι] '*no longer;*' τὸ 'μηκέτι' δείκνυσι πάλαι τοῦτο παθόντας, Chrys. This is not, however, said in reference to Ephesians only, but as the context (πάντες, ver. 13) suggests, in ref. to Christians generally. Eadie somewhat singularly stops to comment on the use of 'μηκέτι not οὐκέτι;' surely to ἵνα in its present sense, 'particula μὴ consentanea est,' Gayler, *Partik. Neg*. p. 168.   κλυδωνιζόμενοι] '*tossed about* like waves' ('usvagidai' Goth., compare Syr., Arm.), — not 'by the waves.' Stier, assuming the latter to be the true meaning of the pass. ('metaphor from a ship lying at hull,' Bramh. *Catching Lev*. ch. 3, Vol. iv. p. 592), adopts the middle (comp. 'fluctuantes,' Vulg.) to avoid the then incongruous κλυδ. ἀνέμῳ. The exx. however, adduced by Wetst. and Krebs, viz., Aristæn. *Epist*. i. 27, κλυδωνίζεσθαι ἐκ τοῦ πόθου, Joseph. *Antiq*. ix. 11. 3, ταρασσόμενος καὶ κλυδωνιζόμενος, confirm the passive use and the former meaning; comp. James i. 6.   ἀνέμῳ τῆς διδασκαλίας] '*wave of doctrine.*' The article does not show 'the prominence which teaching possessed in the Church' (Eadie), but specifies διδασκαλία in the abstract, every kind and degree of it; see Middleton, *Art*. v. 1, p. 89 sq. (ed. Rose). On the apparent distinction between διδασκαλία and διδαχή, see *on* 2 *Tim*. iv. 2.   ἐν τῇ κυβείᾳ κ. τ. λ.] '*in the sleight of men*,' — of men, not the faith and knowledge of the *Son of God*, ver. 13. Ἐν may be plausibly

παντὶ ἀνέμῳ τῆς διδασκαλίας ἐν τῇ κυβείᾳ τῶν ἀνϑρώπων, ἐν

considered instrumental (Arm., Mey.); as, however, this would seem pleonastic after the instrumental, or what Krüger (*Sprachl.* § 48. 151 sq.) more inclusively terms the *dynamic* dat. ἀνέμῳ (see Heb. xiii. 9), and would mar the seeming parallelism with ἐν ἀγάπῃ (ver. 15), the prep. appears rather to denote the *element*, the evil *atmosphere*, as it were, *in* which the varying currents of doctrine exist and exert their force; so Clarom., Vulg., Copt., Æth.-Pol., and perhaps Goth., but see De Gabel. *in loc.*

The term κυβεία (קֻבְיָא Heb.), properly denotes 'playing with dice' (Plato, *Phædr.* 274 D, πεττείας καὶ κυβείας, see Xen. *Mem.* i. 3. 2), and thence, by an easy transition, 'sleight of hand,' 'fraud' (πανουργία, Suid.; comp. κυβεύειν, Arrian, *Epict.* ii. 19, iii. 21, cited by Weist.); ἴδιον δὲ τῶν κυβευόντων τὸ τῇδε κἀκεῖσε μεταφέρειν τοὺς ψήφους καὶ πανούργως τοῦτο ποιεῖν, Theod.; see Suicer, *Thesaur.* s. v. Vol. ii. p. 181, Schoettg. *Hor. Heb.* Vol. i. p. 775.

ἐν πανουργίᾳ πρὸς κ. τ. λ.] '*in craftiness tending to the deliberate system of error,*' 'in astutiâ ad circumventionem erroris,' Vulg.; appositional and partly explanatory clause to the foregoing. The Auth. Ver. (comp. Syr.) is here too paraphrastic, and obscures the meaning of both πρὸς and μεϑοδεία. The former is not equivalent to κατά, Rück., 'with,' Peile, but denotes the *aim*, the *natural tendency*, of πανουργία (compare notes *on Tit.* i. 1); the μεϑοδεία τῆς πλ. is that which πανουργία has in view (compare πρὸς τὸν καταρτ. ver. 12), and to which it is readily and naturally disposed. As πανουργία is anarthrous, the omission of the art. before πρὸς (which induces Rück. incorrectly to refer the clause to φερόμενοι) is perfectly regular; see Winer, *Gr.* § 20. 4, p. 126.   The somewhat rare term μεϑοδεία, a δὶς λεγόμ. in the

N. T. (see ch. vi. 11), must have its meaning fixed by μεϑοδεύω. This verb denotes, 'the pursuit, etc., of a settled plan' — (*a*) honestly (Diod. Sic. i. 81, μ. τὴν ἀληϑείαν ἐκ τῆς ἐμπειρίας), or (*b*) dishonestly (Polyb. *Fr. Hist.* xxxviii. 4. 10), and hence comes to imply 'deception,' 'fraud,' with more or less of *plan* (2 Sam. xix. 27); comp. Chrys. *on Eph.* vi. 11, μεϑοδεῦσαί ἐστι τὸ ἀπατῆσαι καὶ διὰ συντόμου (μηχανῆς Sav.) ἑλεῖν; see also Münthe, *Obs.* p. 367. Thus then μεϑοδεία is 'a deliberate planning or system,' (Peile; τὴν μηχανὴν ἐκάλεσεν, Theod.),' the further idea of 'fraud' (τέχνη ἢ δόλος, Suid.; ἐπιβουλή, Zonar.) being here expressed in πλάνης; see Suicer, *Thesaur.* s. v. Vol. ii. p. 329. The reading is doubtful; *Tisch.* (ed. 7) adopts the form μεϑοδίαν with B¹D¹FG KL; and several mss., but appy. on insufficient authority; changes in orthography which may be accounted for by itacism or some mode of erroneous transcription must always be received with caution; comp. Winer, *Gr.* § 5. 4, p. 47.

πλάνης has not here (nor Matth. xxvii. 64, 2 Thess. ii. 11) the active meaning of 'misleading' (De W., compare Syr. وَلَاخْذُ [ut seducant], nor even necessarily that of 'delusion' (Harl.), but its simple, classical, and regular meaning, 'error' — 'erroris,' Vulgate, 'airzeins,' Goth. The gen. is obviously not the gen. *objecti* (Rück.), but *subjecti*, — it is the πλάνη which μεϑοδεύει, — and thus stands in grammatical parallelism with the preceding gen. τῶν ἀνϑρ. The use of the article must not be overlooked; it serves almost to personify πλάνη, not, however, as metonymically for 'Satan' (Bengel), but as 'Error' in its most abstract nature, and thus renders the contrast to ἡ ἀλήϑεια implied in ἀληϑεύοντες, more forcible and significant.

πανουργίᾳ πρὸς τὴν μεϑοδείαν τῆς πλάνης, ¹⁵ ἀληϑεύοντες δὲ ἐν

15. ἀ λ η ϑ ε ύ ο ν τ ε ς δ έ] 'but holding the truth, walking truthfully;' participial member attached to αὐξήσωμεν, and with it grammatically dependent on ἵνα (ver. 14), — the whole clause, as the use of δέ (after a negative sentence) seems distinctly to suggest (comp. Hartung, Partik. δέ, 2. 11, Vol. i. p. 171), standing in simple and direct opposition to the whole preceding verse (esp. to the concluding πλανή, De W.), without, however, any reference to the preceding negation, which would rather have required ἀλλά; see esp. Klotz, Devar. Vol. ii. p. 3, 361, Donalds. Cratyl. § 201. The meaning of ἀληϑεύειν is somewhat doubtful. On the one hand, such translations as 'veritati operam dare' (Calv.) and even 'Wahrheit festhalten' (Rück.) are lexically untenable (see Rost u. Palm, Lex: s. v. ἀληϑ. Vol. i. p. 97); on the other, the common meaning, 'veritatem dicere' (Gal. iv. 16), seems clearly exegetically unsatisfactory. It is best then to preserve an intermediate sense, 'walking in truth' (Olsh.) or (to preserve an antithesis in transl. between πλάνης and ἀληϑ.) 'holding the truth,' Scholef. (Hints, p. 100), — which latter interpr., if 'holding' be not unduly pressed, is almost justified by Plato, Theæt. 202 B, ἀληϑεύειν τὴν ψυχὴν ['verum sentire,' Ast] περὶ αὐτό; so in effect, but somewhat too strongly, Vulg., Clarom., Goth., 'veritatem facientes,' and sim. Copt.   ἐ ν ἀ γ ά π ῃ] The connection of these words has been much discussed. Are they to be joined — (a) with the participle (Syr., Æth., Theoph., Œcum.), or — (b) with the finite verb (Theod., — who, however, omits ἀληϑ., and appy. Chrys., τῇ ἀγάπῃ συνδεδεμένοι)? It must fairly be conceded that the order, the parallelism of structure with that of ver. 14, and still more the vital association between love and the truest

form of truth (see Stier in loc.), are arguments of some weight in favor of (a); still the absence of any clear antithesis between ἐν ἀγ. and either of the preposit. clauses in ver. 14 forms a negative argument, and the concluding words of ver. 16 (whether ἐν ἀγ. be joined immediately with αὔξησιν ποιεῖται Mey., or with οἰκοδομὴν) supply a positive argument in favor of (b), of such force, that this latter connection must be pronounced the more probable, and certainly the one most in harmony with the context; compare ch. i. 4. The order may have arisen from a desire to keep αὐτὸν as near as possible to its relative.   ε ἰ ς α ὐ τ ό ν] 'into Him,' Auth. Ver.; εἰς not implying merely 'in reference to' (Mey.), — a frigid and unsatisfactory interpretation of which that expositor is too fond (comp. notes on Gal. iii. 27), nor 'for' (Eadie), nor even simply 'unto,' 'to the standard of' (Conyb.; comp. εἰς ἄνδρα τέλειον, ver. 13), but retaining its fuller and deeper theological sense 'into,' so that αὐξ. with εἰς conveys both ideas, 'unto and into.' The growth of Christians bears relation to Christ both as its centre and standard; while the limits of that growth are defined by 'the stature of the fulness of Christ,' its centre is also, and must be, in Him; comp. some profound remarks in Ebrard, Dogmatik, § 445 sq.   τ ὰ π ά ν τ α] 'in all the parts in which we grow' (Mey.), 'in all the elements of our growth;' the article being thus most simply explained by the context. It now need scarcely be said that no 'supplement of κατὰ' (Eadie, Stier) is required; τὰ πάντα is the regular accus. of what is termed the quantitative object (Hartung, Casus, p. 46), and serves to characterize the extent of the action; see Madvig, Gr. § 27, Krüger, Sprachl. § 46. 5. 4.   ὅ ς ἐ σ τ ι ν κ. τ. λ.] 'who is the Head, even

ἀγάπῃ αὐξήσωμεν εἰς αὐτὸν τὰ πάντα, ὅς ἐστιν ἡ κεφαλή, Χριστός, ¹⁶ ἐξ οὗ πᾶν τὸ σῶμα συναρμολογούμενον καὶ συνβιβαζόμε-

Christ.' There is here neither transposition (Grot., comp. Syr.), nor careless-
ness of construct. for εἰς αὐτὸν τὸν Χρ.
(Pisc.). Instead of the ordinary form
of simple, or what is termed *parenthetic*
apposition (see exx. Krüger, *Sprachl.*
§ 57. 9), the Apostle, not improbably for
the sake of making ἐξ οὗ, ver 16, perfectly perspicuous (De W.), adopts the
relative sentence, with the structure of
which the apposition is *assimilated*; see
exx. Winer, *Gr.* § 48. 4, p. 424 (ed. 5),
and Stalb. Plat. *Apol.* 41 A. The
reading is somewhat doubtful; *Rec.* prefixes the art. to Χρ. with DEFGKL;
most mss.; Chrys., Theod. (*De Wette,
Mey.*), — but appy. on authority inferior
to that for its omission, viz. ABC, 3
mss.; Did., Bas., Cyr., al. (*Lachm.,
Tisch., Alf.*). Internal arguments cannot safely be urged, as the preponderance of instances of *real* omission (53)
over those of insertion (31) is not very
decided; see the table drawn up by
Rose in his ed. of Middleton, *Gr. Art.*
Append. II. p. 490 sq., and Gersdorf,
Beiträge, III. p. 272 sq. Under any circumstances the position of the word at
the end of the verse gives it both force
and emphasis.

16. ἐξ οὗ] '*from whom*,' Auth., 'ex
quo,' Syr., Vulgate, Clarom., — not 'in
quo,' Æth. (both); ἐξ οὗ, as the instructive parallel, Col. ii. 19, clearly suggests,
being joined with αὔξησιν ποιεῖται, and
ἐκ, with its proper and primary force of
origin, *source*, denoting the *origin*, the
'fons augmentationis,' Beng.; see notes
on Gal. ii. 16. It is not wholly uninter-
esting to remark that the force of the
metaphor is enhanced by the *apparent*
physiological truth, that the energy of
vital power varies with the distance from
the head; see Schubert, *Gesch. der Seele*,
§ 22, p. 270 (ed. 1).   σ υ ν α ρ μ ο-

λ ο γ ο ύ μ ε ν ο ν] ο '*being fitly framed together*;' pres. part., the action still going
on; see notes ch. ii. 21.   σ υ ν β ι-
β α ζ ό μ ε ν ο ν] '*compacted*,' ܡܬ̈ܩ܊ܠ
[et colligatur] Syr., 'connexum,' Vulg.,
Clarom., 'gagahaftiþ,' Goth., — or more
literally and with more special reference
to derivation [ΒΑ-, βαίνω], '*put together*;'
compare Col. ii. 19, and in a figurative
sense, Acts ix. 22, xvi. 10. The difference of meaning between συναρμ. and
συνβ. has been differently stated. According to Bengel, the first denotes the
harmony, the second the *solidity* and firmness of the structure. Perhaps the
more exact view is that which the simple meanings of the words suggest, viz.,
that συνβ. refers to the *aggregation*, συν-
ναρμ. to the *inter-adaptation* of the component parts. The external author
ity for the form συνβιβ. [AB(?)CD¹FG]
is appy. sufficient to warrant the adoption of this less usual form; see Tisch.
Prolegom. p. XLVII.   δ ι ὰ π ά σ η ς
ἀ φ ῆ ς] '*by means of every joint*,' 'per
omnem juncturam,' Vulg., Clarom., and
sim. all the ancient Vv. Meyer still
retains the interpr. of Chrys., Theod.,
ἀφὴ = αἴσθησις, and connects the clause
with αὔξ. ποιεῖται; but the parallel passage, Col. ii. 19, τῶν ἀφῶν καὶ συνδέσμων
(observe esp. the omission of the 2d article, Winer, § 19. 4) leaves it scarcely
doubtful that the meaning usually assigned (comp. Athen. III. 202 Ε, Plut.
Anton. 27) is correct, and that the clause
is to be connected with the participles.
τ ῆ ς ἐ π ι χ ο ρ η γ ί α ς] '*of the (spiritual)
supply*;' the article implying the specific
ἐπιχορ. which Christ supplies, τῆς χορη-
γίας τῶν χαρισμάτων, Chrysost.; on the
meaning of the word compare notes *on
Gal.* iii. 5. The gen. is not the gen. of
apposition (Rück., Harl.), nor a mere

νον διὰ πάσης ἀφῆς τῆς ἐπιχορηγίας κατ' ἐνέργειαν ἐν μέτρῳ ἑνὸς
ἑκάστου μέρους τὴν αὔξησιν τοῦ σώματος ποιεῖται εἰς οἰκοδομὴν
ἑαυτοῦ ἐν ἀγάπῃ.

Hebraistic genitive of *quality*, 'joint of ministry' = 'ministering joint' (Peile, Green, *Gramm. N. T.* p. 264; compare Winer, *Gr.* § 34. 3. b), but a kind of gen. *definitivus*, by which the predominant use, purpose, or destination of the ἀφὴ is specified and characterized; see Heb. ix. 21, σκεύη τῆς λειτουργίας, and compare the exx. cited by Winer, *Gr.* § 30. 2, β, p. 170. The suggestion of Dobree (*Advers.* Vol. I. p. 573), partly adopted by Scholef., that ἐπιχ. may be 'materia suppeditata,' is not very satisfactory or tenable; see Phil. i. 19.

κατ' ἐνέργειαν κ. τ. λ.] '*according to energy in the measure of* (sc. *commensurate with*) *each individual part*;' τῷ μὲν δυναμένῳ πλέον δέξασθαι, πλέον, τῷ δὲ ἐλάττω, ἔλαττον, Chrys. These words may be connected either (*a*) with ἐπιχορηγίας, — the omission of the art. is no objection (Rück.), as ἡ ἐπιχ. κατ' ἐνέργ. may form one idea (Winer, *Gr.* § 20, 2, p. 123), or (*b*) with the participles, or yet again (*c*) with the finite verb. As the expressions of the clause far more appropriately describe the *nature of the growth* than either the mode of compaction or the degree of the supply, the latter construction is to be preferred. Κατ' ἐνέργ. is then a modal predication, appended to ποιεῖται, defining the *nature* of the αὔξησις; this growth is neither abnormal nor proportionless, but is regulated by a vital power which is proportioned to the nature and extext of the separate parts. Dobree (*Advers.* Vol. I. p. 573) strongly condemns this translation, but, as it would seem, without sufficient reason. His own translation, which connects κατ' ἐνέργ. with ἑνὸς ἑκ. μέρ. and isolates ἐν μέτρῳ, impairs the force of the deep and consolatory truths which the ordinary connection suggests. For a

good practical application see Eadie *in loc.*　　　The reading μέλους is fairly supported [AC; Vulg., Copt., Syr., al.; Cyr., Chrys., al.], but is appy. rightly rejected by most recent editors, as a gloss on μέρους suggested by the preceding σῶμα and the succeeding σώματος.

τὴν αὔξ. τοῦ σώματος ποιεῖται] '*promotes, carries on, the growth of the body*,' — σώματος being probably added for the sake of perspicuity, and so practically taking the place of the reciprocal pronoun; comp. Winer, *Gr.* § 22. 2, p. 130, Krüger, Xenoph. *Anab.* p. 27. Stier, perhaps not incorrectly, finds in the repetition of the noun an enunciation of a spiritual truth, echoed by ἑαυτοῦ, — that the body makes increase of *the body*, and so is a living organism; — that its growth is not due to aggregations from without, but to vital forces from within; comp. Harless.　　　The middle ποιεῖται is perhaps not to be insisted on as confirming this (Alf.), this form appy. being not so much reflexive (Wordsw.), as *intensive* and indicative of the energy with which the process is carried on; see Krüger, *Sprachl.* § 52. 7. 1; compare Donalds. *Gr.* 432. 2.　　　εἰς οἰκοδομὴν ἐν ἀγ.] '*for building up of itself in love*;'

ܣܠܝܩ ܠܒܢܝܢܐ ܕܢܦܫܗ

[ut in caritate perficiatur ædificium ejus] Syr. end and object of the αὔξησιν ποιεῖται; love is the element in which the edification takes place. Meyer connects ἐν ἀγάπῃ with αὔξησιν ποιεῖται, to harmonize with ver. 15, but without sufficient reason, and in opp. to the obvious objection that αὔξησιν ποιεῖται is thus associated with *two* limiting prepositional clauses, and the unity of thought proportionately impaired; comp. Alf. *in loc.*

Do not walk as darkened, hardened, and feelingless heathens. Put off the old, and put on the new man.

¹⁷ Τοῦτο οὖν λέγω καὶ μαρτύρομαι ἐν Κυρίῳ, μηκέτι ὑμᾶς περιπατεῖν καθὼς καὶ τὰ λοιπὰ

17. τοῦτο οὖν λεγω] 'This, I say then;' this, sc. what follows; connecting the verse with the hortatory portion commenced ver. 1—3, by resumption on the negative side (μηκέτι περιπατεῖν) of the exhortation previously expressed on the positive side, ver. 1—3 (παρακ. ἀξίως περιπατῆσαι), but interrupted by the digression, ver. 4—16; πάλιν ἀνέλαβε τῆς παραινέσεως τὸ προοίμιον, Theod. On this resumptive force of οὖν, see Klotz, Devar. Vol. II. p. 718, and notes on Gal. iii. 5. The illative force advocated by Eadie after Meyer (ed. 1), is here improbable, and rightly retracted by Meyer (ed. 2); comp. Donalds. Gr. § 548. 31. μαρτύρομαι ἐν Κυρίῳ] 'testify, solemnly declare, ('quasi testibus adhibitis') in the Lord,' — not 'per Dominum,' (μάρτυρα δὲ τὸν Κύριον καλῶ, Chrysost.; see Fritz. Rom. ix. 1, Vol. II. p. 241), nor even as specifying the authority upon which ('tanquam Christi discipulus,' Fritz. Rom. Vol. II. p. 84), but, as usual, defining the element or sphere in which the declaration is made; compare Rom. ix. 1, ἀλήθειαν λέγω ἐν Χρ.; 2 Cor. ii. 17, ἐν Χρ. λαλοῦμεν (scarcely correctly translated by Fritz. 'ut homines cum Christo nexi'), 1 Thess. iv. 1, παρακαλοῦμεν ἐν Κυρίῳ, and see notes in loc. By thus sinking his own personality, the solemnity of the Apostle's declaration is greatly enhanced. On this use of μαρτ. see notes on Gal. v. 3, and compare Raphel. Annot. Vol. II. p. 478, 595.

μηκέτι ὑμᾶς περιπατεῖν] 'that ye no longer (must) walk;' subject and substance of the hortatory declaration; see Acts xxi. 21, λέγων μὴ περιτέμνειν αὐτοὺς τὰ τέκνα. In objective sentences of this nature (see esp. Donalds. Gr. § 584 sq.) the infinitive frequently involves the same conception that would have been expressed in the direct sentence by the

imperative, and is usually (but incorrectly) explained by an ellipsis of δεῖν; see Winer, Gr. § 45. 2, p. 371, Lobeck, Phryn. 753 sq., and compare Heindorf on Plato, Protag. 346 B. καὶ τὰ λοιπὰ ἔθνη] 'the rest of the Gentiles also;' with tacit reference to their own former state when unconverted; the καὶ introducing a comparison or gentle contrast between the emphatically expressed ὑμᾶς and the ἔθνη, of which they but lately formed a part; see notes on verses 4, 32, and on Phil. iv. 12. The term λοιπὰ is here rightly used, as the Ephesians, though Christians, still fell under the general denomination of Gentiles; it serves also to convey a hint reminding them what they once were, and what they now ought not to be; see Wolf in loc. The external authority for striking this last word (λοιπὰ) out of the text [Lachm. with ABD¹FG; 5 mss., Clarom., Sang., Aug., Boern., Vulg., Copt., Sahid., Æth. (both); Clem., Cyr., al.] is rather strong; still as the probability of its being left out from being imperfectly understood, seems so much greater than the probability of its being a conformation to ch. ii. 3 (Mill, in loc., and Prolegom. p. LX), we may perhaps safely retain the adject. with D²D³EKL; great majority of mss.; Syr. (both), Goth., al.; Chrys., Theod. (Tisch. ed. 2 and 7, Alf., al.]. ἐν ματαιότητι κ τ. λ.] 'in the vanity of their mind;' sphere of their moral walk; comp. Rom. i. 21, ἐματαιώθησαν ἐν τοῖς διαλογισμοῖς αὐτῶν. Chrys. rightly explains the words by τὸ περὶ τὰ μάταια ἠσχολῆσθαι, but is probably not correct in restricting them to idolatry, as μάταιος and ματαιόω do not necessarily involve any such reference; compare Fritz. Rom. Vol. I. 65. The reference seems rather to that general nothingness and depravation of the νοῦς

ἔθνη περιπατεῖ ἐν ματαιότητι τοῦ νοὸς αὐτῶν, ¹⁸ ἐσκοτισμένοι τῇ
διανοίᾳ ὄντες, ἀπηλλοτριωμένοι τῆς ζωῆς τοῦ Θεοῦ διὰ τὴν ἄγνοιαν

(the higher moral and intellectual element), which was the universal characteristic of heathenism ; see Usteri, *Lehrb.*
I. 3, p. 35 sq., and notes *on* 1 *Tim.* vi. 5,
2 *Tim.* iii. 8.

18. *ἐσκοτισμένοι ὄντες*] '*being
darkened:*' participial clause defining
their state, and accounting for the preceding assertion (see Donalds. *Gr.* §
616) ; *ἐσκοτ.* (opp. to *πεφωτισμένοι*, ch.
i. 18; comp. Rom. i. 21, xi. 10, 1 Thess.
v. 4) referring to their state of moral
darkness, and *ὄντες* (rightly referred by
Tisch., Lachm., to *ἐσκοτ.,* not to *ἀπηλλ.*
[Eadie], — a punctuation which mars
the emphatic parallelism of the initial
perf. participles) marking, somewhat
pleonastically after the perf. part., its
permanent and *enduring* state; comp.
Winer. *Gr.* § 45. 5. p. 311. The apparently conjugate nature of the clauses
(comp. *ὄντες*—*οὖσαν*) has led Olsh. and
others to couple together *ἐσκοτ. κ. τ. λ.*
and *διὰ τὴν ἄγν.* as relating to the *intel-
lect, ἀπηλλ. κ. τ. λ.* and *διὰ τὴν πώρ.* as
relating to the *feelings.* This, however,
though at first sight plausible, will not
be found logically satisfactory. The
being *ἐσκοτ. κ. τ. λ.* could scarcely be
said to be the consequence of their *ἄγνοια* ('ignorance' simply, Acts iii. 17,
xvii. 30. and appy. 1 Pet. i.14), but rather *vice versâ,* whereas it seems perfectly
consistent to say that their alienation
was caused by their ignorance, and still
more by the ensuing *πώρωσις.* Hence
the punctuation of the text. The
reading *ἐσκοτισμένοι* is not perfectly certain ; the more classical *ἐσκοτωμένοι* is
found in AB; Ath. (*Lachm., Tisch.* ed.
7), but has not sufficient support to warrant its being received in the text.

τῇ διανοίᾳ] '*in their understanding,*'
'in their higher intellectual nature,'
διέξοδος λογικὴ (Orig.; comp. Beck,

Seelenl. II. 19, p. 58) ; see ch. i. 18, ii.
3, and Joseph. *Antiq.* IX. 4. 3, *τὴν διά-
νοιαν ἐπεσκοτισμένους.* The dat. ('of
reference to') denotes the particular
sphere to which the 'darkness' is limited ; see notes *on Gal.* i. 22, Winer, *Gr.*
§ 31. 3, p. 244. The distinction between
this dat. and the acc., as in Joseph. *l. c.,*
is not very easy to define, as such an
accus. has clearly some of the *limiting*
character which we properly assign to
the dat. ; see Hartung, *Casus,* p. 62.
Perhaps the acc. might denote that the
darkness *extended over* the mind, the dat.
that it has its seat *in* the mind ; see
Krüger, *Sprachl.* § 46. 4. 1.

ἀπηλλοτριωμένοι] '*being alienated
from,*' *ἀλλότριοι καθεστῶτες,* Theod.-
Mops.; see notes on ch. ii. 12.

τῆς ζωῆς τοῦ Θεοῦ] '*from the life
of God.*' This is one of the many cases
(see Winer, *Gr.* § 30. 1. obs. p. 168)
where the nature of the gen., whether
objecti or *subjecti,* must be determined
solely from exegetical considerations.
As *ζωὴ* appears never to denote 'course
of life ' (e. g. *τὴν ἐν ἀρετῇ ζωὴν* Theod.)
in the N. T., but 'the principle of life'
as opp. to *θάνατος* (comp. Trench, *Syn.*
§ XXVII), *τοῦ Θεοῦ* will more naturally
be the gen. *subj.* or *auctoris,* 'the life
which God gives:' comp. *δικαιοσύνη
Θεοῦ,* Rom. i. 17 with *δικ. ἐκ. Θ.,* Phil.
iii. 9. It is, however, *probable* that we
must advance a step farther, and regard
the gen. as *possessive.* This (unique)
expression will then denote not merely
the *παλιγγενεσία,* but in the widest doctrinal application, 'the life of God' in
the soul of man ; comp. Olsh. and Stier
in loc., and see esp. the good treatise on
ζωὴ in Olsh. *Opusc.*　　*τὴν οὖσαν
ἐν αὐτοῖς* seems intended to point out
the *indwelling, deep-seated* nature of the
ἄγνοια, and to form a sort of parallelism

τὴν οὖσαν ἐν αὐτοῖς, διὰ τὴν πώρωσιν τῆς καρδίας αὐτῶν, ¹⁹ οἵτι-
νες ἀπηλγηκότες ἑαυτοὺς παρέδωκαν τῇ ἀσελγείᾳ εἰς ἐργασίαν

to τῆς καρδ. αὐτῶν. Meyer (compare
Peile) conceiving that the words indicate
the subordination of διὰ τὴν πώρ. to διὰ
τὴν ἄγν. removes the comma after αὐτοῖς. This is certainly awkward: St.
Paul's more than occasional use of co-
ordinate clauses (e. g. Gal. iv. 4) leads
us to regard both members as dependent
on ἀπηλλ. (Orig.), and structurally independent of each other, though, as the
context seems to suggest, the latter may
be considered slightly explanatory of the
former, and (like ἀπηλλ.) expressive of
a state naturally consequent; see esp.
Orig. in Cram. Caten. p. 175.　π ώ-
ρ ω σ ι ν] 'callousness,' 'hardness,' — not
'cæcitatem,' Syr. (both), Clarom.,Vulg.,
Æth. (both), Arm. (Suid. πώρωσις, ἡ τυ-
φλωσις), but 'obdurationem' Copt. (thōm,
— which however includes both signifi-
cations), 'daubiþos,' Goth., —ἡ ἐσχάτη
ἀναλγησία, Theod. The word πώρωσις
is not derived from πωρός 'cæcus' ('vox,
ut videtur, a grammaticis ficta,' Fritz.
Rom. xi. 7, Vol. II. p. 452), and certainly
not from πόρος (διαφράττειν), as appy.
Chrys., but from πῶρος, 'tuffstone,' and
thence from the similarity of appearance,
a 'morbid swelling' (Aristot. Hist. An.
III. 19), the 'callus' at the extremity of
fractured bones (Med. Writers). The
adject. πωρός, in the sense of ταλαίπωρος
(Hesych.), is cognate with πηρός, and
derived from ΠΑΩ, πάσχω; comp. Pha-
vor. Eclog. 150. b, p. 396 (ed. Dind.).
19. ο ἵ τ ι ν ε ς] 'who as men;' explanatory force of ὅστις; see notes on Gal. ii.
4, iv. 24.　ἀ π η λ γ η κ ό τ ε ς] 'being
past feeling,' Auth., — an admirable translation. The use of the semi-technical
term πώρωσις, suggests this appropriate
continuation of the metaphor. There is
then no reference to mere 'desperatio,'
comp. Polyb. Hist. ix. 40. 9, ἀπαλγοῦν-
τες ταῖς ἐλπίσι, and exx. in Raphel, An-

not. Vol. II. p. 479), as Syr., Vulg.,
Goth., — but possibly with the reading of
D E, al. ἀπηλπικότες, — nor even to that
feelingless state which is the result of it
(Cicero, Epist. Fam. II. 3, 'desperatione
obduruisse ad dolorem,' aptly cited by
Beng.), but, as the context shows, to
that moral apathy and deadness which
supervenes when the heart has ceased to
be sensible of the 'stimuli' of the conscience; τὸ δὲ ἀπηλγηκότες ὥσπερ τῶν
ἀπὸ πάθους τινὸς μέρη πολλάκις τοῦ σώματος νενεκρωμένων, οἷς ἄλγος οὐδὲν ἐκεῖθεν ἐγγίνεται, Theod.-Mops. The gloss
of Theoph. κατερραθυμηκότες (compare
Chrys.), adopted by Hamm. on Rom. i.
29, but here appy. retracted, is untenable,
as it needlessly interrupts the continuity
of the metaphor.　ἑ α υ τ ο ύ ς] 'themselves,' as Meyer well says, with frightful
emphasis. It has been observed by
Chrys. and others that there is no opposition here with Rom. i. 26, παρέδωκεν
αὐτοὺς ὁ Θεός. The progress of sin is
represented under two aspects, or rather
two stages of its fearful course. By a
perverted exercise of his free-will, man
plunges himself into sin; the deeper de-
mersion in it is the judicial act (no mere
συγχώρησις, Chrys.) of God; compare
Wordsw. in loc.　τ ῇ ἀ σ ε λ γ ε ί ᾳ]
'Wantonness.' On the meaning and derivation of this word, see notes on Gal. v.
19, and comp. Trench, Synon. § xvi.
ε ἰ ς ἐ ρ γ α σ ί α ν] 'to working;' conscious object of the fearful self-abandon-
ment: ἐργασ., φησίν, ἔθεντο τὸ πρᾶγμα.
...ὁρᾷς πῶς αὐτοὺς ἀποστερεῖ συγγνώμης,
Chrys.　π ά σ η ς] 'of every kind,'
whether natural or unnatural; μοιχεία,
πορνεία, παιδεραστία, Chrys. As St.
Paul most commonly places πᾶς before,
and not, as here, after the abstract (anarthrous) subst., it seems proper to express in transl. the full force of πάσης:

ἀκαθαρσίας πάσης ἐν πλεονεξίᾳ. ²⁰ ὑμεῖς δὲ οὐχ οὕτως ἐμάθετε
τὸν Χριστόν, ²¹ εἴγε αὐτὸν ἠκούσατε καὶ ἐν αὐτῷ ἐδιδάχθητε

comp. notes ch. i. 8.　　　ἐν πλεο-
νεξίᾳ] 'in (not 'with') covetousness;'
ἐν marking the condition, the prevailing
state or frame of mind in which they
wrought the ἀκαθ. The word πλεονεξία
('amor habendi,' Fritz., 'boni alieni ad
se redactio,' Beng. on Rom. i. 29), is
here explained by Chrysostom and several Greek Ff. (see Suicer, Thesaur. Vol.
II. p. 750), followed by Hammond (in a
valuable note on Rom. i. 29) and by
Trench, Synon. XXIV., as ἀμετρία, 'im-
moderate, inordinate desire.' In support of this extended meaning the recital
of πλεονεξία with sins of the flesh, 1
Cor. v. 11, Eph. v. 3, Col. iii. 5, is pop-
ularly urged by Trench and others, but
appy., as a critical examination of the
passages will show, without full conclu-
siveness. For example, in 1 Cor. v. 10,
τοῖς πόρνοις ἢ τοῖς πλεονέκταις καὶ ἅρ-
παξιν (Tisch., Lachm.), the use of the dis-
junct. ἢ between πόρν. and πλεον. opp. to
the conjunct. καὶ between πλεον. and ἅρπ.,
and esp. the omission of the art. before
ἅρπ. (Winer, Gr. § 19. 4. d, p. 116)
tend to prove the very reverse. Again,
in Eph. v. 3, πορνεία is joined with ἀκαθαρσία by καί, while πλεονεξ. is disjoined
from them by ἤ; see notes. Lastly, in
Col. iii. 5, the preceding anarthrous,
unconnected nouns, πορν., ἀκαθ., πάθ.,
have no very close union with καὶ τὴν
πλεονεξίαν κ. τ. λ., from which, too, they
are separated by ἐπιθυμίαν κακήν; see
notes in loc. While, therefore, we may
admit the deep significance of the spiritual fact that this sin is mentioned in
connection with strictly carnal sins, we
must also deny that there are grammatical or contextual reasons for obliterat-
ing the idea of covetousness and self-seek-
ing, which seems bound up in the word;
see esp. Müller, Doctr. of Sin, I. 1. 3. 2,
Vol. I. p. 169 (Clark).

20. ὑμεῖς δέ] 'But you;' with distinct and emphatic contrast to these
unconverted and feelingless heathen.
οὐχ οὕτως ἐμάθετε] 'did not thus
learn Christ;' — but on principles very
different; the οὕτως obviously implying
much more than is expressed ('litotes');
τὰ τοῦ δεσπότου Χριστοῦ παντάπασιν ἐναντία, Theodoret. This use of μανθ. with
an accus. personæ is somewhat difficult to
explain, and is probably unique. Raphel
(Annot. Vol. II. p. 480) cites Xenoph.
Hell. II. 1. 1, but the example is illusory.
The common interpr. Χριστὸς = 'doc-
trina Christi' (Grot., Turner) is frigid
and inadmissible, and the use of ἐμάθετε
in the sense of 'learnt to know,' scil.
'who He is and what He desires'
(Rück.), has not appy. any lexical authority. We can only then regard Χρ.
as the object which is learnt (or heard,
ver. 21), the content of the preaching, so
that the hearer, as it were, 'takes up into
himself and appropriates the person of
Christ Himself' (Olsh.); comp. the similar but not identical expression, παρα-
λαμβάνειν τὸν Χριστὸν Ἰησ., Col. ii. 6;
see notes in loc.

21. εἴγε] 'if indeed,' 'tum certe si;'
not 'since,' Eadie; see notes, ch. ii. 2,
Hartung, Partik. Vol. I. p. 407 sq.
The explanation of Chrysost. οὐκ ἀμφι-
βάλλοντος ἐστί, ἀλλὰ καὶ σφόδρα διαβε-
βαιουμένου, is improved on by Œcum.,
ὡσεὶ εἶπεν, ἀμφιβάλλω γὰρ εἴ τις τὸν Χρ.
ἀκούσας καὶ διδαχθεὶς ἐν αὐτῷ τοιαῦτα
πράττει.　　αὐτὸν ἠκούσατε] 'ye
heard HIM;' αὐτὸν being put forward
with emphasis; — 'if indeed it was Him,
His divine voice and divine Self that
you really heard;' Alf. pertinently compares John x. 27, but obs. that the αὐτὸν
is here used in the same sort of inclusive
way as τὸν Χριστόν, ver. 20. No argument can fairly be deduced from this

14

καθώς ἐστιν ἀλήθεια ἐν τῷ Ἰησοῦ, ²² ἀποθέσθαι ὑμᾶς, κατὰ τὴν

that St. Paul had not himself instructed the readers (De W.); see on ch. iii. 2. ἐν αὐτῷ] 'in Him;' not 'by Him,' Arm., Auth., or 'illius nomine,' Beng., but, as usual, 'in union with Him;' see Winer, *Gr.* § 48. a, p. 345. Meyer calls attention to the precision of the language, αὐτὸν ἠκούσατε pointing to the first reception, ἐν αὐτῷ ἐδιδάχ. to the further instruction which they had received as Christians. Both are included in the foregoing ἐμάθετε τὸν Χριστόν.

καθώς ἐστιν ἀλήθ. κ. τ. λ.] 'as, or *according as*, *is truth in Jesus*.' The meaning and connection of this clause are both obscure, and have received many different interpretations, most of which involve errors affecting one or more of the following particulars, — the meaning of καθώς (Rück.), the position of ἐστίν (Olsh.), the meaning of ἀλήθεια (Harl.), the absence of the art. before it (Auth.), the designation of Christ by His *historical* rather than *official* name (Mey.), and finally the insertion of ὑμᾶς (De W.). It is extremely difficult to assign an interpretation that shall account for and harmonize all of these somewhat conflicting details. Perhaps the following will be found least open to exception. The Apostle, having mentioned the teaching the Ephesians had received (ἐδιδάχθ.), notices first (not parenthetically, Beza) the *form* and manner, and then the *substance* of it. Καθὼς κ. τ. λ., is thus a predication of *manner* attached to ἐδιδ., and implies, not 'as truth is in Jesus' (Olsh.), which departs from the order and involves a modification of the simple meaning of ἀλήθ.; nor (as it might have been expressed) 'as is truth,' abstractedly, — but, 'as is truth — in JESUS,' embodied, as it were, in a *personal* Saviour and in the preaching of His cross. The *substance* of what they were taught is then

specified, not without a faint imperative force, by the infin. with ὑμᾶς; the pronoun being added on account of the introduction of the new subject Ἰησοῦ (Winer, *Gr.* § 44. 3, p. 288), or more probably to mark their contrast, not only with the Gentiles before mentioned, but with their own former state as implied in τὴν προτέραν ἀναστροφήν. Mey., following Œcum. 2, connects the inf. with ἐστὶν ἀλήθ., a construction not grammatically untenable (Jelf, *Gr.* § 669, comp. Madvig. *Synt.* § 164. 3), but somewhat forced and unsatisfactory. Stier, after Beng., regards ἀποθ. a resumption of μηκ. περιπ. ver. 17, but yet is obliged to admit a kind of connection with ἐδιδ. κ. τ. λ.

22. ἀποθέσθαι ὑμᾶς] 'that ye put *off*;' objective sentence (Donalds. *Gr.* § 584) dependent on ἐδιδ., and specifying the *purport* and substance of the teaching; see Winer, *Gr.* § 48. a. obs. p. 349, and compare Orig. in Cramer *Caten.* The metaphor is obviously 'a vestibus sumpta,' Beza (Rom. xiii. 12, Col. iii. 12), and stands in contrast to ἐνδύσ. ver. 24; see Usteri, *Lehrb.* II. 1. 3, p. 220. The translation of Peile, 'that you have put off,' is very questionable, as the aor. is here only used in accordance with the common law of succession of tenses (Madvig, *Synt.* § 171, sq.), and *perhaps* with reference [comp. ἐνδύσασθαι ver. 24, as opp. to ἀνανεοῦσθαι] to the speedy, single nature of the act; but compare notes on ch. iii. 4, and *on* 1 *Thess.* v. 27. Equally untenable is the supposition that the inf. is equivalent to the imper. (Luther, Wolf); not, however, because ὑμᾶς is attached to it (Eadie, for see Winer, *Gr.* § 44. 3), but because this usage is only found (excluding Epic Greek) in laws, oracles, etc., or in clauses marked by an especial warmth or earnestness; comp. Bernhardy, *Synt.*

προτέραν ἀναστροφήν, τὸν παλαιὸν ἄνθρωπον τὸν φθειρόμενον κατὰ τὰς ἐπιθυμίας τῆς ἀπάτης, ²³ ἀνανεοῦσθαι δὲ τῷ Πνεύματι

ix. 3, p. 358. But few certain instances, e. g. Phil. iii. 16 (see notes *in loc.*), are found in the language of the N. T.

κατὰ τὴν προτ. ἀναστρ.] '*as concerns your former conversation,*' 'quoad pristinam vivendi, concupiscendi, et peccandi consuetudinem,' Corn. a Lap.; specification of that with regard. to which the ἀποθέσθαι τὸν παλ. ἄνθρ. was especially carried out; κατὰ here not having its more usual sense of *measure,* but, as the context seems to require, the less definite one of *reference to;* compare Rom. ix. 5, and see Rost u. Palm, *Lex.* s. v. Vol. i. p. 1599. The construction τὸν παλ. ἄνθρ. κατὰ κ. τ. λ. (Jerome, Œcum.) is opposed to the order, and to all principles of perspicuity, — not, however, positively to 'the laws of language,' Eadie, for compare Winer, *Gr.* § 19, 2, — and is distinctly untenable. The expressive word ἀναστροφὴ is confined (in its present sense) to the N. T. (Gal. i. 13, 1 Tim. iv. 12, al.), to the Apocrypha (Job. iv. 14, 2 Macc. v. 8), and to later Greek (Polyb. *Hist.* iv. 82, Arrian, *Epict.* i. 9); compare Suicer, *Thes.* Vol. ii. p. 322.   τὸν παλαιὸν ἄνθρωπον] '*the old man,*' i. e. our former unconverted self; personification of our whole sinful condition before regeneration (Rom. vi. 6, Col. iii. 9), and opposed to the καινὸς or νέος ἄνθρωπος (ver. 24, Col. iii. 10), the καινὴ κτίσις (Gal. vi. 15), or, if regarded in another point of view (compare · Chrys.), to the ἔσω ἄνθρ. ch. iii. 16, Rom. vii. 22; see Harless, *Ethik.* § 22, p. 97, and compare Suicer, *Thesaur.* Vol. i. p. 352.

τὸν φθειρόμενον] '*which waxeth corrupt,*' ἀεὶ φθείρεται, Origen (Cram. Caten.); further definition and specification of the progressive condition of the παλαιὸς ἄνθρ., — not however with any *causal* force (ed. 1), as this would be

expressed either by a relative clause (see ὃν 1 *Tim.* ii. 4), or a part. *without* the article. The tense of the part. (*pres.,* — not imperf., Beng.) must here be noticed and pressed, as marking that inner *process* of corruption and moral disintegration which is not only the characteristic (Auth.) but the steadily *progressive* condition of the παλ. ἄνθρ.; contrast κτισθέντα ver. 24. Meyer refers φθειρ. to 'eternal destruction' (comp. Hows.), regarding the pres. as involving a future meaning. This is tenable (see Bernhardy, *Synt.* x. 2, p. 371), but seems inferior to the foregoing, as drawing off attention from the true, present nature of the progressive φθορά; compare Gal. vi. 8, and see notes *in loc.*   κατὰ has here no direct reference to instrumentality (sc. = διά, Œcum., ὑπό, Theoph., compare Syr.), but, as the partial antithesis κατὰ Θεὸν (ver. 24) suggests, its usual meaning of ' accordance to;' in which, indeed, a faint reference to the occasion or circumstances connected with, or arising from the accordance may sometimes be traced; see notes *on Phil.* ii. 3, and on *Tit.* iii. 5. Κατὰ τὰς ἐπιθ. is, however, here simply 'in accordance with the lusts,' 'secundum desideria,' Vulg., ܐܡܶ̈ܐ [secundum concupiscentias] Syr.-Phil., *i. e.* just as the nature and existence of such lusts imply and necessitate; compare Winer, *Gr.* § 49. d, p. 358.   τῆς ἀπάτης] '*of Deceit;*' gen. *subjecti,* ἡ ἀπάτη being taken so abstractedly (Middleton, *Gr. Art.* v. 1, 2) as to be nearly personified (Mey.). The paraphrase ἐπιθυμίαι ἀπατηλαί (Beza, Auth.) is very unsatisfactory, and mars the obvious antithesis to τῆς ἀληθείας ver. 24.

23. ἀνανεοῦσθαι δέ] '*and that ye be renewed;*' contrasted statement on the

τοῦ νοὸς ὑμῶν ²⁴ *καὶ ἐνδύσασθαι τὸν καινὸν ἄνθρωπον τὸν*

positive side ('δὲ alii rei aliam adjicit, ut tamen ubivis quædam oppositio declaretur,' Klotz, *Devar.*, Vol. II. p. 362) of the substance of what they had been taught, previously specified on its negative side (ver. 22). It has been doubted whether ἀνανεοῦσθαι is pass. or middle. The act. is certainly rare (Thom. M. p. 52, ed. Bern.; comp. Aq. Psalm. xxix. 2); still, as Harless satisfactorily shows, the middle; both in its simple and metaphorical sense, is so completely devoid of any reflexive force (comp. even ἀνανέου σεαυτόν, Antonin. IV. 3), and is practically so purely active in meaning, that no other form than the *passive* (opp. to Stier), can possibly harmonize with the context; comp. ἀνακαινοῦσθαι 2 Cor. iv. 16, Col. iii. 10, and see Hofm. *Schriftb.* Vol. II. 2, p. 269. The meaning of ἀνά, *restoration* to a former, not necessarily a primal state, is noticed by Winer (*de Verb. c. Præp.* III. p. 10), and the distinction between ἀνανεοῦσθαι ('recentare,'—more subjective, and perhaps with prevailing ref. to *renovation*,) and ἀνακαινοῦσθαι ('renovare,'—more objective, and perhaps with prevailing ref. to *regeneration*) by Tittmann, *Synon.* p. 60; comp. Trench, *Synon.* § XVIII., and see notes on *Col.* iii. 10.   *τῷ Πνεύματι τοῦ νοός*] '*by the Spirit of your mind.*' In this unique and somewhat ambiguous expression, the gen. νοὸς may be explained either as (*a*) *appositive*, 'spiritus quæ mens vocatur' August. *de Trin.* XIV. 16; so appy. Taylor, *Duct. Dub.* I. 1. 7, comp. ib. *on Repent.* II. 2. 12:— (*b*) *partitive*, 'the governing spirit of the mind' De W., Eadie, τὴν ὁρμὴν τοῦ νόος πνευματικήν, Theodoret; — or (*c*) *possessive*, 'the (Divine) Spirit, united with the human πνεῦμα (comp. Hooker, *Eccl. Pol.* I. 7. 1), with which the νοῦς, as subject, is endued, and of which it is the *receptaculum*;' τῷ Πν. τῷ ἐν τῷ νῷ,

Chrysost. Of these (*a*) is manifestly, as Bp. Bull designates it, 'a flat and dull interpretation;' (*b*), even if not metaphysically or psychologically doubtful, is exegetically unsatisfactory; (*c*) on the contrary, now adopted by Mey., has a full scriptural significance; τὸ Πν. is the Holy Spirit, which by its union with the human πνεῦμα, becomes the agent of the ἀνακαίνωσις τοῦ νοός Rom. xii. 2, and the νοῦς is the seat of His working, — where ματαιότης (ver. 17) once was, but now καινότης. The dat. is thus not, as in (*a*) and (*b*) a mere dat. 'of reference to' (ver. 17), but a dat. *instrumenti*, — scil. διὰ Πν. ἐστι ἀνακαίνισις, Œcum., ὅπερ ἀνανεοῖ ἡμᾶς, Origen (ap. Cram. *Caten.*); see Tit. iii. 5, and comp. Collect for Christmas Day.   This interpr. is ably defended by Bull, *Disc.* V. p. 477 (Engl. Works, Oxf. 1844); see also Waterl. *Regen.* Vol. v. p. 434, Usteri, *Lehrb.* II. 1. 3, p. 227, and Fritz. *Nov. Opusc. Acad.* p. 224. The only modification, or rather explanation which it has seemed necessary to add to the view in ed. 1, is that τῷ Πν. (as above stated) is not the Holy Spirit regarded exclusively and *per se*, but as in a gracious union with the human spirit. With this slight rectification, the third interpr. seems to have a *very* strong claim on our attention; contr. Wordsw. *in loc.*; comp. also Delitzsch, *Bibl. Psychol.* IV. 5, p. 144.

24. *καὶ ἐνδύσασθαι*] '*and put on;*' further and more distinct statement on the *positive* side corresponding to the ἀποθέσθαι on the *negative*; the change of tense (aor.) being appy. intentional; see notes on ver. 22. The arguments of Anabaptists based on this verse are answered by Taylor, *Liberty of Proph.* § 18. ad. 31. It is very improbable that there is here any allusion to baptism: the 'putting on the new

κατὰ Θεὸν κτισθέντα ἐν δικαιοσύνῃ καὶ ὁσιότητι τῆς ἀληθείας.

man' refers to the *renovation* of the heart afterwards; comp. Waterl. *Regen.* Vol. v. p. 434. The metaphorical and dogmatical meaning is investigated in Suicer, *Thesaur.* s. v. Vol. I. p. 1113. τὸν καινὸν ἄνθρ.] '*the new man.*' It is scarcely necessary to observe that the καιν. ἄνθρ. is not Christ (Zanch. ap. Pol. *Syn.*), but is in direct contrast to τὸν παλ. ἄνθρ., and denotes 'the holy form of human life which results from redemption,' Müller, *Doctr. of Sin*, IV. 3. ad. fin., Vol. II. p. 392 (Clark); comp. Col. iii. 10, where νέος ἄνθρ. stands in contrast to a *former* state (Wordsw. aptly compares Matt. ix. 17, Mark ii. 22, Luke v. 38), as καινὸς here to one needing *renewal*; see notes *in loc.*, and Harl. *Ethik*, § 22, p. 97. The patristic interpretations are given in Suicer, *Thesaur.* Vol. I. p. 352.　τὸν κατὰ Θ. κτισθ.] '*which after God hath been created*,' — not '*is* created,' Auth., but 'qui creatus est,' Clarom., Vulg., sim. Copt., with the proper force of the aor. in ref. to the *past* creation in Christ: the new man is, as it were, a holy garb or personality not created in the case of each individual believer, but created once for all ('initio rei Christianæ,' Beng.), and then individually assumed. The key to this important passage is undoubtedly the striking parallel, Col. iii. 10, τὸν νέον τὸν ἀνακαινούμενον εἰς ἐπίγνωσιν κατ' εἰκόνα τοῦ κτίσαντος αὐτόν; from which it would almost seem certain (1) that κτισθέντα in our present passage contains an *allusion* to Gen. i. 27, and suggests a spiritual connection between the first creation of man in Adam and the second new creation in Christ; and (2) that κατὰ Θεόν, as illustrated by κατ' εἰκ. κ. τ. λ. Col. *l. c.*, is rightly explained as 'ad exemplum Dei:' comp. Gal. iv. 28, Gen. i. 27, and see Winer, *Gr.* § 49. d, p. 358. Thus, then, from this passage,

compared with that from Col. we may appy. deduce the great dogmatic truth, — 'ut quod perdideramus in Adam, id est, secundum imaginem et similitudinem esse Dei, hoc in Christo Jesu reciperemus,' Irenæus, *Hær.* III. 20, p. 245 (ed. Grabe); see notes *on Col. l. c.* The justice of this deduction is doubted by Müller (*Doctr. of Sin*, IV. 3, Vol. II. p. 392), but without sufficient reason; see esp. the admirable treatise of Bp. Bull, *State of Man*, etc., p. 445 sq. (English Works, Oxf. 1844), and Delitzsch, *Bibl. Psychol.* II. 2, p. 51. On the nature and process of this revival of the image of God, see Jackson, *Creed*, Book VIII. 35. 1.　ἐν δικαιοσ. καὶ ὁσιότ.] '*in righteousness and holiness;*' tokens and characteristics of the divine image; ἐν defining the state in which a similitude to that image consists and exhibits itself (Olsh.). The usual distinction between these two substantives, ὁσιότης μὲν πρὸς Θεόν, δικαιοσύνη δὲ πρὸς ἀνθρώπους θεωρεῖται, Philo, *de Abrah.* Vol. II. p. 30, ed. Mang. (comp. Tittm. *Synon.* p. 25), is not here wholly applicable; as Harless shows from 1 Tim. ii. 8, Heb. vii. 7, the term ὁσιότης [on the doubtful derivation, see Pott, *Et. Forsch.* Vol. I. p. 126, contrasted with Benfey, *Wurzellex.* Vol I. p. 436] involves not merely the idea of 'piety,' but of 'holy purity,' τὸ καθαρόν, Chrys. There is thus a faint contrast suggested between δικ. and πλεονεξία in ver. 19, and ὁσιότ. and ἀκαθαρσία in the present verse. Olshausen (in an excellent note on this verse) contrasts this passage, Col. iii. 10, and Wisdom, ii. 23 (noticed also by Bull), as respectively alluding to the Divine image under its *ethical, intellectual*, and *physical* aspects.　τῆς ἀληθείας] '*of Truth;*' exactly opp. to τῆς ἀπάτης ver. 22, and of course to be connected with both preceding nouns.

Speak the truth, do not cherish anger, or practise theft : utter no corrupt speech; be not bitter.

²⁵ Διὸ ἀποθέμενοι τὸ ψεῦδος λαλεῖτε ἀλήθειαν ἕκαστος μετὰ τοῦ πλησίον αὐτοῦ, ὅτι ἐσμὲν ἀλλήλων μέλη. ²⁶ Ὀργίζεσθε καὶ μὴ ἁμαρτάνετε· ὁ ἥλιος μὴ

The adjectival solution (Beza, Auth.) wholly destroys the obvious and forcible antithesis, and the reading καὶ ἀληθείᾳ [D¹FG; Clar.; Cypr., Hil., al.] has no claims on our attention.

25. διό] 'Wherefore;' in reference to the truths expressed in the verses immediately preceding: εἰπὼν τὸν παλαιὸν ἄνθρωπον καθολικῶς, λοιπὸν αὐτὸν καὶ ὑπογράφει κατὰ μέρος, Chrys. The previous mention of ἀλήθεια seems to have suggested the first exhortation. On the use of διὸ in the N. T., see notes on Gal. iv. 31.   ἀποθέμενοι τὸ ψεῦδος] 'having put off' (aor., with ref. to the priority of the act; comp. notes on ver. 8) lying, or rather 'falsehood,' in a fully abstract sense (John viii. 44), — not merely τὸ ψεύδεσθαι, scil. τὸ λαλεῖν ψευδῆ : falsehood in every form is a chief characteristic of the παλαιὸς ἄνθρωπος, and, as Müller well shows, comes naturally from that selfishness which is the essence of all sin; see Doctr. of Sin. The positive exhortation which follows is considered by Jerome not improbably a reminiscence of Zachar. viii. 16, λαλεῖτε ἀλήθειαν ἕκαστος πρὸς [is the change to μετὰ intentional, as better denoting 'inter-communion,' etc.?] τὸν πλησίον αὐτοῦ. For a short sermon on this text see August. Serm. CLVI. Vol. v. p. 907 (ed. Migne). ὅτι ἐσμέν κ. τ. λ.] 'because we are members one of another.' The force of the exhortation does not rest on any mere ethical considerations of our obligations to society, or on any analogy that may be derived from the body (Chrys.), but on the deeper truth, that in being members of one another we are members of the body of Christ (Rom. xii. 5), of Him who was ἡ ἀλήθεια καὶ ἡ ζωή ; see Harl. in loc.

26. ὀργίζεσθε καὶ μὴ ἁμαρτάνετε] 'Be angry, and sin not;' a direct citation from the LXX, Psalm iv. 5. The original words are רִגְזוּ וְאַל־תֶּחֱטָאוּ, which, though appy. more correctly translated 'tremble and, etc.' [Gesen., Ewald, J. Olsh. opp. to Hengst. and Hitzig], are adduced by St. Paul from the Greek version, as best embodying a salutary and practical precept; comp. ver. 25. The command itself has received many different, though nearly all ultimately coincident explanations. (1) The usual interpretation 'si contingat vos irasci' ('though ye be angry,' Butler, Serm. VIII.; still maintained by Zyro, Stud. u. Krit. 1841, p. 681 sq.), is founded on the union of two imperatives in Hebrew (Gen. xlii. 18, Prov. xx. 13, Gesen. Gr. § 127. 2), and, in fact, any cultivated language, to denote condition and result. This, however, is here inapplicable, for the solution would thus be not ὀργιζόμενοι μὴ ἁμαρ., but ἐὰν ὀργισθῆσε, οὐκ ἁμαρτήσετε [not -σεσθε in N. T.], which cannot be intended. (2) Winer (Gr. § 43, 1. obs. p. 360 sq.) far more plausibly conceives the first imper. permissive, the second jussive: comp. the version of Symm. ὀργ. ἀλλὰ μὴ ἁμαρτ. It is true that a permissive imper. is found occasionally in the N. T. (1 Cor. vii. 15, perhaps Matt. xxvi. 45), but the close union by καὶ of two imperatives of similar tense, but with a dissimilar imperatival force, is, as Meyer has observed, logically unsatisfactory.   (3) The following interpr. seems most simple : both imperatives are jussive ; as, however, the second imper. is used with μή, its jussive force is thereby enhanced, while the affirmative command is, by juxta-position, so much obscured as to be in effect little more than a participial member, though

ἐπιδυέτω ἐπὶ τῷ παροργισμῷ ὑμῶν, ²⁷ μηδὲ δίδοτε τόπον τῷ

its intrinsic jussive force is not to be denied. There is undoubtedly an anger against sin, for instance, against deliberate falsehood, as the context appy. suggests (see Chrys.), which a good man not only may, but ought to feel (see Suicer, *Thesaur.*, Vol. ii. p. 504), and which is very different from the ὀργή forbidden in ver. 31: compare Trench, *Synon.* § xxxvii. and on the subject of resentment generally, Butler, *Serm.* viii. and the good note of Wordsw. *in loc.*

ὁ ἥλιος κ. τ. λ.] '*let not the sun go down on your irritation.*' The command is the Christian parallel of the Pythagorean custom cited by Hammond, Wetst., and others, εἴποτε προαχθεῖεν εἰς λοιδορίας ὑπ' ὀργῆς, πρὶν ἢ τὸν ἥλιον δῦναι, τὰς δεξιὰς ἐμβάλλοντες ἀλλήλοις καὶ ἀσπασάμενοι διελύοντο, Plutarch, *de Am. Frat.* 488 b [§ 17]. There does not appear any allusion to the possible effect of night upon anger, μήπως ἡ νὺξ πλέον ἀνακαύσῃ τὸ πῦρ διὰ τῶν ἐννοιῶν, Theophyl. (see Suicer, *Thes.* s. v. ἥλιος iii. 2), but to the fact that the day ended with the sunlight: 'quare si quem irascentem nox occuparet, is iram retinebat in proximum diem,' Estius. τῷ παροργισμῷ] '*irritation,*' '*exasperation,*' and therefore to be distinguished from ὀργή, which expresses the more *permanent* state. The word is non-classical and rare, but is found 1 Kings xv. 30, 2 Kings xix. 3, where it is joined with θλίψις and ἐλεγμός, ib. xxiii. 26, Nehem. ix. 18, and Jerem. xxi. 5 (Alex.), where it is joined with θυμὸς and ὀργή. The παρὰ is not merely intensive (Mey.), nor even indicative of a deflection from a right rule (Wordsw.), but probably points to the irritating circumstance or object which provoked the ὀργή; comp. παροξύνω, and Rost u. Palm, *Lex.* s. v. iv. 1, Vol. ii. p. 670. The article before παροργισμῷ is omitted by *Lachm.* with AB;

al., — but appy. incorrectly, as the external authority is not strong, and the omission easy to be accounted for before the sufficiently definite ὑμῶν.

27. μηδέ] '*nor yet;*' '*also do not;*' μηδὲ here serving to connect a *new* clause with the preceding (Jelf, *Gr.* § 776), on the principle that δὲ in negative sentences has often *practically* much of the conjunctive force which καὶ has in affirmative sentences; see Wex, *Antig.* Vol. ii. p. 157. It must, however, be surely *very* incorrect to say that the clauses 'are closely connected, and that μηδὲ indicates this sequence,' (Eadie); there *is* a connection between the clauses, and μηδὲ has practically a conjunctive force (per enumerationem), but it is always of such a nature as δὲ would lead us to expect, 'sequentia adjungit prioribus, non apte connexa, sed potius fortuito concursu accedentia,' Klotz, *Devar.* Vol. ii. p. 707; see esp. Franke, *de Part. Neg.* Part ii. 2, p. 6. On the most appropriate translation of μὴ—μηδὲ, see notes *on* 1 *Thess.* ii. 3 (*Transl.*). The reading μήτε (*Rec.* with a few mss.; Chrys. (1), Theod.) seems clearly to be rejected (opp. to Matth.), not only on critical, but even on grammatical grounds, as the position of μὴ in the previous clause shows that it cannot be regarded as equivalent to μήτε, which supposition, or the strictest union of the clauses (Franke, § 25, p. 27) can alone justify the abnormal sequence; see Winer, *Gr.* § 55. 6, p. 433, Klotz, *Devar.* Vol. ii. p. 709. δίδοτε τόπον] '*give room,*' 'ne detis viam' (*fenot*), Æth.; scil. 'give no room or opportunity to the Evil One to be active and operative;' comp. Rom. xii. 19, and see exx. of this use of τόπον διδόναι in West. Rom. *l. c.*, Loesner, *Obs.* p. 263. τῷ διαβόλῳ] '*to the Devil*' (ch. vi. 11); the constant and regular meaning of ὁ διαβ. (subst.) in

διαβόλῳ. ²⁸ Ὁ κλέπτων μηκέτι κλεπτέτω, μᾶλλον δὲ κοπιάτω

28. ταῖς ἰδίαις χερσὶν τὸ ἀγαθόν] The variations of reading in this passage are great, and, considering the simplicity of the passage, difficult to account for. The choice appears to lie between four. (a) That in the text with AD¹EFG ; 37. 57. 73. 116 ; Vulg., Clarom., Goth., Copt., Sahid., Æth., Arm. ; Bas., Naz., Epiph. ; Hier., Aug., Pel. (Lachm., Tisch. ed. 1, Rück., Wordsw.) (b) Τὸ ἀγ. ταῖς ἰδ. χερ. with K ; mss. (10) ; Syr. (Philox.) ; Theodoret. (c) Ταῖς χερ. τὸ ἀγ. with B : Amit. ; Ambrosiaster (Meyer). (d) Τὸ ἀγ. τ. χερ. with L ; great majority of mss. ; Slav. ; Chrys., Dam., Theophyl., Œcum. (Rec., Griesb., Scholz, Tisch. ed. 2 and 7, Alf.) Harless and Olshausen (see Mill, Prolegom. p. 168) favor a 5th and shorter reading ἐργ. τ. χερ., after Tertull. de Resurr. 45, urging the probability of ἰδ. being interpolated from 1 Cor. iv. 12, and τὸ ἀγ. from Gal. vi. 10. It will be seen, however, that Gal. vi. 10 contains no such allusion to manual labor as might have suggested a ref. to it ; and if ἰδίαις (see notes) is maturely considered, it will seem to have a proper force in this place, though not at first sight apparent. As it seems, then, more likely that ἰδίαις was an intentional omission (its force not being perceived) than an interpolation from 1 Cor. iv. 12, we retain (a) as not improbable on internal grounds, and as supported by a preponderance of external evidence, which the internal objections hitherto adduced do not seem sufficient to invalidate.

the N. T. ; not excluding John vi. 70, and 1 Tim. iii. 6 ; see esp. Stier, Red. Jesu, Vol. IV. p. 345. It is obvious that Σατανᾶς (Æth.) is more a personal appellation ; ὁ διαβ. (ܐܶܟ݂ܶܠܩܰܪܨܳܐ) [calumniatori] Syr.) a name derived from the fearful nature and, so to say, office of the Evil One ; the usage, however, of the N. T. writers is by no means uniform. St. John (in Gosp. and Epp.) once only uses the former ; St. Mark never the latter ; St. Paul more frequently the former, the latter being only found in this and the pastoral Epp. (and once in Heb.). The subject deserves fuller investigation. On the nature of this Evil Spirit generally, see the curious and learned work of Mayer, Historia Diaboli (ed. 2, Tubing, 1780), and in ref. to the question of his real personal nature, the sound remarks on p. 130 sq. ; compare notes on 1 Thess. ii. 18.

28. ὁ κλέπτων] 'He who steals, the stealer ;' not imperf. 'qui furabatur,' Clarom., Vulg., nor for ὁ κλέψας, but a narticipial substantive ; see Winer, Gr.

§ 57, p. 317, and notes on Gal. i. 23. All attempts to dilute the proper force of this word are wholly untenable ; ὁ κλέπτων (not ὁ κλέπτης on the one hand, nor ὁ κλέψας on the other) points to 'the thievish character' ('qui furatur,' Copt.), whether displayed in more coarse and open, or more refined and hidden practices of the sin. Theft, though generally, was not universally condemned by Paganism ; see the curious and valuable work of Pfanner, Theol. Gentilis, XI. 25, p. 336. For a sermon on this text, see Sherlock, Serm. XXXVII. Vol. II. p. 227 (ed. Hughes). μᾶλλον δὲ] 'but (on the contrary) rather ;' οὐ γὰρ ἀρκεῖ παύσασθαι τῆς ἁμαρτίας, ἀλλὰ καὶ τὴν ἐναντίαν αὐτῆς ὁδὸν μετελθεῖν, Theoph. ; see also Kühner, Xen. Mem. III. 13. 6, and notes on Gal. iv. 9, where, however, the corrective force is more strongly marked. ταῖς ἰδίαις χέρσιν] 'with his own hands.' The pronominal adjective ἴδιος (Donalds. Crat. § 139), like οἰκεῖος in the Byzantine writers, and 'proprius' in later Latin (see Krebs, Antibarb. p. 646), appears sometimes in

ἐργαζόμενος ταῖς ἰδίαις χερσὶν τὸ ἀγαθόν, ἵνα ἔχῃ μεταδιδόναι τῷ χρείαν ἔχοντι. ²⁹ Πᾶς λόγος σαπρὸς ἐκ τοῦ στόματος ὑμῶν μὴ

the N. T. to be nearly pleonastic (see exx. in Winer, *Gr.* § 22. 7, p. 139); here, however, there appears an intentional force in the use of the word. The thievish man lives by the labors and hands of others; he is now himself to labor, and with *his own hands*,—those very hands that robbed others (Beng.), to work, not at τὸ κακόν, but at τὸ ἀγαθόν; see Rück. *in loc.* τ ὸ ἀ γα- θ ό ν] '*that which is good*,' 'that which belongs to the category of what is good and honest,' τὸν δίκαιον πορισμόν, Schol. ap. Cramer, *Caten.*; 'τὸ ἀγαθ. antitheton ad furtum, prius manu piceatâ male commissum,' Beng. There may *perhaps* be also involved in τὸ ἀγ. the notion of what is beneficial instead of detrimental to others; comp. notes *on* Gal. vi. 10.

ἵ ν α κ. τ. λ.] '*in order that he may have*,' — not merely 'what is enough for his own wants,' but '*to give to him that needeth;*' the true specific object of all Christian labor (Olsh.); comp. Schoettg. *Hor.* Vol. I. p. 778.

29. Π ᾶ s . . . . μ ή] The negation must be joined with the verb; what is commanded is the *non-utterance* of every σαπρὸς λόγος. On this Hebraistic structure, see Winer, *Gr.* § 26. 1, p. 155, and notes *on Gal.* ii. 16. σ α π ρ ό s λ ό γ ο s] '*corrupt, worthless speech*,' 'sermo malus,' Clarom., Vulg., Copt., sim. Goth., — not necessarily 'filthy,' Hows. (comp. Bp. Taylor, *Serm.* xxii., though he also admits the more general meaning), as this is specially forbidden in ch. v. 4, nor again quite so strong as 'detestabilis,' Syr., but rather 'pravus,' Æth., esp. in ref. to whatever is profitless and unedifying (Chrys.), *e.g.* αἰσχρολογία, λοιδορία, συκοφαντία, βλασφημία, ψευδολογία, καὶ τὰ τούτοις προσόμοια, Theod. The exact shade of meaning will always be best determined by the context. Here

σαπρὸs is clearly opposed, not τῷ διδόντι χάριν (Kypke, *Obs.* Vol. ii. p. 298), but to ἀγαθὸs πρὸs οἰκοδ. τῆs χρείαs; Wetst. cites Arrian, *Epict.* ii. 15, ὑγιὲs opp. to σαπρὸν καὶ καταπίπτον. On the general metaphorical use, see Lobeck, *Phryn.* p. 377, and the exx. collected by Kypke, *loc. cit.* ἀ γ α θ ό s] '*good*,' *i. e.* 'suitable for,' ὅπερ οἰκοδομεῖ τὸν πλησίον, Chrys.; instances of this use of ἀγαθός, with εἰs πρός, and the inf., are of sufficiently common occurrence; see Rost u. Palm, *Lex.* s. v., exx. in Kypke, *Obs.* Vol. ii. p. 298, and Elsner, *Obs.* Vol. ii. p. 219. π ρ ὸ s ο ἰ κ ο δ. τ ῆ s χ ρ ε ί α s] '*for edification in respect of the need*,' 'ad ædificationem opportunitatis,' Vulg. (Amit.). Neither the article nor the exact nature of the genitive has been sufficiently explained. It seems clear that τ ῆ s χρείαs cannot be merely 'quâ sit opus' (Erasm.), but must specify the peculiar need in question (observe εἴ τιs), the χρεία which immediately presses, — τῆs παρούσης χρείαs, Œcum. It would seem to follow then that the gen. χρείαs is not a mere gen. of *quality* ('seasonable edification,' Peile) nor in any way an abstr. for concr. ('those who have need,' Rück., Olsh., comp. Eadie), nor, by inversion, for an accus. ('use of edifying,' Auth., compare Syr.), but is simply a gen. of 'remote reference' (see Winer, *Gr.* 30. 2, p. 169), or, as it has been termed, of 'the point of view' (comp. Scheuerl. *Synt.* § 18, p. 129) — 'edifying as regards the need,' *i. e.* which satisfies the need, ἀναγκαῖον ὂν τῇ προκειμένῃ χρείᾳ as rightly paraphrased by Theophyl. On the practical bearing of this passage, see esp. 4 sermons by Bp. Taylor, *Serm.* xxii.—xxv. Vol. i. p. 734 sq. (Lond. 1836), and Harl., *Ethik*, § 50, p. 261. The reading πίστεως, though found in D¹E¹FG; Vulg. (not

ἐκπορευέσθω, ἀλλ᾽ εἴ τις ἀγαθὸς πρὸς οἰκοδομὴν τῆς χρείας, ἵνα
δῷ χάριν τοῖς ἀκούουσιν, ³⁰ καὶ μὴ λυπεῖτε τὸ Πνεῦμα τὸ ἅγιον
τοῦ Θεοῦ, ἐν ᾧ ἐσφραγίσθητε εἰς ἡμέραν ἀπολυτρώσεως.

Amit., Fuld.) and some Latin Vv., Goth.; Bas., Naz., al. (partially approved of by Griesb.), is still certainly to be rejected both as inferior in external authority to χρείας, and as an almost self-evident correction. δῷ χάριν] 'may impart a blessing.' The ambiguous term χάρις has been explained (a) as χάρις Θεοῦ, Œcum. (who, however, does not refer to Rom. i. 11 for a proof, as Eadie singularly asserts), 'salutis adminicula,' Calv.; (b) as little more than θυμηδία; scil. ἵνα φανῇ δεκτός τοῖς ἀκούουσι, Theod., 'ut invenietis gratiam,' Æth.-Pol., comp. Kypke, Obs. Vol. II. p. 298, — but remove the ref. to Eur. Suppl. 414, which is not in point; (c) as retaining its simple and regular meaning in connection with διδόναι, 'favor, benefit' (Harl., Olsh., Meyer). Of these, (c) is much the most probable (see Exod. iii. 21, Psalm lxxxiii. 12 compared with ver. 13, and perhaps James iv. 6, 1 Pet. v. 5); still, as χάρις has so notably changed its meaning in the N. T., it seems uncritical, even in this phrase, to deny the reference of χάρις to a spiritual 'benefit;' see Stier in loc. The most exact transl. then, here seems 'blessing' ('minister grace,' Auth., is ambiguous), as it hints at the theological meaning, and also does not wholly obscure the classical and idiomatic meaning of the phrase.

30. καὶ μὴ λυπεῖτε κ. τ. λ.] 'and grieve not the Holy Spirit of God;' not a new, unconnected exhortation (Lachm.), but a continued warning against the use of πᾶς λόγος σαπρὸς by showing its fearful results; ἐὰν εἴπῃς ῥῆμα σαπρόν, καὶ ἀνάξιον τοῦ Χριστιανοῦ στόματος, οὐκ ἄνθρωπον ἐλύπησας, ἀλλὰ τὸ Πν. τοῦ Θεοῦ, Theoph. The tacit assumption clearly is that the Spirit dwelt within

them (see Basil, Spir. Sanct. XIX. 50, Hermas, Past. Mand. 10), and that, too, as the solemn and emphatic title τὸ Πν. τὸ ἅγιον τοῦ Θεοῦ and the peculiar term λυπεῖτε, further suggest, in His true holy personality; compare Pearson, Creed, Art. VIII. Vol. I. p. 366 (ed. Burt.), and for an excellent sermon on this text, see Andrewes, Serm. VI. Vol. III. p. 201 sq. (A. C. Libr.); see also a very good practical sermon by Bp. Hall, Serm. XXXVI. Vol. v. p. 489 sq. (Talboys). ἐν ᾧ ἐσφραγίσθητε] 'in whom ye were sealed,' — not 'quo,' Goth., Arm. (compare 'per quem,' Beza), but 'in quo,' Clarom., Vulg., 'in whom, as the holy sphere and element of the sealing.' This clause seems intended to enhance still more the warning by an appeal to the blessings they had received from the Holy Spirit; εἶτα καὶ ἡ προσθήκη τῆς εὐεργεσίας, ἵνα μείζων γένηται ἡ κατηγορία, Chrysost. There does not appear, then, here any reminiscence of Isaiah lxiii. 10, παρώξυναν τὸ Πν. τὸ ἅγ. (cited by Harl.), which would have given the warning a different tone. For the explanation of these words, see notes on ch. i. 13, and for the doctrinal applications, Hammond in loc., Petav. de Trin. viii. 5. 3, Vol. II. 823 sq., and notes on ch. i. 13. For some comments on this clause, see Andrewes, Serm. VI. previously cited, and another serm. by Bp. Hall, Serm. XXXVII. Vol. v. p. 504 (Talboys). εἰς ἡμέραν ἀπολυτρώσεως] 'for the day of redemption,' for the day on which the redemption will be fully realized; see exx. of this use of the gen. in definitions of time in Winer, Gr. § 30. 2, p. 169. On the meaning of ἀπολύτρωσις, see notes on ch. i. 14, and on 'final perseverance,' of

³¹ Πᾶσα πικρία καὶ θυμὸς καὶ ὀργὴ καὶ κραυγὴ καὶ βλασφημία
ἀρθήτω ἀφ᾽ ὑμῶν σὺν πάσῃ κακίᾳ· ³² γίνεσθε δὲ εἰς ἀλλήλους

which Eadie here finds an affirmation (comp. Cocc. *in loc*), see Thorndike, *Cov. of Grace*, ch. xxxi. Vol. iii. p. 615 sq. (A. C. Libr.).

31. πᾶσα πικρία] '*all bitterness,*' *i. e.*, 'every form of it' (see notes on ch. i. 8), and that not merely as shown in expressions, 'sermo mordax,' but, as the context suggests, in feeling and disposition (see Acts viii. 23, Heb. xii. 15), πικρία marking the prevailing temperament and frame of mind ; ὁ τοιοῦτος καί βαρύθυμός ἐστι καὶ οὐδέποτε ἀνίησι τὴν ψυχήν, ἀεὶ σύννους ὢν καὶ σκυθρωπός, Chrys. The contrast is not merely γλυκύτης (comp. Orig. ap. Cram. *Cat.*), but χρηστότης ; see Wetst. *on Rom.* iii. 14, and for an able sermon on this text (the obligations and advantages of goodwill), Whichcote, *Serm.* lxxxii. Vol. iv. p. 198 sq. θυμὸς καὶ ὀργή] '*wrath and anger;*' the emanations from, and products of the πικρία ; ῥίζα θυμοῦ καὶ ὀργῆς πικρία, Chrys. With regard to the distinction between these two words, it may be observed that θυμὸς is properly the agitation and commotion to which πικρία gives rise (ἡ ἐναρχομένη ἐπί τινα γενέσθαι ὀργή, Orig. Cram. *Cat.*, comp. Diog Laert. vii. 1. 63. 114), ὀργὴ the more settled habit of the mind (ἡ ἑτοίμη καὶ ἐνεργητικὴ πρὸς τὴν τιμωρίαν τοῦ ἠδικηκέναι νομιζομένου, Origen, *ib.*) ; see Tittm. *Synon.* p. 132, Trench, *Synon.* s. v., and notes *on Gal.* v. 20.

κραυγὴ καὶ βλασφημία] '*clamor and evil speaking ;*' outward manifestations of the foregoing vices ; ἵππος γάρ ἐστι ἀναβάτην φέρων ἡ κραυγὴ τὴν ὀργήν, Chrys. The distinction between the two words is sufficiently obvious. Κραυγὴ is the cry of *strife* ('in quem erumpunt homines irati,' Est.) ; βλασφημία, a more enduring manifestation of inward anger,

that shows itself in reviling, — not, in the present case, God, but our brethren (λοιδορίαι, Chrys.) ; it has thus nearly the same relation to κρ. that ὀργὴ has to θυμός ; see Col. iii. 8, 1 Tim. vi. 4, and comp. Rom. iii. 8, Tit. iii. 2. For a good practical sermon against evil speaking see Barrow, *Serm.* xvi. Vol. i. p. 447.

κακίᾳ] '*malice ;*' the genus to which all the above-mentioned vices belong, or rather the *active principle* to which they are all due (comp. ch. vi. 23), — uncharitableness in all its forms, 'animi pravitas, humanitati et æquitati opposita,' Calv. ; comp. Rom. i. 28, Col. iii. 8, and on the difference between this word and πονηρία (its outcoming and manifestation), see Trench, *Synon.* § xi.

32. γίνεσθε δὲ] '*but become ye ;*' contrasted exhortation : not 'be ye,' Auth., Alf., but 'vairþaiduh' [fiatis] Goth., — there were evil elements among them that were yet to be taken away ; see ch. vi. 1. *Lachm.* omits δὲ with B ; 4 mss. ; Clem., Dam., al. ; but this omission as well as the variation οὖν [Dˡ FG ; 2 mss. ; Clarom., Sang., Boern.] seems due to a corrector who did not perceive the antithesis between the commands in the two verses. χρηστοί, εὔσπλαγχνοι] '*kind, tender-hearted.*' On the former of these words ('sweet in disposition'), comp. notes *on Gal.* v. 22, and Tittmann, *Synon.* p. 140. The latter εὔσπλαγχνος occurs Orat. Manass. 6, 1 Pet. iii. 8, and designates the exhibition of that *merciful* feeling, of which the σπλάγχνα were the imaginary seat ; comp. Col. iii. 12, and notes *in loc.*, and for additional exx., see Polyc. *Phil.* 5, 6, Clem. Rom. *Cor.* i. 54, *Test. XII. Patr.* p. 537. The substantive εὐσπλαγχνία is found in classical Greek, in the sense of 'good heart,' 'courage' (comp. Eurip.

χρηστοί, εὔσπλαγχνοι, χαριζόμενοι ἑαυτοῖς καθὼς καὶ ὁ Θεὸς ἐν Χριστῷ ἐχαρίσατο ὑμῖν.

Strive then to imitate God, and, like Christ, to walk in love.

V. Γίνεσθε οὖν μιμηταὶ τοῦ Θεοῦ, ὡς τέκνα

Rhesus, 192), and also in the primary and physical sense (comp. Hippocr. 89, ed. Foes.), but the adjective is appy. rare. χαριζόμενοι ἑαυτοῖς] '*forgiving each other;*' participle of concomitant act, specifying the *manner* in which the χρηστότης κ. τ. λ. were to be manifested; comp. Col. iii. 13 and notes *in loc.* Origen (Cram. *Caten.*) calls attention to the use of ἑαυτοῖς (what was done to another was really done to themselves), but this appears *here* somewhat doubtful; see notes *on Col. l. c.,* and for exx. of the use of ἑαυτοῖς for the personal pronoun, Jelf, *Gr.* § 54. 2. καθὼς καὶ ὁ Θεός] '*even as God,*' '*as God also;*' καθὼς (as in ch. i. 4) having a slightly argumentative force, while καὶ introduces a tacit comparison; see Klotz, *Devar.* Vol. II. p. 635 sq., and notes *on Phil.* iv. 12. The two combined do not then simply compare, but argue from an example (Harl.), — τὸν Θεὸν παράγει εἰς ὑπόδειγμα, Theophyl.; comp. ch. v. 2, 25, 29. The context seems clearly to show that the meaning of χαριζόμενοι (and hence of ἐχαρίσατο) is not 'donantes,' Clarom., Vulg., 'largientes, libenter dantes,' Erasm. (comp. Orig. I. ap. Cram. *Cat.*), but 'condonantes,' Copt., Syr., Goth., συγγνωμικοί, Chrys.: they were not only to be χρηστοί and εὔσπλαγχνοι but also merciful and forgiving, following the example of Him who 'præbuit se benignum, misericordem, — condonantem,' Beng. The reading is doubtful: *Lachm.* reads ἡμῖν with B²D EKL; 25 mss.; Amit, Syr. (both), al.; Orig. (Cram. *Cat.*). Chrys. (Comm.), Theod., al., — but scarcely on sufficient authority, as the pronoun of the first person might have been probably sug-

gested by the ἡμᾶς in ch. v. 2: see crit. note *in loc.* ἐν Χριστῷ] 'in Christ;' not 'for the sake of,' Auth., nor 'per Christum,' Calv., but 'in Him,' i. e., in giving Him to be a propitiation for our sins, μετὰ τοῦ κινδύνου τοῦ υἱοῦ αὐτοῦ καὶ τῆς σφαγῆς αὐτοῦ, Theoph.; comp. 2 Cor. v. 19.

CHAPTER V. 1. γίνεσθε οὖν κ. τ. λ.] '*Become then followers (imitators) of God;*' resumption of the previous γίνεσθε, ch. v. 32, the οὖν deriving its force and propriety from the concluding words of the last verse. Stier, on rather insufficient grounds, argues against the connection of these verses, referring οὖν to the whole foregoing subject, the new man in Christ. In this latter case, οὖν would have more of what has been called its *reflexive* force ('lectorem revocat ad id ipsum quod nunc agitur,' Klotz, *Devar.* Vol. II. p. 717); that it is, however, here rather *collective* ('ad ea quæ antea revera posita sunt lectorem revocat,' Klotz, *ib.*) seems much more probable; comp. Hartung, *Partik.* οὖν, 3. 5, Vol. II. p. 22. ἀγαπητά| '*beloved;*' not 'liebe Kinder,' Rück. (compare Chrys.), but 'geliebte.' The reason is given by Œcumen., who, however, does not appear to have felt the full force of the word; τοῖς γὰρ τοιούτοις (ἀγαπητοῖς) ἐξ ἀνάγκης τινὸς ἡ μίμησις. The ἀνάγκη consisted in the fact of God having loved them; love must be returned by love; and in love alone can man imitate God: see 1 John iv. 10, and comp. Charnock, *Attrib.* p. 618 (Bohn). For two practical sermons on this text, see Farindon, *Sermon* LXXXVII. (two Parts), Vol. III. p. 494 sq. (ed. Jackson).

ἀγαπητά, ² καὶ περιπατεῖτε ἐν ἀγάπῃ, καθὼς καὶ ὁ Χριστὸς ἠγάπησεν ἡμᾶς καὶ παρέδωκεν ἑαυτὸν ὑπὲρ ἡμῶν προσφορὰν καὶ θυσίαν τῷ Θεῷ εἰς ὀσμὴν εὐωδίας.

2. ἡμᾶς ... ἡμῖν] Tisch. ὑμᾶς ... ὑμῖν, but his authorities [AB; 8 mss.; San., Æth., Clem. (2), Theophyl., al.] do not appear sufficient to substantiate a reading which seems so very probably to have arisen from a conformation of the text to the second person. We therefore retain the Rec. with Griesb., Scholz, Lachm., Meyer, Alf., and Wordsw. In ver. 3 the order of πᾶσα is reversed (with Tisch.) on nearly the same authority, but there Rec. adopts the more easy reading.

2. καὶ περιπ. ἐν ἀγάπῃ] 'and walk in love;' continuation of the foregoing precept, καὶ serving to append closely a specification of that in which the imitation of God must consist. καθὼς καὶ ὁ Χρ. κ.τ.λ.] 'even as Christ also loved,'—not 'has loved;' the pure aoristic sense is more appropriate and more in accordance with the historic aor. which follows. καὶ παρέδωκεν ἑαυτ.] 'and gave up Himself;' specification of that wherein ('non tantum ut Deus sed etiam ut homo, Est') this love was preëminently shown, καὶ having a slightly explanatory force; see Gal. ii. 20, and comp. notes on Phil. iv. 12. The supplementary idea to παρέδ. must surely be εἰς θάνατον (Harl.), as in every case where παραδ. is used by St. Paul in ref. to Christ, εἰς θάν. or some similar idea, seems naturally included in the verb: see esp. Rom. iv. 25, where παρεδόθη is followed by ἠγέρθη; comp. Rom. viii. 32, Gal. ii. 20, Eph. v. 25. For a sound and clear sermon on this text (Christ's sacrifice of Himself), see Waterl. Serm. xxxi. Vol. v. p. 737 sq. ὑπὲρ ἡμῶν] 'for us,'—and also, as the context indisputably shows, 'in our stead;' on the meaning of ὑπὲρ in this connection, see Usteri, Lehrb. ii. 1. 1, p. 115 sq., and notes on Gal. iii. 13; comp. ib. ch. i. 4. προσφορὰν καὶ θυσίαν] 'an offering and sacrifice;' not 'a sacrifice offered up,' sc. θυσίαν προσφερομένην, Conyb., — a mode of

translation ever precarious and insufficient. It may be doubtful whether θυσ. and προσφ. are intended to specify respectively bloody and unbloody sacrifices, for προσφ. is elsewhere used in ref. to bloody (Heb. x. 10), and θυσ. to unbloody offerings (Heb. xi. 4), and further, the rough definition that θυσία implies 'the slaying of a victim' (Eadie) is by no means of universal application; see esp. John Johnson, Unbl. Sacr. i. 1, p. 73 sq. (A. C. Libr.). Equally doubtful, esp. in reference to Christ, is the definition that a θυσία is a 'προσφ. rite consumpta,' Outram, de Sacrif. viii. 1, p. 182 (ed. 1677). Still it is probable that a distinction was here intended by St. Paul, and that προσφ. as the more general term, relates not only to the death, but to the life of obedience of our blessed Lord (comp. Heb. v. 8), His θυσία ζῶσα (Rom. xii. 1); θυσία, as the more special, more particularly to His atoning death. On this accus., which in its apposition to the foregoing is also practically predicative, and serves to complete the notion of the verb, see Madvig, Synt. § 24. τῷ Θεῷ is commonly explained either (a) as the ordinary transmissive dative, sc. παρεδ. τῷ Θεῷ (Mey.; so appy. J. Johns. Vol. i. p. 161), or (b) as a dat. of limitation to εἰς ὀσμ. answering to the Heb. רֵיחַ נִיחוֹחַ לַיהוֹה (Stier). As, however, the meaning of παρέδωκεν (see above) and the distance of the dat. (De W. compares Rom. xii. 1, but there τῷ

Avoid fornication, covet-
ousness, and all forms of
impurity, for on such comes
the wrath of God.   Ye
were once in heathen darkness, but now are light;
reprove the words of darkness, awake and arise.

³ Πορνεία δὲ καὶ ἀκαθαρσία πᾶσα ἢ πλεονεξία μηδὲ ὀνομαζέσθω ἐν ὑμῖν, καθὼς πρέπει
ἁγίοις, ⁴ καὶ αἰσχρότης καὶ μωρολογία ἢ

Θεῷ is *not* joined with the verb) do not harmonize with the *former*, and the prominent position of τῷ Θεῷ is difficult to be explained on the *latter* hypothesis, it seems more simple to regard τῷ Θεῷ as an ethical dative or dat. *commodi* appended to the two substantives ; so Beng. and appy., by their studied adherence to the order of the original, all the ancient Vv. ; see Scheuerl. *Synt.* § 23. 1, p. 186.   εἰς ὀσμ. εὐωδίας] '*for*, sc. *to become a savor of sweet smell ;*' — sc. a θυσία εὐπρόσδεκτος, Chrys. ; see Phil. iv. 18, Lev. i. 9, 13, 17, ii. 12, iii. 5, comp. Gen. viii. 21. The authors of the *Racov. Catech.* (§ VIII.) have correctly explained the constr., but have erroneously asserted that these words ('quæ de pacificis creberrime ; de expiatoriis autem vix uspiam usurpantur,' — but see Deyling, *Obs.* Vol. I. p. 315, No. 65) do not represent Christ's death as an *expiatory* sacrifice ; comp. even Ust. *Lehrb.* II. 1. 1, p. 113. To this, without needlessly pressing ὑπέρ, we may simply say with Waterland, that the contrary 'is as plain from the N. T. as words can make it,' and that St. Paul's perpetual teaching is that Christ's death was 'a true and proper expiatory sacrifice for the sins of mankind ;' see proof texts, Vol. IV. p. 513, and esp. Jackson, *Creed*, Book IX. 55, Vol. IX. p. 589 sq. (Oxf. 1844). The nature of the gen. εὐωδίας is rightly explained by Wordsw. as that of the *characterizing* quality ; see notes *on Phil.* iv. 18, and comp. Winer, *Gr.* § 34. 2, p. 211.

3 πορνεία δέ] '*But fornication ;*' gentle transition to another portion of the exhortation, with a resumption of the negative and prohibitive form of address (ch. iv. 31) ; the δὲ being mainly

μεταβατικόν (see *on Gal.* i. 11), though perhaps not without some *slight* indication of contrast to what has preceded. On the Apostle's constant and emphatic condemnation of the deadly sin of πορνεία, as one of the things which the old Pagan world deemed ἀδιάφορα, compare Mey. *on Acts* xv. 20. ἢ πλεονεξία] '*or covetousness ;*' the ἢ is not explanatory (Heins. *Exercit.* p. 467), but has its full and proper *disjunctive* force, serving to distinguish πλεον. from more special sins of the flesh ; see notes on ch. iv. 19. μηδὲ ὀνομαζέσθω] '*let it not be even named,* — not, 'ut facta' (Beng. 1), a meaning which ὀνομαζ. will scarcely justify ; but, 'let it not be even mentioned by name' (Beng. 2), οἱ γὰρ λόγοι τῶν πραγμάτων εἰσὶν ὁδοί, Chrys. ; see ver. 12, and comp. Psalm xv. 4. Mey. cites Dio Chrys. 360 b, στάσιν δὲ οὐδὲ ὀνομάζειν ἄξιον παρ᾽ ὑμῖν.   καθὼς πρέπει ἁγίοις] '*as becometh saints,*' — sc. to thus avoid all mention by name even of these sins, ἱκανῶς τὸ μυσαρὸν τῶν εἰρημένων ὑπέδειξε, καὶ αὐτὰς αὐτῶν προσηγορίας τῆς μνήμης ἐξορίσαι κελεύσας Theod.

4. καὶ αἰσχρότης] '*and filthiness,*· not merely in words (Æth., Theoph., Œcum.), which would be αἰσχρολογία (Col. iii. 8), but, as the abstract form suggests, τὸ αἰσχρόν, whether actively exhibited or passively approved, in word, gesture, or deed. The context obviously limits its reference to ἀκαθ. and sins of the flesh ; αἰσχρότης δὲ τίς ἐστιν καθ᾽ ἕκαστον εἶδος ἀκολασίας, Origen (Cram. *Caten.*).   *Lachm.* reads ἢ αἰσχρ. ἢ μωρολ. with AD¹E¹FG ; mss. ; Clarom., Vulg., Sahid. ; Bas., al. (*Meyer*), but in opp. to good external authority [BD³E² KL ; nearly all mss. ; Copt., Æth.-Platt,

εὐτραπελία, τὰ οὐκ ἀνήκοντα, ἀλλὰ μᾶλλον εὐχαριστία. ⁵τοῦτο

al.; Clem., Chrysost., al.], and to the internal probability of a conformation to the following ἡ. μωρολογία] '*foolish talking*,' stultiloquium, Clarom., Vulg., ܡܙܥ݂ ܕܫܛܝܘܬܐ [sermones stultitiæ] Syriac; an ἅπαξ λεγόμ. in the N. T. of which the exact meaning must be defined by the context. Of the two definitions of Origen, the first, ἡ ἀσκουμένη ὑπὸ τῶν μωρολόγων καὶ γελωτοποιῶν, is too lax; the second, τὸ μωρὸν εἶναι ἐν τοῖς δογματιζομένοις, too restrictive. The terms with which it stands in connection seem certainly to preclude any reference to positive profanity (compare Calv.), still Trench is probably right in here superadding to the ordinary meaning of idle, aimless, and foolish talk, a ref. to that sin and vanity of spirit which the talk of fools is certain to bewray; see *Synon.* § xxxiv., and Wordsw. *in loc.* εὐτραπελία] '*jesting*,' '*wittiness*;' a second ἅπαξ λεγόμ.: ἔνθα γέλως ἄκαιρος ἐκεῖ ἡ εὐτραπελία, Chrysost. The word, as its derivation suggests, properly means *versatility*, whether in motion, manners, or talk (Dissen, Pind. *Pyth.* I. 93); from which a more unfavorable signification, 'polished jesting,' (εὐτράπελος· ὁ δυνάμενος σκῶψαι ἐμμελῶς, Aristot. *Moral.* I. 31), 'use of witty equivoque' (ingenio nititur,' Beng.), is easily and naturally derived; see Trench, *Synon.* xxxiv., and the excellent sermon by Barrow on this text, *Serm.* xiv. Vol. I. p. 383 sq. The disjunctive (surely not 'conjunctive,' Bp. Taylor, *Serm.* xxiii.) ἤ marks it as a different vice to μωρολ., and thus appy. as not only a sin of the tongue (Trench), but as including the evil 'urbanitas' (in manners or words) of the witty, godless man of the world. The practical application may be found in Taylor, *Serm.* xxiii. (Gold. Grove),

and esp. in the latter part of Chrysost. *Hom.* xvii. τὰ οὐκ ἀνήκοντα] '*things which are not convenient*;' in apposition to the 'last two words, to which both εὐχ., as denoting oral expression yet *implying* inward feeling, forms a clear contrast. It is instructive to compare Rom. i. 28, τὰ μὴ καθήκοντα, there the subjective denial seems appropriately introduced ('facere quæ (si quæ) essent indecora,' Winer, *Gr.* § 59. 4, p. 564, ed. 5); here is a plain objective fact that such things — οὐκ ἀνῆκεν. Such indeed (ἃ οὐκ ἀνῆκεν) is the reading of AB; 3 mss.; Clem., al. (*Lachm.*), — authority, however, too weak to justify a change in the present text. On the use of οὐ and μὴ with participp., see Gayler, *Partic. Neg.* p. 287, but observe the caution suggested in notes *on* 1 *Thess.* ii. 15, iii. 1. εὐχαριστία] '*giving of thanks*;' the meaning of this word, adopted by Hammond, several of the older, and some later expositors, 'edifying discourse,' 'devoutness,' cannot be justified by St. Paul's use either of the verb or the subst.; comp. Petav. *Dissert. Eccl.* II. 10. 4, 5, and on the true force of the ethical connection, see Harl. *Ethik,* § 32. a. On the duty generally, so frequently inculcated by St. Paul, see notes and reff. *on Phil.* iv. 6, and *on Col.* iii. 15. The verb here omitted, 'per brachylogiam' (Jelf, *Gr.* § 895), is differently supplied; perhaps γινέσθω ἐν ὑμῖν is the supplement *most* natural, ἀνήκει (Beng.) that *least* so.

5. τοῦτο γὰρ ἴστε γινώσκ.] '*For this ye know, being aware*, or, *as ye are aware*;' confirmation of the preceding prohibitions, by an appeal to their own knowledge of the judgment against those who practise them. It is scarcely critically exact to connect this with the Hebraistic (but compare also Jelf, *Gr.* § 705. 3) mode of expression, γινώσκων

γὰρ ἴστε γινώσκοντες ὅτι πᾶς πόρνος ἢ ἀκάθαρτος ἢ πλεονέκτης,
ὅς ἐστιν εἰδωλολάτρης, οὐκ ἔχει κληρονομίαν ἐν τῇ βασιλείᾳ τοῦ

γνώσῃ, Gen. xv. 13, 'thou shalt know full well,' etc. (Stier), as ἴστε and γινώσκ. are not portions of the same verb. The part. must be joined more immediately with ὅτι, and seems used with a slightly *causal* force which serves to elucidate and justify the appeal; see Winer, *Gr.* § 45. 8, p. 318. Whether ἴστε be taken as *imperative* or *indicative* must be left to individual judgment. The former interpr. is adopted by Clarom., Vulg., Arm. (comp., — but with different reading, Syr., Æth.), and by some Ff., *e. g.* appy. Clem. Alex. (*Pœdag.* III. 4), but seems scarcely so impressive as the latter (Copt.), and somewhat tends to diminish the force of the now isolated and emphatic imperative in ver. 6; comp. Alf. *in loc.* The reading ἐστε γιν. (*Rec.*) is supported by D³E KL; mss.; Syr. (both), al.; Theod., Dam., but is distinctly inferior to ἴστε in external authority [ABD¹FG; 30 mss.; Vulg., Clarom., Copt., al.; Clem., al.], and is rejected by nearly all recent editors.   πᾶς — οὐκ] On this Hebraistic mode of expression, see notes on ch. iv. 29.   ὅς ἐστιν refers immediately to πλεονέκτης, not to the three preceding substantives; comp. Col. iii. 5, τὴν πλεονεξίαν ἥτις ἐστιν εἰδωλολατρεία. Covetousness is truly a definite form of · idolatry, it is the worship of Mammon (Matth. vi. 24) instead of God; comp. Theodoret. To this, therefore, rather than to the other sins, which are veritable, but more subtle forms of the same sin, the Apostle gives the above specific designation. The passages adduced by Wetst. and Schoettg. illustrate the form of expression, but nothing more.   The reading ὅ adopted by *Lachm., Alf.,* is only found in B.; 3. 67**, al.; Cyr., Jerome, — and has no claim to be received in the text on such

weak external authority.   οὐκ ἔχει κληρον.] '*hath no inheritance;*' a weighty present, involving an indirect reference to the eternal and enduring principles by which God governs the world, — not so much, 'has no inheritance, and *shall* have none' (Eadie), as 'has, etc., and *can* have none;' compare ver. 6, and Col. iii. 6, δι' ἃ ἔρχεται ἡ ὀργὴ τοῦ Θεοῦ; see Winer, *Gr.* § 40. 2, p. 237.   τοῦ Χριστοῦ καὶ Θεοῦ] '*of Christ and God,*' — not '*of God,*' Auth. This is the first decided instance (the reading being doubtful in Acts xx. 28) adduced by Granville Sharp, to prove that the same Person in Scripture is called Christ and God, see Middleton, *Greek Art.* p. 362 sq. (ed. Rose), and ch. III. 4. 2, p. 57 sq. When, however, we maturely weigh the context, in which no dogmatic assertions relative to Christ find a place (as in Tit. ii. 13, 14), when we recall the frequent use of Θεὸς without· an article, even where it might have been expected (compare Winer, *Gr.* § 19. 1, p. 110), — and lastly, when we observe that the presence of the art. τοῦ Θεοῦ would really have even suggested a thought of subordination (as if it were necessary to specify that the kindom of Christ was also the kingdom of God, — the inadvertence of the Auth.), we seem forced to the conviction that Sharp's rule does not apply *here.* Christ and God are united together in the closest way, and presented under a single conception ·(compare Winer, *Gr.* § 19. 4, p. 116), — an indirect evidence of Christ's divinity of no slight value, — still the identity of the two substantives ('of Him who is Christ and God,' Wordsw.) cannot be safely or certainly maintained from this passage. On the meaning of the term βασιλεία Θεοῦ, see notes and reff. *on Gal.* v. 21.

Χριστοῦ καὶ Θεοῦ. ⁶ μηδεὶς ὑμᾶς ἀπατάτω κενοῖς λόγοις· διὰ ταῦτα γὰρ ἔρχεται ἡ ὀργὴ τοῦ Θεοῦ ἐπὶ τοὺς υἱοὺς τῆς ἀπειθείας. ⁷ μὴ οὖν γίνεσθε συμμέτοχοι αὐτῶν.

6. μηδεὶς ὑμᾶς κ.τ.λ.] 'Let no one deceive you with vain words, sophistries;' emphatic warning (without any particle) against all who sought to deceive them as to the real nature of the sins condemned. It does not seem necessary to limit the regular meaning of κενός ('empty,' οὐδαμῶς ἐπὶ τῶν ἔργων δεικνύμενοι, Chrys., — hence ' a veritate alieni,' Kypke, Obs. Vol. ii. p. 299), and to refer the κενοὶ λόγοι specially to heathen philosophers (Grot.), to Judaizers (Neand. Planting, Vol. i. p. 184, note, Bohn), or to Christian Antinomians (Olsh.). The Apostle generally condemns all apologists for vice, whoever they might be. These would of course be most commonly found among the heathens, and to them the passage most naturally points. The palliation or tacit toleration of vice, especially sensuality, was one of the most fearful and repulsive features of heathenism; see esp. Tholuck, Influence of Heathenism, Part IV. 2.   διὰ ταῦτα γάρ] 'for on account of these sins :' confirmation of the preceding warning; it is on account of these things (obs. the emphasis on διὰ ταῦτα), that God's wrath and vengeance is directed against the perpetrators. The reference of ταῦτα is clearly to the sins above mentioned (τούτων ἕκαστον ἔδρων, Theodoret); comp. Col. iii. 6, δι' ἅ, — in reference to a foregoing list of vices, and Gal. v. 21, ἅ προλέγω ὑμῖν. The pronoun has been referred to the ἀπάτη of the κενοὶ λόγοι (Theoph. 2), or to the ἀπάτη and the foregoing vices. The first interpr. is not grammatically untenable, as the plural ταῦτα may be idiomatically used to denote a single object, etc., in its different manifestations (see Bernhardy, Synt. VI. 8. d, p. 282, Winer, Gr.

§ 23. 5, p. 146], but, equally with the second, is open to the contextual objection, that ver. 7 seems a general warning against Gentile sins, to which consequently the present verse will be more naturally referred.   ἡ ὀργὴ τοῦ Θεοῦ] 'the wrath of God;' certainly not to be restricted to this life, 'ordinaria Dei judicia,' Calv., but as the solemn present (see last verse) indicates, to be extended also, and perhaps more especially, to the judgments ἐν τῇ βασ. τοῦ Χρ. καὶ Θεοῦ.   υἱοὺς τῆς ἀπειθ.] 'Sons of disobedience;' scil., in effect, τοὺς σφόδρα ἀπειθεῖς, Chrys., ἔχοντες τὸν τῆς μητρὸς χαρακτῆρα, Origen; see esp. notes on ch. ii. 2, and Suicer, Thes. Vol. ii. p. 1357. The ἀπειθ. here is disobedience to the principles and practice of the Gospel; see more on ch. ii. 2.

7. μὴ οὖν γίνεσθε] 'Do not then become;' οὖν having its full collective force (see on ver. 1), and referring to the previous statement that the wrath of God certainly does come on all such. The γίνεσθε (Clarom., 'nolite fieri,' Vulg., 'nolite effici,' — perhaps somewhat too strongly) is not to be explained away: the Apostle does not warn them only against being (Alf.), but against becoming ('ni vairþaiþ,' Goth.) partakers with them, against allowing themselves to lapse into any of their prevailing sins and depravities.   συμμέτοχοι αὐτῶν] 'partakers with them;' not in their punishment (Holzh.), nor their punishment and sins (Stier), but, as the context, esp. ver. 11, obviously suggests, their sins; 'nolite similia facere,' Estius. On συμμέτοχος, see notes ch. iii. 6, and on the orthography (which has here the authority of AB¹D¹FG) comp. Tisch. Prolegom. p. XLVII.

16

⁸ ἦτε γάρ ποτε σκότος, νῦν δὲ φῶς ἐν Κυρίῳ· ὡς τέκνα φωτὸς περιπατεῖτε, ⁹ ὁ γὰρ καρπὸς τοῦ φωτὸς ἐν πάσῃ ἀγαθωσύνῃ καὶ

8. ἦτε γάρ] 'For ye WERE;' emphatic, the time is now past, Rom. vi. 17. It is this very difference between the *past* and *present* state that confirms and proves (γὰρ) the propriety of the preceding warning; 'as that state is past, do not recur to it, — do not lapse again into a participation in vices which you have now turned away from;' comp. note on γίνεσθε (ver. 7), of which the present verse seems tacitly confirmatory. The assertion of Rück. that in this and several other passages in St. Paul's Epp. (*e. g.* Rom. v. 13, vi. 17, 1 Cor. iii. 12, 21, Gal. ii. 6, 15, vi. 8) μὲν ought to be inserted is sufficiently refuted by Harless. The rule is simple, — if the first clause is intended to stand in connection with and prepare the reader for the opposition in the second, μὲν is inserted; if not, not : see the excellent remarks of Klotz, *Devar.* Vol. ii. p. 356 sq., Fritz. *Rom.* x. 19, Vol. ii. p. 423, and notes *on Gal.* ii. 15. σκότος] '*darkness;*' not merely living or abiding in it (comp. Rom. ii 19, 1 Thess. v. 4), but themselves actual and veritable darkness; for examples of this vigorous and appropriate use of the abstract term, see Jelf, *Gr.* § 353. 1. φῶς ἐν Κυρίῳ] '*light in the Lord;*' not διὰ τῆς θείας χάριτος, Theoph., but 'in fellowship with the Lord;' extra Christum Satan omnia occupat,' Calv. The continued and corresponding use of the abstr. for concr. (see above) suitably prepares for the energetic exhortation (without οὖν) which follows. They were φῶς, not only in themselves (πεφωτισμένοι), but to others (comp Matth. v. 14), and were to pursue their moral walk in accordance with such a state of privilege. On the use of the terms φῶς and σκότος, see Usteri, *Lehrb.* ii. 1, 3, p. 229. ὡς τέκνα φωτὸς περιπ.] '*walk as children of light,*' as those who stand in nearest and truest connection with it; see notes on ch. ii. 3. The absence of the article can hardly be pressed (Alf.), as it appears due only to that common principle of correlation, by which, if the governing noun is without the article, the governed will be equally so; see Middleton, *Art.* iii. 3, 7, p 49 (ed Rose). On the meaning of περιπατεῖν, which, however, must not always be too strongly pressed, see notes *on Phil.* iii. 18, and *on* 1 *Thess.* iv. 12.

9. ὁ γὰρ κ. τ. λ.] '*For the fruit of the light;*' parenthetic confirmation of the foregoing command, and incitement to follow it. Γὰρ is thus not simply explanatory (ὥσπερ ἐφερμηνεύει τί ἐστι τὸ τέκνα τοῦ φωτός, Theoph.), but, as the order seems to suggest, confirms the propriety of using the term περιπατεῖτε, and also supplies its fuller explanation : 'As children of the light walk ye, for the fruit of light is shown in a moral walk, in practical instances of ἀγαθωσύνη.' The modal participle δοκιμάζοντες (see below) is thus closely joined with περιπατεῖτε, and ver. 9, though not fully so in form, is clearly parenthetical in sense : contra Stier, who, however, fails properly and grammatically to explain the use of the participle. The reading πνεύματος [*Rec.* with D³E²KL; great majority of mss.; Syr.-Phil., al.; Chrys., Theod]. seems clearly a gloss from Gal. v. 25, and is rightly rejected by nearly all recent editors. ἐν] 'consistit *in,*' Beng., or, more exactly, 'continetur, ponitur in :' the assertion that ἐν is here the 'Beth essentiæ' (compare Gesen. § 151. 3. a) is distinctly untenable; see Winer, *Gr.* § 47. 3. obs. p. 420. πάσῃ ἀγαθωσύνῃ] '*all goodness,*' *i. e.* all forms and instances of it ; see notes ch. i. 8. On the meaning of ἀγαθ. see

δικαιοσύνη καὶ ἀληθείᾳ, ¹⁰ δοκιμάζοντες τί ἐστιν εὐάρεστον ' τῷ
Κυρίῳ· ¹¹ καὶ μὴ συνκοινωνεῖτε τοῖς ἔργοις τοῖς ἀκάρποις τοῦ
σκότους, μᾶλλον δὲ καὶ ἐλέγχετε. ¹² τὰ γὰρ κρυφῇ γινόμενα ὑπ'

notes on Gal. v. 22. The special appo-
sitions which Chrys. finds in these three
nouns, πρὸς τοὺς ὀργιζομένους, πρὸς τοὺς
πλεονεκτοῦντας, πρὸς τὴν ψευδῆ ἡδονήν,
are too limited. As Meyer correctly
observes, the whole of Christian moral-
ity is presented under its three great
aspects, the good, the right, the true;
ἀνίστοιχα are κακία, ἀδικία, ψεῦδος; compare Harl. in loc., and for a sermon on
this text, see Tillotson, Serm. CXLVIII.
Vol. II. p. 311 (Lond. 1717).

10. δοκιμάζοντες] 'proving,' 'testing;' predication of. manner appended
to περιπατεῖτε, defining its character and
distinctive features. The verb δοκιμάζειν
is not 'to have a just conception of,'
Peile, nor 'examinando cognitum ha-
bere,' Borger, ad Rom. p. 12 (cited by
Fritz.), but, in its simple and primary
sense, 'to prove, to try,' the word marking the activity and experimental energy
that should characterize the Christian
life; see Rom. xii. 2, and Fritz. in loc.,
and notes on Phil. i. 10, where the meanings of this word are briefly discussed.
The sense then is well expressed by
Eadie; 'the one point of the Christian's
ethical investigation is, Is it well pleas-
ing to the Lord?' ἄρα ἀδοκίμου καὶ παιδι-
κῆς διανοίας τὰ ἀλλά, Œcum.

11. μὴ συνκοινωνεῖτε] 'have no
fellowship with,' Auth.—a good and accurate translation; comp. ܡܫܘܬܦܝܢ
[commercium habentes] 'gadailans,'
Goth. The version of Eadie and De
W., 'take no part in,' is questionable,
if not erroneous, as this would imply a
genitive; comp. Rom. xi. 17, 1 Cor. ix.
23, Phil. i. 7. Though the sense is
nearly the same, there is still no reason,
either here, Phil. iv. 4, or Rev. xviii. 4,
for departing from the exact translation.

The form συνκοιν. is found AB¹D¹FGL,
and on such evidence is appy. rightly
adopted by Tisch. (ed. 7); see Prolegom.
p. XLVII.   τοῖς ἔργοις τοῖς
ἀκάρπ.] 'the unfruitful works;' comp.
Gal. v. 19, 22, where there is a similar
opposition between καρπὸς and ἔργα.
The comment of Jerome (cited by Harless) is very good, 'vitia in semet ipsa
finiuntur et pereunt, virtutes frugibus
pullulant et redundant;' see notes on
Gal. v. 22.   μᾶλλον δὲ καὶ cannot be correctly considered as a single
formula, 'yea, much more,' Eadie: μᾶλλον δὲ is corrective (see notes on Gal. iv.
9), while καὶ is closely connected with
the verb, preserving its full ascensive
force, 'not only μὴ συγκ., but rather even
ἐλέγχετε;' 'non satis abstinere est,'
Bengel; comp. Fritz. Rom. viii. 34, Vol.
II. p. 216.   ἐλέγχετε] 'reprove
them,' 'redarguite,' Clarom., Vulg.,—
not by the passive, virtual reproof of
your holy lives and conversation (Peile),
but, as St. Paul's use of the word (see
esp. 1 Cor. xiv. 24, 2 Tim. iv. 2, Tit. i.
9, 13, ii. 15), and still more the context,
suggest,—by active and oral reproba-
tion. The antithesis is thus most fully
marked; 'do not connive at them or
pass them over unnoticed, but take
aggressive measures against them; try
and raise the Gentiles to your own
Christian standard;' see Olsh. in loc.

12. τὰ γὰρ κ. τ. λ.] 'For the things,
etc.;' confirmatory reason for the command in the preceding clause. The
connection of this verse with the preceding has been differently explained. If
the correct meaning of ἐλέγχ. (see
above) be retained, there seems but little
difficulty; γὰρ then gives the reason for
the καὶ ἐλέγχετε; 'reproof is indeed
necessary, for some of their sins, their

αὐτῶν αἰσχρόν ἐστιν καὶ λέγειν·   ¹³ τὰ δὲ πάντα ἐλεγχόμενα ὑπὸ

secret vices for instance, are such that it is a shame even to speak of them, much less connive at them or join in them.' Harl. refers γὰρ more to μὴ συγκ.; 'do not commit these sins, for they are too bad even to mention.' This, however, assumes a perfect identity between τὰ ἔργ. τοῦ σκ. and τὰ κρυφῇ γιν., which (see below) is highly doubtful; and also gives to the negative part of the command (which, as the corrective μᾶλλον δὲ suggests, is obscured by the positive) an undue and untenable prominence. τὰ κρυφῇ γιν.] 'the things which are done in secret by them,' sc. by the υἱοῖς τῆς ἀπειθείας. There is not enough in the context to substantiate a reference to the mysteries and orgies of heathenism (Elsner, Obs. Vol. II. p. 223). The use of κρυφῇ (which obviously has here a simple, and not an ethical meaning like σκότος) and its emphatic position seem alike to show that τὰ κρυφῇ γιν. are sins, not simply identical with τὰ ἔργα τ. σκότους, ver. 11 (Harl.), but a specific class of the genus. These 'deeds done in secret,' then, were all those 'peccata occulta' which presented the worst features of the genus, and which, from their nature and infamy, shunned the light of day and of judgment. καὶ λέγειν] 'even to speak of,' 'only to mention.' This is an instance of what may be termed the descensive force of καί; see exx. in Hartung, Partik. καί, 2. 9, Vol. I. p. 136; comp. Klotz, Devar. Vol. II. p. 364, and notes on Gal. iii. 4. Elsner compares, not inappropriately, Isocr. Demon. p. 6, ἃ ποιεῖν αἰσχρόν, ταῦτα νόμιζε μηδὲ λέγειν εἶναι κάλον.

13. τὰ δὲ πάντα] 'But all of them,' 'they all' ܟ݁ܽܠܗܶܝܢ ܕܶܝܢ [illa omnia] Syr.-Phil.; continuation of the reason for the command μᾶλλον δὲ καὶ ἐλέγχ., — with antithetical reference to

the κρυφῇ γινόμενα, δὲ retaining its proper force in the opposition it suggests to any inference that might have been deduced from ver. 12; 'it is true these deeds are done in secret, but all of them, etc.;' see Klotz, Devar. Vol. II. p. 363, 365. Τὰ πάντα is not 'all things,' taken generally (Rück., Alf.), but, as the antithesis between κρυφῇ and φανερ. (compare Mark iv. 22) clearly suggests, 'all the κρυφῇ γινόμ.,' 'haud dubie quin ea quæ occulte fiunt,' Hieron.; so rightly De W. and Meyer in loc. ἐλεγχόμενα] 'when they are reproved' ܡܶܬܟ݁ܰܣܣܺܝܢ ܟ݁ܰܕ [dum redarguuntur] Syr.-Phil.; predication of manner or perhaps rather of time appended to τὰ πάντα. The absence of the art. before ἐλεγχ. distinctly precludes the translation 'quæ arguuntur' (Clarom., Vulg., Auth., — comp. Copt.), and shows that the participle is not an epithet but a secondary predicate; see Scholef. Hints, p. 103. ὑπὸ τοῦ φωτὸς φανεροῦται] 'are made manifest by light.' It is somewhat difficult to decide whether these words are to be connected with the part. (Syr., Copt.), or with the finite verb (Æth., Syr.-Phil., — appy.); a connection with both (Scholef., comp. Stier) is an evasion, but not an explanation, of the difficulties. The following positions will perhaps serve to narrow the discussion. (a) Ἐλεγχόμενα, both in tense as well as meaning (contr. Hamm., Peile), must stand in closest reference to ἐλέγχετε; it may still be said, however, that the secondary meaning of the word (compare Clem. Al. Protrept. II. p. 19, ἐλέγχει τὸν Ἴακχον τὸ φῶς) may have suggested the metaphorical language which follows. (b) Φῶς (φάος, φανερός) and φανερόω are closely allied terms; the one so obviously explains, elucidates, and implies the other, that the connec-

τοῦ φωτὸς φανεροῦται· πᾶν γὰρ τὸ φανερούμενον φῶς ἐστιν·
¹⁴ διὸ λέγει Ἔγειρε ὁ καθεύδων καὶ ἀνάστα ἐκ τῶν νεκρῶν, καὶ
ἐπιφαύσει σοι ὁ Χριστός.

tion of the two in the same clause seems in a high degree natural and probable. (c) Φῶς must have the same meaning in both clauses; if simply *metaphorical* in the latter clause, then also simply *metaphorical* (not *ethical*, as in τέκνα φωτός) in the former. (d) The voice of φανερόω must be the same in both clauses, and is certainly *passive*; the verb occurs nearly fifty times in the N. T., and never in a middle sense; see Winer, *Gr.* § 38. 6, p. 231. Applying these premises, it seems clear that if we adopt the first-mentioned connection, ἔλεγχ. ὑπὸ φωτ. (Chrys., al.), conditions (a) and (c) cannot be fully satisfied; for either ἔλεγχ. must be taken as nearly synonymous with φανερ. (De W.), or φῶς must have an ethical reference ('lux verbi,' Croc.) in the former clause, which it can scarcely bear in the latter; and further, ἐλεγχόμ. will thus have a specification attached to it, which is not in harmony with ver. 12, where the act alone is enjoined without any *special* concomitant mention of the agent. It would thus seem to be almost certain that ὑπὸ φωτός must be joined with φανεροῦται, which it somewhat emphatically precedes. We translate then, in accordance with (a), (b), (c), (d), as follows: '*but all things* (though so κρυφῇ γιν.) *when reproved are made manifest by the light* (thus shed upon them), *for everything that is made manifest is light* (becomes daylight, is of the nature of light); compare Scholef. *l. c.*, and Wordsw. *in loc.* In a word, the reasoning depends on the logical proposition which Meyer has adduced,— 'quod est in effectu (φῶς ἐστί), id debet esse in causâ (ὑπὸ τοῦ φωτός).' That this φανέρωσις, however, does not *necessarily* imply or involve a 'mutatio in melius' (Jerome, comp. Wordsw.),

seems clear from (c). All that is asserted is, that 'whatever is illumined is light;' whether that tend to condemnation or the contrary, depends upon the nature of the case, and the inward opera-° tion of the outwardly illuminating influence; see Alf. *in loc.*

14. δ ι ό] '*On which account;*' since this ἔλεγξις is so urgent and necessary a duty, and its nature such as described. On the use of διό, see notes *on Gal.* iv. 31. λ έ γ ε ι] '*He saith;*' scil. ὁ Θεός, according to the usual form of St. Paul's quotations; see notes on ch. iv. 8, and *on Gal.* iii. 16. The words here quoted are not found exactly in the same form in the O. T., but certainly occur in substance in Isaiah lx. 1 sq. Meyer represents it as a quotation from an apocryphal writing which the Apostle introduces by a lapse of memory; De W., as an application from a passage in the O. T., which he had so constantly used as at last to mistake for the original text. Alii alia. It seems much more reverent, as well as much more satisfactory, to say that St. Paul, speaking under the inspiration of the Holy Spirit, is expressing, in a condensed and summary form, the spiritual meaning of the passage. The prophet's immediate words supply, in substance, the first part of the quotation, קוּמִי אוֹרִי כִּי בָא אוֹרֵךְ; the concluding part is the spiritual application of the remainder of the verse, viz. וּכְבוֹד יְהֹוָה עָלַיִךְ זָרָח, and of the general tenor of the prophecy; see esp. ver. 19, and comp. Surenhus, Βιβλ. Καταλλ. p. 588. Any attempt to explain λέγει impersonally ('one may say,' Bornem. *Schol.* in *Luc.* p. XLVIII.) is not only opposed to St. Paul's constant use of λέγει, but is grammatically unsupported: φησὶ (compare Lat. 'inquit') is so used

Walk strictly: avoid excess, but be filled with the Spirit; sing psalms outwardly with your lips, and make melody with thankfulness in your hearts within.

^{15} Βλέπετε οὖν πῶς ἀκριβῶς περιπατεῖτε, μὴ

especially in later writers, but no instances have been adduced of a similar use of λέγει: comp. Bernhardy, *Synt.* XII. 4, p. 419.   ἔγειρε] 'Awake,' 'Up!' This expression is now generally correctly explained: it is not an instance of an 'act. pro medio' (Porson, Eurip. *Orest.* 288), or of an ellipsis of σεαυτόν, but simply a 'formula excitandi;' consult the excellent note of Fritz. *Mark* ii. 9, p. 55. The reading of the *Rec.* ἔγειραι, found only in some cursive mss., is undoubtedly a correction, and is rejected by all the best editors.   ἀνάστα] 'arise.' This shortened form occurs Acts xii. 7, and may be compared with κατάβα (*Rec.*), Mark xv. 30, ἀνάβα, Rev. iv. 1; see Winer, *Gr.* § 14, 1, p. 73.   καὶ ἐπιφαύσει] 'and Christ shall shine upon thee,' — obviously not in the derivative sense, 'Christus tibi propitius erit' (Bretsch.), but simply, 'illucescet tanquam sol' (Beng.), 'per gratiam te illuminabit' (Est.): ὅταν οὖν ἐγερθῇ τις ἀπὸ τῆς ἁμαρτίας, τότε ἐπιφαύσει αὐτῷ ὁ Χριστός, τουτέστιν, ἐπιλάμψει ὥσπερ καὶ ὁ ἥλιος τοῖς ἐξ ὕπνου ἐγερθεῖσιν, Theoph.

15. βλέπετε οὖν] 'Take heed then;' resumption of the preceding exhortations (ver. 8) after the digression caused by the latter part of ver. 11. It is quite unnecessary to attempt to connect closely this with the preceding verse (Harless, Eadie); this resumptive use of οὖν being by no means of rare occurrence (see Klotz, *Devar.* Vol. ii. p. 718, notes *on Gal.* iii. 5), and indeed involved in the nature of the particle, which nearly always implies *retrospective reference* rather than direct inference; see Donalds. *Gr.* § 548. 31, p. 571. It is scarcely necessary to add that βλέπετε has no reference whatever to the φῶς previously alluded to (comp. Est.), but simply implies 'take heed;' see 1 Cor. xvi. 10, Col. iv. 17, and notes *in loc.*   πῶς ἀκ-

ριβῶς περιπατεῖτε] 'how ye walk exactly, or, with strictness,' scil. 'quomodo illud efficiatis ut provide vivatis' (πῶς τὸ ἀκριβῶς ἐργάζεσθε), Fritz. *Fritz. Opusc.* p. 208, 209, note, — where this passage is carefully investigated; see also Winer, *Gr.* § 41. 4. c. obs. p. 268, who has long since given up the assumption that the text is an abbreviated expression for βλέπετε οὖν πῶς περιπατεῖτε, δεῖ δὲ ὑμᾶς ἀκριβῶς περιπατεῖν, though still referred to by Meyer (ed. 2, 1853), as retaining it. Thus then the indic. is not used for the *subj.* (Grot.), which (if an admissible structure) would be 'quomodo provide vivere possitis,' nor for the *future*, which would be 'quomodo provide vitam sitis acturi,' but simply calls attention to that in which τὸ ἀκριβῶς περιπατεῖν finds its present manifestation, and which is specified more precisely in the clause which follows. As περιπ. appy. here implies little more than ζῆν (see Fritz. *Rom.* xiii. 13, Vol. iii. p. 141, comp. notes on ver. 8), there is no necessity to depart from the literal meaning of ἀκριβῶς, — not 'caute,' Vulg., Syr., still less, 'without stumbling,' Conyb., but '*exactly*,' 'accurate,' Beza, 'tanquam ad regulam et amussim,' Fritz. *Opusc. l. c.*; see Neander, *Planting*, Vol. i. p. 486 (Bohn).

μὴ ὡς ἄσοφοι κ.τ.λ.] 'to wit, not as unwise but as wise;' more exact specification of the terms of the preceding clause. It is thus not necessary to supply either περιπατοῦντες to this clause (Harl.), or περιπατῆτε to its second member (as, *in effect*, Fritz., 'sed ut homines sapientes [vitam instituatis '], *loc. cit.*, p. 209): the clause is simply dependent on περιπατεῖτε, explaining first on the negative, and then on the affirmative side the foregoing adverbs; both the strictness of their walk and the way in which that strictness was to be shown were to reflect the spirit of wise men and not of

ὡς ἄσοφοι ἀλλ᾽ ὡς σοφοί,   ¹⁶ ἐξαγοραζόμενοι τὸν καιρόν, ὅτι
αἱ ἡμέραι πονηραί εἰσιν.   ¹⁷ διὰ τοῦτο μὴ γίνεσθε ἄφρονες, ἀλλὰ

fools: comp. Gayler, *Part. Neg.* p. 63, where similar positions of the neg. clause are incidentally cited.

16. ἐξαγοραζόμενοι τὸν καιρόν] '*buying up for yourselves (making your own) the opportunity, the fitting season;*' part. of *manner* exemplifying the wise spirit of action specified in the foregoing member. This expression occurs twice in the N. T.; here with, and in Col. iv. 5, without an appended causal sentence; compare also Dan. ii. 8, καιρὸν ἐξαγοράζετε (*appy.* 'hanc opportunitatem capiatis,' see Schoettg. *Hor.* Vol. I. p. 780, not 'dilationem quaeritis,' Schleusn.). The numerous, and, in most cases, artificial explanations of this passage arise from the attempts to specify (a) *those from whom* ('mali homines,' Beng., 'Diabolus,' Calv., etc.) the καιρὸς is to be purchased, or (b) *the price* (all worldly things, τὰ πάντα, Chrys., Theophyl., Schrader) paid for it; both of which are left wholly undefined. The force of ἐκ does not appear *intensive* (Mey., comp. Plutarch, *Crass.* § 2), or simply latent (a Lap.), but directs the thoughts to the undefined time or circumstances *out of* which, in each particular case, the καιρὸς was to be bought; comp. Gal. iii. 13, iv. 5, where however the meaning is more special, and the reference of the preposition better defined by the context. The expression then seems simply to denote that we are to make a wise use of circumstances for our own good or that of others, and, as it were, like prudent merchants (comp. Beza, Corn. a Lap.) to '*by up* the fitting season' for so doing; 'diligenter observare tempus, ut id tuum facias, eique ut dominus imperes,' Tittm. *Synon.* p. 42; so Sever. (ap. Cram. *Caten.*), and in effect Origen (ib.), though he has too much mixed up the ideas of a right purchase of the time and

a right expenditure of it. For sermons on this text see August. *Serm.* CLXVIII. Vol. V. p. 909 sq. (ed Migne).

τὸν καιρόν] '*the opportunity;*' not 'hoc tempus, scil. tempus breve quod restat huic aevo,' Bretsch. (Sever. ὁ καιρὸς ὁ παρών, comp. Stier), but, as rightly explained by Cornel. a Lap., 'occasionem et opportunitatem scil. mercandi.' On the use of καιρὸς ('tempus, seu punctum temporis opportunum') and its distinction from αἰών, χρόνος, and ὥρα, see Tittm. *Synon.* p. 39 sq.   πονη- ραῖ] 'evil,' in a moral sense (Gal. i. 4), not 'difficultatum et asperitatis plena,' Beza (comp. Gen. xlvii. 9), which would introduce an idea foreign to the context. Christians are bidden to walk ἀκριβῶς, and to seize every opportunity, because 'the days' (of their life, הַיָּמִים, or of the period in which they lived) were marked by so much moral evil and iniquity; ἐπεὶ οὖν ὁ καιρὸς δουλεύει τοῖς πονηροῖς, ἐξαγοράσασθε αὐτόν, ὥστε καταχρήσασθαι αὐτῷ πρὸς εὐσέβειαν, Sever. ap. Cram. *Caten.*

17. διὰ τοῦτο] '*For this cause;*' commonly referred to the clause immediately preceding, ἐπειδὴ ἡ πονηρία ἀνθεῖ, Œcum., Theophyl. (so De W., Olsh.), but far more probably (see Mey.) to ver. 15, 16, — 'for this cause, sc. because ye ought to walk with such exactness;' εἰ γὰρ ἔσεσθε ἄφρονες ἀκριβῶς οὐ περιπατήσετε, Schol. ap. Cram. *Caten.* συνιέντες] '*understanding;*' 'plus est συνιέναι quam γινώσκειν, ut apparet ex hoc loco cum Luc. xii. 47; γινώσκειν est nosse, συνιέναι attente expendere,' Grot. (Pol. *Syn.*). The reading is slightly doubtful. *Lachm.* reads συνίετε with AB; 6 mss.; Chrys. (ms.), but on external evidence inferior to that for the participle [συνιέντες, D³EKL (συνίοντες, D¹FG, Alf.); nearly all mss.; Clarom.,

συνιέντες τί τὸ θέλημα τοῦ Κυρίου. ¹⁸ καὶ μὴ μεθύσκεσθε οἴνῳ,
ἐν ᾧ ἐστιν ἀσωτία, ἀλλὰ πληροῦσθε ἐν Πνεύματι, ¹⁹ λαλοῦντες

Vulg., Goth., Syr.-Phil., al., and many Ff.], and in the face of the high probability that the imper. is due to a conformation to ver. 18.   ἄφρονες] 'unwise,' 'senseless;' 'ἄφρων est qui mente non recte utitur,' Tittm. *Synon.* p 143, — where the distinction between this word, νήπιος, ἀνόητος, and ἀσύνετος is investigated; but see notes *on Gal.* iii. 1.   18. καὶ μὴ μεθύσκ.] '*And be not made drunk with wine ;*' specification of a particular instance ; καὶ being here used to append the *special* to the *general :* on this and on the converse use, see notes *on Phil.* iv. 12, and comp. the good note of Fritz. *Mark* i. 5, p. 11.   ἐν ᾧ] '*wherein,*' Auth.; referring not simply to οἶνος (Schoettg.), but to μεθύσκεσθαι οἴνῳ, scil., 'in inebriatione,' Beza; so rightly Orig. 1, ap. Cram. *Cat.* ἀσωτία] '*dissoluteness,*' Hamm., 'luxuria,' Vulg., Clarom.; not inappropriately Goth., 'usstiurei' [unyokedness]; τοὺς ἀκρατεῖς καὶ εἰς ἀκολασίαν δαπανηροὺς ἀσώτους καλοῦμεν, Arist. *Ethic. Nic.* IV. 1 ; comp. Cic. *de Fin.* II. 8. Ἄσωτος (σώζω) appears to have two meanings, the rarer, 'qui servari non potest,' a meaning which Clem. Alex. (*Pædag.* II. 2, p. 184, ed. Pott.) applies to this place, τὸ ἄσωστον τῆς μέθης διὰ τῆς ἀσωτίας αἰνιξάμενος, — and the more common, 'qui servare nequit ;' see Trench, *Synon.* § XVI. The latter meaning passes naturally into that of 'dissoluteness,' the only sense in which ἀσωτία and ἀσώτως are used in the N. T., *e. g.*, Luke xv. 13, Tit. i. 6, 1 Pet. iv. 4 ; the substantive is found Prov. xxviii. 7 (Trench), to which add 2 Macc. iv. 6, where it is joined with κῶμοι; see also Tittm. *Synon.* p. 152   ἐν Πνεύματι] '*with the Spirit ;*' ἐν being appy. primarily, though not exclusively, *instru-*

mental (Vulg., Arm.; see Origen ap. Cram. *Cat.*), — though an unusual construction with πληρόω; see however ch. i. 23. Meyer cites also Phil. iv. 19, but this is a doubtful instance ; still more so are Col. ii. 10, iv. 12 (cited by Eadie after Harl.), as in the first of these passages ἐν is obviously 'in,' and in the second the reading is more than doubtful ; see notes *in loc.* There would seem to have been an intentional inclusiveness in the use of this prepp., as Matthies (misrepresented by Eadie) suggests ; the Spirit is not the bare instrument *by* which, but that *in* which and *by* which the true Christian is fully filled Whether the passive πληροῦσθε hints at our 'reluctant will' (Mey.) seems doubtful ; there is no doubt, however, that the opposition is not between οἶνος and Πνεῦμα, but, as the order of the words suggests, between the two states expressed by the two verbs. On the omission of the article (which is inserted in FG), see notes on ch. ii. 22, and *on Gal.* v. 5.

19. λαλοῦντες ἑαυτοῖς] '*speaking to one another ;*'—not 'to yourselves,' Auth.; ἑαυτοῖς being used for ἀλλήλοις, as in ch. iv. 32 ; comp. Col. iii. 16, and see Jelf, *Gr.* § 654. 2. Scholefield (*Hints,* p. 103) and, before him, Bull (*Prim. Trad.* I. 12), compare the well-known quotation, 'carmen Christo quasi Deo dicere secum *invicem,*' Pliny, *Epist.* x. 97. Whether the reference is here to social meetings (compare Clem. Alex. *Pædag.* II. 4, p. 194, Pott.), or expressly to religious service (Olsh.), or, more probably, to both, can hardly be determined from the context.   ψαλμοῖς κ. τ. λ.] '*with psalms and hymns and spiritual songs.*' The distinctions between these words have been somewhat differently estimated. Olsh. and

ἑαυτοῖς ψαλμοῖς καὶ ὕμνοις καὶ ᾠδαῖς πνευματικαῖς, ᾄδοντες καὶ ψάλλοντες ἐν τῇ καρδίᾳ ὑμῶν τῷ Κυρίῳ, ²⁰ εὐχαριστοῦντες πάν-

Stier would confine ψαλμ. to the Psalms of the Old Test., ὕμνος to any Christian song of praise; this does not seem borne out by 1 Cor. xiv. 26 (see Alford), compare James v. 13. Harless refers the former to the Jewish, the latter to Gentile Christians; Orig. (Cram. Cat.) still more arbitrarily defines the ψαλμ. as περὶ τῶν πρακτέων, the ᾠδὴ as περὶ τῆς τοῦ κόσμου τάξεως καὶ τῶν λοιπῶν δημιουργημάτων. In a passage so general as the present, no such rigorous distinctions seem called for; ψαλμὸς most probably, as Meyer suggests, denotes a sacred song of a character similar to that of the Psalms (ὁ ψαλμὸς ἐμμελής ἐστιν εὐλογία καὶ σώφρων, Clem. Alex. Pædag. ΙΙ. 4, p. 194); ὕμνος, a song more especially of praise, whether to Christ (ver. 19), or God (ver. 20; comp. Acts xvi. 25, Heb. ii. 12); ᾠδή, a definition generally of the genus to which all such compositions belonged (ᾠδὴν πνευματικὴν ὁ Ἀπόστολος εἴρηκε τὸν ψαλμόν, Clem. Alex. l. c.). To this last the epithet πνευματικαῖς is added, — sc. not merely, 'of religious import,' Olshaus. ('sancta,' Æth.), but in accordance with the last clause of ver. 18, 'such as the Holy Spirit inspired and gave utterance to;' ψάλλοντες γὰρ Πνεύμ. πληροῦνται ἁγίου, Chrys. Much more curious information will be found in the article 'Hymni a Christianis decantandi,' in Deyling, Obs. No. 44, Vol. III. p 430 sq.; for authorities, see Fabricius, Bibliogr. Antiq. XI. 13, and for specimens of ancient ὕμνοι, ib. Bibl. Græca, Book v. 1. 24.   Lachm. inserts ἐν in brackets before ψαλμοῖς, but on authority [B; 5 mss.; Clarom., Sangerm., Vulg., Goth., al; Chrys.] nearly the same and apparently equally insufficient with that [B; Clarom., Sangerm.; Ambrst. ed.] on which he (so Alford) similarly en-

closes the scarcely doubtful πνευματικαῖς. ᾄδοντες καὶ ψάλλοντες] 'singing and making melody in your heart;' participial clause, coördinate with (Mey.), not subordinate to (so as to specify the moral quality of the psalmody, μετὰ συνέσεως, Chrys.) the foregoing λαλοῦντες κ. τ. λ. Harl. very clearly shows that ἐν τῇ καρδίᾳ, without ὑμῶν, could not indicate any antithesis between the heart and lips, much less any qualitative definition, — 'without lip-service' (compare Theod., Eadie), or 'heartily,' like ἐκ τῆς καρδίας (κατὰ τὴν καρδ. Œcum.), but that simply another kind of psalmody is mentioned, that of the inward heart; 'canentes intus in animis et cordibus vestris, Bulling. (cited by Harl.)   The reading ἐν ταῖς καρδίαις, though fairly supported [Lachmann with ADEFG; mss.; Clarom., Vulg., Syr., Goth., Copt., Syr.-Phil. in marg.; Bas., Chrys. (2), al.] is still properly rejected by Tisch., al. as an emendation of ἐν τῇ καρδίᾳ [B (omits ἐν) KL; nearly all mss.; Syr.-Phil.; Chrys., Theod., al.] derived from Col. iii. 16.

20. εὐχαριστ. πάντ.] 'giving thanks always;' third and more comprehensive participial member, specifying the great Christian accompaniment of this and of all their acts (ch. v. 4, Phil. iv. 6, Col. iv. 2, see notes), and preparing the way for the further duty expressed in ver. 21. It would thus appear that the imperative πληρ. ἐν Πν. has four participial clauses appended, two of which specify more particular, and the third a more pervading manifestation of the fruits of the Holy Spirit, viz. ᾠδαὶ χειλέων (Ecclus. xxxix. 15), ᾠδαὶ ἐν τῇ καρδίᾳ, and εὐχαριστία, while the fourth, ὑποτασσ. passes onward to another form of Christian duty; see notes ver. 21, and for two good sermons on this text, Barrow, Serm. VIII., IX. Vol. I., p. 179

17

τοτε ὑπὲρ πάντων ἐν ὀνόματι τοῦ Κυρίου ἡμῶν Ἰησοῦ Χριστοῦ
τῷ Θεῷ καὶ πατρί, ²¹ ὑποτασσόμενοι ἀλλήλοις ἐν φόβῳ Χριστοῦ.

Wives be subject to your ²² Αἱ γυναῖκες, τοῖς ἰδίοις ἀνδράσιν ὡς τῷ
husbands as the Church is
to Christ.   Husbands love your wives as Christ loved His Church.   Marriage is a type of the mystical
union of Christ and the Church.

22. ἀνδράσιν] *Tisch.* has, with good judgment, rejected the addition of ὑποτάσσεσθε, — whether after γυναῖκες with DEFG ; Lect. 19 ; Vulg., al., or after ἀνδράσιν,

sq.   ὑ π ὲ ρ π ά ν τ ω ν] 'for all things,'
Auth. ; not masc., sc. ὑπὲρ πάντων τῶν
τῆς εὐεργεσίας μετειληχότων, Theodoret.
Meyer needlessly limits the πάντα to
blessings ; surely it is better to say, with
Theophyl., οὐχ ὑπὲρ τῶν ἀγαθῶν μόνον,
ἀλλὰ καὶ τῶν λυπηρῶν, καὶ ὧν ἴσμεν, καὶ
ὧν οὐκ ἴσμεν, καὶ γὰρ διὰ πάντων εὐεργε-
τούμεθα κἂν ἀγνοῶμεν. Numerous instances of similar cumulation and παρή-
χησις are cited by Lobeck, *Paralipom.*
p. 56, 57.   ἐ ν τ ῷ ὀ ν ό μ α τ ι] 'in
the name ;' obviously not 'ad honorem'
(Flatt.), nor even 'per nomen,' scil. 'per
Christum' (a Lap.), but 'in nomine,'
Clarom , Vulg., Copt., al. : the name of
Christ is that general and holy element,
as it were, in which everything (as Harl.
forcibly remarks) is to be received, to be
enjoined, to be done, and to be suffered ;
see Col. iii. 17. The context will always
indicate the precise nature of the application ; see the exx. cited by Alf. *in loc.*
τ ῷ Θ ε ῷ κ α ὶ Π α τ ρ ί] 'to God and the
Father ;' see notes on ch. i. 3, and on
Gal. i. 4. The most appy. suitable mode
of translating this special and august
title is noticed in notes to *Transl. of Gal.*
p. 146 (ed. 2).
    21. ὑ π ο τ α σ σ ό μ ε ν ο ι ἀ λ λ ή λ.]
'submitting yourselves to one another ;' not
for the finite verb (Flatt. ; see contra
Hermann, *Viger*, No. 227, Winer, *Gr.* §
45. 6, p. 314), but a fourth participial
clause appended to πληροῦσθε. The
first three name three duties, more or
less special, in regard to *God*, the last a
comprehensive moral duty in regard to
man, which seems to have been sug-

gested by the remembrance of the humble and loving spirit, which is the moving principle of εὐχαριστία. In the following paragraph, and under a somewhat
similar form (ὑπακοή), in v. 1 sq. and vi.
5 sq., this general duty is inculcated in
particular instances : ἐπειδὴ κοινὴν τὴν
περὶ τῆς ὑποταγῆς νομοθεσίαν προσήνεγκε
κατ' εἶδος, λοιπὸν παραινεῖ τὰ κατάλληλα,
Theod. On the distinction between ὑποτασσ. (*sponte*) and πειθαρχεῖν (*coactus*),
see Tittm. *Synon.* Part II. p. 3. It
must be admitted that there is *some* difficulty in the connection between this and
the foregoing participial member. We
can, however, hardly refer the clause to
the remote μὴ μεθύσκ. ('don't bluster,
. . . but be subject,' Eadie, Alf.), but
may reasonably retain the connection in-
dicated above, the exact connecting link
being perhaps the ὑπὲρ πάντων ; 'thank-
ing God for *all things* (joys — yea sor-
rows, submitting yourselves to Him. yea),
submitting yourselves to one another :'
compare Chrys., ἵνα πάντων κρατῶμεν
τῶν παθῶν, ἵνα τῷ Θεῷ δουλεύωμεν, ἵνα
τὴν πρὸς ἀλλήλους ἀγάπην διασώζωμεν.
ἐ ν φ ό β ῳ Χ ρ.] 'in the fear of Christ ;'
the prevailing feeling and sentiment in
which ὑποταγὴ is to be exhibited ; 'ex
[in] timore Christi ; quia scilicet Christum reveremur, eumque timemus offend-
ere,' Corn. a Lap.   The reading
Θεοῦ (*Rec*) is only supported by cursive
mss., Clem., and Theod., and is rightly
rejected by nearly all modern editors.
    22. α ἱ γ υ ν α ῖ κ ε ς] '*Wives*, — sc. be
subject ;' first of the three great ex-
emplifications (husbands and wives, —

Κυρίῳ, ²³ *ὅτι ἀνήρ ἐστιν κεφαλὴ τῆς γυναικὸς ὡς καὶ ὁ Χριστὸς*

with KL; very many Vv.; Chrys., al. (*Rec., Scholz*),— though supported in the omission only by B, *all Gr. MSS. used by Jerome*, and Clem. (*Harl., Mey. De W.*), *Lachm.* inserts *ὑποτασσέσθωσαν* after *ἀνδράσιν* with A; 10 mss.; Vulg., Copt., Goth.; Clem. (1), Bas., al.; the variations, however, and still more the absence of the word in the MSS. mentioned by Jerome, render it in a very high degree probable that the original text had no verb in the sentence.

parents and children, ch. vi. 1 sq.,— masters and servants, ch. vi. 4 sq.) of the duty of subjection previously specified. A verb can easily and obviously be supplied from the preceding verse,— either *ὑποτασσέσθωσαν* (*Lachm.*), or more probably, as the imper. in ver. 25 and Col. iii. 18 suggests, *ὑποτάσσεσθε* (*Rec.*).　*τοῖς ἰδίοις ἀνδράσιν*] '*your own husbands:*' those specially yours, whom feeling therefore as well as duty must prompt you to obey; comp. 1 Pet. iii. 1. The pronominal adject. *ἰδίοις* is clearly more than a mere possess. pronoun (De W.), or, what is virtually the same, than a formal designation of the husband, 'der Ehemann' (Harl., Winer), for St. Paul might have equally well used *τοῖς ἀνδράσιν*, as in Col. iii. 18. It seems rather, both here and 1 Pet. iii. 1, to retain its proper force, and imply, by a latent antithesis, the *legitimacy* (comp. John iv. 18), *exclusiveness* (1 Cor. vii. 2), and *speciality* (1 Cor. xiv. 35) of the connection; see esp. 1 Esd. iv. 20, *ἐγκαταλείπει τὴν ἰδ. χώραν καὶ πρὸς τὴν ἰδ. γυναῖκα κολλᾶται.* We may also adduce against Harl. his own quotation, Stobæus, *Floril.* p. 22, Θεανὼ — ἐρωτηθεῖσα, τί πρῶτον εἴη γυναικί, τὸ τῷ ἰδίῳ, ἔφη, ἀρέσκειν ἀνδρί; clearly '*her own* husband,— no one except in that proper and special relationship.' It may still be remarked that the use of *ἴδιος* in later writers is such as to make us cautious how far in *all* cases in the N. T. (see Matth. xxii. 5, John i. 42) we press the usual meaning; see Winer, *Gr.* § 22, 7, p. 139, and notes on ch. iv. 28.

ὡς τῷ Κυρίῳ] '*as to the Lord;*' clearly not 'as to the lord and master,' which perspicuity would require to be *τοῖς κυρίοις*, but,— *to Christ;* 'vir Christi imago,' Grot.; *καλὸν τῇ γυναικὶ Χριστὸν αἰδεῖσθαι διὰ τοῦ ἀνδρός*, Greg.-Naz. The meaning of *ὡς* is somewhat doubtful. Viewed in its simplest grammatical sense as the pronoun of the relative (Klotz, *Devar.* Vol. II. p. 737), the meaning would seem to be 'yield that obedience to your husbands which you yield to Christ;' comp. Beng. As, however, the immediate context and, still more, the general current of the passage (comp. ver. 32) represent marriage in its typical aspect, *ὡς* will seem far more naturally to refer (as in ch. vi. 5, 6, comp. Col. iii. 23) to the *aspect* under which the obedience is to be regarded ('quasi Christo ipsimet, cujus locum et personam viri repræsentant,' Corn. a Lap.) than to describe the nature of it (Eadie), or the manner (De W.) in which it is to be tendered; see notes *on Col.* iii. 23. Still less probable is a reference merely to the *similarity* between the duties of the wife to the husband and the Church to Christ (Kop, comp. Eadie), as this interpr. would clearly require *ὡς ἡ ἐκκλ. τῷ Κυρ.*; see Mey. It is thus well and briefly paraphrased by Chrys., ὅταν ὑπείκῃς τῷ ἀνδρί, ὡς τῷ Κυρίῳ δουλεύουσα ἡγοῦ πείθεσθαι (Sav.): see also Greg.-Naz. *Orat.* XXXI. p. 500 (ed Morell.).

23. *ἀνήρ*] '*a husband.*' The omission of the article [with all the uncial MSS., and nearly all modern editors] does not affect the meaning of the proposition, but only modifies the form in which it is

κεφαλὴ τῆς ἐκκλησίας, αὐτὸς σωτὴρ τοῦ σώματος. ²⁴ ἀλλ' ὡς ἡ

expressed; ὁ ἀνήρ would be 'the husband,' i. e. 'every husband' (see notes on *Gal.* iii. 20); ἀνήρ is 'a husband,' i. e. any one of the class; comp. Winer, *Gr.* § 19. 1, p. 111; γυνή, on the contrary, has properly the article as marking the definite relation it bears to the ἀνήρ ('his wife'), on which the general proposition is based.   ὡς καὶ ὁ Χρ. κ. τ. λ.] 'as Christ also is head — of the Church ;' the 'being head' is common to both ἀνήρ and Χρ.; the bodies, to which they are so, are different. In sentences thus composed of correlative members, when the enunciation assumes its most complete form, καὶ appears in *both* members, e. g. Rom. i. 13; comp. Kühner, Xen. *Mem.* i. 1. 6. Frequently it appears only in the *demonstrative*, or, as here, only in the *relative* member; see Hartung, *Partik.* καί, 2. 2, Vol. i. p. 126. In all these cases, however, the particle καὶ preserves its proper force. In the former case, 'per aliquam cogitandi celeritatem,' a double and reciprocal comparison is instituted between the two words to each of which καὶ is annexed; see Fritz. *Rom.* Vol. i. p. 38; in the two latter cases a single comparison only is enunciated between the word qualified by καὶ and some other, whether expressed or understood; see Klotz, *Devar.* Vol. ii. p. 635, and compare Winer, *Gr.* § 53. 5, p. 390, who, however, on this construction is not wholly satisfactory.   αὐτος σωτήρ] 'He Himself is the saviour of the body ;' declaration, apparently with a paronomasia (σωτὴρ ..... σώματος), of an important particular in which the comparison did not hold ; the clause not being appositional (Harl.), but, as the use of ἀλλὰ in the following verse seems distinctly to suggest (see notes on ver. 24), independent and emphatic (Mey.) ; 'He — and, in this full sense, none other than He — is the σωτὴρ of the body.'

The reading καὶ αὐτός ἐστι [*Rec.* with D²D³E²KL; majority of mss; Syr. (both), Goth., al.; many Ff.] seems clearly an explanatory gloss, and is rightly rejected by nearly all recent editors.

24. ἀλλά] '*Nevertheless.*' The explanation of this particle is here by no means easy. According to the usual interpr. αὐτὸς κ. τ. λ. (ver. 23) forms an apposition to the preceding words, the pronoun αὐτὸς (comp. Bernhardy, *Synt.* vi. 10, p. 287) being inserted with a rhetorical emphasis. The proof is then introduced by ἀλλά, which, according to De W., preserves its adversative character in the fresh aspect under which it presents the relation; '*But* as the Church, etc.;' see Winer, *Gr.* § 57. 8, p. 529. This is plausible, but, as Meyer has ably shown, cannot be fairly reconciled with the clear adversative force of ἀλλά, — 'aliud jam esse, de quo sumus dicturi' (Klotz, *Devar.* Vol. ii. p. 2); δὲ or οὖν would have been appropriate; ἀλλὰ is wholly out of place. Rückert and Harless explain it as resumptive (Hartung, *Partik.* ἀλλά, 2. 7, Vol. ii. p. 40), but surely, after a digression of only four words, this is inconceivable. Eadie supposes an ellipsis, 'be not disobedient, etc.,' an assumption here still more un-tenable; as in all such uses of ἀλλά, and in all those which he has adduced (some of which, e. g. Rom. vi. 5, 2 Cor. vii. 11, are not correctly explained) the ellipsis is simple, and almost self-evident; compare Klotz, *Devar.* Vol. i. p. 7. Amid this variety of interpretation, that of Calv., Beng., Meyer, and recently Alf. alone seems simple and satisfactory. Αὐτὸς κ. τ. λ. is to be considered as forming an independent clause; it introduces a particular peculiar only to Christ, and therefore in the conclusion is followed, not by οὖν or δέ, but by the fully

ἐκκλησία ὑποτάσσεται τῷ Χριστῷ, οὕτως καὶ αἱ γυναῖκες τοῖς
ἀνδράσιν ἐν παντί.　　²⁵ Οἱ ἄνδρες, ἀγαπᾶτε τὰς γυναῖκας
ἑαυτῶν, καθὼς καὶ ὁ Χριστὸς ἠγάπησεν τὴν ἐκκλησίαν καὶ ἑαυτὸν
παρέδωκεν ὑπὲρ αὐτῆς,　²⁶ ἵνα αὐτὴν ἁγιάσῃ καθαρίσας τῷ

25. τὰς γυναῖκας ἑαυτῶν] The reflexive pronoun was omitted in ed. 1, with AB;
5 or 6 mss.; Clem., Origen, al. (Lachmann, Tisch.), but is apparently more rightly
inserted with DEKL (FG add ὑμῶν); most mss.; Chrys., Theod., al. (Rec., Mey.,
Alf., Wordsw.), as the introduction is not easy to account for, and the omission
might have arisen from a conformation to the preceding verse.

adversative ἀλλά : ʻHe is the saviour of
the body (that certainly man is not), nevertheless, as the Church is subject unto
Christ, so, etc.'· The various attempts
to explain the σωτηρία in reference to
the other members of the comparison,
the husband and wife (comp. Bulling.,
Beza, Hofm. Schriftb. Vol. II. 2, p. 115),
are all forced and untenable.　　The
reading ὥσπερ for ὡς [Rec. with D³E
KL; most mss.; Theod., Dam.] is
rightly rejected by most recent editors.
οὕτως καὶ κ.τ.λ.] ʻ so let wives also
be (subject) to their husbands in everything,'
— scil. ὑποτασσέσθωσαν, supplied from
the preceding member. The Rec. inserts
ἰδίοις before ἀνδράσιν with AD³E²K;
many mss., Vv. and Ff., — but in opp.
to preponderant authority; BD¹E¹FG;
2 mss.; Clarom., Sangerm., al., and to
the internal objection that the word was
an interpolation in accordance with ver.
22.
25. οἱ ἄνδρες κ.τ.λ] ʻ Husbands
love your own wives;' statement of the
reciprocal duties of the husband; ἄκουε
καὶ πῶς σε πάλιν ἀναγκάζει ἀγαπᾶν αὐτήν,
ἀλλ' οὐχὶ δεσποτικῶς προσφέρεσθαι. ἀγάπα
γὰρ αὐτὴν· ποίῳ μέτρῳ; ᾧ καὶ ὁ Χρ. τὴν
ἐκκλησίαν. προνόει αὐτῆς, ὡς καὶ ὁ Χρ.
ἐκείνης· κἂν δέῃ τι παθεῖν, κἂν ἀποθανεῖν
δι' αὐτήν, μὴ παραιτήσῃ, Theophyl. On
this and the two following verses, see a
good sermon by Donne, Serm. LXXXV.
Vol. IV. p. 63 sq. (ed. Alf.).
καθὼς καὶ κ.τ.λ.] ʻ even as Christ
also loved the Church and gave Himself

for it;' nearly a repetition of the latter
part of ver. 2, where see the notes on
the different details.
26. ἵνα αὐτὴν ἁγ.] ʻ in order that
He might sanctify it;' immediate, not (as
De W.) remote purpose of the παραδιδό-
ναι, — sanctification of the Church attendant on the remission of sins in baptism; see Pearson, Creed, Vol. I. p. 435
(Burt.), Taylor, Bapt. IX. 17, Waterland, Eucharist. IX. 3, Vol. IV. p. 645.
Both sanctification and purification are
dependent on the atoning death of
Christ, the former as an act contemplated by it, the latter as an act included
in it.　There is thus no necessity to
modify the plain and natural meaning
of the verb; ἁγιάζ. here neither implies
simple consecration (Eadie) on the one
hand, nor expiation, absolution (Matth.),
on the other, but the communication and
infusion of holiness and moral purity;
see Pearson, Creed, Vol. I. p. 404, comp.
Suicer, Thesaur, s. v. II. a, Vol. p. 54.
καθαρίσας] ʻ having purified it;' temporal participle, here more naturally
denoting an act antecedent to ἁγιάσῃ
(Olsh., Mey.) than one contemporaneous with it, as appy. Syr., Vulg., al.,
and, as it would seem, our own Version.
Eadie is far too hasty in imputing ʻerror'
to Harl. for maintaining the latter; it is
clearly tenable on grammatical (see
Bernhardy, Synt. x. 9, p. 383, notes ch.
i. 9), but less probable on dogmatical
grounds; compare 1 Cor. vi. 11, ἀλλὰ
ἀπελούσασθε, ἀλλὰ ἡγιάσθητε.　　τῷ

λουτρῷ τοῦ ὕδατος ἐν ῥήματι,　　　²⁷ ἵνα παραστήσῃ αὐτὸς ἑαυτῷ

λουτρῷ τοῦ ὕδατος] 'by the [well-known] *laver of the water;*' gen. 'materiæ,' Scheuerl *Synt.* § 12, p. 82; comp. Soph. *Œd. Col.* 1599. The reference to baptism is clear and distinct (see Tit. iii. 5, and notes *in loc.*), and the meaning of λουτρόν ('lavacrum,' Vulg., Clarom., ‎ܠܡܣ Syr., 'þvahla.' Goth.) — indisputable: instances have been urged in behalf of the active sense of λοῦτρον, adopted by Auth. (and *perhaps* Copt., Æth.), — but in all that have yet been adduced (Ecclus. xxxiv. 25 [30], τί ὠφέλησεν τῷ λουτρῷ αὐτοῦ), the peculiar force of the termination (instrumental object; comp. Donalds. *Crat.* § 267, Pott, *Etym. Forsch.* Vol. ii. p. 403) may be distinctly traced: see exx. in Rost u. Palm, *Lex.* s. v. Vol. ii. p. 83, and comp. Suicer, *Thesaur.* s. v. Vol. ii. p. 277. It seems doubtful whether Olsh. is perfectly correct in positively denying that there is here any allusion to the bride's bath before marriage (Elsner, *Obs.* Vol. ii. p. 226); see ver. 27, which, considered in reference with the context, and compared with Rev. xxi. 2, makes such an allusion far from improbable.　　ἐν ῥήματι] '*in the word,*' 'in verbo,' Clarom, Vulg., Copt, Goth. There is great difficulty in determining (1) the exact *meaning*, (2) the grammatical *connection* of these words. With regard to the former, we may first remark that ῥῆμα occurs (excluding quotations) five times in St. Paul's Epp. and four in Heb., and in all cases, directly Rom. x. 17, Eph. vi. 17, Heb. vi. 5, xi. 3) or indirectly (Rom. x. 8, 2 Cor. xii. 4, Heb. i. 3, xii 19) refers to words proceeding ultimately or immediately *from God*. The ancient and plausible reference to the words used in baptism (Chrysost., Waterl. *Justif.* Vol. vi. p. 13) would thus, independently of the omission of the article, scarcely seem probable; see Estius

in loc. The same observation applies with greater or less force to every interp. except 'the Gospel,' τὸ ῥῆμα τῆς πίστεως, Rom. x. 8, the word of God preached and taught preliminary to baptism (comp. notes ch. i. 13); the omission of the article being either referred to the presence of the prep. (Middleton, *Gr. Art.* vi. 1), or, more probably, to the fact that words of similarly definite import (e. g. νόμος, χάρις, κ. τ. λ.) are frequently found anarthrous; see Winer, *Gr.* § 19, p. 112. (2) Three constructions obviously present themselves; (*a*) with ἁγιάσῃ; (*b*) with λουτρῷ τοῦ ὕδατος; (*c*) with καθαρίσας, or rather *with the whole expression*, καθ. λουτρ. τ. ὕδ. Of these (*a*), though adopted by Jerome, and recently maintained by Rück., Winer, (*Gr.* § 20. 2, p. 125) and Meyer, is seriously opposed to the order of the words, and (if ἐν be considered simply instrumental) introduces an idea (ἁγ. ἐν ῥήμ.) which is scarcely doctrinally tenable; the second (*b*) is plainly inconsistent with the absence of the article, this being a case which is not referable to any of the three cases noticed on ch. i. 17, — appy. the only ones in which, in constructions like the present, the omission can be justified; — the third (*c*) though not without difficulties, is on the whole fairly satisfactory. According to this view, ἐν ῥήματι has neither a purely instrumental, nor, certainly, a simple modal force (' verheissungsweise,' Harl.), but specifies the necessary *accompaniment*, that *in which* the baptismal purification is vouchsafed (comp. John xv. 3), and without which it is not granted; comp. Heb. ix. 22, ἐν αἵματι πάντα καθαρίζεται κ. τ. λ., where the force of the prep. is somewhat similar.

27. ἵνα παραστήσῃ] '*in order that He might present;*' further and more ultimate purpose of ἑαυτὸν παρέδωκεν ὑπὲρ αὐτῆς (ver. 25), the full accomplishment

ἔνδοξον τὴν ἐκκλησίαν, μὴ ἔχουσαν σπίλον ἢ ῥυτίδα ἤ τι τῶν
τοιούτων, ἀλλ' ἵνα ᾖ ἁγία καὶ ἄμωμος· ²⁸ οὕτως καὶ οἱ ἄνδρες

of which must certainly be referred to ὁ αἰὼν μέλλων (August., Est.), not to ὁ αἰὼν οὗτος (Chrysost., Beng., Harl.), see Pearson, *Creed*, Vol. I. p. 406 (ed. Burt.). Schoettg. appositely cites the Rabbinical interpr. of Cant. i. 5, שְׁחוֹרָה אֲנִי וְנָאוָה, in which the swarthiness is referred to the Synagogue בְּעוֹלָם הֲזֶה [in hoc seculo], the comeliness to it, בְּעוֹלָם הַבָּא [in seculo futuro]; see Petersen, *von der Kirche*, III. 220. The verb παραστήσῃ is here used as in 2 Cor. xi. 2, of the presentation of the bride to the bridegroom, — not of an offering (Harl.; Rom. xii. 1), which would here be a reference wholly inappropriate.

αὐτὸς ἑαυτῷ] 'Himself to Himself;' not 'for Himself,' *i. e.* for His joy and glory (Olsh.), but, with local reference, 'to Himself.' Christ permits neither attendants nor paranymphs to present the Bride: He alone presents, He receives. The reading παραστ. αὐτὴν ἑαυτῷ [*Rec.* with D³EK; most mss.; Chrys., Theod.] is rightly rejected on preponderant evidence [ABD¹FGL; 15 mss.; Clarom., Goth., Vulg., al.; Greek and Lat. Ff.] by most modern editors.

ἔνδοξον τὴν ἐκκλησίαν] 'the Church glorious;' the tertiary predicate ἔνδοξον (Donalds. *Gr.* § 489) being placed emphatically forward, and receiving its further explanation from the participial clause which follows: so, with a correct observance of the order, Syr., Copt., Æth., probably Clarom., Vulg., and all the best modern commentators. μὴ ἔχουσαν σπίλον] 'not having a spot.' The word σπίλος (μιασμός, ῥύπος. Suid.) is a δὶς λεγόμ. in the N. T. (2 Pet. ii. 13), and belongs to later Greek, the earlier expression being κηλίς; see Lobeck, *Phryn* p. 28. *Lachmann*, Bruder (*Concord.*), Meyer, and others, still retain the accentuation σπίλος. As the iota is

short (comp ἄσπῖλος, Antiph. ap. *Anthol.* Vol. VI. 252) the accentuation in the text seems most correct; comp. Arcad. *Accent.* VI. p. 52 (ed. Barker). ῥυτίδα] 'a wrinkle;' ῥυτίς· ἡ συνελκυσμένη σάρξ, *Etym. M.*; derived from ΡΥΩ, ἐρύω, see Benfey, *Wurzellex.* Vol. II. p. 317. Ruga and 'wrinkle' are probably cognate forms; see ib. p. 314, and comp. Diffenbach, *Lex.* Vol. I. p. 236.

ἀλλ' ἵνα] 'but in order that it might be;' change of construction, as if ἵνα μὴ ἔχῃ had preceded: similar exx. of 'oratio variata' are cited by Winer, *Gr.* § 63. II. 1, p. 509. On the true meaning of ἁγία, as applied to the Church, see Pearson, *Creed*, Art. IX. Vol. I. p. 403 (Burton), Jackson, *Creed*, XII. 4. 3, and on ἄμωμος, see notes ch. i. 4. The context might here seem to favor the translation, 'omni maculâ carens' (comp. Cant. iv. 7), but it seems more correct to say that the first part of the verse presents the conception of purity, etc., in *metaphorical* language, the second in words of simply *ethical* meaning.

28. οὕτως] 'Thus,' 'in like manner; 'ita, scilicet uti Christus dilexit ecclesiam quemadmodum jam dixi,' Corn. a Lap. Even if the reading of the *Rec.* be retained (οὕτως ὀφ. οἱ ἄνδρ. ἀγ. κ. τ. λ.; see below), the reference must still clearly be to καθώς καὶ ὁ Χρ. κ. τ. λ. ver. 25—27, not as Est. (comp. De W.) suggests, to the *following* ὥς; this latter construction being contrary, not necessarily 'to grammatical law' (Eadie; for comp. John vii. 46, 1 Cor. iv. 1), but to the natural use of οὕτως, of which 'non alia est vis quam quæ naturæ ejus consentanea est, ut eo confirmentur *præcedentia*,' Herm. *Viger*, Append. x. p. 747. In passages like 1 Cor. *l. c.* there is an obvious emphasis, which would here be out of place. The reading is doubtful, as in addition to the

ὀφείλουσιν ἀγαπᾶν τὰς ἑαυτῶν γυναῖκας ὡς τὰ ἑαυτῶν σώματα.
ὁ ἀγαπῶν τὴν ἑαυτοῦ γυναῖκα ἑαυτὸν ἀγαπᾷ·   ²⁹ οὐδεὶς γάρ ποτε

evidence in favor of *Rec.* [KL; nearly all mss.; perhaps Syr., Arm.; Chrys., Theod., al.] that of B (ὀφείλ. καὶ οἱ ἄνδρες) may now be urged for the inversion; still the authority in favor of the text [ADEFG; 2 mss.; Clarom., Vulg., Goth., Copt.; Clem., Lat. Ff.] seems fairly to preponderate, and owing to the testimony of B being of a divided nature, may perhaps be most safely followed.   ὡς τὰ ἑαυτῶν σώματα] '*as (being) their own bodies*;' not '*wie* ihre eigenen Leiber,' Meier (comp. Alf.), but '*als* ihre eigenen Leiber,' Luth., Mey. The context clearly implies that Christ loved the Church not merely *just* as (comparatively) He loved His own body (scil. ὡς ἑαυτόν, Schoettg.), but *as being* His own body, the body of which He is the Head. In the hortatory application, therefore, ὡς must have a similarly semi-argumentative force; otherwise, as Harl. remarks, we should have two comparisons, the one with οὕτως, the other with ὡς, which certainly mar the perspicuity of the passage. In the present view, on the contrary, the distinction is logically preserved; οὕτως alone introduces the comparison; ὡς with its regular and proper force marks the *aspects* (see notes on ver. 22) in which the wives were to be regarded ('as being, in the light of, their own bodies'), and thus tacitly supplies to the exhortation an argument arising from the thus acknowledged nature of the case. For a defence of the simply comparative use of ὡς, see Alf. *in loc.* ὁ ἀγαπῶν κ. τ. λ.] '*He that loveth his own wife, loveth himself*;' explanation of the preceding ὡς τὰ ἑαυτῶν σώμ. The Apostle's argument rests on the axiom that a man's wife is a part of his very self. Husbands are to love them as being their own bodies; thus their love

to them is in fact self-love; it is not κατ' ὀφειλήν, but κατὰ φύσιν.

29. οὐδεὶς γάρ κ. τ. λ.] '*For no one ever hated*;' confirmation and proof of the position just laid down, ὁ ἀγαπῶν κ. τ. λ.; first, it is ultimately based on a general law of nature, οὐδείς ποτε κ. τ. λ. ('insitam nobis esse corporis nostri caritatem,' Senec. *Epist.* 14, cited by Grot.); secondly, it is suggested by the example of Christ, καθὼς καὶ ὁ Χρ. κ. τ. λ. The whole argument then seems to run, 'Men ought to love their wives as Christ loves His Church, as being in fact (I might add) their own (ἑαυτῶν) bodies; yes, I say the man who loves his wife loves himself (ἑαυτόν); for if he hated her he would hate (according to the axiom; see above) his own flesh, whereas, on the contrary, unless he acts against nature, he nourishes it, even as (to urge the comparison again) Christ nourishes His Church.' τὴν ἑαυτοῦ σάρκα] '*His own flesh.*' This word appears undoubtedly to have been chosen in preference to σῶμα, on account of the allusion to Gen. ii. 23, which is still further sustained by the longer reading of ver. 30 and the quotation in ver. 31.   ἀλλὰ ἐκτρέφει] '*but nourisheth,*' 'ministers to its outward growth and development.' The prep. does not appear intensive ('valde nutrit,' Beng.), but marks the evolution and development produced by the τρέφειν; comp. Xenoph. *Œcon.* xvii. 10, ἐκτρέφει ἡ γῆ τὸ σπέρμα εἰς καρπόν.   καὶ θάλπει] '*and cherisheth*;' 'fovet' Clarom., Vulg., — more derivatively, Syr.,

[et curam habet] sim. Æth.-Platt, 'solicite conservat,' Meyer maintains the literal meaning, 'warmeth' (comp. Goth. 'varmeiþ'), citing Beng., 'id spectat amictum, ut *nutrit* victum.'

τὴν ἑαυτοῦ σάρκα ἐμίσησεν, ἀλλὰ ἐκτρέφει καὶ θάλπει αὐτήν,
καθὼς καὶ ὁ Χριστὸς τὴν ἐκκλησίαν· ³⁰ ὅτι μέλη ἐσμὲν τοῦ

30. ἐκ τῆς σαρκὸς αὐτοῦ, καὶ ἐκ τῶν ὀστέων αὐτοῦ] Tisch. (ed. 2) and Lachm. omit
these words, with AB ; 17. 67** ; Copt., Æth. (both) ; Method. (?) Ambrst. (Mill,
Prolegom. p. 69). The external authorities for their insertion are DEFGKL ;
nearly all mss., and Vv. ; Iren., Chrys., Theodoret, Dam., al. ; Hieron., al. (Rec.,
Scholz, Harl., Mey., De W. (?) Alf., Words., — to which now may be added Tisch.,
ed. 7). The preponderance of external authority is thus very decided ; paradiplomatic considerations (See Pref. to Galat. p. xvi.) also suggest the probability of an
accidental omission, from the transcriber's eye having fallen on the third αὐτοῦ
instead of the first ; and lastly, internal considerations seem to suggest that the
words, if an insertion from the LXX, would have been cited more exactly, while
the omission might so easily have arisen from the appy. material conception presented by the clause. On these grounds we retain the longer reading.

This seems, however, here an interpr. far too definite and realistic ; θάλπειν certainly primarily and properly implies 'to warm,' but still may, as its very etymological affinities (θηλή Θάω) suggest, bear the secondary meaning, 'to cherish,' the fostering warmth of the breast (compare Theocr. Idyll. xiv. 38) being the connecting idea ; see 1 Thess. ii. 7, ὡς ἂν τροφὸς θάλπῃ τὰ ἑαυτῆς τέκνα. καθὼς καὶ κ. τ. λ.] 'Even as Christ the Church,' scil. ἐκτρέφει καὶ θάλπει, with general reference to the tender love of Christ towards His Church. Any special applications ('nutrit eam verbo et Spiritu, vestit virtutibus,' Grot.) seem doubtful and precarious. The reading of Rec. (ὁ Κύριος τὴν ἐκκλ.) rests only on D³KL ; majority of mss. ; Dam., Œcum.. and is rightly rejected by nearly all modern editors.
30. ὅτι μέλη ἐσμέν] 'because we are members ;' reason why Christ thus nourishes and cherishes His Church. The position of μέλη seems emphatic ; 'members,' — not accidental, but integral parts of His body (Meyer), united to Him not only as members of His mystical body, the Church, but by the more mysterious marital relation in which Christ in His natural and now glorified body stands to His Church. On the

important dogmatical application of this passage to the Holy Communion, see Waterland, Eucharist, ch. vii. Vol. iv. p. 600, 608, and compare J. Johnson, Works, Vol. ii. p. 129 sq. (A. C. Libr.). ἐκ τῆς σαρκὸς κ. τ. λ.] 'being of His flesh and of His bones ;' more exact specification of the foregoing words, ἐκ with its primary and proper force pointing to the origin, to which we owe our spiritual being ; comp. notes on Gal. ii. 16. The true and proper meaning of these profound words has been much obscured by a neglect of their strict reference to the context, and by the substitution of deductions and applications for the simple and grammatical interpretation. We must thus set aside all primary reference to the sacraments (Theod.), to the Holy Communion (Olsh.), to Baptism (comp. Chrys.), and certainly to the Crucifixion ('per corporis ejus et sanguinis pretium redempti,' Vatabl. ap. Poli Syn.). A reference to the ἐνσάρκωσις (Irenæ, Hær. v. 2) is plausible, but untenable ; for Christ, thus considered, is of our flesh, not we of His, John i. 14 ; and even if this be explained away ('quia in hâc naturâ ipse caput est,' Est., comp. Stier) the reference would have to be extended to all mankind, not, as the context requires, limited to the members of Christ's

18

σώματος αὐτοῦ, ἐκ τῆς σαρκὸς αὐτοῦ, καὶ ἐκ τῶν ὀστέων αὐτοῦ.
³¹ ἀντὶ τούτου καταλείψει ἄνϑρωπος πατέρα καὶ μητέρα καὶ προσ-

Church. The most simple and natural view (comp. Chrys., Beng., Mey.) then seems to be this, that the words are cited (in substance) from Gen. ii. 23, to convey this profound truth, — that our real (spiritual) being and existence is as truly, as certainly, and as actually (not ὥσπερ, Theod.-Mops., but γνησίως ἐξ αὐτοῦ, Chrysost.) 'a true native extract from His own body' (Hooker), as was the physical derivation of Eve from Adam ; see esp. the forcible language of Hooker, *Eccl. Pol.* v. 56. 7, and comp. Bp. Hall, *Christ Mystical*, ch. III. § 2, 3, and the good note of Wordsw. *in loc.* This is the general truth, which of course admits a forcible *secondary* application to the sacraments (comp. Kahnis, *Abendm.* p. 143 sq.) ; we may truly say, with Waterland, that 'the true and firm basis for the economy of man's salvation is this, that in the sacraments we are made and continued members of Christ's *body, of His flesh and of His bones.*' Our union with the Deity rests entirely in our mystical union with our Lord's humanity, which is *personally* united with His divine nature, which is *essentially* united with God the Father, the head and fountain of all,' *Charge*, A. D. 1739, Vol. v. p. 212. These are weighty words.

31. ἀ ν τ ὶ   τ ο ύ τ ο υ] '*For this cause ;*' ἕνεκεν τούτου, Gen. ii. 24. The meaning is practically the same ; ἀντὶ passes by a natural transition from its primary idea of *local opposition* (Xenoph. *Anab.* IV. 7. 6) through that of *counterchange* (see Winer, *Gr.* § 47. a, p. 326) to that of mere ethical relation. It can scarcely be doubted that this verse is nothing more than a free citation from Genes. ii. 24, ἀντὶ taking the place of ἕνεκεν, and referring to the same fact, — the derivation of woman from man, which is

clearly presupposed in the allusions of ver. 30. Meyer refers ἀντὶ τούτου with punctilious accuracy to the words immediately preceding, and gives the passage a directly mystical interpretation in reference to the final and *future* union of Christ with His Church. Somewhat differently, and more probably, Chrys., Theodoret, Theophyl., Jerome, refer to Christ's coming in the flesh ; compare Taylor, *Serm.* XVII. 1, 'Christ descended from His Father's bosom, and contracted His divinity with flesh and blood, and married our nature, and we became a church ;' see Beng. *in loc.* To denounce summarily such an interpr. as 'wild and visionary' (Eadie), seems alike rash and inconsiderate. That St. Paul adduces the verse as containing a definite allegorical meaning, may perhaps be considered doubtful ; but that St. Paul intended his readers to make some such *application*, seems to have been the general opinion of the early commentators, is by no means incompatible with the context, and cannot be confidently denied ; see Alford *in loc.* Thus, then, in a *certain* sense, we may with Hofmann (*Weiss. u. Erf.* Vol. I. p. 71), recognize in this the first prophecy in Scripture ; 'primus vates Adam,' Jerome.   κατα- λ ε ί ψ ε ι κ. τ. λ.] '*shall leave father and mother.*' Meyer presses the tense somewhat unnecessarily, as referring to something yet to come. Even if in the original passage it designate something positively future, there is no reason why, in this application and free citation, it may not state, not only what *will*, but whatever *shall* and *ought* to happen ; on this ethical force of the future, see Winer, *Gr.* § 40. 6, p. 250, Thiersch., *de Pent.* III. 11, p. 158 sq. The longer reading of *Rec.* τὸν πατ. αὐτοῦ καὶ τὴν μητ. is fairly supported [AD³EKL ;

κολληθήσεται πρὸς τὴν γυναῖκα αὐτοῦ, καὶ ἔσονται οἱ δύο εἰς
σάρκα μίαν. ³²τὸ μυστήριον τοῦτο μέγα ἐστίν, ἐγὼ δὲ λέγω εἰς

most mss.; Syr., Copt., al.; Orig., al.],
but is rightly rejected by *Lachm.*, *Tisch.*,
Meyer, al., as a conformation to the
LXX.; see especially the critical comment of Origen, cited by *Tisch. in loc.*
προσκολλ. πρὸς τὴν γυναῖκα]
'*shall be closely joined unto his wife;*'
comp. Matt. xix. 5, προσκολληθήσεται
τῇ γυναικὶ αὐτοῦ, where the dat. is used,
but with little difference of meaning.
On the close affinity between the dat.
and the accus. with εἰς and πρός, and
their interchange in many passages, see
Winer, *Gr.* § 31. 5, p. 190. The reading, however, is somewhat doubtful;
Lachm. maintains the dat. with AD¹E¹
FG; 3 mss.; Meth., Epiph. (compare 1
Cor. vi. 16); but owing to the fair evidence for the text [BD³EKL; nearly all
mss.; Orig., Chrys., Theod.], and the
distinct notice by Origen (see *Tisch. in
loc.*), with less probability than the accus.
with πρός (*Tisch.*, *Mey.*, al.).

32. τὸ μυστήριον τοῦτο] '*This
mystery is great*, sc. *deep;*' explanatory
comment on the preceding verse. But
what mystery? The answer is not easy,
as four antecedents are possible; — (*a*)
the text immediately preceding; τὸ εἰρη-
μένον, τὸ γεγραμμένον, Stier, Meyer,
compare Chrys., Theodorus; — (*b*) the
whole preceding subject, the strict parallelism between the conjugal relation and
that between Christ and his Church; —
(*c*) the spiritual purport, 'non matrimo-
nium humanum sed ipsa conjunctio
Christi et ecclesiæ,' Beng.; — (*d*) the
simple purport and immediate subject
of the text, 'arctissima illa conjunctio
viri et mulieris,' Est. Of these, (*a*),
though not otherwise untenable, involves
a meaning of μυστήριον, which cannot
be substantiated by St. Paul's use of the
word; μυστ. being only used by the
Apostle to imply either something not

cognizable by (ch. i. 9, iii. 4, and appy.
vi. 19), or not fully *comprehensible* by
unassisted human reason (1 Cor. xiv. 2,
1 Tim. iii. 9, 16), but not, as here (compare Schoettg. *Hor.* Vol. i. p. 783), 'a
passage containing an allegorical import:' see Tholuck, *Rom.* xi. 25, and
compare Lobeck, *Aglaoph.* Vol. i. p. 85,
89. Of the rest, (*b*) and (*c*) are less
plausible, as in both cases — more especially in the latter — the remark ἐγὼ δὲ
λέγω κ. τ. λ. would seem superfluous,
and the force of the pronoun obscure.
On the whole, then, (*d*) seems best to
harmonize with the context. Thus,
then, ver. 29 states the exact similarity
(καθὼς) of the relationship; ver. 30 the
ground of the relation in regard of
Christ and the Church; ver. 31 the
nature of the conjugal relation, with a
probable application also to Christ; ver.
32 the mystery of that conjugal relation
in itself, and still more so in its typical
application to Christ and to His Church.
It is needless to observe that the words
cannot possibly be urged in favor of the
sacramental nature of marriage (Concil.
Trid. xxiv. init.), but it may fairly be
said that the very fact of the comparison
(see Olsh.) does place marriage on a far
holier and higher basis than modern theories are disposed to admit; see Harl. *in
loc.*, and for two good sermons on this
text, Bp. Taylor, *Serm.* xvii. xviii.
Vol. i. p. 705 sq. (Lond. 1836).
ἐγὼ δὲ λέγω] '*but I am speaking;*'
antithetical comment on the foregoing;
ἐγὼ having no special reference to his
own celibacy (comp. Stier), but, as De
W. admits, marking, and with emphasis,
the subjective character of the application and comparison (Winer, *Gr.* § 22.
6, p. 138, *ed.* 6), while the slightly op-
positive δὲ contrasts it with any other
interpretation that might have been

Χριστὸν καὶ εἰς τὴν ἐκκλησίαν. ³³ πλὴν καὶ ὑμεῖς οἱ καθ᾿ ἕνα ἕκαστος τὴν ἑαυτοῦ γυναῖκα οὕτως ἀγαπάτω ὡς ἑαυτόν, ἡ δὲ γυνὴ ἵνα φοβῆται τὸν ἄνδρα.

Children, obey and honor your parents according to God's commandment: fathers provoke not your children, but educate them holily.

VI. Τὰ τέκνα, ὑπακούετε τοῖς γονεῦσιν ὑμῶν

adduced (Mey.) : ' the mystery of this closeness of the conjugal relation is great, *but* I am *myself* speaking of it in its still deeper application, in reference to Christ and the Church; ' μέγα ὄντως μυστήριον, τέως μέντοι εἰς Χριστὸν ἐκλαμβάνεται, παρ᾿ ἐμοῦ τουτό, φησιν, ὡς προφητικῶς περὶ αὐτοῦ λεχθέν, Theoph. On the general use of λέγω δέ, formula ' explanandi atque pressius eloquendi ea quæ antea obscurius erant dicta,' see Raphel *on* 1 *Cor.* i. 12, and notes *on Gal.* iv. 1.   εἰς Χριστόν] '*in reference to;*' not ' of,' Conyb. (comp. Syr.), still less ' in Christo,' Vulg., but ' in Christum,' Beza (comp. Æth., Syr.-Phil.), the preposition correctly marking the ethical *direction* of the speaker's words ; comp. Acts ii. 25, and see Winer, *Gr.* § 49. a, p. 354, and notes *on* 2 *Thess.* i. 11. The prep. is omitted by BK ; 10 mss. ; Iren., Epiph., Marc., and is bracketed by *Lachm.*, but without sufficient reason, as the external authorities against it are weak, and the þrobability of an omission, from not being understood, by no means slight.

33. πλήν] '*Nevertheless,*' i. e. not to press the mystical bearings of the subject any further ; the particle not being resumptive (Beng., Olsh.), but, in accordance with its primary meaning, *comparative,* and thence contrasting and slightly *adversative;* see esp. Klotz, *Devar.* Vol. II. p. 725, Donalds. *Gr.* § 548. 33, and notes *on Phil.* i. 18, where the derivation and force of πλήν are briefly discussed. καὶ ὑμεῖς οἱ καθ᾿ ἕνα] '*Ye also severally ;*' ye also — as well as Christ towards His Church. The plural thus specified by the distributive οἱ καθ᾿ ἕνα, 'vos singuli' (comp. 1 Cor. xiv. 27, 31,

and see Winer, *Gr.* § 49 a, p. 357), passes easily and naturally into the singular in the concluding member of the sentence. On the striking equivalence of κατά with ἀνά in nearly all its meanings (here evinced in the distributive use), see esp. Donalds. *Cratyl.* § 183 sq. ὡς ἑαυτόν] '*as himself,*' scil. ' as being one with himself,' see notes on ver. 28.   ἡ δὲ γυνὴ κ. τ. λ.] '*and the wife (I bid), that she fear her husband :*' emphatic specification (with slight contrast) of the duties of the wife : ἡ γυνὴ being a simple and emphatic nominative absolute (Mey. ; contra Eadie, — but erroneously), though not of a kind so definitely unsyntactic as Acts vii. 40 and exx. cited by Winer (*Gr.* § 28. 3, p. 207, ed. 5 ; see p. 507 ed. 6), and most probably dependent, not on an imper., but on some verb of command which can easily be supplied from the context ; see Mey. *on* 2 *Cor.* viii. 7, Fritz. *Diss. in* 2 *Cor.* p. 126, Winer, *Gr.* § 44. 4, p. 365 (ed. 5). Alford (*Cor. l. c.*) suggests βλέπετε, citing 1 Cor. xvi. 10, but this is not fully in point, as the subject of the imperative and the subjunctive is not the same : more pertinent is Soph. *Œd. Col.* 156, where, as Ellendt correctly observes, ' φύλαξαι adsignificatum habet loquentis consilium ; *hæc tibi dico ne,*' etc., *Lex. Soph.* Vol. I. p. 840.

Chapter VI. 1. ὑπακούετε κ.τ.λ.] '*obey your parents in the Lord ;*' ἐν Κυρίῳ (*Christ,* — not God, as Chrys., Theod. ; compare ch. iv. 7, v. 21) as usual, denoting the *sphere* to which the action is to be limited (not for κατὰ Κύρ., Chrys.), and obviously belonging, not to τοῖς γονεῦσιν, nor to τοῖς γον. and to ὑπακ.

ἐν Κυρίῳ· τοῦτο γάρ ἐστιν δίκαιον. ² τίμα τὸν πατέρα σου καὶ τὴν μητέρα, ἥτις ἐστὶν ἐντολὴ πρώτη ἐν ἐπαγγελίᾳ, ³ ἵνα εὖ

(comp. Origen ap. Cramer, *Caten.*), but simply to the latter, — serving thus to define and characterize the nature, and possibly limits, of the obedience ; ἐν οἷς ἂν μὴ προσκρούσῃς [Κυρίῳ], Chrys. On the more exact nature of these limits (here, however, not perhaps very definitely hinted at ; comp. Alf.), see Taylor, *Duct. Dub.* iii. 5, Rule 1 and 4 sq. The reading is somewhat doubtful, as ἐν Κυρίῳ is omitted by *Lachm.* on fair authority [BD¹FG ; Clarom., Sang., Aug., Boern. ; Clem., al.]. The external authorities, however, for its insertion [AD³ EKL ; nearly all mss. and Vv. ; Chrys. (expressly), Theod.] seem clearly to predominate, and the internal arguments are in its favor, as if it had come from Col. iii. 20 it would have been inserted after δίκαιον ; see Meyer, p. 238.

τοῦτο γὰρ ἐστιν δίκ.] '*for this is right ;*' not merely πρέπον, nor merely κατὰ τὸν τοῦ Θεοῦ νόμον (Theod.), but 'in accordance with nature' (τέκνα γονεῦσιν) and, as the next verse shows, the law of God : καὶ φύσει δίκαιον, καὶ ὑπὸ τοῦ νόμου προστάσσεται, Theophyl. ; comp. Coloss. iii. 20. On the position of children in the early church, and the relation such texts bear to infant-baptism, see Stier, *Reden Jes.* Vol. vi. p. 924 sq.

2. τίμα κ. τ. λ.] '*Honor thy father and thy mother ;*' specification of the commandment as an additional confirmation of the foregoing precept, and as supplying the reason on which it was based. Had δίκαιον referred only to this command, some causal particle would more naturally have been appended. As it stands, however, the solemn recitation of the commandm. blends the voice of God with that of nature.   ἥτις] '*the which ;*' the pronoun not having here a strongly *causal*, but rather an *explanatory* force ; see notes on Gal. ii. 4,

v. 24.   πρώτη ἐν ἐπαγγελίᾳ] '*the first in regard of promise,*' scil., 'as a command of promise ;' compare Syriac

ܩ‍ܕ‍ܡ‍ܝ‍ܐ   ‍ܕ‍ܡ‍ܘ‍ܠ‍ܟ‍ܢ   [primum quod promittit] : not exactly 'with promise' Beza, Alf., al., as the prep. here seems naturally used not so much to state the accompaniment as to specify the exact point in which the predication of πρώτη was to be understood ; so rightly Chrys. (οὐ τῇ τάξει ['in regard of order,' notes on Gal. i. 22] εἶπεν αὐτὴν πρώτην, ἀλλὰ τῇ ἐπαγγελίᾳ), and expressly Winer, *Gr.* § 48. a. obs. p. 349. Meyer cites Diod. Sic. xiii. 37, ἐν δὲ εὐγενείᾳ καὶ πλούτῳ πρῶτος. Some little difficulty has been found in the use of πρώτη, owing to the 2nd commandm. seeming to involve a kind of promise ; see Orig. ap. Cram. *Cat.* If this be considered as not a definite ἐπαγγελία (Calv.), still πρώτη would seem unusual, as the fifth commandm. would then be the *only* one which has a promise : nor would the assumption that it is 'first' on the *second* table (not such a recent division as Meyer after Erasm. seems to think, see Philo, *de Special. Legg.* Vol. ii. p. 300, ed. Mang.) relieve the difficulty, as the same objection would still remain. We may perhaps best explain the statement of priority by referring it, not to all other *foregoing* commands (Harl.), but to all the *other* Mosaic commands (Mey.), of which the decalogue forms naturally the chief and prominent portion ; simply, then, 'the first command we meet with which involves a promise.'   It may be observed that the article is not needed with πρῶτος ; ordinals being from their nature sufficiently definite ; comp. Acts xvi. 12, and see Middleton, *Greek Art.* vi. 3, p. 100.

3. ἵνα εὖ σοι κ. τ. λ.] '*in order that*

σοι γένηται καὶ ἔσῃ μακροχρόνιος ἐπὶ τῆς γῆς. ⁴ Καὶ οἱ πατέρες,

it may be well with thee;' a slightly varied citation from the LXX, Exod. xx. 12, Deuteron. v. 16, ἵνα εὖ σοι γένηται καὶ ἵνα μακροχρόνιος γένῃ ἐπὶ τῆς γῆς [τῆς ἀγαθῆς, Exod. l. c.] ἧς Κύριος ὁ Θεός σου δίδωσί σοι. The omission of the latter words can scarcely have arisen from the Apostle's belief that his hearers and readers (Gentiles) were so familiar with the rest of the quotation, that it would be unnecessary to cite it (see Mey.); for thus τῆς γῆς must be translated 'the land' (of Canaan, — simply and historically, Meyer) and the promise denuded of all its significance to Christian children. It is far more probable (see Eadie) that the omission was intended to generalize the command, and that, not merely 'toti genti' (Beng.), nor in typical ref. to heaven (Hamm., Olsh., see Barrow, Decal. Vol. VI. 524), but simply and plainly, to individuals, subject, of course, to the conditions which always belong to such temporal promises; see Leighton, Expos. of Command., p. 487 (Edinb. 1845). καὶ ἔσῃ μακρ.] 'and (that) thou be long-lived,' 'et sis longævus,' Vulgate. The future is commonly explained as a lapse into the 'oratio directa' (see Winer, Gr. § 41. b. 1, p. 258), but is more probably to be regarded as dependent on ἵνα (so Vulg., Æth., Arm., all of which use the subjunct.), — a construction which though not found in Attic Greek (see Klotz, Devar. Vol. II. p. 630) certainly does occur in the N. T. (comp. 1 Cor. ix. 18, Rev. xxii. 14, and see Winer, l. c.), harmonizes perfectly with the classical use of ὅπως (see the numerous exx. cited by Gayler, Partic. Neg. p. 209, sq.), and is here eminently simple and natural; compare Meyer in loc. Whether, however, we can here recognize a 'logical climax' {Mey.), is doubtful; the future undoubtedly does often express the more lasting

and certain result (compare Rev. l. c., where the single act is expressed by the aor. subj., the lasting act by the future); still, as the present formula occurs in substance in Deut. xxii. 7 (Alex.), and might have thence become a known form of expression, it seems better not to press the future further than as representing the temporal evolution of the εὖ γένεσθαι.

4. καὶ οἱ πατέρες] 'And ye fathers;' corresponding address to the parents in the persons of those who bore the domestic rule, the πατέρες; compare Meyer in loc. Bengel remarks on the presence of the καὶ here and ver. 9, and its absence, ch. v. 25; 'facilius parentes et heri abutuntur potestate suâ quam mariti.' This distinction is perhaps over-pressed; καὶ here and ver. 9 introduces a marked and quick appeal (see Hartung, Partikel. καί, 5. 7, Vol. I. 149), and also marks that the obligation was not all on one side, but that the superior also had duties which he owed to the inferior. The duty is then expressed negatively and positively. μὴ παροργίζετε] 'provoke not to wrath;' see Col. iii. 21, μὴ ἐρεθίζετε τὰ τέκνα (Rec., Tisch.); negative side of exhortation (οὐκ εἶπεν, ἀγαπᾶτε αὐτά. τοῦτο γὰρ καὶ ἀκόντων ἡ φύσις ἐπισπᾶται, Chrys.), not with reference to any stronger acts such as by disinheriting, etc. (Chrys.), but, as Alf. rightly suggests, by all the vexatious circumstances which may occur in ordinary intercourse; θεραπεύειν καὶ μὴ λυπεῖν ἐκέλευσε, Theod. ἐκτρέφετε] 'bring up, educate;' in an ethical sense, καλῶς ἐκτρέφει πατὴρ δίκαιος, Prov. xxiii. 24; so, frequently in Plato; compare Polyb. Hist. I. 65. 7, ἐν παιδείαις καὶ νόμοις ἐκτεθραμμένων (Winer). In ch. v. 29, the reference is simply physical, but the force of the compound is the same in both passages;

μὴ παροργίζετε τὰ τέκνα ὑμῶν, ἀλλὰ ἐκτρέφετε αὐτὰ ἐν παιδείᾳ
καὶ νουθεσίᾳ Κυρίου.

Servants obey and faith-　　　5 Οἱ δοῦλοι, ὑπακούετε τοῖς κυρίοις κατὰ
fully do your duty to your
masters as unto Christ, and ye shall receive your reward; masters do the like in return.

see notes *in loc.*　　　ἐν παιδείᾳ
καὶ νουθεσίᾳ] '*in the discipline and
admonition;*' 'in disciplinâ et conrep-
tione,' Vulg.; not instrumental, but as
usual 'in the sphere and influence of;'
see Winer, *Gr.* § 48. a, p. 346 note.
These two words are not related to one
another as the *general* (παιδ.) to the
special (Harl., Mey.), but specify the two
methods in the Christian education of
children, training by act and discipline,
and training by word; so Trench, *Syn-
onymns,* § XXXII., and before him, Grot.,
'παιδ. hic. significare videtur institutio-
nem *per pœnas;* νουθ. autem est ea insti-
tutio quæ fit *verbis.*' This Christian
meaning of παιδεύω and παιδεία, 'per
molestias eruditio' (August.), seems
occasionally faintly hinted at in earlier
writers; comp. Xen. *Mem.* I. 3. 5, and
Polyb. *Hist.* II. 9. 6, where the adverb
ἀβλαβῶς marks that the παιδεύειν was a
word that needed limitation. On the
later form νουθεσία instead of νουθέτη-
σις, see Moeris, *Lex.* p. 248 (ed. Koch),
Lobeck, *Phryn.* p. 512, 520.
Κυρίου] '*Of the Lord;*' subjecti, —
belonging to the general category of the
possessive genitive, and specifying the
Lord (Christ), as Him by whom the
νουθεσία and παιδεία were, so to say, prescribed, and by whose Spirit they must
be regulated; so Harl., Olsh., Meyer.
The gen. *objecti* 'about the Lord' ('mo-
nitis ex verbo Dei petitis,' Beza), though
apparently adopted by all the Greek
commentators (compare Theodoret. τὰ
θεῖα παιδεύειν), seems far less satisfactory. Meyer reads τοῦ Κυρίου but as it
would seem, by accident; there is no
trace of such a reading in any of the
critical editions.
5. τοῖς κυρίοις κατὰ σάρκα]

'*to your masters according to the flesh;*'
κατὰ σάρκα here, as in Col. iii. 22 (where
it precedes κυρ.), serving to define and
qualify κυρίοις, 'your bodily, earthly
masters; see notes on ch. i. 19, ii. 11.
Both here and Col. *l. c.* (where the mention of ὁ Κύριος immediately follows)
the adverbial epithet would seem to have
been suggested by the remembrance of
the different relation they stood in to
another Master, τῷ κατὰ πνεῦμα καὶ κατὰ
σάρκα Κυρ. Whether anything *consolatory,* (κατὰ σάρκα ἐστὶν ἡ δεσποτεία, πρόσ-
καιρος καὶ βραχεῖα, Chrys.) or *alleviating*
('manere nihilominus illis intactam libertatem,' Calv.) is further couched in
the addition, is perhaps doubtful (see
Harl.), still both, especially the latter,
are obviously *deductions* which must
have been, and which the Apostle might
possibly have intended to be made. On
the stricter but here neglected distinction between κύριος and δεσπότης, see
Trench, *Synon.* § XXVII.　　Lachm.
places κατὰ σάρκα before κυρίοις with
AB; 10 mss; Clem., Chrys. (1), Dam.,
al., — but such a position is rightly rejected by *Tisch.,* and most recent editors,
as so probable a conformation to Col. iii.
22.　　μετὰ φόβου καὶ τρόμου]
'*with fear and trembling.*' By comparing
1 Cor. ii. 3, 2 Cor. vii. 15, Phil. ii. 12,
where the two words are united, it does
not seem that there is any allusion to the
'durior servorum conditio' (Wolf, Bengel, compare Chrys.), but only to the
'anxious solicitude' they ought to feel
about the faithful performance of their
duties; comp. Hammond *on Phil.* ii. 12,
where, however, the idea of ταπεινοφροσύνη (Hamm.) is not so prominent as
that of distrust of their own powers,
anxiety that they could not do enough;

σάρκα μετὰ φόβου καὶ τρόμου, ἐν ἁπλότητι τῆς καρδίας ὑμῶν, ὡς
τῷ Χριστῷ· ⁶ μὴ κατ᾿ ὀφθαλμοδουλείαν ὡς ἀνθρωπάρεσκοι, ἀλλ᾿

see notes *in loc.*　　ἐν ἁπλότητι
τῆς καρδίας ὑμ.] '*in singleness of
heart;*' 'in simplicitate cordis,' Clarom.,
Vulg., Syr.; element in which their
anxious and solicitous obedience was to
be shown : it was to be no hypocritical
anxiety, but one arising from a sincere
and single heart; καλῶς εἶπεν, ἔνι γὰρ
μετὰ φ. καὶ τρ. δουλεύειν οὐκ ἐξ εὐνοίας δέ,
ἀλλ᾿ ὡς ἂν ἐξῇ, Chrys. The term ἁπλό-
της occurs seven times (2 Cor. i. 12 is
doubtful) in the N. T. (only in St. Paul's
Epp.), and in all marks that *openness* and
sincerity of heart (not *per se* 'liberality,'
see the good note of Fritz. *Rom.* Vol.
III. 62) which repudiates *duplicity*, in
thought (2 Cor. xi. 3) or action (Rom.
xii. 8). It is joined with ἀκακία (Philo,
Opif. § 41, p. 38, § 55, p. 61), with ἀγα-
θότης (Wisdom i. 1), and is opposed to
ποικιλία, πολυτροπία (Plato, *Rep.* 404 E ;
comp. *Hipp. Min.* 364 E, where Achilles
is contrasted with Ulysses), κακουργία,
and κακοηθεία (Theoph., Theod., *in loc.*) ;
see Suicer, *Thesaur.* Vol. I. p. 436, comp.
Tittm. *Synon.* p. 29, and on the scriptural aspects of *singleness* of heart, Beck,
Seelenl. III. § 26, p. 105 sq.

6. μὴ κατ᾿ ὀφθαλμοδουλείαν]
'*not in the way of eye service;*' further
specification on the negative side of the
preceding ἐν ἁπλότ., the prep. with its
usual force designating the rule or '*nor-
mam* agendi,' which in this case they
were not to follow; see exx. in Winer,
Gr. § 49. d, p. 358. The word ὀφθαλ-
μοδ. appears to have been coined by St.
Paul, being only found here and Col. iii.
22: the adj. ὀφθαλμόδουλος occurs in
Constitut. Apost. Vol. I. p. 299 A (ed.
Cotel.), but in reference to this passage.
The meaning is well expressed by Clarom., Vulg., 'non ad oculum servientes'
(comp Syr.), the ref. being primarily to
the *master's eye* (μὴ μόνον παρόντων τῶν

δεσποτῶν καὶ ὁρώντων ἀλλὰ καὶ ἀπόντων,
Theophyl.; compare Xen. *Œcon.* XII.
20), and thence generally, and as in the
present case, ἡ οὐκ ἐξ εἰλικρινοῦς καρδίας
προσφερομένη θεραπεία, ἀλλὰ τῷ σχήματι
κεχρωσμένη, Theodoret. The more correct form seems ὀφθαλμοδουλία, see L.
Dindorf in Steph. *Thesaur.* Vol. v. p.
1088, 2446.　　ἀνθρωπάρεσκοι]
'*men-pleasers;*' Psalm lii. 6, ὁ Θεὸς διεσ-
κόρπισεν ὀστᾶ ἀνθρωπαρέσκων. Lobeck
(*Phryn.* p. 621) remarks on the questionable forms εὐάρεσκος, δυσάρεσκος, but ex-
cepts ἀνθρωπάρεσκος.　　ἀλλ᾿ ὡς
δοῦλοι Χρ.] '*but as bondservants of
Christ;*' contrasted term to ἀνθρωπάρ.;
τίς γὰρ Θεοῦ δοῦλος ὢν ἀνθρώποις ἀρέσκειν
βούλεται ; τίς δὲ ἀνθρώποις ἀρέσκων Θεοῦ
δύναται εἶναι δοῦλος ; Chrys. : comp. ver.
7, where the opposition is more fully
seen. Rückert removes the stop after
Χρ., thus regarding ποιοῦντες as the principal member in the opposition, δοῦλοι
Χρ. only a subordinate member which
gives the reason and foundation of it.
This, though obviously harsh, and completely marring the studied antithesis
between ἀνθρωπάρεσκοι and δοῦλοι
Χριστοῦ is reintroduced by *Tisch.* (ed.
7), but properly rejected by other recent
editors. The article before Χριστοῦ [Rec.
with D³EKL; most mss.; Chrys.,
Theod.] is rightly struck out by *Lachm.,
Tisch.,* al., on preponderant external
authority.　　ποιοῦντες κ. τ. λ.]
'*doing the will of God from the soul;*' participial clause defining the manner in
which their δουλεία to Christ was to be
exhibited in action. The qualifying
words ἐκ ψυχῆς are prefixed by Syr.,
Æth.-Platt., Arm., Chrys., and some
recent editors and expositors (*Lachm.,*
De W., Harl., Alf., al.) to the participial
clause which follows. but more naturally
and it would seem correctly connected

ὡς δοῦλοι Χριστοῦ, ποιοῦντες τὸ θέλημα τοῦ Θεοῦ ἐκ ψυχῆς,
[7] μετ' εὐνοίας δουλεύοντες ὡς τῷ Κυρίῳ καὶ οὐκ ἀνθρώποις,
[8] εἰδότες ὅτι ὃ ἐάν τι ἕκαστος ποιήσῃ ἀγαθόν, τοῦτο κομίσεται

8. ὃ ἐάν τι ἕκαστος] So *Tisch.* with KL; great majority of mss.; Syr. (both), al.;
Chrys. (3), but ἄνθρ. for ἔκ. (2), Theod. (adds ἡμῶν), Dam., Theoph., Œcum. (*Rec.*,
Griesb., Scholz, De W., Meyer). The shorter and inverted reading, ἕκαστος ὃ ἐάν,
is supported by *very* strong external authority, viz., by ADEFG; many mss.;
Vulg., Clarom., al.; Bas., al. (*Lachm., Rück., Wordsw.*); still the internal arguments derived from *paradiplomatic* (see Pref. to *Gal.* p. xvi.) considerations are so
decided that we seem fully authorized in retaining the reading of *Tisch.* The example is instructive, as it would seem the numerous variations can all be referred
either to (*a*) correction, or (*b*) error in transcription, or both united. For example,
(*a*) the tmesis seems to have suggested a correction ὅ τι ἐάν, and then, on account
of the juxtaposition of ὅτι ὅ τι, the further correction of AB, al. Again it is (*b*)
not improbable that owing to the homœoteleuton, ὃ ἐάν τι was, in some mss. acci-
dentally omitted, and that the unintelligible reading ὅτι ἕκαστος ποιήσῃ then received various emendations: thus we may account for the insertion of ὃ ἐάν τις (I.
27. 31), ἐάν τις (62. 179), ἐάν τι (46. 115), ὃ ἐάν (23. 47), between ὅτι and ἕκ., all
of which have this value, that they attest the position of ἕκαστ. adopted in the
text.

by Clarom. (where ἐκ ψυχῆς concludes
the στίχος), Copt., Æth.-Pol., Syr.-Phil.,
Auth. (*Tisch.*, Mey., Wordsw., al.), with
the present participial clause. Far from
there thus being any tautology (De W.),
there is rather a gentle climactic explanation of the characteristics of the δοῦλ.
Χρ.; he does his work heartily, and besides this, feels a sincere good-will to his
master: comp. Col. iii. 23, ἐκ ψυχῆς ἐργάζεσθε, which, though claimed by De
W. as supporting the other punctuation,
is surely more in favor of that of the
text. On the varied uses of ψυχή (here
in ref. to the inner principle of action),
see Delitzsch, *Psychol.* iv. 6, p. 159 sq.

7. μετ' εὐνοίας δουλ.] '*with good
will doing service;*' further specification
of the nature and character of the service; μετ' εὐνοίας implying not merely
'lubenti animo' (Grinf. *Hell. Test.*), but
'cum benignitate,' Clarom., 'cum cogi-
tatione bonâ,' Copt., in reference to the
well-disposed ('well-affected,' Eadie)
mind with which the service was to be
performed. Raphel (*Obs.* Vol. II. p.

489) very appositely cites Xenoph.
Œcon. p. 673 [XII. 5], οὐκοῦν εὔνοιαν
πρῶτον, ἔφην ἐγώ, δεήσει αὐτὸν [τὸν ἐπίτ-
ροπον] ἔχειν σοὶ καὶ τοῖς σοῖς εἰ μέλλοι
ἀρκέσειν ἀντὶ σοῦ παρών. ἄνευ γὰρ εὐνοίας
τί ὄφελος κ. τ. λ. This quotation certainly seems to confirm the distinction
made by Harl. (to which Mey. objects)
that while ἐκ ψυχῆς seems to mark the
relation of the servant to his *work*, μετ'
εὐνοίας points to his relation to his
master: so also the author of the *Constit.
Apost.* IV. 22, εὔνοιαν εἰσφερέτω πρὸς τὸν
δεσπότην, Vol. I. p. 302 (ed. Cotel.):
see exx. in Elsner, *Obs.* Vol. I. p. 228.
The Atticists define εὔν. as both ἀπὸ τοῦ
μείζονος πρὸς τὸν ἐλάττονα and *vice versâ*,
εὐμένεια as only the former, see Thom.
Mag. p. 368 (ed. Jacobitz), and exx. in
Wetst. *in loc.* The insertion of ὡς
before τῷ Κυρ. [*Rec.* omits with D³EKL;
mss.; Theod., al.] is supported by preponderant authority.

8. εἰδότες] '*seeing ye know;*' concluding participial member, giving the
encouraging *reason* (σφόδρα θαρρεῖν περὶ

παρὰ Κυρίου, εἴτε δοῦλος εἴτε ἐλεύθερος. ⁹ Καὶ οἱ κύριοι, τὰ
αὐτὰ ποιεῖτε πρὸς αὐτούς, ἀνιέντες τὴν ἀπειλήν, εἰδότες ὅτι καὶ

τῆς ἀμοιβῆς, Chrys.) why they were to
act with this honesty and diligence.
The imperatival translation, 'atque sci-
tote' (Raphel, Annot. Vol. II. p. 491),
is not grammatically tenable (compare
Winer, Gr. § 45. 6, p. 313), and mars
the logical connection of the clauses.
The translation of participles, it may be
observed, must always be modified by
the context; see Winer, Gr. § 45. 2, p.
307, but correct, there what cannot be
termed otherwise than the erroneous
observation that such participles admit
of a translation by means of relatives;
the observation so often illustrated in
these commentaries — that a participle
without the article can never be strictly
translated as a part. with the article —
appears to be of universal application;
see esp. Donalds. Gr. § 490.
ὃ ἐάν τι κ. τ. λ.] 'whatsoever good thing
each man shall have done;' ἐὰν coalescing
with the relative and being in such connections used simply for ἂν both by
writers in the N. T., LXX, and late
Greek generally. In the passages collected by Viger (Idiom. VIII. 6), from
classical authors, ἂν clearly must be
written throughout; see Herm. in loc.
and Winer, Gr. § 42. 6. obs. p. 277.
The relative is separated from τι by a
not uncommon 'tmesis,' instances of
which are cited by Meyer, e. g. Plato,
Legg. IX. 864 E, ἣν ἄν τινα καταβλάψῃ
[Lysias], Polystr. p. 160, ὃς ἄν τις ὑμᾶς
εὖ ποιῇ, — but here some edd. read ὅταν.
The reading κομιεῖται [Rec. with D³E
KL; most mss.; Bas., Chrys., Theod]
is rightly rejected by recent editors, both
on preponderant external authority, and
as derived from Col. l. c. The τοῦ is
also rightly struck out before Κυρίου.
τοῦτο κομ. παρὰ Κυρίου] 'this
shall he receive (back) from the Lord
(Christ);' 'this, — and fully this,' ex-

pressed more at length Col. iii. 24, 25.
The 'appropriative' middle κομίζεσθαι
(see esp. Donalds. Gr. § 432. bb, and §
434, p. 450) refers to the receiving back
again, as it were, of a deposit; so that
in κομιεῖται ὃ ἠδίκησε, Col. l. c. (comp.
2 Cor. v. 10), there is no brachylogy;
see Winer, Gr. § 66. 1. b, p. 547, and
compare notes in loc. The tense seems
obviously to refer to the day of final
retribution; ἐπειδὴ εἰκός ἐστι πολλοὺς
τῶν δεσποτῶν μὴ ἀμείβεσθαι τῆς εὐνοίας
τοῖς δούλοις, ἔκει αὐτοῖς ὑπισχνεῖται τὴν
ἀμοιβήν, Œcum.　　εἴτε δοῦλος
εἴτε ἐλ.] 'whether he be bond-slave or
free;' whatever be his social condition
here, the future will only regard his
moral state; μετὰ τὴν ἐντεῦθεν ἐκδημίαν
[ἔδειξε] οὐκ ἔτι δουλείας διαφοράν, Theod.
9. καὶ οἱ κύριοι] 'And ye masters;'
corresponding duties of masters similarly
enunciated positively and negatively
(ἀνιέντες τὴν ἀπ.), and concluded with a
similar participial clause expressing the
motive. The negative statement of the
duty is omitted in the parallel passage,
Col. iv. 1. On the use of καὶ, see notes
on ver. 4.　　τὰ αὐτὰ ποιεῖτε]
'do the same things towards them;' 'evince
in action the same principles and feelings towards them; preserve the 'jus
analogum' (Calv.) in your relations to
them.' It does not seem necessary to
restrict τὰ αὐτὰ to μετ' εὐνοίας δουλεύειν (Chrys.), or to ποιεῖν τὸ θέλ. κ. τ. λ.
(Rück.), or, on the other hand, to extend it to ἐν ἀπλ., as well as to the other
details (Origen, Cram. Caten.; compare
Eadie), the reference being rather to the
general expression of feeling, the εὔνοια
which was to mark all their actions, ἵνα
εὐνοϊκῶς — θεραπεύσωσι, Theodoret, or,
as more correctly modified by Stier, —
κυριεύσωσι; 'ea quæ benevolentiæ sunt
compensate,' Beng.　　ἀνιέντες

αὐτῶν καὶ ὑμῶν ὁ Κύριός ἐστιν ἐν οὐρανοῖς καὶ προσωπολημψία
οὐκ ἔστιν παρ᾽ αὐτῷ.

Put on the panoply of God; **10** Τὸ λοιπόν, ἐνδυναμοῦσθε ἐν Κυρίῳ καὶ ἐν
arm yourselves against your
spiritual foes with all the defensive portions of Christian armor and the sword of the Spirit. Pray that we
may be bold.

τὴν ἀπειλήν] 'giving up your threatening,' 'the too habitual threatening,' 'quemadmodum vulgus dominorum solet,' Erasm. *Paraphr.* (cited by Meyer); explanatory participial clause (De W., here wholly miscited by Eadie), specifying a course of action, or rather of non-action, in which the feeling was to be particularly exhibited. As ἀπειλὴ expresses, by the nature of the case, a certain and single course of action, the article does not appear to be used, as with ἀδικία, ἀκολασία, al., to specify the particular acts (Middleton, *Art.* v. i. 1), but to hint at the common occurrence of ἀπειλή, see ib. v. 1. 4. It is thus not necessary to modify the meaning of ἀπ. ('hardness of heart,' Olsh.); St. Paul singles out the prevailing vice, and most customary exhibition of bad feeling on the part of the master, and in forbidding this, naturally includes every similar form of harshness. εἰδότες ὅτι κ. τ. λ.] 'seeing ye know that both their and your master is in heaven;' causal participial member exactly similar to that in ver. 8; see notes *in loc.* The reading is somewhat doubtful; the order in the text is adopted by *Lachmann, Tischendorf,* and long since by Simon Colinæus (ed. N. T. 1534) with ABD[1] (supported partially by L; 6 mss., al., καὶ ὑμ. καὶ αὐτ.); mss., Vulg., Goth., Copt., al.; 'Clem., al., — but designated by Mill, *Prolegom.* p. 115, as 'argutius quam verius.' This is not a judicious criticism, for the probability of an omission of καὶ ὑμῶν, owing to homœoteleuton, is far from small, and seems very satisfactorily to account for the various readings; see Mey. *in loc.* (Crit. Notes), p. 239. προσωπολημψία] 'respect of persons;' personarum accep-

tio, Clarom., Vulg., 'vilja haþei,'Goth.; on the meaning of this word, see notes *on Gal.* ii. 6, and on the orthography, Tisch. *Prolegom. in N. T.* p. XLVII.

10. τὸ λοιπόν] 'Finally,' 'as to what remains for you to do;' μετὰ τὸ διατάξαι, φησί, τὰ εἰκότα τοῦτο ἀκόλουθον καὶ ὑπόλοιπον, Œcum.; 'formula concludendi [see Chrys.], et ut ad magnam rem excitandi,' Beng.; see 2 Cor. xiii. 11, Phil. iii. 1, iv. 8, 2 Thess. iii. 1, and compare notes *on Phil. l. c.* On the distinction between τὸ λοιπὸν and τοῦ λοιποῦ [adopted here by *Lachm.* with AB; 3 mss.; Cyr., Dam., — evidence obviously insufficient], see notes *on Gal.* vi. 17; and between it and τὸ μέλλον (merely 'in posterum') the brief distinctions of Tittmann, *Synon.* p. 175. The insertion of ἀδελφοί μου before ἐνδυν. [*Rec.*, Wordsw. with KL (FG, al. omit μου); most mss.; Syr., Copt., al.; Theod., al.] has the further support of A, which adds ἀδελφοὶ after ἐνδ., — but is appy. rightly rejected by *Lachm., Tisch.,* al. on good external authority [BDE; Clarom., Sang., Goth., Æth. (both) Arm.; Cyr., al.], and as appy. alien to the style of an Epistle in which the readers do not elsewhere appear so addressed; see Olsh. and Alf. *in loc.* ἐνδυναμοῦσθε] 'be strengthened;' ܩܘܪܒܡܝ [corroboremini] Syr., — less definitely, 'be strong,' Auth.; not middle, 'corroborate vos,' Pisc., but (as always in the N. T.) *passive;* compare Acts ix. 22, Rom. iv. 20, 2 Tim. ii. 1, Heb. xi. 34, and see Fritz. *Rom. l. c.* Vol. I. p. 245. The active occurs, Phil. iv. 13, 1 Tim. i. 12, 2 Tim. iv. 17, in each case in reference to Christ. The simple form [here adopted by B; 17

τῷ κράτει τῆς ἰσχύος αὐτοῦ. ¹¹ ἐνδύσασθε τὴν πανοπλίαν τοῦ
Θεοῦ, πρὸς τὸ δύνασθαι ὑμᾶς στῆναι πρὸς τὰς μεθοδείας τοῦ
διαβόλου· ¹² ὅτι οὐκ ἔστιν ἡμῖν ἡ πάλη πρὸς αἷμα καὶ σάρκα,

Orig. *Cat.*] is only found once, Col. i.
11, see Lobeck, *Phryn.* p. 605.
καὶ ἐν τῷ κ. τ. λ.] '*and in the power
of His might;*' not an ἐν διὰ δυοῖν, Beng.,
but with a preservation of the proper
sense of each substantive; see notes on
ch. i. 19. This appended clause (καὶ)
serves to explain and specify the principle in which our strength was to be
sought for, and in which it abided; compare 2 Cor. xii. 9, ἵνα ἐπισκηνώσῃ ἐπ᾽ ἐμὲ
ἡ δύναμις τοῦ Χριστοῦ. On the familiar
ἐν Κυρίῳ ('in the Lord,' our only element
of spiritual life), see notes ch. iv. 1.
    11. ἐνδύσ. τὴν πανοπλίαν] '*Put
on the whole armor, the panoply.*' The
emphasis rests on this latter word (Mey.)
as the repetition in ver. 13 still more
clearly shows, not τοῦ Θεοῦ (Harless);
'significat debere nos *ex omni parte*
instructos esse, ne quid desit,' Calv.;
the term here clearly denoting not
merely the 'armatura,' Vulg., but the
'*universa* armatura,' Beza, the armor in
all its parts, offensive and defensive;
'omnia armorum genera, quibus totum
militis corpus tegitur,' Raphel, *Annot.*
Vol. ii. 491; see Judith, xiv. 4, πανο-
πλίας, compared with ver. 2, τὰ σκεύη τὰ
πολεμικά, and comp. παντελὴς πανοπλία,
Plato, *Legg.* vii. 796 b. It has been
doubted whether St. Paul is here alluding to the armor of the Hebrew or the
Roman soldier; the latter is most probable, but both were substantially the
same; see esp. Polyb. *Hist.* vi. 23, a
good Art. in Kitto, *Cyclop.* ('Arms,
Armour'), and Winer, *RWB.* Art.
'Waffen,' Vol. ii. p. 667. For a sermon on this text see Latimer, *Serm.* iii.
p. 25 (ed. Corrie). Θεοῦ] '*of God;*'
'quæ a Deo donantur,' Zanch.; gen. of
the *source, origin,* whence the arms came
(Hartung. *Casus,* p. 23, notes, *on* 1 *Thess.*

i. 6), well expressed by Theod. ἅπασιν
διανέμει τὴν βασιλικὴν παντευχίαν.
    πρὸς τὸ δύνασθαι κ. τ. λ.] '*in order
that ye may be able to stand against;*'
object and purpose contemplated in the
equipment; compare notes on ch. iii. 4
with those on iv. 12. The verb στῆναι,
as Raphel (*Annot.* Vol. ii. p. 493) shows,
is a military expression, 'to stand one's
ground,' opp. to φεύγειν; see esp. Kypke,
Obs. Vol. ii. p. 301. The second πρὸς
in this connection has thus the meaning
'adversus' (Clarom., Vulg.), with the
implied notion of *hostility* ('contra')
which is otherwise less usual, unless it
is involved in the verb; see Winer, *Gr.*
§ 49. h, p. 361 note.   τὰς μεθοδείας τοῦ διαβ.] '*the wiles of the
Devil,*'— or perhaps, as more in harmony with the context, '*the stratagems*'
(Eadie; μεθοδεῦσαί ἐστι τὸ ἀπατῆσαι καὶ
διὰ μηχανῆς ἑλεῖν, Chrysost.); the
plural denoting the various concrete
forms of the abstract singular; see notes
on Gal. v. 20. On the form μεθοδίας,
which it must be admitted is here
very strongly supported [AB¹D¹EGKL;
many mss.], see notes on ch. iv. 14.
The only reason for not accepting it is,
that in cases of apparent *itacism* caution
is always required in estimating the
value of external evidence.
    12. ὅτι οὐκ ἔστιν ἡμῖν ἡ
πάλη] '*because our struggle is not,*' '*the
struggle in which we are engaged;*' reason for the special mention of the μεθοδείας τοῦ διαβόλου, ver. 11. 'It is commonly asserted that the metaphor is not
here fully sustained, on the ground that
πάλη (πάλλω) is properly 'lucta;' see
Plato, *Legg.* vii. 795 d. As, however,
we find πάλη δορός (Eur. *Heracl.* 160),
πάλην μίξαντες λόγχης (Lycophron, *Cas-
sand.* 1358), it is clear such a usage as

ἀλλὰ πρὸς τὰς ἀρχάς, πρὸς τὰς ἐξουσίας, πρὸς τοὺς κοσμοκράτο-

the present can be justified ; indeed it is not unlikely that the word (an ἅπ. λεγόμ. in New Test., not found in LXX) was designedly adopted to convey the idea of the *personal, individualizing* nature of the encounter.　　　The reading ὑμῖν adopted by *Lachm.* is well supported [BD¹FG ; 3 mss. ; Clarom., Sang., Aug., Boern., Syr., Goth., al. ; Lucif., Ambrst.], but appy. less probable than ἡμῖν [AD³EKL ; nearly all mss. ; Vulg., Copt., Syr.-Phil., al. ; Clem., Orig., al.], for which it might have been easily substituted as a more individualizing address.　　　πρὸς αῖμα καὶ σάρκα] '*against flesh and blood,*' mere *feeble* man ; οὐ πρὸς τοὺς τυχόντας ἔχομέν φησιν, οὐδὲ πρὸς ἀνθρώπους ὁμοιοπαθεῖς ἡμῖν καὶ ἰσοδυνάμους, Theophyl. ; comp. Polylænus, *Strateg.* iii. 11, μὴ ὡς πολεμίοις συμβάλλοντες ἀλλ' ἀνθρώποις αῖμα καὶ σάρκα ἔχουσι [the exhortation of Chabrias to his soldiers], and see notes *on Gal.* i. 16, where the formula is more fully explained.　　　ἀλλά] There is here no ground for translating οὐκ ἀλλά, 'non tam . . . . quam ;' comp. Glass. *Philolog.* i. 5. 22, Vol. i. p. 420 sq. (ed. Dathe). The negation and affirmation are both absolute ; '*non* contra homines ['vasa sunt, alius utitur,' August.], *sed* contra dæmones,' Cornel. a Lap. ; see esp. Winer, *Gr.* § 55. 8, p. 439, where this formula is very satisfactorily discussed, and comp. Kühner on Xenoph. *Mem.* i. 6. 2, and notes *on* 1 *Thess.* iv. 8. In those exx. where the negation cannot, by the nature of the case, be considered completely absolute, it will be observed, as Winer ably shows, that the negation has designedly a *rhetorical* coloring, which, in a faithful and forcible translation, ought always to be preserved without any toning down ; see Fritz. *Mark,* Excurs. ii. p. 773 sq., Klotz, *Devar.* Vol. ii. p. 9, 10.　　　πρὸς τὰς

ἀρχάς] '*against the principalities ;*' see esp. notes on ch. i. 23, and observe that the same terms which are there used to denote the classes and orders of *good,* are here similarly applied to *evil* angels and spirits ; comp. Usteri, *Lehrb.* ii. 2. b, p. 355.　　　τοὺς κοσμοκράτορας κ. τ. λ.] '*the world-rulers of this darkness ;*' those who extend their worldwide sway over the present (comp. ch. ii. 1) spiritual and moral darkness ; ποίου σκότους ; ἆρα τῆς νυκτός [compare Wetst.] ; οὐδαμῶς, ἀλλὰ τῆς πονηρίας, Chrys., see ch. v. 8. Meyer rightly maintains (against Harless) the full meaning of κοσμοκρ, as not merely 'rulers' ('magnates,' Æth.), ' fairwuhabandans,' Goth. (comp. Syr.), but 'rulers over the world,' *munditenentes,* Tertull. (*Marc.* v. 18), κόσμος preserving its natural and proper force. So even in the second of the three exx. cited by Schoetgg. *Hor.* Vol. i. p. 790, out of Rabbinical writers ('qui vocem hanc, קוזמיקרטור civitate suâ donarunt'), which Harl. here adduces, — 'Abraham persecutus est quatuor קוזמיקרטורין, sc. reges,' — the word appears used designedly with a rhetorical force ; ex. 3 is perfectly distinct.　　　Further exx. from later writers are cited by Elsner, *Obs.* Vol. i. p. 219. The dogmatical meaning is correctly explained by the Greek commentators ; the evil spirits exercise dominion over the κόσμος, not in its mere material nature (οὐχὶ τῆς κτίσεως κρατοῦντες, Theophyl.), but in its ethical and perhaps intellectual character and relations (ὡς κατακρατοῦντες τῶν τὰ κοσμικὰ φρονούντων, Œcumen.), the depravation of which is expressed by τοῦ σκ. τούτου ; see John xvi. 11, ὁ ἄρχων τοῦ κ. τούτου, i. ib. v. 19, ὁ κ. ὅλος ἐν τῷ Πονηρῷ [see notes, ver. 16] κεῖται, 2 Cor. iv. 4, ὁ Θεὸς τοῦ αἰῶνος τούτου, compare John xiv. 30. On the meanings of κόσ-

ρας τοῦ σκότους τούτου, πρὸς τὰ πνευματικὰ τῆς πονηρίας ἐν τοῖς

μos, see Bauer, *de Regno Divino*, iii. 2, 3 (*Comment: Theol.* Vol. ii. p. 144, 154), and comp. notes *on Gal.* iv. 3. The insertion of τοῦ αἰῶνος before τούτου [*Rec.* with D³FKL; majority of mss. ; Syr.-Phil. with an ast. ; Orig., Chrys., Theod., al.] seems clearly explanatory, and is rightly rejected by nearly all modern editors. τὰ πνευματικὰ τῆς πονηρίας] '*the spiritual hosts, communities, of wickedness*,' sc. characterized by essential πονηρία ; gen. of ' the characteristic quality' (Scheuerl. *Synt.* § 16. 3, p. 115, Winer, *Gr.* § 34. 3. b, p. 211) ; ἐπειδὴ γάρ εἰσι καὶ οἱ ἄγγελοι πνεύματα, προσέθηκε τῆς πονηρίας, Theoph., comp. Œcumen. *in loc.* Τὰ πνευματικὰ are not, however, merely τὰ πνεύματα (Elsn. 1, comp. Syr., Æth.), but, in accordance with the force of the collective neut. adject. (Bern. *Synt.* vi. 2, p. 326, Jelf, *Gr.* § 436, i. δ.), denote the *bands, hosts,* or confraternities of evil spirits : Winer and Meyer aptly cite τὰ λῃστρικά ('robber-hordes), Polyæn. *Strateg.* v. 14. 1 [τὰ δοῦλα, τὰ αἰχμάλωτα, cited by Mey. after Bernhardy, are not fully appropriate ; see Lobeck, *Phryn.* p. 378] ; comp. τὰ δαιμόνια, and see esp. Winer, *Gr.* § 34. 3. b. obs. 3, p. 213. The gloss of Auth. 'spiritual wickedness,' does not seem tenable, for if τὰ πνευματικὰ be taken as the abstract neuter (so perhaps Copt.,— which adopts the singular πνευματικὸν) expressive of the properties or attributes (the 'dynamic neut. adj.' of Krüger, *Sprachl.* § 43. 4. 27 ; comp. Stier), the meaning must be, not 'spiritales malignitates,' Beza, but 'spiritualia nequitiæ,' Vulg., Clarom. (comp. Goth.), *i. e.* 'spiritual elements, properties, of wickedness' (see Jelf, *Gr.* § 436, obs. 2),— an abstract meaning which obviously does not harmonize with the context; see Meyer *in loc.* The concrete interpretation, on the other hand, is grammati-

cally correct, and far from unsuitable after the definite τοὺς κοσμοκράτορας. ἐν τοῖς ἐπουρανίοις] 'in the heavenly regions,' ' in the sky or air ;' Dobree, *Adv.* Vol. i. p. 574 : see notes ch. i. 20, ii. 6. Here again we have at least three interpretations ; (*a*) that of Chrys. and the Greek commentators. who give τὰ ἐπουρ. an ethical reference, ' heavenly blessings ;' (*b*) that of Rück., Matth., Eadie, al., who refer the expression to the scene, the locality of the combat, ' the celestial spots occupied by the church ;' (*c*) the ancient interpr. (see Jerome *in loc.*; comp. Tertull. *Marc.* v. 18, where, however, the application is too limited) according to which ἐν τοῖς ἐπ. is to be joined with τὰ πν. τῆς πον. as specifying the *abode* or rather *haunt* of the τὰ πνευματ. ; 'qui infra cælum,' Æth. (both). Of these (*a*) is opposed to the previous local interpretations of the words, and involves an explan. of ἐν (= ὑπέρ, Chrys., or περί, Theod., wholly untenable; (*b*) seems vague and not fully intelligible ; (*c*) on the contrary is both grammatically admissible (as the clause thus presents a single conception, 'supernal spirits of evil,' see notes on ch. i. 19) and exegetically satisfactory. The haunt of the evil spirits was indirectly specified in ch. ii. 2 as being in the regions τοῦ ἀέρος ; here the latent opposition, αἷμα καὶ σάρξ (on earth) and τὰ πνευμ. (in supernal regions), suggests a word of greater antithetical force, which, still *can* include the same lexical meaning; comp. Matth. vi. 26, τὰ πετεινὰ τοῦ οὐρανοῦ. As in ch. ii. 2 there was no reason for limiting the term to the mere physical *atmosphere*, so here still less need we adopt any more precise specification of locality; see notes *in loc.*, and comp. generally Hofm. *Schriftb.* Vol. i. p. 401 sq. The repetition of πρὸς before each of the substantives is somewhat of

ἐπουρανίοις. ¹³ διὰ τοῦτο ἀναλάβετε τὴν πανοπλίαν τοῦ Θεοῦ, ἵνα δυνηθῆτε ἀντιστῆναι ἐν τῇ ἡμέρᾳ τῇ πονηρᾷ καὶ ἅπαντα κατεργασάμενοι στῆναι. ¹⁴ στῆτε οὖν περιζωσάμενοι τὴν ὀσφὺν ὑμῶν ἐν

a rhetorical nature, designed to give emphasis to the enumeration; see Winer, *Gr.* § 50. 7. obs. p. 374.

13. δ ι ὰ τ ο ῦ τ ο] '*On this account,*' '*wherefore;*' since we have such powerful adversaries to contend with; ἐπειδή φησι, χαλεποὶ οἱ ἐχθροί, Œcum.

ἀ ν α λ ά β ε τ ε] '*assume,*' '*take up,*' not necessarily 'to the field of battle,' Conyb., but with simple local reference, as opposed to καταγίζεσθαι; ἀναλαμβ. τὰ ὅπλα κ. τ. λ. being the technical expression: see Deut. i. 41, Jer. xxvi. 3, Judith xiv. 3, 2 Macc. x. 27, xi. 7, and exx. in Kypke, *Obs.* Vol. ii. p. 302, Elsner, *Obs.* Vol. i. p. 231, and Wetst. *in loc.*

ἐ ν τ ῇ ἡ μ έ ρ ᾳ τ ῇ π ο ν η ρ ᾷ] '*in the evil day* — of violent temptation,' Fell, Cocc.: ἡμέραν πονηρὰν τὴν τῆς παρατάξεως ἡμέραν καλεῖ, ἀπὸ τοῦ ἐνεργοῦντος αὐτῇ διαβόλου τὸ ὄνομα τεθεικώς, Theod.; Schoettg. compares רעה בשעה '*in hora mala,* quando periculum nobis imminet,' *Hor. Hebr.* Vol. i. p. 793. The use of ἡμέρᾳ rather than αἰῶνι (Gal. i. 4) is opposed to the interpr. of Chrys., Œcum., Theophyl., τὸν παρόντα βίον φησί; and the foregoing earnest tone of exhortation to the idea that any consolation (scil. τὸ βραχὺ ἐδήλωσε, Theophyl., comp. Chrys.) was implied in the use of ἡμέρᾳ. Still more untenable is the view of Meyer, that St. Paul is here specifying the day when the last great Satanic outbreak was to take place (comp. notes on *Gal* i. 4); the Apostle has at heart what he knew was much more present and more constantly impending; 'bellum est perpetuum; pugna alio die minus, alio die magis fervet,' Beng.

ἅ π α ν τ α κ α τ ε ρ γ α σ ά μ ε ν ο ι] '*having accomplished, fully done all,*' not merely *before* the fight, Beng., but as στῆναι ('to stand your ground') obviously suggests,

in and *appertaining to* the fight; all things that the exigences of the conflict required. The special interpr. of Œcum. (comp. Chrys.) κατεργασ. = καταπολεμήσαντες, *i. e.* 'having overcome all,' Auth. in Marg. (comp. Ezek. xxxiv. 4, 3, Esdr. iv. 4), though adopted by Harl., is very doubtful; for, in the first place, the masc. would have seemed more natural than the neut. ἅπαντα (Est., contr. De W.); and secondly, though κατεργάζ. occurs 20 times in St. Paul's Epp., it is only in one of two senses, either *perficere* ('notat rem arduam,' Fritz.), as here, Rom. vii. 18, Phil. ii. 12, al., or *perpetrare* ('de rebus quæ fiunt non honeste'), Rom. i. 27, ii. 9, al.; see Fritz. *Rom.* ii. 9, Vol. i. p. 109, and the numerous exx. cited by Raphel, *Annot.* Vol. ii. p. 495 sq. The concluding στῆναι is, then, not 'stare tanquam triumphatores' (Zanch. ap. Pol. *Syn.*, comp. even Meyer), but as in ver. 11, 'to stand firm' (the battle is life-long), 'ut non cadatis aut loco cedere cogamini,' Est.

14. σ τ ῆ τ ε ο ὖ ν] '*Stand then,*' not as in ver. 13, *in* the fight, but, as the context obviously requires, *ready for* the fight; 'kampffertig,' De Wette. The several portions of the πανοπλία are then specified in regular order; παραθαρσύνας αὐτούς, λοιπὸν αὐτούς καὶ καθοπλίζει, Chrys. π ε ρ ι ζ ω σ ά μ ε ν ο ι τ ὴ ν ὀ σ φ ύ ν] '*having girt your loins about;*' comp. Isaiah, xi. 5, ἔσται δικαιοσύνη ἐζωσμένος τὴν ὀσφὺν αὐτοῦ, καὶ ἀληθείᾳ εἰλημένος τὰς πλευράς. The remark of Holz., that the aorists are improperly used for presents, is wholly mistaken; the different acts specified by the participles were all completed before the soldier took up his position; comp. notes on ch. iv. 8. It may be observed that the girdle was no mere ornament (Harless,

ἀληθεία, καὶ ἐνδυσάμενοι τὸν θώρακα τῆς δικαιοσύνης, ¹⁵ καὶ

compare Eadie), but the first and most necessary part of the equipment; a στρατιώτης ἄζωστος was, as Meyer observes, a very 'contradictio in adjecto.' Independently of serving to keep the armor in its proper place, it appears also, — except in the Homeric age, when it formed a part of the cuirass, and in later times, when ornamented 'baltei' came into use (Smith, *Dict. of Antiq.* Art. 'Balteus '), to have been commonly used to support the sword ; see plates in Montfaucon, *L'Antiq. Expl.* Vol. ɪᴠ. 1, p. 19 sq. and *Suppl.* Vol. ɪᴠ. p. 14 sq., Smith, *Dict.* Art. 'Zona,' and Winer, *RWB.* Art. 'Gürtel,' Vol. ɪ. p. 448.

ἐν ἀληθείᾳ] '*with truth,*' as the girdle which bound all together, and served to make the Christian soldier expedite and unencumbered for the fight ; ἐν being instrumental, or perhaps rather semi-local, with a ref. to the cincture and equipment ; see Isaiah xi. 5 quoted above, Psalm lxiv. 7, περιεζωσμένος ἐν δυναστείᾳ, and comp. Green, *Gramm.* p. 289. It has been doubted (see Œcumen. *in loc.*) whether by ἀλήθεια is meant what is termed *objective* truth (ἀλήθεια δογμάτων Œcum. 1), *i. e.* 'the orthodox profession of the Gospel' (Hamm. *on Luke,* xii. 35), or *subjective* truth; the latter is most probable, provided it is not unduly limited to mere 'truthfulness' (Chrysost. 1) or sincerity (Calv., Olsh.). It must be taken in its widest sense ἀλήθ. ἐν Ἰησοῦ, ch. iv. 21, the inward practical acknowledgment of the truth as it is in Him ; δύνῃ δὲ ὡς πρὸς τὸν Χρ. νοῆσαι, τὸν ὄντως ἀλήθειαν, Œcum.; comp. Reuss, *Théol. Chrét.* ɪᴠ. 16, Vol. ɪɪ. p. 169.   τῆς δικαιοσύνης] '*of righteousness ;*' gen. of *apposition* or *identity ;* see Winer, *Gr.* § 59. 8, p. 470, comp. Scheuerl. *Synt.* § 12. 1, p. 82; so similarly in regard of sentiment, Isaiah, lix. 17, καὶ ἐνεδύσατο δικαιοσύνην

ὡς θώρακα, Wisdom, v. 19, ἐνδύσεται θώρακα δικαιοσύνην. This δικαιοσύνη is not 'righteousness' in its deeper scriptural sense, scil. by faith in Christ (Harless), as πίστις is mentioned independently in ver. 16, but rather Christian moral rectitude (Meyer, Olsh., Usteri, *Lehrb.* ɪɪ. 1. 2, p. 190 ; τὸν καθολικὸν καὶ ἐνάρετον βίον, Chrys.), or, more correctly speaking, the righteousness which is the result of the renovation of the heart by the Holy Spirit ; see Waterl. *Regen.* Vol. ɪᴠ. p. 434. Eadie presses the article, but without grammatical grounds ; its insertion is merely due to the common principle of correlation ; see Middl. *Art.* ɪɪɪ. 1. 7, p. 36.

15. ὑποδησάμενοι τοὺς πόδα,] '*having shod your feet,*' 'calceati pedes,' Clarom., Vulg. It does not seem necessary to refer this *specially* to the Roman 'caliga' (Mey.; see Joseph. *Bell. Jud.* ᴠɪ. 1. 8), as the reference to the Roman soldier, though probable, is not certain ; any strong *military* sandal (Heb. מִנְעָל, Isaiah ix. 4, see Gesen. *Lex.* s. v.) is perhaps all that is implied ; compare Lydus, *Synt. Sacr.* ɪɪɪ. 2, p. 46 sq.

ἐν ἑτοιμασίᾳ] '*with the readiness ;*' not 'in præparationem,' Clarom. but 'in præparatione,' Amit., Copt. ; ἐν being instrumental, or semi-local, as in ver. 14. The somewhat peculiar form ἑτοιμασία, used principally in the LXX and eccl. writers, denotes properly 'preparation' in an active sense (Wisdom xiii. 12, ἑτοιμ. τροφῆς, Mart. Polyc. § 18, ἄσκησίν τε καὶ ἑτοιμ.), then 'a state of readiness,' whether outwardly considered (Joseph. *Antiq.* x. 1. 2, ἵππους εἰς ἑτοιμ. παρέχειν) or inwardly estimated (Hippocr. *de Dec. Habitu.* Vol. ɪ. p. 74, ed. Kühn ; compare Psalm ix. 38, ἑτοιμ. καρδίας, *i. e.* τὸ ἐμπαράσκευον, Chrys.), and thence by a conceivable transition (esp. as הֵכִין admits both meanings, see

ὑποδησάμενοι τοὺς πόδας ἐν ἑτοιμασίᾳ τοῦ εὐαγγελίου τῆς εἰρήνης·
16 ἐπὶ πᾶσιν ἀναλαβόντες τὸν θυρεὸν τῆς πίστεως, ἐν ᾧ δυνήσεσθε

Gesen. Lex. s. v.), 'something fixed, settled' (compare Theodot. Prov. iv. 18, ἑτοιμασία ἡμέρας = σταθερὰ μεσημβρία), and further even 'a basis, a foundation,' Heb. יְכֹן (Dan. xi. 7, τῆς ῥίζης αὐτῆς, τῆς ἑτοιμασίας αὐτοῦ, compare Esra ii. 68, Psalm lxxxviii. 14). This last meaning, however, may possibly have originated from a misconception of the translator (see Holzh. and Meyer in loc.), but at any rate is very inappropriate in this place. There is then no reason to depart from the more correct meaning, 'readiness,' 'preparedness' (ܡܛܝܒܘܬܐ, Syr., 'manviþa,' Goth.), not, however, ὥστε ἑτοίμους εἶναι πρὸς τὸ εὐαγγέλιον (Chrys.), but, as the context and metaphor suggest, 'ad militiam, impedimentis omnibus soluti,' Calv.   τοῦ εὐαγγ. τῆς εἰρήνης] 'of the Gospel of peace;' scil. caused by the εὐαγγ. τῆς εἰρήνης; the first gen. εὐαγγελίου being that of the source or agent (see notes on 1 Thess. i. 6, Scheuerl. Synt. § 17, p. 126), the second, εἰρήνης, that of the purport and contents; comp. ch. i. 13, τὸ εὐαγγέλ. τῆς σωτηρίας, where see notes, and Bernhardy, Synt. iii. 44, p. 161. The sum and substance of the Gospel was ἡ εἰρήνη, Peace, not with one another merely, but with God (Est.), a peace that can only be enjoyed and secured if we war against His enemies; ἂν τῷ διαβόλῳ πολεμῶμεν εἰρηνεύομεν πρὸς τὸν Θεόν, Chrys. On the different terms with which εὐαγγ. is associated in the N. T., see Reuss, Théol. Chrét. iv. 8, Vol. ii. p. 81.

16. ἐπὶ πᾶσιν] 'in addition to all;' not, with local ref., 'super omnibus, quæcumque induistis,' Beng. (comp. Goth. 'ufar all'), nor, with ethical ref., 'above all,' Auth., — but simply in ref. to the last accompaniment; comp. Luke iii. 20,

προσέθηκε τοῦτο ἐπὶ πᾶσι, and see Winer, Gr. § 48. c, p. 350. Eadie cites Col. iii. 14, ἐπὶ πᾶσι τούτοις, but neither this passage nor Luke xvi. 26 are strictly similar, as the addition of τούτοις implies a reference to what has preceded, while ἐπὶ πᾶσιν is general and unrestricted, and more nearly approaches a 'formula concludendi;' see Harless, and exx. collected by Wetst. on Luke xvi. 26. In both the force of ἐπὶ is the same, 'accession,' 'superaddition;' comp. Donalds. Gr. § 483. aa.   The reading ἐν πᾶσιν, adopted by Lachm., with B; a few mss; Clarom.; Vulgate (appy.); Method., Greg.-Naz.; al., has not sufficient external support, and may have been a correction for the ambiguous ἐπί. τὸν θυρεόν] 'the shield,' 'scutum,' Clarom., Vulg. The term θυρεός, as its derivation suggests, is properly ânything, 'quod vicem januæ præstat' (Homer, Od. ix. 240, 313, 340), thence in later writers (see Lobeck, Phryn. p. 366) a large oblong or oval shield (οἵα τις θύρα φυλάττων τὸ σῶμα, Theophyl.), differing both in form and dimensions from the round and lighter ἀσπίς ('clypeus'); see esp. Polyb. Hist. vi. 23. 2, comp. Lips. de Milit. Rom. iii. 2, and exx. in Kypke, Elsner, and Alberti in loc. Harl. doubts whether θυρεὸς was intentionally used instead of ἀσπίς, and cites the very similar passage, Wisdom v. 20, λήψεται ἀσπίδα ὁσιότητα; it is not, however, improbable that in the time of St. Paul (perhaps 150 years later) the distinction had become more commonly recognized; see Plutarch, Flamin. § 12.   τῆς πίστεως] 'of faith;' appositional gen. similar to δικαιοσύνης, ver. 14.   ἐν ᾧ δυνήσεσθε] 'with which ye will be able;' scil. as protected by and under cover of which (comp. ver. 16), or, with a still more definite instrumental force

πάντα τὰ βέλη τοῦ πονηροῦ τὰ πεπυρωμένα σβέσαι· ¹⁷ καὶ τὴν

(Goth., Arm.), as specifying the defensive implement by which the extinction of the fire-tipped darts will be facilitated and effected; ἡ πίστις οὖν ταῦτα σβέννυσιν, Theoph. The future must not be unduly pressed (Mey.); it points simply and generally to the time of the contest, whenever that might be: the future is only 'a conditioned present;' see Bernhardy, *Synt.* x. 5, p. 377.

τοῦ πονηροῦ] 'the wicked One;' 'nequissimi,' Clarom., Vulg.; not 'evil,' τὸ πονηρόν, but in accordance with the individualizing and *personal* nature of the conflict which the context so forcibly depicts, — the Devil; μόνον ἐκεῖνος πονηρὸς κατ᾽ ἐξοχὴν λέγεται, Chrys. *de Diab.* II. Vol. II. p. 309 (ed. Ben. 1834), comp. 2 Thess. iii. 3, 1 John v. 18, probably Matth. v. 37, John xvii. 15, al., and see Suicer, *Thesaur.* s. v. Vol. II. p. 807, notes *on* 1 *Thess. l. c.*, and on the conflict generally, the instructive remarks of Mayer, *Hist. Diab.* § 7, p. 681 sq. comp. also Reuss, *Théol. Chrét.* IV. 20, Vol. II. p. 226 sq. τὰ βέλη τὰ πεπυρ.] 'the fire-tipt, or fiery darts;' the addition of the epithet serving to mark the fell nature of the attack, and to warn the combatant; πεπ. δὲ αὐτὰ κέκληκεν διεγείρων τοὺς στρατιώτας, καὶ κελεύων ἀσφαλῶς περιφράττεσθαι, Theodoret. Allusion is here distinctly made to the πυρφόροι ὀϊστοί, arrows, darts, etc., tipped with some imflammable substance, which were used both by the Hebrews (Psalm vii. 14), Greeks (Herodotus, VIII. 52, Thucyd. II. 75, Arrian, *Alex.* II. 18), and Romans ('malleoli,' Cicero *pro Milone,* 24 : 'falaricæ,' Livy XXI. 8, were much larger), in sieges, or, under certain circumstances, against the enemy in the field; see Vegetius, *de Re Mil.* IV. 18, Winer, *RWB.* Art. 'Bogen,' Vol. I. p. 190. Any reference to 'poisoned' darts (Hamm. al.) is not in accordance

with the meaning and tense of the part. πεπυρωμένα. It may be remarked that the art. is not found in BD¹FG, and is rejected by *Lachm.*; in which case πεπυρ. will become a 'tertiary' predicate, and must be translated 'fire-tipt as they are,' see esp. Donalds. *Gr.* § 489 sq., and comp. Winer, *Gr.* § 20, 1. obs. p. 122. It seems, however, much more probable that the art. was omitted by an oversight, than that the transcriber felt any grammatical difficulty, and sought to remedy it by insertion. σβέσαι] 'to quench.' It seems too much to say with Calv., 'improprie loquitur.' That the use of σβέσαι was suggested by πεπυρ. is not improbable; as, however, it is certain that the larger shields, which for lightness were made of wood, were covered with hides (μοσχείῳ δέρματι, Polyb. *Hist.* VI. 23. 3, Lips. *de Milit.* III. 2) and similar materials designed to prevent the full effect of the βέλη πεπυρ., the particular verb cannot in any way be considered here as inappropriate; comp. Arrian, *Alex.* II. 18.

17. καὶ τὴν κ.τ.λ.] Meyer rightly objects to the punctuation of *Lachm.* and *Tisch.*: a comma, or perhaps rather a colon (Wordsw.), is here far more suitable than a period. We have here only one of St. Paul's rapid transitions from the participial structure to that of the finite verb; see Col. i. 6, and notes ch. i. 20. δέξασθε] 'receive,' as from Him who furnishes the armor (ver. 13), and whose Spirit puts in our hands the sword; 'accipite, oblatam a Domino,' Beng. The verb is omitted by D¹ FG; Clarom.; Cypr., Tertull., al., and converted into δέξασθαι by Matth. with AD³ (E?) KL; mss.; Cypr. (1), — but in neither case on sufficient external evidence. τοῦ σωτηρίου] 'of salvation;' gen. of apposition, as in ver. 14, 16. The use of this abstract neuter is,

περικεφαλαίαν τοῦ σωτηρίου δέξασθε, καὶ τὴν μάχαιραν τοῦ Πνεύ
ματος, ὅ ἐστι ῥῆμα Θεοῦ· ¹⁸ διὰ πάσης προσευχῆς καὶ δεήσεως
προσευχόμενοι ἐν παντὶ καιρῷ ἐν Πνεύματι, καὶ εἰς αὐτὸ ἀγρυπ

with the exception of this place, confined
to St. Luke (see Luke ii. 30, iii. 6, Acts
xxviii. 28), though sufficiently common
in the LXX; compare Isaiah lix. 17,
περικεφ. σωτηρίου, — a passage to which
its present occurrence may perhaps be
referred. There is no ground for supposing that τοῦ σωτ. is masculine ('salu-
taris, sc. Christi,' Beng.), either here or
Acts l. c., nor can we say with Mey. that
τὸ σωτήριον is 'any ideal possession :'
in 1 Thess. v. 8, the περικεφαλαία is the
ἐλπὶς σωτηρίας, in the present case there
is no such limitation. Salvation in
Christ, as Harl. remarks, forms the subject of faith ; in faith (by grace, ch. ii. 5)
it is apprehended, and becomes even, in a
certain sense, a present possession ; see
notes, ch. ii. 8.　　τοῦ Πνεύματος]
'of the Spirit;' sc. given by, supplied by
the Spirit ; the gen. of the source or
origin, as in verse 13, τὴν πανοπλ. τοῦ
Θεοῦ. The gen. is clearly not appositional (Œcum. 1., Theophyl. 1., and even
Harl., Olsh.), as the explanatory clause
would thus be wholly out of place. Still
less probable is a gen. of quality, ἡ μά
χαιρα πνευματική (Chrys. 2), or a simple
gen. of possession, in reference to the
τιμωρητικὴ ἐνέργεια (Sever. ap. Cram.
Cat.) of the Spirit, both of which seem
at variance with the general tenor of the
passage, which represents the 'armatura' as furnished to us by God. Thus
then it is from the Spirit that we receive
the sword, that sword being the Word
of God, the Gospel (ver. 15), which is
the δύναμις Θεοῦ (Rom. i. 16, 1 Cor. i.
18) to every one who believeth; comp.
Heb. iv. 12.
　　18. διὰ πάσης κ.τ.λ.] 'with all
(every form of) prayer and supplication
praying;' participial clause expressive
of the manner and accompaniments of

the action, dependent on the principal
imperative στῆτε οὖν (Mey.), not on the
subordinate aor. imper. δέξασθε, which is
only a variation of the participial structure, and with which the idea of duration expressed in πάσης and παντὶ καιρῷ
would not be consistent. The seeming
tautology and an imaginary logical difficulty in προσεύχεσθαι διὰ πάσης προσ. ἐν
παντὶ καιρῷ have induced Mey. to disconnect διὰ πάσης κ. τ. λ. and προσευχόμενοι.
This, though not inconsistent with the
use of διὰ ('conditio in quâ locatus aliquid facias,' Fritz. Rom. ii. 27, Vol. 1. p.
138), is still neither necessary nor satisfactory : διὰ πάσης κ. τ. λ. simply and
correctly denotes the earnest (because
varied) character of the prayer (see
Theophyl.) ; ἐν παντὶ καιρῷ, the constancy of it (ἐνδελεχῶς, Theod., comp.
Luke xviii. 1, 1 Thess. v. 17, 2 Thess. i.
11) ; ἐν Πνεύματι (see infra), the holy
sphere of it. Conyb. (comp. Syr., but
not Æth., Syr.-Phil.) translates the part.
as a simple imperat., and makes ver. 18
the beginning of a new paragraph ; this,
however, cannot be justified ; see Winer,
Gr. § 45. 6, p. 313.　　It has been
doubted whether there is here any exact
distinction between προσευχὴ (חְפִלָּה) and
δέησις (חְחִנָּה). Chrys. and Theodoret
on 1 Tim. ii. 1 explain προσ. as αἴτησις
ἀγαθῶν (see Suicer, Thesaur. s. v. 1),
δέησ. as ὑπὲρ ἀπαλλαγῆς λυπηρῶν ἱκετεία
(so Grot., as ἀπὸ τοῦ δεοῦς, but see 2
Cor. i. 11) ; comp. Origen, de Orat. § 33,
Vol. xvii. p. 292 (ed. Lomm.). Alii
alia. The most natural and obvious distinction is that adopted by nearly all recent commentators, viz. that προσευχὴ is
a 'vocabulum sacrum' (see Harl.) denoting 'prayer' in general, precatio, δέ
ησις, a 'vocabulum commune,' denoting
a special character or form of it, 'pe-

νοῦντες ἐν πάσῃ προσκαρτερήσει καὶ δεήσει περὶ πάντων τῶν
ἁγίων, ¹⁹ καὶ ὑπὲρ ἐμοῦ, ἵνα μοι δοθῇ λόγος ἐν ἀνοίξει τοῦ

tition,' *rogatio;* see Fritz. *Rom.* x. 1,
Vol. ii. p. 372, and notes *on* 1 *Tim. l. c.*
ἐν παντὶ καιρῷ] '*in every season.*'
There is no necessity to restrict this to
'every fitting season,' Eadie; the *mind*
of prayer (τὸ ὁμιλεῖν τῷ Θεῷ, Theophyl.
on 1 *Thess.* v. 17) is alluded to as much
as the outward act; see Alford *on Luke*
xviii. 1. ἐν Πνεύματι] '*in the
Spirit;*' certainly not the *human* spirit
('cum devoto cordis effectu,' Est.), nor
as in contrast to βαττολογεῖν (Chrys.),
but, the Holy Spirit (Jude 20), *in* whose
blessed and indwelling influence, and by
whose merciful aid we are enabled to
pray (Rom. viii. 15, Gal. iv. 6), yea, and
who Himself intercedes for us (Rom.
viii. 26). εἰς αὐτὸ] '*for this,*'
thereunto; scil. τὸ προσεύχεσθαι ἐν παντὶ
καιρῷ ἐν Πνεύματι. The reference is
obviously not to what follows (Holzh.),
but to what *precedes.* It was 'for *this*'
(scarcely more than 'in respect of *this,*'
Mey.) that the Ephesians were to be
watchful; not that *all* should abide in
continual prayer (Olsh., Harl.), for the
prayer for the Apostle (ver. 19) is to be
for a different spiritual grace, but that
they themselves might have that grace
('ut quotidie oretis,' Est.), and exercise
it in general, persistent, and appropriate
supplications for all saints. The
addition of τοῦτο after αὐτὸ [*Rec.* with
DᵍEKL; mss.; Chrys.-text, Theod.,
al.] is rightly rejected by *Lachm., Tisch.,*
al., with AB (D¹FG; αὐτὸν); Clarom.,
Vulg., Copt., al., as a mere explanatory
addition: 'αὐτὸς sæpius dicitur de eo de
quo cummaxime sermo est,' Kühner
Xen. *Mem.* iii. 10, 14, comp. Matth. *Gr.*
§ 469. 7. ἀγρυπ. ἐν πάσῃ
προσκαρτ. κ. τ. λ.] '*watching in all
perseverance and supplication,*' 'in omni
instantiâ et observatione,' Vulg.; supplementary clause, specifying a particu-

lar accompaniment to their prayer and
watchfulness in regard to themselves,
and a particular phase and aspect which
it was to assume; 'in praying for themselves, they were uniformly to blend
petitions for all the saints,' Eadie; compare Col. iv. 2, γρηγοροῦντες ἐν αὐτῇ
(προσευχῇ) ἐν εὐχαριστίᾳ, where ἐν εὐχ.
denotes the attendant, *concomitant* act,
one of the forms which προσευχὴ was to
assume. The two substantives
προσκαρτ. καὶ δεήσ., though not merely
equivalent to 'precantes sedulo' (Syr.
comp. Æth.), still *practically* amount to
a 'hendiadys.' According to the regular rule, the substantive which contains
the 'accidens' ought to *follow* rather
than precede (see Winer, *de Hypall. et
Hendiad.* p. 19), still here προσκ. so
clearly receives its explanation from καὶ
δεήσει, that the expression, though not a
strict and grammatical, is yet a virtual,
or what might be termed a *contextual* ἓν
διὰ δυοῖν; see esp. Fritz. *Matth.* p. 857.
On προσκαρτ. comp. notes *on Col.* iv. 2.

19. καί] '*and*, to add a particular
case;' on this use of καί in appending a
special example to a general classifica-
tion, see Winer, *Gr.* § 53. 3, p. 388,
notes on ch. v. 18, and *on Phil.* iv. 21.
ὑπὲρ ἐμοῦ] '*for me,*' '*in behalf of me.*'
Eadie (after Harl.) endeavors to trace a
distinction between ὑπὲρ here, and περὶ
ver. 18, as if the former was more special and individualizing, the latter more
general and indefinite; 'sorgt um Alle,
auch *für* mich,' Harl. This, in the present case, where the two prepp. are so
contiguous, is *plausible,* but, as a general
rule, little more can be said than that
ὑπὲρ in its ethical sense perhaps retains
some stronger trace of its local meaning
than περί; see notes *on Gal.* i. 4, *on
Phil.* i. 7, and compare Krüger, *Sprachl.*
§ 68. 28. 3. ἵνα μοι δοθῇ

στόματός μου ἐν παῤῥησίᾳ γνωρίσαι τὸ μυστήριον τοῦ εὐαγγελίου,
²⁰ ὑπὲρ οὗ πρεσβεύω ἐν ἁλύσει, ἵνα ἐν αὐτῷ παῤῥησιάσωμαι ὡς
δεῖ με λαλῆσαι.

λόγος] 'that there may be given to me;' particular object of the ἀγρυπν. ἐν προσ-καρτ., with an included reference to the subject of the prayer; comp. notes on ch. i. 17. The δοθῇ, as its position seems to indicate, is emphatic: it was a special gift of God, and felt to be so by the Apostle, 'non nitebatur Paulus habitu suo,' Beng. The reading of Rec., δοθείη (which rests only on the authority of a few cursive mss.), would give the purpose a more subjective reference, and represent the feeling of a more dependent realization; comp. ch. i. 17, and see esp. Klotz, Devar. Vol. ii. p. 622, Herm. Soph. Elect. 57.   ἐν ἀνοίξει στόμ.] 'in the opening of my mouth;' act in which and occasion at which the gift was to be realized, the connection clearly being with the preceding (Syr., Chrysost., al.), not with the following words (Auth., Kypke), and the meaning not 'ad apertionem,' i. e. 'ut os aperiam' (Beza), or, in passive reference to himself, and active to God, 'ut Deus aperiat os meum' (comp. Æth.), i. e. 'that my mouth may be opened' (a Lap., Olsh.; comp. Psalm l. 17), but simply 'in the opening of my mouth' ('occasione datâ,' Grot.), 'dum os aperio,' Est.; so Mey., Eadie, al.; see esp. Fritz. Dissert. ii. ad 2 Cor. p. 99 sq.   The expression ἀνοίγειν στόμα may be briefly noticed. When not specially modified or explained by the context (comp. 2 Cor. vi. 11), it does not, on the one hand, appear to have any prelusive reference to the nature or quality of the discourse (οὐκ ἄρα ἐμελέτα ἅπερ ἔλεγεν Chrysost., 'ore semiclauso proferuntur ambigua,' Calv.), nor, on the other, is to be considered as merely graphic and unemphatic (Fritz. loc. cit., and on Matth. v. 2), but nearly always appears to specify the

solemnity of the act and the occasion; compare Matth. v. 2, Job iii. 1, Dan. x. 16, Acts viii. 35, and appy. xviii. 14 [it was a grave answer before a tribunal], and see Tholuck, Bergpr. p. 60 sq. ἐν παῤῥησίᾳ γνωρίσαι] 'with boldness (of speech) to make known,' 'cum fiduciâ, notum facere,' Clarom., Vulg.; specification of the result contemplated in the gift ('ut mihi contingat λόγος, inde autem nascatur τὸ ἐν παῤῥ. γνωρίσαι,' Fritz. ad 2 Cor. p. 100), and of the spirit by which it was to be marked. As ἐν ἀνοίξ. τοῦ στόμ. hinted at the solemn and responsible nature of the act, so ἐν παῤῥ. refers qualitatively to the character and spirit of the preaching; θάρσος καὶ λόγου χορηγίαν ἵνα κατὰ τὸν θεῖον λόγον πληρώσω τὸν δρόμον, Theodoret. On the meaning of παῤῥησία, see notes on 1 Tim. iii. 13.   τὸ μυστ. τοῦ εὐαγγελ.] 'the mystery of the Gospel.' The gen. is somewhat different to τὸ μυστήρ. τοῦ θελήματος, ch. i. 9; there it was 'the mystery in the matter of, concerning the θέλημα,'—gen. objecti; here it is rather 'the mystery which the εὐαγγέλ. has, involves,'—gen. subjecti. The distinction between these two forms of gen. is briefly but ably stated by Krüger, Sprachl. § 47. 7. On the meaning of μυστήριον, comp. notes on ch. v. 32.   The concluding words τοῦ εὐαγγελ. are omitted by BFG; Boern.; Tert., Ambrst., and bracketed by Lachmann, but rightly retained by Tisch., Alf., Wordsw. on distinctly preponderating evidence.

20. ὑπὲρ οὗ] 'in commodum cujus,' 'to preach which.' The reference of οὗ is doubtful; it can, however, scarcely be 'to the preceding clause,' Eadie; for as this involves two moments of thought, ἐν παῤῥ. and γνωρ., and as αὐτὸ would

I have sent Tychicus to tell you of my state and to comfort you.

²¹ Ἵνα δὲ εἰδῆτε καὶ ὑμεῖς τὰ κατ᾽ ἐμέ, τί

certainly seem to have the same reference as ὅ, there would be an inevitable tautology in ἐν αὐτῷ (scil. τὸ ἐν παῤῥ. κ. τ. λ.) παῤῥησιάσωμαι. The reference must then be either simply to τὸ εὐαγγέλ. (Harl.) or more probably to τὸ μυστ. τοῦ εὐαγγελ. (Mey.), as this was what the Apostle ἐγνώρισεν, and in the matter of which he prayed for the grace of παῤῥησία. πρεσβεύω ἐν ἁλύσει] 'I am an ambassador in a chain,' 'in catenâ,' Clarom., Vulg., but ܐܣܝܪܐ [in catenis] Syr., and similarly Copt., Goth., Arm. [gābānok, no sing.]; a noticeable and appy. designedly antithetical collocation, 'I am an ambassador — in chains;' 'alias legati jure gentium sancti et inviolabiles,' Wetst., compare Theoph. It seems doubtful whether any historical allusion to a 'custodia militaris' (Beza, Grot.; on which see esp. Wieseler, Synops. p. 394, note) is actually involved in the present use of the singular; comp. Acts xxviii. 20, 2 Tim. i. 16, Joseph. Antiq. XVIII. 6, 10, and see Paley, Hor. Paul. VI. 5, Wieseler, Synops. p. 420. As the singular is not conclusive, being often used, especially in the case of material objects, in a collective sense (see Krüger, Sprachl. § 44. 1, 1, Bernhardy, Synt. II. 1, p. 58), and as the use of the word in St. Paul's Epp. (here and 2 Tim. i. 16) is confined to the singular, it seems uncritical to press the allusion, though it still may be regarded as by no means improbable: ἅλυσις is used in the singular (εἰς τὴν ἅλυσιν ἐμπίπτειν), but with the article and in a more general sense, in Polyb. Hist. XIX. 3. 3, IV. 76. 5. ἵνα κ. τ. λ.] 'in order that I may speak boldly;' second purpose and object of the ἀγρυπν. κ. τ. λ., ver. 18. There seems no reason to depart from the ordinary interpr.; the second ἵνα κ. τ. λ. is not dependent

on πρεσβ. ἐν ἁλύσει (Beng.), nor subordinate to (Harl.), but coördinate with ἵνα δοθῇ (comp. Rom. vii. 13, Gal. iii. 14), and involves no tautology. The first of the two final sentences relates to the gift of utterance and παῤῥ. generally, the second, to the gift of a conditioned παῤῥ., — scil. ὡς δεῖ με λαλῆσαι. ἐν αὐτῷ] 'in it,' 'therein;' scil. ἐν τῷ μυστ. τοῦ εὐαγγελ., — 'occupied with it, engaged in preaching it.' Ἐν here marks, not so much the (official) sphere in which. (see Rom. i. 9, λατρεύω ἐν εὐαγγελίῳ), as the substratum on which the παῤῥησία was to be displayed and exercised; see Krüger, Sprachl. § 68. 12. 6, and notes on Gal. i. 23. It can scarcely denote the source or ground of the παῤῥ., Harl.; for, as 1 Thess. ii. 2, ἐπαῤῥησιασάμεθα ἐν τῷ Θεῷ κ. τ. λ. (cited by Harless) clearly shows, God was the source and causal sphere of the παῤῥ (see notes in loc.); the Gospel (here 'the mystery of the Gosp.') the object in which and about which it was to be manifested: see exx. in Bernhardy, Synt. v. 8. b, p. 212.

21. ἵνα δὲ εἰδῆτε καὶ ὑμ.] 'But in order that ye also may know;' transition by means of the δὲ μεταβατικόν, see notes on Gal. i. 11, to the last and valedictory portion of the Epistle. In the words καὶ ὑμεῖς the καὶ is certainly something more than a mere 'particle of transition' (Eadie, Ruck.). It indisputably refers to others besides the Ephesians, but who they were cannot be satisfactorily determined. If the Epistle to the Colossians was written first, καὶ might point to the Colossians (Harl., Einleit. p. 60, Wiggers, Stud. u. Krit. 1841, p. 453, Meyer, Einleit. p. 17, Wieseler, Synops. p. 432), but as the priority of that Ep., though by no means improbable both from internal (Neander, Planting, Vol. I. p. 329 Bohn, comp. Schleierm.

πράσσω, πάντα ὑμῖν γνωρίσει Τύχικος ὁ ἀγαπητὸς ἀδελφὸς καὶ
πιστὸς διάκονος ἐν Κυρίῳ, ²²ὃν ἔπεμψα πρὸς ὑμᾶς εἰς αὐτὸ τοῦτο,
ἵνα γνῶτε τὰ περὶ ἡμῶν καὶ παρακαλέσῃ τὰς καρδίας ὑμῶν.

Stud. u. Krit. 1832, p. 500) and perhaps external considerations (see Wieseler, *Syn.* p. 450 sq.), is still very doubtful (see Credner, *Einleit.* § 157, Reuss, *Gesch. des N. T.* § 119), this seems all that can be said, — that the use of καὶ is certainly noticeable, and not to be explained away, and that though *per se* it cannot safely be relied upon as an argument in favor of the priority of the Ep. to the Colossians, it still, on that hypothesis, admits of an easy and natural explanation. The article by Wiggers, above referred to, though in several points far from conclusive, deserves perusal. The reading is somewhat doubtful: *Lachm.* adopts the order καὶ ὑμεῖς εἰδ. with ADEFG (AD¹FG ἰδ.); Clarom., Vulg., al.; Theod., Lat. Ff.,— but appy. with less probability than the text, which is found in BKL; great majority of mss.; Syr. (both), Basm.; Chrys., Dam., Jerome, al., and adopted by *Tisch.*, and most recent editors.
τί πράσσω] '*how I fare;*' not 'quid (in carcere) agam' (Wolf), but simply 'quid agam,' Clarom., Vulg., — in simple explanation of τὰ κατ᾽ ἐμέ; see Arrian, *Epict.* I. 19, τί πράσσει Φηλικίων, Ælian, *Var. Hist.* II. 35, ἤρετο, τί πράττοι [ὁ ὑπὸ ἀσθενείας καταληφθείς], comp. Hor. *Sat.* I. 9. 4. Illustrations of τὰ κατ᾽ ἐμέ, 'res meas' (Phil. i. 12, Col. iv. 7), are cited by Elsner, *Obs.* Vol. II. p. 234: see Wetst. and Kypke. Τύχικος] Not Τυχικός (*Griesb.*, *Tisch.* ed. 7), see Winer, *Gr.* § 6, p. 49. Tychicus was an Ἀσιανός, and is mentioned Acts xx. 4, Col. iv. 7, 2 Tim. iv. 12, Tit. iii. 12. Tradition represents him as afterwards bishop of Chalcedon in Bithynia, of Colophon, or of Neapolis in Cyprus; see *Acta Sanct.* April 29, Vol. III. p. 613. The order γνωρίσει ὑμῖν, though found in BD

EFG; 3 mss.; Clarom., Sangerm. Aug., Boern., Goth., al; Ambrst. (*Lachm.*), is rightly reversed by *Tisch.*, Alf., Wordsw., on fair evidence [AKL; nearly all mss.; Vulg. (Amit., Demid., — not Fuld), Syr.-Phil., al.; Chrys., Theod., al.], being not unlikely a conformation to Col. iv. 7.   πιστός] '*faithful,*' '*trusty;*' not ἀξιόπιστος, scil. οὐδὲν ψεύσεται ἀλλὰ πάντα ἀληθεύσει, Chrys., Beng.; for, as Mey. remarks, he was probably known to the Ephesians (comp. Acts xx. 4), though probably not to the Colossians.
διάκονος ἐν Κυρίῳ] '*minister in the Lord;*' Christ was the sphere of his ministrations, Christ's Spirit animated and actuated his labors. It does not seem necessary to refer the term διάκονος to any special ('sacrâ ordinatione diaconum fuisse,' Est.), or any general office ('qui Evangelio navat operam,' Grot.) in relation to the Gospel, but merely in reference to his services *to St. Paul;* see Col. iv. 7, πιστὸς διάκονος καὶ σύνδουλος, where, as Meyer and De W. observe, the latter term is intended to heighten and dignify the former; comp. also 2 Tim. iv. 7.

22. ὃν ἔπεμψα πρὸς ὑμᾶς] '*whom I have sent to you;*' not 'I send' (Words.) — which, though not appy. inconsistent with the usage of the New Testament (see Winer, *Gr.* § 40. 5. 2, p. 249), does not seem accordant with the probable circumstances. Tychicus appears to have been sent with Onesimus to Colossæ on a special mission (Col. iv. 8), of which the Apostle availed himself so far as to send this letter by him; this mission, however, the Apostle naturally regards as an act belonging to the past, and so probably uses ἔπεμψα in its ordinary sense.   εἰς αὐτὸ τοῦτο] '*for this very purpose,* and no other,'

Peace be to the brethren, and grace to all true Christians.

²³ Εἰρήνη τοῖς ἀδελφοῖς καὶ ἀγάπη μετὰ πίστεως ἀπὸ Θεοῦ πατρὸς καὶ Κυρίου Ἰησοῦ Χριστοῦ. ²⁴ Ἡ χάρις μετὰ πάντων τῶν ἀγαπώντων

viz., in reference to, and further explained by what follows; not 'for the same purpose,' Auth.; comp. Phil. i. 28, Col. iv. 8, and notes *in loc.* The preposition is sometimes omitted; see Plat. *Sympos.* 204 A, and Stalb. *in loc.*; comp. ib. *Legg.* III. 686 c, *Protag.* 310 E.

ἵνα γνῶτε κ. τ. λ.] 'in order that ye may know the things concerning us;' obviously similar in meaning to εἰδῆτε τὰ κατ' ἐμέ, but perhaps with a more inclusive reference both to himself and those with him.   παρακαλέσῃ] 'comfort,' 'consoletur,' Vulg. (comp. Goth. 'gaþvasstjai'), here judiciously changed from the 'exhorte[n]tur' of Clarom.; see Col. iv. 7. The subject of the παράκλησις may have been 'ne offenderetis in meis vinculis' (Bengel), or 'ne animis deficiatis ob meas tribulationes' (Est.; compare ch. iii. 13); so also Œcum., Theophyl.; it is better, however, from our ignorance of the exact state of the church to leave the precise reference undefined, and to extend it generally to all particulars in which they needed it. On the meaning of the word, see notes on ch. iv. 1, and *on* 1 *Thess.* v. 11.

23. εἰρήνη] '*Peace*,' simply; not 'concordia,' Calvin, 'peaceableness,' Hamm. (comp. εἰρηνεύετε, 2 Cor. xiii. 11), as the Epistle, though εἰρηνικὸς (De Wette) in relation to the doctrinal aspects of the union of Jews and Gentiles (see ch. ii.), contains no special exhortations on the subject of concord generally. Εἰρήνη is however no mere parting salutation (comp. notes ch. i. 3, and *on Gal.* i. 3), but is in effect a valedictory prayer for that γαληνὴ καὶ εὐδία ψυχῆς (Orig. ap. Cram. *Cat.*) which was the blessed result of reconciliation with God, and His Spirit's special gift; see Steiger *on* 1 *Pet.* i. 2, Reuss, *Théol. Chrét.* IV.

18, Vol. II. p. 200 sq.   τοῖς ἀδελφοῖς] '*the brethren* at Ephesus.' Wieseler (*Synops.* p. 444) refers ἀδελφ. specially to the *Jewish* Christians, πάντων to the *Gentile* Christians. This is surely a very doubtful, and even improbable interpretation; for is it likely that, in an epistle so opposed in its tenor to all national distinctions, any such special recognition of their existence would be found? Clearly οἱ ἀδελφοὶ can only mean 'the whole Christian brotherhood.' ἀγάπη μετὰ πίστεως] '*love with faith*,' not ἀγάπη καὶ πίστις; the Apostle does not simply pray for the presence of each of these graces in his converts, for, as Olsh. correctly observes, he assumed πίστις to be there already; what he prays for is their *coëxistence*. As love (not here the divine love, Beng.) is the characteristic of a true faith, the medium by which its energy is displayed (Gal. v. 6), so here faith is represented as the perpetual *concomitant* of a true love. If it had been ἀγάπ. σὺν πίστει it would rather have conveyed the here scarcely realizable conception of their *coherence*; compare ch. iv. 31, πικρία . . . . . . σὺν κακίᾳ [badness of heart was the 'fermentum,' the active principle]; 1 Cor. x. 13, σὺν τῷ πειρασμῷ καὶ τὴν ἔκβασιν [not the one without the other]; see Krüger, *Sprachl.* § 68. 13. 1. On the connection of love and faith, compare Reuss, *Théol. Chrét.* IV. 19, Vol. II. p. 205, and on the whole verse, a short but not very connected sermon of Augustine, *Serm.* CLXXVIII. Vol. v. p. 911 (ed. Migne).

24. ἡ χάρις] '*Grace*,' κατ' ἐξοχήν; the grace of God in Jesus Christ (Mey.). The use of the article is in harmony with the immediately preceding and succeeding mention of Him through whom

τὸν Κύριον ἡμῶν Ἰησοῦν Χριστὸν ἐν ἀφθαρσίᾳ.

(John i. 17) ἡ χάρις ἐγένετο. μετὰ πάντων κ. τ. λ.] 'with all that love our Lord, J. C.;' second and more general and comprehensive form of benediction. Meyer compares the similar maledictory form in 1 Cor. xvi. 22.

ἐν ἀφθαρσίᾳ] 'in incorruption,'
ܠ ‍ ‍ ‍ [sine corruptione] Syr., 'in incorruptione,' Vulg., Copt., 'incorruptione,' Clarom., Arm., 'in unriurein,' Goth., 'in non-interitu,' Æth.-Platt. The connection of this clause and the meaning of the words are both somewhat doubtful, and must be noticed separately. (1) *Meaning;* excluding all arbitrary interpretations of the preposition, e. g. ὑπέρ (Chrys. 2), διά Theophyl.), μετά (Theod.), εἰς (Beza), and all doubtful explanations of ἀφθαρσίᾳ, whether temporal (sc. εἰς τὸν αἰῶνα, Matth.), brachylogical (ἵνα ζωὴν ἔχωσιν ἐν ἀφθ., Olsh.), abstr. for concrete — really (ἐν ἀφθάρτοις, Chrys. 2) or virtually ('in unvergänglichem Wesen,' Harless), — we have *three* probable interpr.; (a) *ethical,* 'sincerity,' Auth. Version, Chrys., compare 1 Pet. iii. 4; (b) *quasi-local,* in reference to the sphere of the ἀγάπη; comp. ἐν ἐπουρανίοις; (c) simply *qualitative, i. e.* '*imperishableness,*' Œcum., Mey., al. To (a) the lexical meaning of the word is seriously opposed; see Meyer. St. Paul's use of ἀφθαρσίᾳ is perhaps rather in favor of (b), as in all the six other passages where it occurs (Tit. ii. 3 [*Rec.*] is very doubtful) ἀφθ. refers directly or indirectly to a higher sphere than the present; still as ἀφθ. is

anarthrous, and the explanation difficult, unless the unsatisfactory construction (β), see below, be adopted, we decide in favor of (c), and regard ἐν as marking the manner, or rather conditioning *sphere,* in which the action takes place; comp. esp. Tit. iii. 15. (2) *Connection;* three constructions have been suggested; (a) with Ἰησ. Χρ., scil. ' Christum immortalem non humilem,' Wetst.; — (β) with ἡ χάρις, Harl., Stier; — (γ) with ἀγαπώντων, Chrys., Theod. Of these (a) is inadmissible, being exegetically unsatisfactory, and, on account of the absence of the article, grammatically suspicious; (β) is harsh, especially in a simple benediction, on account of the intercalation of so many words between the nom. and the modal factor of the sentence; (γ) is adopted by all the Greek commentators, and seems most simple and satisfactory; we translate, therefore, 'grace be with all who love our Lord Jesus Christ *in incorruption, i. e.* in a manner and in an element that knows neither change, diminution, nor decay;' ἡ γὰρ εἰς τὸν Χρ. ἀγάπη ἄφθαρτος καὶ ἀμείωτος μᾶλλον δὲ καθ' ἑκάστην ἐπιδιδοῦσα τὴν ἡμέραν ὤφελεν εἶναι, Œcumen. Thus, then, this significant clause not only defines what the essence of the ἀγάπη is, but indicates what it ought to be, — perennial, immutable, incorruptible. The concluding ἀμὴν [Rec. with DEKL; most Vv. and Ff.] is perhaps rightly rejected by Lachm., Tisch., al. [with ABFG; 2 mss., Aug., Boern., Amit*., Tol., Basm., Æth.-Pol., and some Ff.], as a liturgical addition.

21

TRANSLATION.

NOTICE.

THE principles on which this translation is based are explained in the general Preface to the commentary *on the Galatians*, and in the notice prefixed to the translation of that Epistle. The English Versions with which the translation is compared, and the editions which have been used, are the same as those used in the Translation of the former Epistle, with this exception, that I have also made extracts from the second *edition* (if indeed that be a right title) of the Genevan Version published in 1560. My attention has been particularly called to this Version by a kind correspondent (Mr. H. Craik), who appears to me to have so far successfully confirmed the statements in Kitto's *Biblical Cyclopædia* (Art. ' Versions '), relative to this Version, as to make it seem *very* doubtful whether the edition of 1557, reprinted by Messrs. Bagster, has in any degree the same claims to be considered *THE* GENEVAN VERSION, as that published three years later. Without venturing to come to a positive decision on a question which requires much investigation, I have still thought it highly desirable to place before the student, under the title of *Gen.* 2, extracts from this later and for a long time popular edition, and to call attention to the apparently slender authority of the edition of 1557 as a formal representation of the views of the translators of Geneva. Fresh citations from the other Versions have in a few cases been added, and some errors detected and rectified.

THE EPISTLE TO THE EPHESIANS.

CHAPTER I. 1.

PAUL, an apostle of Christ Jesus by the will of God, to the saints which are in Ephesus, and to the faithful in Christ Jesus. ² Grace *be* to you, and peace, from God our Father and the Lord Jesus Christ.

³ Blessed be God and the Father of our Lord Jesus Christ, who blessed us with every blessing of the Spirit in the heavenly *regions*

---

1. *Christ Jesus*] * ' Jesus Christ,' *Auth.* *In Ephesus*] ' At Ephesus,' *Auth.* and all the other Vv.

2. *And the Lord*] So *Wicl., Cov., Rhem.:* ' and *from* the Lord,' *Auth.* and remaining Vv. The prep. in such cases as the present should certainly be omitted, as tending to make that unity of source from whence the grace and peace come less apparent than the Greek; comp. notes *on Phil.* i. 2. *God and the Father*] So *Wicl., Cov.* (Test.), *Rhem.:* ' the God and Father,' *Auth.*; ' God the Father,' *Tynd.* and remaining Vv. except *Gen.* 2, ' God even the Father.'

3. *Blessed us*] ' Hath blessed us,' *Auth.* and all the other Vv. The aorist here ought certainly to be maintained in translation, as the allusion is to the past act of the Redemption. The idiom of our language *frequently* interferes with the regular application of the rule, but it

is still no less certain that the English præterite is the nearest equivalent of the Greek aor., see Latham, *Engl. Lang.* § 360, 361, and compare Scholef. *Hints* (Pref.), p. xi. It is possible that there are cases when the English present, owing to its expressing an habitual action (Latham, § 573), might *seem* to correspond to the Greek aor., but as the iterative force of the latter tense, even if admitted (see notes *on Gal.* v. 24), seems radically to differ from that of the Engl. pres. (the one expressing indefinite recurrence in the *past*, see Jelf, *Gr.* § 402, 1, the other indef. recurrence in the *present*), it will seem best not to venture on any such translation. *Every blessing*] So *Cov.* (Test.), and sim. *Tynd., Cov., Cran., Gen.* 1: ' all,' *Auth.* and the remaining Vv. *Of the Spirit*] ' Spiritual,' *Auth.* and all the other Vv.; see notes. *The heavenly regions*]

in Christ : ⁴ even as He chose us in Him before the foundation of the world, that we should be holy and blameless before Him ; ⁵ having foreordained us IN LOVE for adoption through Jesus Christ into Himself, according to the good pleasure of His will, ⁶ to the praise of the glory of His grace, wherein He bestowed grace on us in the Beloved ; ⁷ in whom we are having redemption through His blood, the forgiveness of our transgressions, according to the richness of His grace, ⁸ which He made to abound towards us in all wisdom

'Heavenly places,' *Auth.* and all Vv. except *Rhem.*, 'in cœlestials.'

4. *Even as*] 'According as,' *Auth.*, *Tynd.*, *Cov.*, *Cran.*, *Gen.*, *Bish.* ; 'as,' *Wicl.*, *Cov.* (Test.), *Gen.* 2, *Rhem.* *Chose*] So *Rhem.* : 'hath chosen,' *Auth.*, *Wicl.*, *Coverd.* (Test.), *Gen.* 2 ; 'had chosen,' *Tynd.*, *Cran.*, *Gen.* *Blameless*] 'Without blame,' *Auth.*, *Tynd.*, *Cov.*, *Cran.*, *Gen.* (both), *Bish.* ; 'without wemme,' *Wicl.*; 'unspotted,' *Cov.* (Test.); 'immaculate,' *Rhem.* The slight change has been made for the sake of retaining the same translation both here and ch. v. 27. On the distinction between ἄμωμος ('in quo nihil est quod reprehendas') and ἄμεμπτος ('in quo nihil desiderari potest'), see Tittm. *Synon.* p. 29.

5. *Having, etc.*] *Auth.* and all the other Vv. connect with the preceding verse; see notes. The participle expresses probably a *temporal* relation, 'after He had, etc.,' but in so profound a subject it seems best to retain the more undefined transl. of *Auth.* *Fore-ordained*] Sim. *Wicl.*, 'bifore ordeyned ;' *Tynd.*, *Cov.*, *Cran.*, 'ordeyned before ;' 'predestinated,' *Auth.*, and sim. the remaining Vv. *For adoption*] 'Unto the adoption of children,' *Auth.*, sim. *Rhem.* : well translated by *Gen.* (both), 'to be adopted through J. C.,' but perhaps scarcely sufficiently literal. *Through*] So *Tynd.* and the other Vv. except *Auth.*, *Wicl.*, *Bish.*, *Rhem.*, 'by.' *Into Himself*] 'To Himself,' *Auth.*; 'into Him,' *Wicl.*, 'unto Him silfe,' *Tynd.*,

Cran., *Gen.* (both), *Bish.*, *Rhem.*; 'in Hymselfe,' *Cov.* (Test.). Whether we adopt the translation 'into' or 'unto' matters but little, both approximating to, but neither *fully* expressing the meaning of the inclusive εἰς, perhaps English idiom ('adopt into') is slightly in favor of the former. It seems also best in English, for the sake of *perspicuity*, to return to the reflexive form : 'into Him' (ed. 1), though literal, perhaps may seem ambiguous.

6. *Bestowed grace on us*] 'Hath made us accepted,' *Auth.* and all Vv. except *Wicl.*, 'hath glorified us,' *Rhem.*, 'hath gratified us.'

7. *We are having*] *Auth.* and all Vv., 'we have.' In the next words we must appy. be content to omit (with all the Vv.) the expressive article 'the redemption;' our idiom seeming to require some adject., e. g. 'the *promised* red.,' to make the article perfectly intelligible. *Our transgressions*] 'Sins,' *Auth.* and all Vv.

8. *Which He made to abound*] 'Hath abounded,' *Auth.*, *Bish.*; 'He shed on us abundantly,' *Tynd.*, and sim. *Cov.*; 'He hath ministered unto us abundantly,' *Cran.*; 'He hath been abundant towarde us,' *Gen.* 2 ; 'He abounded toward us,' *Gen.* On this clause a friend and accurate scholar has made the observation, that as all verbs of the character of περισσεύω may practically be resolved into a 'verbum faciendi' with an appended accus. elicited from the verb

and discernment ; [9] having made known unto us the mystery of His will, according to the good pleasure which He purposed in Himself [10] in reference to the dispensation of the fulness of times, to gather up again together all things in Christ, the things that are in heaven and the things that are on earth, *even* in Him ; [11] in whom we were also chosen as *His* inheritance, having been foreordained according to the purpose of Him who worketh all things after the counsel of His will ; [12] that we should be to the praise of His glory, who have

('make an abundance of') the gen. ἧς may here receive a simple explanation without reference to the principles of attraction. This remark appears to deserve consideration.   *Discernment*] 'Prudence,' *Auth.*, *Wicl.*, *Cov.* (both), *Cran.*, *Bish.*, *Rhem.* ; 'perceavaunce,' *Tynd.* ; 'understanding,' *Gen.* (both). The transl. 'prudence' appears to give the word a more decided reference to *practice* than the context will admit ; 'understanding,' on the other hand, is too abstract, and fails to recognize the distinction between σύνεσις and φρόνησις. Perhaps the transl. in the text, or 'intelligence,' as indicating an application and exercise of the φρήν, and a result of (spiritual) σοφία (comp. 1 Cor. ii. 13), approaches more nearly to the true meaning of the word in this passage

9. *The good, etc.*] ' His,' *Auth. Purposed*] So *Wicl.*, *Tynd.*, *Cov.* (Test.), *Rhem.* : 'hath purposed,' *Auth.* ; 'had purp.,' *Cov.*, *Cran.*, *Gen.* (both), *Bish.*

10. *In reference to*] ' That in the dispens.,' etc., *Auth.*, sim. *Gen.* (both) *Bish.* ; 'to have it declared when the tyme were full come,' *Tynd.*, *Cran.*, sim. *Cov.* ; 'in the dispens.,' *Cov.* (Test.) *Rhem.* The translation in the text, or 'with a view to ' (see notes), seems to make the meaning a little more distinct than the more usual ' for.'   *To gather up again together*] So *Gen.*, omitting 'up,' but with a different turn of sentence : ' He might gather together in one,' *Auth.*, *Gen.* 2, *Bish.* ; ' shuld be gaddered toge-

ther,' *Tynd.*, *Cov.* ; ' to enstore,' *Wicl.* ; ' to set up all things perfectly,' *Cov.* (Test.), sim. *Cran.* .   *The things, etc.*] So *Cov.* (Test.), and sim. *Cov.*, *Tynd.*, *Cran.*, ' both which are in heaven, and which are,' *Auth.*, *Bish.* : the repetition which the older translators thus preserve is perhaps not without force in this solemn enunciation of the eternal purpose of God.

11. *We were also, etc.*] 'Also we have obtained an,' *Auth.*, ' we ben clepid bi sorte,' *Wicl.*, sim. *Cov.* (Test.), *Rhem.* ; ' we are made heyres,' *Tynd.*, sim. *Cran.* ; ' by whom also we are come to the inheritaunce,' *Cov.* ; ' in whom also we are chosen,' *Gen.* (both), *Bish. Having been fore-ordained*] ' Being predestinated,' *Auth.* Some of the Vv. resolve the part. into a finite verb with the copula (' and were thereto predestinate,' *Tynd.*, *Cran.*), others, as *Gen.* 1, express more fully the temporal meaning (' when we were ') : the simpler translation of the text (comp. *Wicl.*, *Rhem.*) is appy. to be preferred.   *His will*] So *Wicl.*, *Rhem.* : ' His own will,' *Auth.* and remaining Vv.

12. *Who have, etc.*] ' Who first trusted,' *Auth.*, sim. *Gen.* (both) ; ' that had hoped bifor,' *Wicl.* ; ' even we whyche afore have hoped,' *Cov.* (Test.), sim. *Rhem.* ; ' we which before believed,' *Tynd.*, *Cran.*, sim. *Bish.* The force of the *perf.* part. should be retained in transl., esp. as this can so easily be done by the inserted ' have,' as *Cov.*, *Rhem.* ; the English

before hoped in Christ : [13] in whom ye too, having heard the word of truth, the gospel of your salvation, — in whom, *I say*, having also believed, ye were sealed with the holy Spirit of promise, [14] which is the earnest of our inheritance, for the redemption of the purchased possession, unto the praise of His glory.

[15] For this cause I also, having heard of the faith which is among you in the Lord Jesus, and the love which ye have unto all the saints, [16] cease not to give thanks for you, making mention of you in my prayers ; [17] that the God of our Lord Jesus Christ, the Father of glory, would give unto you the Spirit of wisdom and

perfect expresses the past in connection, by its efforts or consequences, with the present: see Latham, *Engl. Lang.* § 579 (ed. 3).

13. *Ye too having, etc.*] So with a similarly suspended member, *Rhem.*, 'in whom you also, when you had heard,' etc. : 'ye also *trusted* after that, etc.,' *Auth.*, sim. *Gen.* (both) ; 'in whom ye also (after that, etc , wherein ye beleved) were sealed,' *Tynd.* ; 'on whom also ye beloved after that,' *Coverd.*, similarly *Cov.* (Test.) ; 'we also believe forasmoch as we have,' *Cran.* ; 'in whom also ye hoped after that ye heard,' *Bish.*   *I say, having, etc.*] 'Also after that ye,' *Auth.* The change to the particip. structure in both members seems to make the sentence a little more distinct, and to preserve in the latter, the close connection of καί with πιστεύσαντες ; see notes. *The*] So all the Vv. except *Auth.*, 'that holy Spirit.'

14. *Which*] On the form 'which,' see notes *on Gal.* i. 2 (*Transl.*).   *For*] So *Cov.* (Test.), sim. *Cran.* : 'until,' *Auth.*, *Gen.* 2 (*Gen.* 1, paraphrases, 'that we might be fully restored to libertie') ; 'into the red.,' *Wicl.* ; 'to redeme the,' *Tynd.* ; 'unto the red.,' *Bish.* ; 'to the red. of,' *Rhem.* The translation of Turnbull, *Epp. of Paul*, p. 92, 'in the redeemed possession,' is very insufficient and inexact.

15. *For this cause, etc.*] 'Wherefore I also after .I heard,' *Auth.*, sim. *Tynd.*, *Bish.* ; 'wherefore,' *Tynd.*, *Cov.* (both), *Cran.*, *Gen.* 1, *Bish.* ; 'therefore,' *Wicl.*, *Gen.* 2, *Rhem.* The transl. 'for this cause' is more consonant with the general style of *Auth.* than the equally literal and correct 'on this account,' and so substituted accordingly. 'Wherefore' (*Auth.*) is rather the transl. of διό. *The faith which is among you*] 'Your faith,' *Auth.*, *Wicl.*, *Cov.* (Test.), *Rhem* ; 'the fayth which ye have,' *Tynd.*, *Cov.*, *Cran.*, *Gen.* (both), *Bish.*   *And the love which ye have*] 'And love,' *Auth.*, *Tynd.*, *Cran.*, *Gen.*, and similarly *Bish.*, *Gen.* 2, *Rhem.* ; 'the love into,' *Wicl.*

17. *Would give*] 'May give,' *Auth.*, *Cov.* (both), *Cran.*, *Bish.* ; 'myght geve,' *Tynd.*, *Gen.* (both), *Bish.* The change in the text is made as an *attempt* to express the conditioned, hoped for, realization (' would please to give') expressed by the opt. δῴη ; comp. Latham, *Engl. Lang.* § 592, Wallis, *Gramm. Angl.* p. 107. Hermann (Soph. *Elect.* 57) asserts that in German the distinction may be observed by translating the Greek subj. by the German ind. pres., the opt. by the German imperf. subjunctive. The transl. of *Tynd.*, etc., though practically preserving the correct shade of meaning, violates the law of 'the succession of tenses ;' see Latham, *Engl. Lang.* § 616.

revelation in true knowledge of Him ; [18] having the eyes of your heart enlightened, that ye may know what is the hope of His calling, and what the riches of the glory of His inheritance *are* among the saints, [19] and what the surpassing greatness of His power *is* to us-ward who believe, according to the operation of the power of His might, [20] which He wrought in Christ, when He raised Him from the dead, — and He set *Him* on His right hand in the heavenly *regions*, [21] over above all Principality, and Power, and Might, and Dominion, and *indeed* every name that is named not only in this world, but also in that which is to come ; [22] and put all *things* under His feet, and gave HIM as Head over all

---

True knowledge] ' The knowledge,' *Auth.*, and all the other Vv.

18. *Having the eyes, etc.*] ' The eyes of your* understanding being enlightened,' *Auth.*, sim. *Bish.* ('lightened') ; ' and lighten the eyes of youre myndes,' *Tynd.*, *Cran.*, *Gen.* 1, sim. *Cov.* ; ' the eyes of youre harte beynge lyghtened,' *Cov.* (Test.) : ' the eies of your hart illuminated,' *Rhem.*   *Are among*] ' In,' *Auth.* and the other Vv. except *Tynd.*, *Cov.*, *Cran.*, 'apon the sainctes.' It may be observed that *Tynd.*, *Cov.*, *Cran.* (both), similarly insert the verb immediately before the prep., showing that they did not consider ἐν τοῖς ἁγίοις as merely κληρονομ. αὐτοῦ ; see notes.

19. *What*] ' What is,' *Auth.* and the other Vv. except *Wicl.*, *Rhem.*, 'whyche is.'   *Surpassing*] ' Excellent,' *Wicl.* : ' passing,' *Rhem.* ; ' exceeding,' *Auth.* and other Vv.   *Is to us-ward*] ' To us-ward,' *Auth.*, *Tynd.*, *Cran.*, *Gen.* 1, *Bish.* ; ' in to us,' *Wicl.* ; ' toward us,' *Cov.* (Test.), *Gen.* 2, *Rhem.* *Operation*] So *Rhem.* : ' working,' *Auth.* and the remaining Vv. ; see notes on ch. iii. 7.   *The power of His might*] ' His mighty power,' *Auth.*, *Cov.*, *Bish.*, sim. *Tynd.*, *Cran.*, *Gen.* ; ' the myght of His vertu,' *Wicl.* ; ' the myght of His power,' *Cov.* (Test.), *Rhem.*

20. *And He set*] ' And set,' *Auth.* : the change in the original from the participial structure to that of the aor. indic. is better preserved by inserting the pronoun.

On His right hand] So *Tynd.*, *Cov.*, *Cran.*, *Bish.*, *Rhem.*, sim. *Wicl.* : ' at His own right hand,' *Auth.* ; so also *Cov.* (Test.), *Gen.* (both), but omit ' own.'   *Heavenly regions*] ' Heavenly places,' *Auth.*, *Gen.* (both), *Bish.* ; ' heavenli thingis,' *Wicl.*, *Tynd.*, *Cov.* (both), *Cran.* ; ' celestials,' *Rhem.*

21. *Over above*] ' Far above,' *Auth.*, *Gen.* (both), *Bish.* : ' above,' *Wicl.* and remaining Vv.   *And indeed*] ' And,' *Auth.*, see notes.

22. *Put*] ' Hath put,' *Auth.*, *Tynd.*, *Cov.*, *Cran.*, *Bish.*, *Rhem.* : ' hath appointed,' *Gen.* (both : *Wicl.* alone omits the auxiliary verb, ' and made alle thingis,' etc.   *And gave* HIM, *etc.*] ' And gave Him to be head over all things to, etc.,' *Auth.*, *Bish.*, (' the head ') ; ' and hath made Him above all thynges, the heed of, etc.,' *Tynd.*, *Cov.*, *Cran.* ; ' and made Hym heade over all the congr.,' *Cov.* (Test.) ; ' hath appointed Him aboue all thinges, the heade of, etc.,' *Gen.* 1 ; ' to be the heade of,' *Gen.* 2 ; ' and hath made Him head ouer al the church,' *Rhem.* The emphatic position of αὐτόν in the original should not be left unnoticed.

things to the church, [23] which indeed is His body, the fulness of Him that filleth all with all.

CHAPTER II.

And you also being dead by your trespasses and your sins, — [2] wherein ye once walked according to the course of this world, according to the prince of the empire of the air, of the spirit that now worketh in the sons of disobedience ; [3] among whom even we

23. *Which indeed*] 'Which,' *Auth.* and the other Vv. except *Wicl.*, 'that is.' If the distinction usually made between 'that' and 'which' is correct, viz., that the former is *restrictive*, the latter *resumptive* (see Brown, *Gramm. of Grammars*, II. 5, p. 293, and notes *on Col.* iii. 1, *Transl.*), 'that' will often be a correct translation of ἥτις when used *differentially* (see notes *on Gal.* iv. 24), e. g., ἡ πόλις ἥτις ἐν Δέλφοις κτίζεται ; in the present case, however, *Wicl.* is not correct, as ἥτις appears here used *explicatively*.   *With all*] 'In all,' *Auth.*, *Cov.*, *Cran.*, *Bish.*, *Rhem.*, and similarly the remaining Vv.

Chap. II. 1. *And you also who, etc.*] 'And you *hath He quickened* who, etc.,' *Auth.* The participle ὄντας has been differently translated : 'whereas ye were,' *Cran.* : 'when ye were,' *Cov.* (probably following Vulg.) ; 'that were,' *Tynd.*, *Gen.* (both), *Bish.* ; 'who were,' *Auth.* Of these, the first two, though more correct in point of grammar than *Tynd.*, al., which tacitly apply an article, seem scarcely so satisfactory as the more simple translation in the text, esp. if the present verse be compared with verse 5. The part. ὄντας obviously marks the state in which they were at the time when God quickened them. While in verse 5 this is brought prominently forward by the καί; here, on the contrary,

the καί is joined with, and gives prominence to ὑμᾶς. In the present case, then, a simple indication of their state without any temporal or causal adjunct, 'when,' 'whereas,' etc., seems most suitable to the context, as less calling away the attention from the more emphatic ὑμᾶς.
By] So *Rhem.* ; 'in,' *Auth.* and other Vv.   *Your trespasses, etc.*] 'Trespasses and sins' *Auth.*, *Cov.*, *Cran.*, *Gen.* (both), *Bish.*, similarly *Tynd.* : *Wicl.*, *Cov.* (Test.), *Rhem.* insert 'your' before the first substantive only.
2. *Once walked*] 'In time past ye walked,' *Auth.* and the other Vv. except *Wicl.*, 'ye wandriden sumtyme,' and sim. *Cov.* (Test.), *Rhem.*   *Empire*] 'Power,' *Auth.*, *Wicl.*, *Cov.* (Test.), *Rhem.* ; 'the governor that ruleth in,' *Tynd.*, *Cran.*, *Gen.*, sim. *Cov.* This somewhat modern form of expression seems the only one that exactly represents the view taken in the notes of the collective term ἐξουσίας.   *Of the spirit*] So *Wicl.*, *Rhem.* : 'the spirit,' *Auth.*, *Tynd.*, *Cov.* (Test.), *Cran.*, *Bish.* ; 'namely after the sp.,' *Cov.* ; 'and the sp.,' *Gen.* 1 ; 'even the sp.,' *Gen.* 2. *Sons*] So *Wicl.* ; 'children,' *Auth.* and the other Vv.
3. *Even we all*] 'Also we all,' *Auth.* ; 'we also had,' *Tynd.*, *Cov.*, *Gen.* (both) ; 'we all had,' *Bish.*   *Once had our convers.*] 'Had our convers. in times past,' *Auth.*, and sim. the other Vv.

all once had our conversation in the lusts of our flesh, doing the desires of the flesh and of the thoughts, and we were children by nature — of wrath, even as the rest : — ⁴ but God, being rich in mercy, because of His great love wherewith. He loved us, ⁵ even while we were dead by our trespasses, quickened us together with Christ (by grace have ye been saved), ⁶ and raised *us* up with *Him*,

except *Wicl.*, 'lyueden sumtyme ; *Cov.* (Test.), 'somtyme ;' *Rhem.*, 'conversed sometime.' This lighter translation of πoτε seems preferable both here and in ver. 2. The order of the Greek would seem to require 'had our conversation once,' but this would lead to ambiguity when read in connection with the succeeding words. *Doing*] So *Wicl.*, *Cov.* (Test.), *Rhem.*, and similarly *Cov.* : 'fulfilling,' *Auth.*, and sim. the remaining Vv. *Thoughts*] *Wicl.*, *Cov.* (Test.), *Rhem.* ; 'mind,' *Auth.* and remaining Vv. *We were*] 'Were,' *Auth.* *Children*] 'The children,' *Auth.* and all other Vv. except *Wicl.*, 'the sons.' *By nature — of wrath*] 'By nature the children of wrath,' *Auth.* and sim. all other Vv. All attempts to explain away the simple and ordinary meaning of these words must be, somewhat summarily, pronounced as both futile and untenable. Such a translation as 'children of impulse' (Maurice, *Unity*, p. 538), has only to be noticed to be rejected. The substantive ὀργὴ is used in *thirty-four* other places in the N. T., and in none does it appear even to approach to the meaning thus arbitrarily assigned to it. *The rest*] So *Rhem.*: 'others,' *Auth.*, *Gen.* 2 ; 'other men,' *Wicl.* ; 'other,' *Tynd.* and the remaining Vv.

4. *Being rich*] 'Who is rich,' *Auth.* ; 'that is,' *Wicl.* ; 'which is,' *Tynd.* and the remaining Vv. *Because of*] 'For,' *Auth.*, *Wicl.*, *Cov.* (Test.), *Cran.*, *Bish.*. *Rhem.* ; 'through,' *Tynd.*, *Cov.*, *Gen.* (both).

5. *While*] 'When,' *Auth.* and all Vv. The change is only made to express more forcibly the existing state ; see notes. *By our trespasses*] Similarly *Tynd.*, 'by sinne ;' *Cran. Gen.* (both), *Bish.*, *Rhem.*, 'by synnes ;' *Cov.* (Test.), 'thorow synnes :' 'in sins,' *Auth.*, *Wicl.*, *Cov.* *Quickened*] So *Wicl.*, *Cran.*, *Rhem.* ; 'hath quickened,' *Auth.* and the remaining Vv. *Have ye been*] 'Ye are,' *Auth.* On the simplest practical rule of choosing between 'am' and 'have been' in the translation of the Greek perf. pass., see notes *on Col.* i. 16 (*Transl.*). 'Are' might indeed still be retained on the ground that 'am' with the part. does involve an essentially *past* element (Latham, *Engl. Lang.* § 568), still the change seems a little more in harmony with the context.

6. *Raised*] So *Wicl.*, *Cran.*, *Rhem.*: 'hath raised,' *Auth.* and the remaining Vv. *Up with him*] So *Cov.* (both), *Rhem.* : 'up together,' *Auth.* and the remaining Vv. except *Wicl.*, which omits 'up.' *Sit with him*] So *Cov.* (Test.), *Rhem.* ; 'sit together,' *Auth.* and the remaining Vv. except *Cov.* ; 'set us with Him.' *The heavenly regions*] 'Heavenly places,' *Auth.* ; sim. *Gen.* (both), 'the heavenly places :' 'hevenly thingis,' *Wicl.*, *Tynd.*, *Cov.* (both), *Bish.* ; 'among them of heaven,' *Cran.* ; 'the celestials,' *Rhem.*

7. *That He might, etc.*] So as to order, *Wicl.*, *Tynd.*, *Gen.* (both), *Rhem.* ; 'that in the ages to come He might,' *Auth.*, and sim. *Cov.* (both), *Cran.*, *Bish.* *That are coming*] 'To come,' *Auth.* **and**

and made *us* sit with Him in the heavenly *regions*, in Christ Jesus;
[7] that He might show forth in the ages that are coming the exceeding riches of His grace in kindness towards us in Christ Jesus.
[8] For by GRACE have ye been saved through faith; and this *cometh*
not of yourselves, the gift is GOD'S; [9] not of works, that no man
should boast: [10] for His workmanship are we, created in Christ
Jesus for good works, which God before prepared that we should
walk in them.

[11] Wherefore remember, that aforetime ye, Gentiles in the flesh,
who are called the Uncircumcision by the so-called Circumcision,

the other Vv. except *Wiclif*, 'above comyng,' *Rhem.* 'succeeding.' *Shew forth*] 'Shew,' *Auth.*, and all the other Vv. *In kindness*] So *Tynd.*, *Cov.*, *Cran.*; 'in *His* kindness,' *Auth.*, *Gen.* (both), *Bish.*; 'in goodness,' *Wicl.*, *Cov.* (Test.); 'in bountie,' *Rhem.* *In*] So all the Vv. except *Auth.*, *Cran.*, *Bish.*, 'through.'

8. *Have ye been*] 'Are ye,' *Auth.*: see notes on ver. 5. *And this cometh*] Sim. *Wicl.*: 'and that not,' *Auth.* and remaining Vv. It does not seem neces-sary to change 'of' into 'from,' the former being frequently a very suitable translation of ἐκ; see notes *on Gal.* ii. 16. *The gift is God's*] 'It is the gift of God,' *Auth.* and all the other Vv. The emphasis is maintained, appy. more in accordance with English idiom, by placing the gen. at the end rather than at the beginning.

9. *That no man*] So *Wicl.*, *Rhem.*: 'lest any man.' *Auth.* and the remain-ing Vv.

10. *His workmanship are we*] 'We are His workmanship,' *Auth.*, *Tynd.*, *Cov.* (both), *Cran.*, *Gen.* (both), *Bish.*; 'we ben the makynge of Hym,' *Wicl.*; 'we are His work,' *Rhem.* The emphatic position of αὐτοῦ should not be neglected. *For good, etc.*] 'Unto,' *Auth.*, and the other Vv. except *Wicl.*, *Cov.* (Test.), *Rhem.*, 'in.' *Prepared*] So *Cov.*

(Test.), but omits 'before;' sim. *Rhem.*, but inserts 'hath:' 'hath before or-dained,' *Auth.*, and sim. remaining Vv., some of which, *Wicl.*, *Gen.* (both), omit 'before;' some 'hath,' *Tynd.*, *Cov.*, some both words, as *Cran.*, *Gen.*

11. *That aforetime*] * 'That ye *being* in time past,' *Auth.* This translation of ποτὲ (*Cov.*) is perhaps a little simpler than that of *Auth.* (and remaining Vv. except *Wicl.*, *Cov.* (Test.), *Rhem.*, 'sum-tyme'), and serves equally well to keep up the antithesis between ποτὲ and τῷ καιρῷ ἐκείνῳ in ver. 12. *By the so-called, etc.*] 'By that which is called the circumcision,' *Auth.*, and similarly all Vv. *Performed by hand*] So, as to order, *Wicl.*, 'made bi hand in fleisch;' *Cov.* (Test.), 'made wyth the hande in the flesh;' 'in the flesh made by hands,' *Auth.*, sim. *Gen.* 2, *Bish.*; 'which circumcision is made by hondes,' *Tynd.*, *Cran.*, sim. *Cov.*; 'and which is made by handes,' *Gen.* 1. The trans-position in the text seems desirable as precluding any connection of ἐν σαρκὶ with λεγομένης, the error of *Tynd.*, *Cran.*, and most of the other Vv.; 'made with the hande,' *Cov.*, and sim. remaining Vv.

12. *Ye were at that time*] So *Tynd.*, *Gen.* (both), sim. *Wicl.*, *Rhem.*: 'at that time ye were,' *Auth.* and the remaining Vv. except *Cov.*, 'that ye at the time were.' *The promise*] So *Cran.*,

performed by hand in the flesh, — [12] that ye were at that time without Christ, being aliens from the commonwealth of Israel, and strangers from the covenants of the promise, having no hope, and without God in the world, [13] but now in Christ Jesus ye who once were far off are become nigh by the blood of Christ. [14] For He is our Peace, who made both one, and broke down the middle wall of the partition — [15] *to wit*, the enmity — in His flesh, having abolished the law of commandments *expressed* in decrees ; that he might make the two in Himself into one new man, *so* making peace, [16] and might reconcile again both of us in one body unto God by the cross, having slain the enmity thereby. [17] And He came and preached peace to you which were afar off, and peace to them that were nigh ; [18] since through Him we both in one Spirit have our

Coverd. (Test.), *Rhem.*: ' promise,' *Auth.* and the remaining Vv.

13. *Once were*] So *Gen.* (both) : 'sometimes,' *Auth.* and the remaining Vv. except *Tynd.*, ' a while agoó ;' *Cov.*, 'aforetyme.' *Are become*] ' Are made,' *Auth.* and all the other Vv. The change, however, seems desirable, if only to obviate the supposition that ἐγενήθητε is here used with a passive force ; see notes on ch. iii. 7. The aorist cannot be preserved in English when in association with the particle of present time (νυνί) ; comp. notes on ch. iii. 5.

14. *Made — broke*] ' Hath made . . . . . hath broken,' *Auth.* and sim. the other Vv. except *Wicl.*, ' made . . . . . and unbindynge ;' *Rhem.*, ' hath made . . . . . and dissolving.' *The partition*] So *Rhem.*, and sim. *Gen.* (both) : ' partition,' *Auth.* ; ' the myddel-walle,' *Wicl.* ; ' that was a stoppe bitwene us,' *Tynd.*, *Cov.*, *Cran.*, *Bish.*

15. *To wit, the enmity, etc.*] ' Having abolished in His flesh the enmity *even*,' *Auth.*, and similarly as to connection the other Vv. except *Wicl.*, *Cov.* (Test.), *Rhem*, which separate ἐν σαρκὶ from καταργήσας, and appy. connect it with τὴν ἐχθραν ; see notes. *Expressed in decrees*] Similarly *Cov.* (Test.), *Rhem.*:

' *contained* in ordinances,' *Auth.*, *Bish.* ; ' maundementis, bi domes,' *Wicl.* ; ' *which standeth* in ordinances,' *Gen.* 2.

That he might make, etc.] Similarly *Cov.* (both), *Rhem.* ; ' for to make in Himself of twain,' *Auth.*, and similarly *Tynd.*, *Cran.*, *Gen.* (both) ; 'that he make two in Hym Silf into a newe man,' *Wicl.* ; ' for to make of twaine one new man in Hymselfe,' *Bish.*

16. *And might*] 'And that He might,' *Auth.* *Reconcile again*] ' Reconcile,' *Auth.* and the other Vv. ; see notes *in loc.* *Both of us*] 'Both,' *Auth.* *In one body unto God*] Similarly *Wicl.*, *Cov.* (Test.), *Rhem.* : ' unto God in one body,' *Auth.* and remaining Vv.

17. *And He came*] 'And came,' *Auth.* and the other Vv. except *Wicl.*, *Coverd.* (Test.), 'and He comynge ;' *Rhem.*, ' and coming He.' *And peace to*] 'And to,' *Auth.*

18. *Since*] 'For,' *Auth.* and all the other Vv. *We both, etc.*] ' We both have access by one Spirit,' *Auth.* ; ' han nyg comynge,' *Wicl.* ; ' have an open waye,' *Tynd.*, *Gen.* 1 ; ' an intraunce,' *Cov.* (Test.) *Cran.*, *Gen.* 2, similarly *Cov.* ; ' we have both an entrance,' *Bish.* ; ' have access,' *Rhem.*

admission unto the Father. [19] So then ye are no more strangers and sojourners, but ye are fellow-citizens with the saints, and of the household of God, [20] built up upon the foundation of the apostles and prophets, Jesus Christ himself being the chief corner *stone;* [21] in whom all the building being fitly framed together groweth into an holy temple in the Lord; [22] in whom ye also are builded together for an habitation of God in the Spirit.

CHAPTER III.

FOR this cause I Paul, the prisoner of Christ Jesus for you Gentiles, — [2] if indeed ye have heard of the dispensation of the grace of God which was given me to you-ward; [3] how that BY REVELATION the mystery was made known unto me, as I have before written in few words; [4] agreeably to which, when ye read, ye can perceive my understanding in the mystery of Christ,

19. *So then*] 'Now therefore,' *Auth.* and the other Vv. except *Wicl.*, 'therefor now;' *Coverd.* (Test.), 'therefore;' *Rhem.*, 'now then.'   *Sojourners*] 'Foreigners,' *Auth.* and the other Vv. except *Wicl.*, *Cov.* (both), 'straungers.' *But ye are*] * 'But,' *Auth.*

20. *Built up*] 'And are built,' *Auth.* and the other Vv. except *Wicl.*, 'aboue bildid;' *Cov.* (both), *Rhem.*, 'built.'

21. *All the building*] So *Auth.*, *Gen.* (both), *Bish.*; 'eche bildynge,' *Wicl.*; 'every bildynge,' *Tynd.*, *Cov.* (both); 'what buildyng so ever,' *Cran.*: see notes.   *Being fitly*] 'Fitly,' *Auth.*

22. *In the Spirit*] So *Wicl.*, *Tynd.*, *Coverd.* (both), *Rhem.*: 'through the Spirit,' *Auth.*, *Cran.*, *Bish.*; 'by the Spirit,' *Gen.* (both).

CHAP. III. 1. *Christ Jesus*] 'Jesus Christ,' *Auth.* and other Vv., but without any difference of reading in the *Rec. Text.*

2. *If indeed*] 'If ye,' *Auth.*, *Tynd.*, *Cran.*, *Gen.* (both), *Bish.*; 'if netheless,'

Wicl.; 'accordinge as,' *Cov.*; 'if so be that,' *Cov.* (Test.); 'if yet,' *Rhem.*
Which, etc.] It is nearly impossible (without paraphrase) to imply that 'which' refers to 'grace:' in the original edition 'God' was followed by a comma. *Was given*] 'Is given,' *Auth.* and all the other Vv.

3. *The mystery, etc.*] * 'He made known unto me the mystery,' *Auth.* *As I have before written*] 'As I wrote afore,' *Auth.*, *Cran.*, *Bish.*; 'wrote above,' *Tynd.*, *Cov.*, *Gen.* (both), and similarly *Wicl.*

4. *Agreeably to which*] 'Whereby,' *Auth.* and the other Vv. except *Wicl.*, 'as;' *Cov.*, (Test.), 'like as;' *Rhem.*, 'according as.'   *Can*] 'May,' *Auth.* and all the other Vv., but perhaps not with perfect exactness; the rule apparently being, 'may et can potentiam innuunt, cum hoc tamen discrimine, *may* et *might* vel de jure vel saltem de rei possibilitate dicuntur, at *can* et *could* de viribus agentis,' Wallis, *Gramm. Angl.* p. 107.   *Perceive my understanding*]

[5] which in other generations was not made known unto the sons of men, as it hath now been revealed unto His holy apostles and prophets by the Spirit; [6] *to wit*, that the Gentiles are fellow-heirs, and of the same body, and joint-partakers of the promise, in Christ Jesus, through the Gospel; [7] whereof I became a minister, according to the gift of the grace of God which was given unto me according to the operation of His power. [8] Unto me, who am less than the least of all saints, was this grace given, — to preach among the Gentiles the unsearchable riches of Christ, [9] and to make all *men* see what *is* the dispensation of the mystery, which from the ages hath been hid in God, who created ALL THINGS;

So *Cov.*: 'understand my knowledge,' *Auth.*, *Cran.*, *Bish.*; 'know myne understondynge, *Tynd.*, *Gen.* (both); undurstonde my prudence,' *Wicl.*, *Cov.* (Test.), 'und. my wisdom,' *Rhem.*

5. *Generations*] So *Wiclif*, *Cov.* (Test.), *Rhem.*: 'ages,' *Auth.*, *Gen.* 2, *Bish.*; 'tymes passed,' *Tynd.*, and remaining Vv. *It hath now been*] 'It is now,' *Auth.* and the other Vv. except *Rhem.*, 'now it is.' This is a case where the strict translation cannot be maintained; in English the aorist has no connection with pres. time (Latham, *Engl. Lang.* § 579), and therefore cannot here properly be connected with νῦν; in Greek this is possible, from the greater temporal latitude of the tense; comp. notes *on* 1 *Tim.* ch. v. 15 (*Transl.*).

6. *To wit, that*] Similarly *Coverd.*, 'namely, that:' 'that,' *Auth.* and the remaining Vv. except *Rhem.* (which is excessively harsh), 'the Gentiles to be, etc.' *Are*] So *Wicl.*, *Cov.* (Test.): 'should be,' *Auth.* and the remaining Vv. except *Rhem.*, supr. cit. *Joint-partakers*] Sim. *Cov.* (Test.), 'lyke partakers:' 'partakers,' *Auth.* and the remaining Vv. except *Wicl.*, 'parteneris to gidre;' *Rhem*, 'comparticipant.' *The promise*] * 'His promise,' *Auth.* *Christ Jesus*] * 'Christ,' *Auth.* *Through*] So *Cov.* (Test): 'by,' *Auth*,

Wicl., *Cov.*, *Gen.* 2, *Bish.*, *Rhem.*; 'by the means of,' *Tynd.*, *Cran.*, *Gen.* 1.

7. *I became*] * 'I was made,' *Auth.* *Which was given*] Sim. *Wicl.*, *Coverd.* (both), *Cran.*, *Rhem.*, 'which is given:' *Auth.* and remaining Vv., 'given.' *According to*] So *Cov.*, *Rhem.*: 'by,' *Auth.*, *Wicl.*: 'thorow,' *Tynd.*, *Gen.* (both): 'after the,' *Cov.* (Test.), *Cran.*, *Bish.* *Operation*] So *Rhem.*: 'effectual working,' *Auth.*; 'worchynge,' *Wicl.* and all the remaining Vv. This word is always difficult to translate: 'effectual working' is perhaps too strong; 'working' alone is appy. too weak. Perhaps the term in the text as marking a more formal nature of working is slightly preferable; comp. notes *on* 2 *Thess.* ii. 12, where, however, the present translation would seem less suitable.

8. *Was this*] 'Is this,' *Auth.* and all the other Vv. *To preach*] So *Wicl.*, *Cov.* (Test.), sim. *Rhem.*; 'that I should preach,' *Auth.* and all the remaining Vv. The change is made to preserve a similar translation of the two infinitives; see Scholef. *Hints*, p. 190.

9. *Dispensation*] * 'Fellowship,' *Auth.* *From the ages*] 'From the beginning of the world,' *Auth.* and the other Vv. except *Wicl.*, *Rhem.*, 'fro worldis,' and *Cor.* (Test.), 'sence the worlde beganne.' *All things*] * 'All things by J. C.,' *Auth.*

[10] to the intent that now unto the Principalities and the Powers in the heavenly *regions*, might be made known through the church the manifold wisdom of God, [11] according to the purpose of the ages which he wrought in Christ Jesus our Lord ; [12] in whom we have our boldness and our admission, in confidence, through the faith in Him. [13] Wherefore I entreat you not to lose heart in my tribulations for you, seeing it is your glory.

[14] For this cause I bow my knees unto the Father, [15] from whom every race in heaven and on earth is *thus* named, [16] that he would grant you, according to the riches of His glory, to be strengthened with might through His Spirit into the inner man, [17] so that Christ may dwell in your hearts by faith, — [18] ye having been rooted and

10. *The powers*] 'Powers,' *Auth.* and the other Vv. except *Wicl., Rhem.,* 'potestatis.'   *The heavenly regions*] 'Heavenly places,' *Auth., Gen.* (both); 'hevenly thingis,' *Wicl., Cov.* (Test.), *Cran., Bish.* : 'in heven,' *Tynd., Cov.* : 'in the celestials,' *Rhem.*   *Might be made known*] 'Might be known,' *Auth.* and the other Vv. except *Wicl.,* 'be knowun ;' *Rhem.,* 'may be notified.' *Through*] 'By,' *Auth.* and all the other Vv.

11. *Purpose of the ages*] 'Eternal purpose,' *Auth.* and the other Vv. except *Wicl.,* 'ordenaunce of worldis,' and *Rhem.,* 'prefinition of worldes.' *Wrought*] So *Cran., Gen.* (both), *Bish :* 'purposed,' *Auth., Tynd.* : 'made,' *Wicl., Rhem.* : 'hath shewed,' *Cov.* (both).

12. *Our boldness*] 'Boldness,' *Auth.* *Our admission*] 'Access,' *Auth., Rhem.;* 'intraunce,' *Cov.* (both), *Cran., Gen.* (both), *Bish.*   *In confidence*] So, as regards the prep., *Wicl., Cov.* (both), *Rhem., Bish.* ; 'with,' *Auth., Cran., Gen.* (both). The words προσαγωγὴν ἐν πεποιθήσει are joined together by *Tynd.* and appy. all Vv. except *Wicl.,* and *Auth.* (orig. ed.).

13. *I entreat you, etc.*] 'I desire that ye faint not,' *Auth., Gen.* 2, *Bish.,* and similarly the remaining Vv. except *Wicl.,*

'axe that ye faile not.'   *Seeing it is, etc.*] 'Which is,' *Auth.* and all the other Vv.

14. *The Father*] 'The Father* of our Lord Jesus Christ,' *Auth.*

15. *From*] 'Of,' *Auth., Gen., Bish., Rhem.*   *Every race*] 'The whole family,' *Auth., Gen.* (both), 'eche fadirheed,' *Wicl.,* similarly *Coverd.* (Test.) ; 'which is father over all that ys called father,' *Tynd , Cran.,* sim. *Cov.* : 'all the familie,' *Bish.* ; 'al paternitie,' *Rhem.* On the difficulty of properly translating this clause, see Trench *on Auth. Ver.* ch. ii. p. 26 (ed. 2).   *And on earth*] 'And earth,' *Auth.*   *Is thus named*] 'Is named,' *Auth.* The word *thus* is introduced only to make the paronomasia in the original a little more apparent.

16. *Through*] 'By,' *Auth.* and all the other Vv.   *Into*] 'In,' *Auth.* and all the other Vv.

17. *So that*] 'That,' *Auth.,* and the other Vv. except *Rhem.,* 'Christ to dwel, etc.'

18. *Ye having been, etc.*] Similarly *Cov.* (Test.), *Rhem.* : 'that ye being,' *Auth.* and the remaining Vv. except *Wicl.* which omits 'being.'   *That ye may be fully able*] 'May be able,' *Auth.* and sim. all the other Vv.

grounded in love, — that ye may be fully able to comprehend with all saints what *is* the breadth, and length, and depth, and height, [19] and to know the love of Christ which passeth knowledge, that ye may be filled up to all the fulness of God.

[20] Now unto Him that is able to do beyond all things, abundantly beyond what we ask or think, according to the power that worketh in us, [21] unto Him *be* glory in the church, in Christ Jesus, to all the generations of the age of the ages. Amen.

CHAPTER IV.

I EXHORT you, therefore, I the prisoner in the Lord, that ye walk worthy of the vocation wherewith ye were called, [2] with all lowliness and meekness, with longsuffering, forbearing one another in love ; [3] striving to keep the unity of the Spirit in the bond of peace. [4] *There is* one body, and one Spirit, even as ye

19. *May*] So *Cov.* (both), *Gen.* (both), *Rhem.* : 'might,' *Auth., Tynd., Cran., Bish.;* change made to avoid the violation of the law of 'succession of tenses;' see Latham *Engl. Lang.* § 616.   *Up to*] 'With,' *Auth.* and the other Vv. except *Wicl.,* 'in;' *Cov.* (Test.), 'into;' *Rhem.,* 'unto.'

20. *To do beyond, etc.*] 'To do exceeding abundantly above all that, etc., *Auth.* and the other Vv. except *Wicl.,* 'more plenteously than we axen ;' *Cov.* (Test.), *Rhem.,* 'more abundantly than we desire.'

21. *In Christ Jesus*] 'By J. C.,' *Auth. Cran., Gen.* (both), *Bish.;* 'and in J. C.,' *Wicl., Cov.* (Test.), *Rhem.;* 'which is in,' *Cov.*   *To all the generation, etc.*] 'Throughout all ages, world without end,' *Auth., Bish.,* sim. *Rhem.;* 'to alle the generaciouns of the worldis,' *Wicl.;* 'thorow out all gen. from tyme to tyme,' *Tynd., Cran.;* 'throughout all gen. for ever,' *Gen.* (both).

CHAP. IV. 1. *I exhort you, etc.*] 'I, therefore, the prisoner, etc., beseech you

that,' *Auth.,* and in similar order all the other Vv. It seems, however, desirable to maintain the emphatic collocation ('ad excitandum affectum, quo cit efficacior exhortatio,' *Est.*) of the original. There is some variation in the translation of παρακαλῶ. The translation in the text is found in *Tynd., Cov., Cran., Bish.* : 'beseech,' *Auth., Wicl., Cov.* (Test.), *Rhem.;* 'praye,' *Gen.* (both).   *In the Lord*] So *Coverd.* (both), *Gen.* (both), *Bish., Rhem.;* 'of the Lord,' *Auth., Cran.;* 'for the Lord,' *Wicl.;* 'for the Lordes sake,' *Tynd.*   *Were called*] 'Are called,' *Auth.* and all the other Vv.

3. *Striving*] 'Endeavouring,' *Auth.* The present current use of the verb 'endeavour' seems to fall so short of the real meaning of the σπουδάζειν as to warrant the change in the text or the adoption of 'being diligent' (*Tynd., Cran.*), 'using diligence,' — terms more clearly indicative of the σπουδή and zeal that was evinced in the matter; see Trench on *Auth. Ver.* ch. iii. p. 43.

4. *There is, etc.*] It can scarcely be doubted that the *Auth.* is right in retain-

23

were called in one hope of your calling ; [5] one Lord, one faith, one baptism ; [6] one God and Father of all, who *is* over all, and through all, and in all.

[7] But unto each one of us the grace *which he has* was given according to the measure of the gift of Christ. [8] Wherefore He saith, When He ascended up on high, He led captivity captive, He gave gifts unto men. [9] Now that He ascended, what doth it imply but that He also descended into the lower *parts* of the earth. [10] HE THAT DESCENDED, He it is that ascended up above all the heavens, that He might fill all things. [11] And Himself gave some *to be* Apostles ; and some, Prophets ; and some, Evangelists ; and some Pastors and Teachers ; [12] with a view to the perfecting of the saints,

---

ing (after *Gen.* i. 2) this assertory form. Some of the older Vv., *Wicl., Cov.* (both), *Bish.*, supply nothing ; others, *Tynd., Cran.*, supply the participle 'being one body, etc.,' both of which forms fail to convey the force of the original ; see notes.   *Were called*] 'Are called,' *Auth.* and all the other Vv.

6. *Over*] So *Rhem.* : 'above all,' *Auth.* and all the remaining Vv.   *In all*] 'In *you all,' *Auth.*

7. *Each one*] Sim. *Wicl.* : 'every one,' *Auth.* and the remaining Vv. This change seems desirable to avoid a confusion with the usual translation of παντί. *The grace which, etc.*] 'Is given grace,' *Auth.* and the other Vv. except *Wicl.*, 'grace is gouun.'

8. *He gave*] ' *And gave,' *Auth.* *What doth it imply*] 'What is it,' *Auth., Cov.* (both), *Gen.* ii., *Rhem.* ; 'what meaneth it,' *Tynd., Cran., Gen.* i. *Descended*] 'Descended *first,' *Auth.*

10. *He it is*] So *Wicl.* : 'is the same also that,' *Auth.*   *Above*] 'Far above,' *Auth.*   *The heavens*] So *Cov.* (Test.), *Rhem.* ; 'heavens,' *Auth.* and the remaining Vv.

11. *Himself*] 'He,' *Auth., Wicl., Rhem.* ; 'and the very same,' *Tynd., Cran.* ; 'and the same,' *Cov.* (both) ; 'He therefore,' *Gen.* (both).   *To be Apostles*]

So *Cov.* (both), *Gen.* (both) ; 'some,' *Auth., Wicl., Bish., Rhem.* ; 'made some,' *Tynd. Cran.* The insertion of the words in italics seems necessary to make the sense perfectly clear.

12. *With a view to*] 'For,' *Auth., Cov.* (Test.), *Gen.* ii. ; 'to the ful endynge,' *Wicl.*, ; 'that the sainctes might have all things,' *Tynd.* ; 'whereby the sayntes mighte be coupled together,' *Cov.* ; 'to the edifyeng,' *Cran.* ; 'that the sainctes might be gathered together,' *Gen.* i. ; 'to the gathering togeather,' *Bish.* ; 'to the consummation,' *Rhem.*   *Of ministration*] So *Bish.* ; 'of the ministry,' *Auth.* ; 'of mynsteri,' *Wicl.* ; 'work and minystracyon,' *Cran.*   *For the building up*] 'For the edifying,' *Auth., Cov.* (Test.) ; 'to the edifying,' *Tynd., Cov.* ; 'even to the edifying,' *Gen.* i. ; 'edification,' *Gen.* ii. ; 'unto the edifying.' *Bish., Rhem.* This translation is perhaps slightly preferable to that of *Auth.*, and to that adopted in ed. i. ('edification'), as both verb and substantive are now commonly associated with what is simply *instructive* or *improving*, without necessarily suggesting the wider sense which seems to prevail in the present passage. The article is required by the principles of English idiom, though confessedly thus not in exact harmony with the Greek.

for the work of ministration, for the building up of the body of Christ; [13] till we all arrive at the unity of the faith and of the true knowledge of the Son of God, unto a full-grown man, unto the measure of the stature of the fulness of Christ: [14] that we may no longer be children, tossed to and fro and borne about by every wind of doctrine, in the sleight of men, in craftiness *tending* to the settled system of Error ; [15] but holding the truth may in love grow up into Him in all things, which is the head, *even* Christ: [16] from whom the whole body being fitly framed together and compacted by means of every joint of the *spiritual* supply, according

13. *Arrive at*] 'Come in,' *Auth.*; 'rennen into,' *Wicl.*; 'growe up unto,' *Tynd., Gen.* 1 ; 'come to,' *Cran.*; 'al meete together (in the etc.), unto,' *Gen.* 2 ; 'meete together into,' *Bish.*; 'meete al into,' *Rhem.* *The true knowledge*] 'The knowledge,' *Auth.* : the other Vv. omit the article *Full-grown*] 'Perfect,' *Auth.* and the other Vv.

14. *May, etc.*] '*Henceforth* be no more,' *Auth.* *Borne about by*] 'Carried about with,' *Auth.* and the other Vv. except *Wicl.*, 'borun aboute with ;' *Tynd.*, 'caryed with.' *In — in*] So *Wicl., Coverd.* (Test.), *Bish., Rhem.*: 'by — and,' *Auth.*, *Tynd.*; 'by — through,' *Cran.* *In craftiness, etc.*] 'And cunning craftiness, whereby they lie in wait to deceive,' *Auth.* and the other Vv. except *Wicl.*, 'to the disceyuynge of errour ;' *Cov.* (Test.), 'to the deceatfulness of errour ;' *Bish.*, 'in craftiness to the laying in wayte of errour ;' *Rhem.*, 'to the circumvention of errour.' It is by no means easy to devise a literal and at the same time perfectly intelligible translation of the last clause of this verse. The difficulty is mainly in the brief and almost elliptical form of expression introduced by the prep. : of the translations that have hitherto been proposed, that in the text, or 'furthering, promoting the system, etc.' (but see notes *on Phil.* iv. 17 *Transl.*), or more

simply, 'with a view to the system,' etc., seems the most suitable.

15. *Holding the truth*] 'Speaking the truth,' *Auth.*; 'folowe the truth,' *Tynd., Coverd., Cran., Gen.* (both), 'do truthe ;' *Wicl.*, 'perfourmyng ye truth,' *Coverd.* (Test.); 'folowing the truth,' *Bish.*; 'doing the truth,' *Rhem.* *May in love*] 'In love may,' *Auth.*

16. *Being fitly framed together*] 'Fitly joined together,' *Auth.* It seems desirable to retain the same translation here and ch. ii. 21. The translation of several of the older Vv. *e. g.* 'coupled and knet togedder,' *Tynd., Cov.* (Test.),*Cran., Gen.* (both), is not unsatisfactory ; 'compacted' has, however, the advantage of preserving the σὺν in each verb without repetition ; otherwise, 'knit together' would perhaps have been a more genuinely English translation. *Active working*] 'The effectual working,' *Auth.*; 'worchynge,' *Wicl.*; 'the operacion,' *Tynd., Cran., Rhem.*; 'the effectual power,' *Gen.* 1. The addition of the epithet 'active' or 'vital,' Alf., — if in italics (see notes on ch. iii. 7, and on 2 *Thess.* ii. 11), may perhaps here be rightly admitted as serving slightly to clear up the meaning. *By means of*, etc.] 'By that which every joint supplieth,' *Auth.*; 'in every joint wherwith one ministreth to another,' *Tynd., Gen.* 1, and similarly *Cov., Cran.*;

to *active* working in the measure of each single part, promoteth the increase of the body for the building up of itself in love.

[17] This then I say and testify in the Lord, that ye no longer walk as the other Gentiles also walk, in the vanity of their mind, [18] being darkened in their understanding, alienated from the life of God because of the ignorance that is in them, because of the hardness of their heart : [19] who as men past feeling have given

'bi eche joynture of undir seruynge,' *Wicl.*; 'every joynt of subministration,' *Cov.* (Test.), and sim. *Rhem.* ; 'by every joint for the furniture *thereof*,' *Gen.* 2 ; 'by every joint yeelding nourishment,' *Bish.*   *Each single*] Sim. *Wicl.*, 'each :' 'every,' *Auth.* and all the remaining Vv. ; see notes on ver. 7.

Promoteth the increase] 'Maketh increase,' *Auth.*; 'makith encreesynge,' *Wicl.*; 'maketh the increase,' *Rhem.* ; *Tynd.*, al. paraphrase. The more modern term 'promoteth,' seems admissible as both literal, and also tending to clear up the sense.   *For the building up of itself*] 'Unto the edifying,' *Auth.*: it seems desirable, for the sake of uniformity, to preserve the same translation as in ver. 12 ; the simplest (paraphrastic) translation would be 'so as to build itself up in love.'

17. *This then I say*] 'This I say therefore,' *Auth.* and the other Vv. except *Rhem.*, 'this therefore I say.' The resumptive character of the address is appy. here best preserved by the more literal translation of οὖν ; comp. notes on 1 *Tim.* ch. ii. 1.   *Ye must no longer*] 'Ye henceforth walk not,' *Auth.*, *Tynd.*, *Cran.*, *Gen.* (both), *Bish.*; 'ye walke not now,' *Wicl.*, *Cov.* (Test.), sim. *Rhem.*   *As the other . . . . also*] Sim. *Cov.*: 'as other,' *Auth.* and the other Vv. except *Wicl.*, *Coverd.* (Test.), *Rhem.*, which omit τὰ λοιπὰ in translation.

18. *Being darkened, etc.*] 'Having the understanding darkened,' *Auth.*, *Cov.* Test. ('an und.' etc.) ; 'that han undir-

stondynge derkned with derknesses,' *Wicl.*; 'blynded in their und' *Tynd.*, *Cov.*; 'whyle they are blinded, etc.' *Cran.*; 'having their cogitation darkened,' *Gen.* (both) ; 'darkened in cogitation,' *Bish.* ; 'having their und. obscured with darkness,' *Rhem.*   *Alienated*] 'Being alienated,' *Auth.* On account of the absence of ὄντες in the second member, it seems best to omit the part. of the verb substantive.   *Because of*] So *Tynd.*, *Cran.*, *Gen.* 1 : 'through,' *Auth.*, *Cov.* (both), *Gen.* 2; 'bi,' *Wicl.*, *Bish.*, *Rhem.*   *Hardness*] So *Gen.* (both) : 'blindness,' *Auth.* and remaining Vv. ; see Trench *on Auth. Ver.* ch. vii. p. 117.

19. *Who as men*] 'Who being,' *Auth.*, and sim., as to the translation of the relative, all the other Vv.   *Wantonness*] So *Tynd.*, *Cov.*, *Cran.*, *Gen.* (both), *Bish.*; 'lasciviousness,' *Auth.*; 'unchastite,' *Wicl.*; 'unclennesse,' *Cov.* (Test.) ; 'impudicitie,' *Rhem.* The article joined with it tends almost to personify it, hence the capital.   *For the working*] Sim. *Wicl.*,' in to the worchynge ;' *Cov.* (Test.), 'in the workinge ;' 'unto the operation,' *Rhem.*: 'to work,' *Auth.* and the remaining Vv.

All manner of] So *Tynd.*, *Cov.*, *Cran.*, *Gen.* 1 : 'all,' *Auth.* and the remaining Vv. ; see notes on ver. 31.   *In greediness*] 'With greediness,' *Auth.* and the other Vv. except *Wicl.*, 'in coueitise ;' *Cov.* (Test.), 'unto gr. ;' *Rhem.*, 'unto avarice.' This translation of πλεονεξία may be retained if qualified

THEMSELVES over unto Wantonness, for the working of all man·
ner of uncleanness in greediness. [20] But YE did not so learn
Christ; [21] if indeed ye heard HIM, and were taught in HIM, as is
truth in Jesus [22] that ye *must* put off, as concerns your former conversation, the old man, which waxeth corrupt according to the lusts
of Deceit, [23] and *rather* become renewed by the Spirit of your
mind, [24] and put on the new man, which after God's *image* hath
been created in righteousness and holiness of Truth.

[25] Wherefore, having put away Falsehood, speak truth each man
with his neighbor; because we are members one of another.

by the remarks *in loc.*, and not understood as indicating a mere general
$\dot{a}\mu\epsilon\tau\rho\dot{i}a$. The true idea of $\pi\lambda\epsilon\sigma\nu\epsilon\xi\dot{i}a$ is
' amor habendi : ' the objects to which it
is directed will be defined by the context.

20. *Did not so learn*] ' Have not so
learned Christ,' *Auth.* and all the other
Vv.

21. *If indeed*] ' If so be that,' *Auth.*,
Bish., and sim. other Vv. except *Wicl.*,
' if nethless ;' *Rhem.*, ' if yet.'
Ye heard him] Sim. *Wicl.* : ' have heard
Him,' *Auth.* and all the remaining Vv.
Were taught in Him] ' Have been taught
by Him,' *Auth.*, *Gen.* (both); ' ben
taugte in Him,' *Wicl.*, *Tynd.*, *Cov.*; ' be
instructe in Him,' *Cov.* (Test.); ' haue
bene taught in Him,' *Cran.* and the remaining Vv.　　　*As is, etc.*] So
Wicl.; ' as the truth is in Jesus,' *Auth.*,
Bish., and sim. remaining Vv.

22. *That ye must*] ' That ye,' *Auth.*
As concerns your former] ' Concerning
the former, etc.' *Auth.*　　*Which
waxeth, etc.*] ' Which is corrupt,' *Auth.*,
and the other Vv. except *Cov.*, ' which
marreth himselfe.　　　*The lusts of
Deceit*] ' The deceitful lusts,' *Auth.*; ' bi
the desiris of errour,' *Wicl.*, sim. *Cov.*
(Test.), *Rhem.*; ' the deceavable lustes,'
Tynd., *Cov.*, *Cran.*, *Gen.* (both); ' the
lustes of errour,' *Bish.*

23. *And rather*] ' And,' *Auth.*
Become renewed] ' Be renewed,' *Auth.*

This change is made as an attempt to
express the contrast between the pres.
$\dot{a}\nu a\nu\epsilon o\hat{v}\sigma\vartheta a\iota$ and the aor. $\dot{\epsilon}\nu\delta\dot{v}\sigma a\sigma\vartheta a\iota$.
By the Spirit] ' In the spirit,' *Auth.* and
all the other Vv.

24. *And put on*] ' And that ye put on,'
Auth.　　　*After the image of God*]
So *Tynd.*, ' after the ymage of God : '
' after God,' *Auth.* and the other Vv.
except *Rhem.*, ' according to God.' The
order of the Greek $\tau\dot{o}\nu$ $\kappa a\tau\dot{a}$ $\Theta\epsilon\dot{o}\nu$ $\kappa\tau\iota\sigma\vartheta$.
is similarly retained by all the Vv.
except *Wicl.*, *Cov.* (both). It may be
observed that the transl. of *Rhem.*, ' according to,' has the advantage of pre-
serving the antithesis $\kappa a\tau\dot{a}$ $\tau\dot{a}s$ $\dot{\epsilon}\pi\iota\vartheta$.
$\kappa. \tau. \lambda.$(ver. 23), and $\kappa a\tau\dot{a}$ $\Theta\epsilon\dot{o}\nu$, but fails
in bringing out clearly the great doc-
trinal truth appy. implied · in the latter
words.　　　　*Hath been created*] ' Is
created,' *Auth.*, and similarly all the
other Vv. The transl. ' hath been,' is
perhaps here slightly preferable to ' was,'
as the latter tends to throw the $\kappa\tau\iota\sigma\iota s$
further back than is actually intended;
the ref. being to the new $\kappa\tau\iota\sigma\iota s$ in Christ.
Holiness of Truth] So *Wicl.*, *Cov.* (Test.),
Bish., similarly *Rhem.* : ' true holiness,'
Auth. and the other Vv. except *Cov.*,
where it is *more* correctly, ' true righteousness and holynes.'

25. *Having put away*] ' Putting away,'
Auth.　　　*Falsehood*] ' Lying,' *Auth.*
and the other Vv. except *Wicl.*, ' lesynge.'

²⁶ Be angry, and sin not : let not the sun go down upon your angered mood ; ²⁷ nor yet give place to the devil. ²⁸ Let the stealer steal no more : but rather let him labor, working with his own hands the thing that is good, that he may have to give to him that needeth. ²⁹ Let no corrupt communication proceed out of your mouth, but that which is good for edification of the need, that it may minister a blessing unto the hearers ; ³⁰ and grieve not the Holy Spirit of God, in whom ye were sealed for the day of redemption. ³¹ Let all bitterness, and wrath and anger, and

Truth each man] So *Wicl.* ; 'every man truth,' *Auth.* and the other Vv. except *Cov.* (Test.), *Rhem.* (omits 'the'), 'the truth every man.'   *Because*] 'For,' *Auth.*, *Gen.* 1, al. ; 'for as moch,' *Tynd.*, *Cran.* ; 'because,' *Rhem.*

26. *Be angry*] So the other Vv. except *Auth.*, *Cov.* (Test.), *Bish.*, 'be ye angry ;' *Wicl.*, 'be ye wrooth.'
Angered mood] 'Wrath,' *Auth.* and all the other Vv. The change may perhaps be considered scarcely necessary, as the expression has become so familiar ; still παροργισμός, 'exacerbatio,' 'exasperation,' cannot strictly be translated 'wrath.'

27. *Nor yet*] *'Neither,' *Auth.* ; see notes on 1 *Thess.* ii. 3 (*Transl.*)

28. *The stealer*] 'Him that stole,' *Auth.*, *Bish.*, and sim. all other Vv. except *Cov.*, 'he that hath stollen ;' *Cov.* (Test.), 'he that dyd steale.' The *Auth.* in ver. 29 supplies a precedent for this idiomatic translation of the present part. with the article.   *His own*] 'His,' *Auth.* and all the other Vv.
The thing that] 'The thing which,' *Auth.*, *Cran.*, *Bish.* ; 'that that,' *Wicl.* ; 'some good,' *Cov.* ; 'some good thing,' *Tynd.* ; 'that which,' *Bish.*, *Rhem.* The slight change to 'that' is perhaps more critically exact ; see Brown, *Gram. of Gramm.* II. 5, p. 293, and notes on ch. i. 23.

29. *For edification*] 'To the use of edifying,' *Auth.*, *Gen* (both) ; 'good to

edefye with all,' etc., *Tynd.*, *Cov.*, *Cran.*, *Bish.* ; ' to the edificatioun of feith,' *Wicl.*, sim. *Cov.* (Test.), *Rhem.* On the difficulty of properly translating these words, see Trench *on Auth. Ver.* ch. x. p. 178.   *A blessing*] 'Grace,' *Auth.* and the other Vv. except *Cov.*, 'that it be gracious to hear ;' *Tynd.*, 'that it may have faveour.'

30. *In whom*] Sim. *Wicl.*, *Rhem.*, 'in whiche :' 'whereby,' *Auth.* ; 'by whom,' *Tynd.*, *Cran.*, *Gen.* (both), *Bish.* ; 'wherewith,' *Cov.* (both).   *Ye were*] 'Ye are,' *Auth.* and all the other Vv.   *For*] 'Unto,' *Auth.*, *Cov.*, *Tynd.*, *Cran.*, *Gen.* (both), *Bish.* ; 'in the,' *Wicl.* : ' agaynst the,' *Cov.* (Test).

31. *All bitterness*] So *Auth.* It is not always desirable to preserve the more literal transl. of πᾶς ('all manner of'), esp. when it is prefixed to more than one abstract substantive, as it tends to load the sentence without being much more expressive. When the adj. follows, as in ver. 19, the longer translation will often be found more admissible.
Wrath] So *Auth.*, *Wicl.*, *Coverd.* (Test.), 'fearsness,' *Tynd.*, *Cov.*, *Cran.*, *Gen.* ; 'anger,' *Bish.*, *Rhem.* The translation may be retained, whenever θυμὸs and ὀργὴ occur together, as sufficiently exact, provided that by ' wrath ' we understand rather the *outbreak* ('excandescentia,' Cicero, *Tusc. Disput.* IV. 9), by 'anger' the more settled and abiding habit. It is perhaps doubtful whether 'wrath'

clamour, and evil speaking, be put away from you, with all malice; [32] but become kind one to another, tender-hearted, forgiving one another, as God also in Christ forgave you.

CHAPTER V.

BECOME then followers of God, as beloved children; [2] and walk in love, even as Christ also loved us, and gave Himself for us, an offering and a sacrifice to God, for a savour of sweet smell.

[3] But fornication, and all manner of uncleanness or covetousness,

does not imply a greater permanence than ϑυμός, see Cogan *on the Passions*, I. 1. 2. 3, p. 111, still as it is several times applied to God as well as man, it seems generally the most proper and satisfactory translation.   *Malice*] So *Auth. Wicl., Cov.* (Test.), *Rhem.;* 'maliciousness,' *Tynd.* and remaining Vv. except *Bish.,* 'noughtiness.' As κακία points rather to the evil habit of the mind, as distinguished from πονηρία, the outcoming of the same (Trench, *Synon.* § xi.), — 'malice,' which is defined by Crabb (*Synon.* s. v.) as 'the essence of badness lying in the heart,' would appear a correct translation; see Cogan *on the Passions*, I. 3. 2, 1, p. 159.

32. *But*] 'And,' *Auth.*   *Become kind*] 'Be ye,' *Auth.* and other Vv.; corresponding to ἀρϑῆτω ἀφ' ὑμῶν, ver. 31.   *As God also in Christ*] Similarly *Wicl., Cov.* (Test.), *Rhem.;* 'even as God for Christ's sake,' *Auth., Tynd.,* and the remaining Vv.

Forgave] So *Wicl., Tynd., Gen.* (both), *Bish.;* 'hath forgiven,' *Auth.* and the remaining Vv. The aorist seems more exact, as pointing to the past act of God's mercy and forgiveness displayed in 'Christ,' *i. e.* in giving Him to die for the sins of the world.

:CHAPTER V. 1. *Become then followers*]

'Be ye therefore followers,' *Auth.* and the other Vv. except *Wicl.,* 'therfor be ye folowers;' *Cov.,* 'be ye the folowers therefore;' *Cov.* (Test.), 'be ye therfore the folowers.' The more literal transl. of γίνεσϑε might perhaps be here dispensed with, as necessarily involved in the action implied in μιμηταί; as, however, it seems an echo and resumption of the preceding γίνεσϑε (ch. iv. 32), it will be most exact to retain this more literal translation.   *Beloved*] 'Dear,' *Auth.* and the other Vv. except *Wicl.,* 'dereworthe;' *Cov.* (Test.), *Rhem.,* 'most deare.'

2. *Even as*] So all the other Vv. except *Wicl., Rhem., Auth.,* 'as;' *Cov.* (Test.), 'lyke as;' see notes *on* 1 *Thess.* i. 5 (*Transl.*).   *Loved us, etc.*] So all Vv. except *Auth., Gen.* 2, *Bish.* (similarly *Cov.*), 'hath loved us and hath given.'   *Savour of sweet smell*] 'Sweet smelling savour,' *Auth., Gen.* (both), *Bish.;* 'in to the odour of swetnes,' *Wicl.,* sim. *Cov.* (Test.); 'sacr. of a swete saver,' *Tynd., Cov., Cran.;* 'in an odour of sweetness,' *Rhem.*

3. *All manner of uncleanness*] * 'All uncleanness,' *Auth.;* see notes on ch. iv. 31.   *Be even*] 'Be once,' *Auth., Cran., Gen.* 2, *Bish.,* sim. *Tynd., Gen.* 1; 'so much as be,' *Rhem.;* *Wicl.* omits καὶ in transl.

let it not be even named among you, as becometh saints ; ⁴ and *no*
filthiness, and foolish talking or jesting, — things which are unbe-
coming, — but rather giving of thanks. ⁵ For this ye know, being
aware that no whoremonger, nor unclean person, nor covetous man
who is an idolater, hath an inheritance in the kingdom of Christ
and God. ⁶ Let no man deceive you with vain words: for because
of these *sins* cometh the wrath of God upon the children of disobedience. ⁷ Do not then become partakers with them. ⁸ For ye
WERE once darkness, but now *are ye* light in the Lord : walk as
children of light, — ⁹ for the fruit of the light *is* in all goodness
and righteousness and truth, — ¹⁰ proving what is well-pleasing
unto the Lord. ¹¹ And have no fellowship with the unfruitful
works of darkness, but rather even reprove *them*. ¹² For the
things which are done by them in secret it is a shame even to
speak of. ¹³ But all *these* things, when they are reproved, are
made manifest BY THE LIGHT ; for everything that is made mani-

4. *And no — and*] 'Neither — nor,' *Auth.* As several MSS., *e. g.* AD¹E¹ FG ; 4 mss. ; Vulg., Clarom., al. (*Lachm., Meyer, al.*), read ἤ—ἤ, it seems desirable to mark in the translation the reading adopted. *Or*] 'Nor,' *Auth. Jesting*] So *Auth.* and the other Vv. except *Wicl.*, 'harlotrie ;' *Rhem.*, 'scurrility.' *Things which are, etc.*] 'Which are not convenient,' *Auth.* ; 'which are not comely,' *Tynd., Cov., Cran., Bish.* ; 'which are things not comely,' *Gen.* (both).

5. *Ye know, being aware*] 'Ye know that, etc.,' *Auth. An inheritance*] 'Any inheritance,' *Auth.* and the other Vv. except *Wicl.*, 'eritage ;' *Cov.* (both), *Rhem.*, 'inheritaunce.' *Of Christ and God*] 'Of Christ and of God,' *Auth.* and all the other Vv.

6. *These sins*] 'These things,' *Auth.*

7. *Do not then become*] Sim. *Rhem.*, 'become not therefore ;' 'be not ye therefore,' *Auth., Cov.* (both), *Cran., Gen.* 2, *Bish.* ; 'therfor nyle ye be made,' *Wicl.* ; 'be not therefore,' *Tynd.*,

Gen. 1 : the insertion of 'ye' is not in accordance with the original.

8. *Once*] So *Tynd., Gen.* (both) : 'sometimes,' *Auth., Bish.* ; 'sometime,' *Wicl., Cov.* (both), *Cran., Rhem.*

9. *The light*] 'The * Spirit,' *Auth.*

10. *Well-pleasing*] So *Wicl., Cov.* (Test.), *Rhem.* ; 'acceptable,' *Auth., Bish.* ; 'pleasinge,' *Tynd.* and the remaining Vv.

11 *But rather even*] Similarly, but rather awkwardly, *Gen.* 2, 'but even reprove them rather ;' 'but rather,' *Auth.* and remaining Vv. except *Wicl.*, 'but more ;' *Bish.*, 'but even rebuke.'

12. *For the things, etc.*] 'For it is a shame even to speak of those things which are done of them in secret,' *Auth.* and in similar order, the other Vv. except *Wicl., Rhem.*

13. *All these*] 'All,' *Auth. When they are*] So *Tynd., Cov., Cran., Gen.* (both), *Bish.* ; 'that are,' *Auth., Wicl., Cov.* (Test.) *Rhem. For everything, etc.*] 'For whatsoever doth make manifest is light,' *Auth.* ; 'for

fest is light. [14] Wherefore He saith, Up! thou that sleepest, and arise from the dead, and Christ shall give thee light.

[15] Take heed then how ye walk with strictness, not as fools, but as wise, [16] buying up for yourselves the opportunity, because the days are evil. [17] For this cause do not become unwise, but understanding what the will of the Lord *is*. [18] And be not made drunk with wine, wherein is dissoluteness, but be filled with the Spirit; [19] speaking to one another in psalms and hymns and spiritual songs, singing and making melody in your heart to the Lord, [20] giving thanks always for all things unto God and the Father in the name of our Lord Jesus Christ, [21] submitting yourselves one to another in the fear of Christ.

[22] Wives, *submit yourselves* unto your own husbands, as unto the Lord; [23] for a husband is head of his wife, as Christ also is head of the church; He *is* the saviour of the body. [24] Nevertheless as the church is subject unto Christ, so *let* the wives also *be* to their hus-

---

al thing that is schewed is light,' *Wicl.*; 'for whatsoever is manifest, that same is light,' *Tynd., Cov., Cran.*; 'for euery thinge that is manifest is light,' *Cov.* (Test.): 'for it is light that discouereth all things,' *Gen.* 1; 'for it is light that makes all things manifest,' *Gen.* 2; 'for all that which doeth make manifest is light,' *Bish.*; 'for al that is manifested is light,' *Rhem.*

14. *Up! thou that sleepest*] So *Coverd.* (Test.): 'awake thou that sleepest,' *Auth.* and the remaining Vv. except *Wicl., Rhem.*, 'rise thou that,' etc.

15. *Take heed*] So all the other Vv. except *Wicl., Rhem., Auth.*, 'see.' *How ye*] So *Cran., Cov.* (both), *Rhem.*, similarly *Wicl.*; 'that ye,' *Auth.* and the remaining Vv.　　*With strictness*] 'Circumspectly,' *Auth.* and the other Vv. except *Wicl., Rhem.*, 'warily.'

16. *Buying up, etc.*] 'Redeeming the time,' *Auth., Tynd., Cov.* (Test.), similarly *Cov., Gen.* (both), *Bish., Rhem.*; 'agenbiynge tyme,' *Wicl.*; 'avoydyng occasion,' *Cran.*

17. *For this cause*] 'Wherefore,' *Auth.*,

Tynd., Cov., Cran., Gen. (both), *Bish.*; 'therfor,' *Wicl., Cov.* (Test.), *Rhem.*

Do not become] Sim. *Rhem.*; 'be ye not,' *Auth.* and the remaining Vv.

18. *Made drunk*] 'Be not drunk,' *Auth.* and the other Vv. except *Wicl.*, 'nyle ye be drunken;' *Cov.*, 'be not dronken;' *Cov.* (Test.), 'be not ye dronken,'　　*Dissoluteness*] 'Excess,' *Auth., Tynd., Cov., Cran., Gen.* (both), *Bish.*; 'leccherie,' *Wicl.*; 'voluptuousnesse,' *Cov.* (Test.); 'riotousness,' *Rhem.*

19. *One another*] 'Yourselves,' *Auth.* and all the other Vv.

21. *Of Christ*] 'Of *God,' *Auth.*

22. *Submit yourselves*] Italics; but not so in *Auth.* which adopts the insertion.

23. *A husband*] *'The husband,' *Auth.*　　*Head of his*] 'The head of the,' *Auth.*　　*As Christ also*] 'Even as Christ,' *Auth.* and the other Vv. except *Wicl Cov.* (Test.), *Rhem.*, 'As Christ is.'　　*He is*] *'And he is,' *Auth.*

24. *Nevertheless*] 'Therefore,' *Auth.* and the other Vv. except *Wicl., Cov.*

bands. [25] Husbands, love your own wives, *even* as Christ also loved the church, and gave Himself for it; [26] that He might sanctify it, having cleansed it by the laver of the water in the word, [27] that He might Himself present to Himself the church *in* glorious *beauty*, not having spot, or wrinkle, or any such thing; but that it should be holy and blameless. [28] Thus ought husbands also to love their own wives, as *being* their own bodies. He that loveth his own wife loveth himself. [29] For no man ever hated his own flesh; but nourisheth it and cherisheth it, even as Christ also *doth* the church: [30] because we are MEMBERS of His body, of His flesh, and of His bones. [31] For this cause shall a man leave his father and mother, and shall be joined unto his wife, and they two shall be one flesh. [32] This mystery is a great one; I however am

---

(Test.), *Bish., Rhem.,* 'but.'

Also be] 'Be,' *Auth.*   *Their husbands*] * 'Their own husbands,' *Auth.*

25. *Your own*] 'Your,' *Auth.* and all the other Vv.

26. *Sanctify it, etc.*] 'Sanctify it and cleanse it,' *Auth., Gen.* 2; 'to sanctifie it, and clensed it,' *Tynd., Cov., Cran., Gen.* 1; 'to sanctifie it, when he had clensed it,' *Bish.;* 'sanctifie it, cleansing it,' *Rhem.*   *By the laver of the, etc.*] So *Rhem.* (' of water'): 'with the washing of water by the word,' *Auth.;* 'with the, etc., in the word,' *Wicl.:* 'in the fountayne of water thorow the worde,' *Tynd., Cran.;* 'in the f. of w. by the worde,' *Cov.;* 'with the f. of w. in the worde,' *Cov.* (Test.); 'in the washing of w. through the worde,' *Gen.* 1; 'in the fountain of water in the word,' *Bish.*

27. *He might Himself, etc.*] 'He might present it * to Himself a glorious church,' *Auth., Bish.* ('unto'); 'to make it unto Himselfe a glorious congregacion,' *Tynd., Cov., Cran.,* similarly *Gen.* 1; 'to geue the chirche glorious to Him self,' *Wicl.* *Blameless*] 'Without blemish,' *Auth.;* 'that it hadde no wemme,' *Wicl.;* 'with-

out blame,' *Tynd., Cov., Cran., Gen.* (both), *Bish.;* 'undefyled,' *Cov.* (Test.); 'unspotted,' *Rhem.;* see notes on ch. i. 4.

28. *Thus also, etc.*] * 'So ought men to love,' *Auth.*   *Own wife — wives*] *Auth.* omits 'own.' *As being*] 'As,' *Auth.* and all the other Vv.

29. *Ever*] So *Wicl., Rhem.;* 'ever yet,' *Auth.* and the remaining Vv. except *Cov.* (Test.), 'at ony tyme.' *Christ also, etc.*] * 'The Lord, the Church,' *Auth.*

30. *Because*] So *Rhem.:* 'for,' *Auth.* and the remaining Vv. except *Wicl.,* 'and.'

31. *Father*] * 'His father,' *Auth.*

32. *This mystery, etc.*] 'This is a great mystery,' *Auth., Cov.* (Test.); 'this sacrament is great,' *Wicl.;* 'is a great sacr.' *Rhem.;* 'is a great secrete,' *Tynd., Cov., Cran., Gen.* (both), *Bish.* *I however am, etc.*] 'But I speak,' *Auth.* and the Vv. except *Wicl.,* 'ye I seie;' *Cov.* (Test.), 'but I say;' 'I speake,' *Bish.*   *In reference to*] 'Concerning,' *Auth., Gen.* 2; 'in,' *Wicl., Cov.* (Test.) *Rhem.;* 'bitwene,' *Tynd.;* 'of,' *Cov., Cran., Gen.*

speaking in reference to Christ and to the church. ³³ Nevertheless ye also severally, let each one *of you* thus love his own wife as himself; and the wife, let her reverence *her* husband.

Chapter VI.

Children, obey your parents, in the Lord; for this is right. ² Honour thy father and thy mother, the which is the first commandment in regard of promise; ³ that it may be well with thee, and that thou mayest live long upon the earth. ⁴ And, ye fathers, provoke not your children to wrath; but bring them up in the discipline and admonition of the Lord.

⁵ Bond-servants, be obedient to your masters according to the flesh, with fear and trembling, in singleness of your heart, as unto Christ; ⁶ not with eye-service, as men-pleasers, but as bond-servants of Christ; doing the will of God from the heart; ⁷ with good will doing service, as to the Lord, and not to men: ⁸ seeing ye know that whatsoever good thing each man shall do, THIS shall

---

33. *Ye also, etc.*] 'Let every one of you in particular,' *Auth.*; 'do ye so, that every one,' *Tynd., Cov., Cran.*; 'you also let every one loue,' *Cov.* (Test.); 'every one of you, *do ye so*,' *Gen.* (both), *Bish.* The slight asyndeton in the original is perhaps best retained.   *Thus love his own wife as*] 'So love his wife as,' *Auth.*
Let her reverence] '*See* that she reverence,' *Auth.*; 'and let the wife se that,' *Tynd., Gen.* (both); 'but let,' etc., *Cov.* (both); 'and let the wife feare,' *Cran., Rhem.*; 'and let the wyfe reverence,' *Bish.*

Chap. VI. 2. *Thy mother*] So *Wicl., Cov.* (both), *Rhem.*; 'mother,' *Auth.* and the remaining Vv.   *The which*] 'Which,' *Auth., Cov.* (Test.), *Gen.* 2, *Bish., Rhem.*; 'that is,' *Wicl., Cov., Tynd., Gen.* 1; 'the same is,' *Cran.*
In regard of promise] 'With promise,' *Auth., Gen.* 2; 'that hath eny promes,'

Tynd., Cov., Gen. 1; 'in the promyse,' *Cov.* (Test.), *Cran., Bish.* (omits 'the') *Rhem.*; 'in behest,' *Wicl.*
3. *And that thou*] 'And thou,' *Auth. Upon*] 'On,' *Auth.*
4. *Discipline*] So *Rhem.*; 'nurture,' *Auth., Tynd., Coverd.* (both), *Cran.*; 'techynge,' *Wicl.*; 'instruction,' *Gen.* (both), *Bish.*
5. *Bond-servants*] 'Servants,' *Auth.*; change to maintain the opposition in ver. 8.   *Your*] 'Them that are,' *Auth.*
6. *Bond-servants*] 'The servants,' *Auth.*
8. *Seeing ye know*] 'Knowing,' *Auth.*, and similarly other Vv. except *Tynd.*, 'and remember;' *Cov.*, 'and be sure;' *Gen.* (both, 'and know ye.')
Each man] So *Wicl.*, 'any man,' *Auth.* and the remaining Vv. except *Cov.*, 'a man;' *Cov.* (Test.), 'he doth;' *Rhem.*, 'he shall do.'   *Shall do*] So *Wicl., Rhem.*; 'doeth,' *Auth.* and the remaining Vv.   *This*] 'The

he receive of the Lord, whether *he be* bond or free. [9]And, ye
masters, do the same things unto them, giving up your threatening: seeing ye know that both their Master and yours is in
heaven, and there is no respect of persons with Him.

[10]Finally, be strengthened in the Lord, and in the power of His
might. [11]Put on THE WHOLE ARMOUR of God, that ye may be
able to stand against the stratagems of the devil: [12]because our
struggle is not against flesh and blood, but it is against Principalities,
against Powers, against the World-Rulers of this darkness, against
the spiritual hosts of wickedness in the heavenly *regions*. [13]For
this cause take up THE WHOLE ARMOUR of God, that ye may be
able to withstand in the evil day, and having fully done all, to
stand. [14]Stand therefore, having girt your loins about with truth,

same,' *Auth., Cov.* (Test.), *Cran.*; 'that
same,' *Gen.* (both); 'that,' *Tynd., Bish.*;
'it,' *Cov.*

9. *Giving up your*] 'Forbearing,' *Auth.*;
'puttinge awaye,' *Tynd., Cov.* (both),
Cran., Gen. (both), *Bish.*; 'remitting,'
Rhem.   *Seeing ye know, etc.*]
'Knowing that your * Master also is in
h. neither is there,' *Auth.*

10. *Finally*] *'Finally my brethren,'
Auth.   *Be strengthened*] So
Rhem.; 'be strong,' *Auth.* and the remaining Vv. except *Wicl.*, 'be ye coun-
fortide.'

11. *Stratagems*] 'Wiles,' *Auth.*; 'as-
piyngis,' *Wicl.*; 'crafty assautes,' *Tynd.,
Cov., Gen.* 1; 'assaultes,' *Cov.* (Test.),
Cran., Gen. 2, *Bish.*; 'deceites,' *Rhem.*
The translation in the text seems best to
convey the idea of a fixed and settled
plan: see notes on ch. iv. 14.

12. *Because our wrestling*] 'For we
wrestle not,' *Auth.* and remaining Vv.
except *Wicl.*, 'for why stryuynge;'
Rhem., 'for our wrestling.'   *But
it is*] 'But,' *Auth.*   *The World-
Rulers*] 'The rulers,' *Auth.*; 'govern-
ouris of the world,' *Wicl., Cov.* (Test.),
sim. *Cov.*; 'worldly rulers,' *Tynd.,
Cran.*; 'the worldly gouernours,' *Gen.*
(both), *Bish.* (omits 'the'); 'the rec-

tors of the world,' *Rhem.*   *Of
this darkness*] *' Of the darkness of
this world,' *Auth.*   *The spiritual
hosts of wickedness*] 'Spiritual wickedness,' *Auth., Bish.*; 'spiritual thingis of
w.' *Wicl., Cov.* (Test); 'spretual w.'
Tynd.; 'ye spretes of w.' *Cov.*: 'spretual craftynes,' *Cran.*; 'spiritual wicked-
nesses,' *Gen.* (both); 'the spirituals of
w.' *Rhem.*   *In the heavenly
regions*] 'In high places,' *Auth.*; 'in
hevenli thingis,' *Wicl., Coverd.* (Test.),
Cran.; 'for hevenly thinges,' *Tynd.*:
'under the heauen,' *Cov.*; 'which are
above,' *Gen.* 1; 'which are in the hie
places,' *Gen.* 2; 'in heavenly places,'
Bish.; 'in the celestials,' *Rhem.*

13. *For this cause*] So *Tynd., Cov.,
Gen.* (both): 'wherefore,' *Auth., Bish.,
Cran.*; 'therfor,' *Wicl., Rhem.*

Up] 'Unto you,' *Auth.*   *Fully
done*] 'Done,' *Auth.*; 'and in alle
thingis stonde parfigt,' *Wicl.*: 'having finished all thynges,' *Gen.* (both),
Bish.

14. *Having girt, etc.*] 'Having your
loins girt about,' *Auth., Bish.*; 'and
your loynes gyrd aboute,' *Tynd., Cov.,
Gen.* (both), sim. *Cran.*; 'having your
loins girded in,' *Rhem.*   *Having put on*] 'Having on,' *Auth.*

and having put on the breastplate of righteousness, [15] and having shod your feet with the preparedness of the gospel of peace ; [16] in addition to all, having taken up the shield of faith, wherewith ye shall be able to quench all the fiery darts of the wicked One ; [17] and receive the helmet of salvation, and the sword of the Spirit, which is the word of God ; [18] with all prayer and supplication praying always in the Spirit, and watching thereunto, with all perseverance and supplication for all the saints ; [19] and *in particular* for me, that utterance may be GIVEN unto me in the opening of my mouth, so that with boldness I may make known the mystery of the gospel, [20] for which I am an ambassador in a chain ; that therein I may speak boldly, as I ought to speak.

[21] But that ye also may know my condition, how I fare, Tychicus, the beloved brother and faithful minister in the Lord, shall make known to you all things : [22] whom I have sent unto you for this

15. *And having shod*] 'And your feet shod,' *Auth.*   *Preparedness*] 'With the preparation,' *Auth.*, *Gen.* (both) ; 'in makynge rede of,' *Wicl.;* '(showes) prepared by the, etc.' *Tynd.*; 'that ye may be prepared,' *Cov.*, similarly *Cran*, 'that ye may be prepared for ;' 'in the preparation,' *Bish.·;* 'to the prep.' *Rhem.*

16. *In addition to*] 'Above all,' *Auth.* and the other Vv. except *Wicl., Cov.* (Test.), *Rhem.*, 'in alle thingis.' *Having, etc.*] 'Taking,' *Auth.*, *Bish.*, *Rhem.;* 'take to you,' *Tynd., Cran.*, *Gen.* 1 ; 'take holde of,' *Cov.* *Wicked one*] Sim. *Rhem.*, 'of the most wicked one :' 'the wicked,' *Auth.* and the remaining Vv. except *Wicl.*, 'the worst;' *Cov.* (Test.), 'the most wicked.' The addition in the text seems desirable as marking the personality of τοῦ πονηροῦ.

17. *Receive*] 'Take,' *Auth.* and all the other Vv.

18. *With all prayer, etc.*] 'Praying always with all, etc.' *Auth.* *All the saints*] So *Rhem.;* 'all saints,' *Auth.* and the remaining Vv. except *Wicl.*, 'alle holi men.'

19. *And in particular*] 'And,' *Auth.:* use of καὶ to add the particular to the general; see Fritz. *on Mark*, p. 11, 713, and comp. notes on Phil. iv. 12. *In the opening, etc.*] 'That I may open my mouth boldly to,' etc., *Auth.*, *Tynd*, *Cov.*, *Cran.*, *Gen.* (both; 'in openynge of my mouth,' *Wicl.*, similarly *Cov.* (Test.), *Rhem.:* 'that I may open my mouth freely to utter,' etc., *Bish.*

20. *A chain*] So *Wicl.;* 'in this ch.," *Cov.* (Test.), *Rhem.;* 'in bonds,' *Auth.* and the remaining Vv.

21. *Condition*] Sim. *Tynd.*, *Cran.;* 'affairs,' *Auth.*, *Bish.;* 'what case I am in,' *Cov.;* change merely to avoid the homœoteleuton.   *How I fare*] 'And how I do,' *Auth.:* all the other Vv., 'what I do;' but as this might be misunderstood and referred to what the Apostle was actually engaged in (see Wolf *in loc.*), it seems best, with Harl., to refer τὰ κατ' ἐμέ to 'meine Lage,' τὶ πράσσω to 'mein Befinden.' *The beloved*] Sim. *Cran.*, *Cov.* (Test.), 'the :' 'a beloved,' *Auth.;* 'my,' *Wicl.*, *Tynd.*, *Coverd.*, *Gen.*, *Rhem.;* 'a,' *Bish.*

22. *This very purpose*] 'The same,'

very purpose, that ye may know our affairs, and *that* he may comfort your hearts.

23 Peace *be* to the brethren, and love with faith, from God the Father and the Lord Jesus Christ. 24 Grace *be* with all them that love our Lord Jesus Christ in incorruption.

Auth. and all the other Vv. except *Wicl.,* 'this same.'   *May — may*] 'Might — might,' *Auth.:* change in accordance with the law of the succession of tenses, Latham, *Engl. Lang.* § 616.

24. *In incorruption*] So *Wicl., Rhem.;* 'in sincerity,' *Auth., Bish.;* 'in puernes,' *Tynd.;* 'unfaynedly.' *Cov., Cran.;* 'sincerely,' *Cov.* (Test.); 'to *their* immortalitie,' *Gen* (both).